"To honor who we are as chefs is hard enough. To do so unapologetically, deliciously, and with style is even more difficult. To do all that and inspire others to cook, to create food so irresistible that I am insistent that you buy this book that my friend made for you, well, that is pure magic. And magic is indeed what's inside these covers. Melissa King is a phenomenal talent, a superb cook in every sense of the word, and her recipes—several of which I have had the pleasure of eating—are incomparably craveable. You will be cooking out of this book for years and years. And wowing whoever is at your table."

—ANDREW ZIMMERN

"Chef Melissa is one of the most talented chefs in the country. I have had the privilege to have her food many times, and now we all can cook her food at home. I can't wait to eat through this book with my family."

—MARCUS SAMUELSSON, award-winning chef, author, and restaurateur

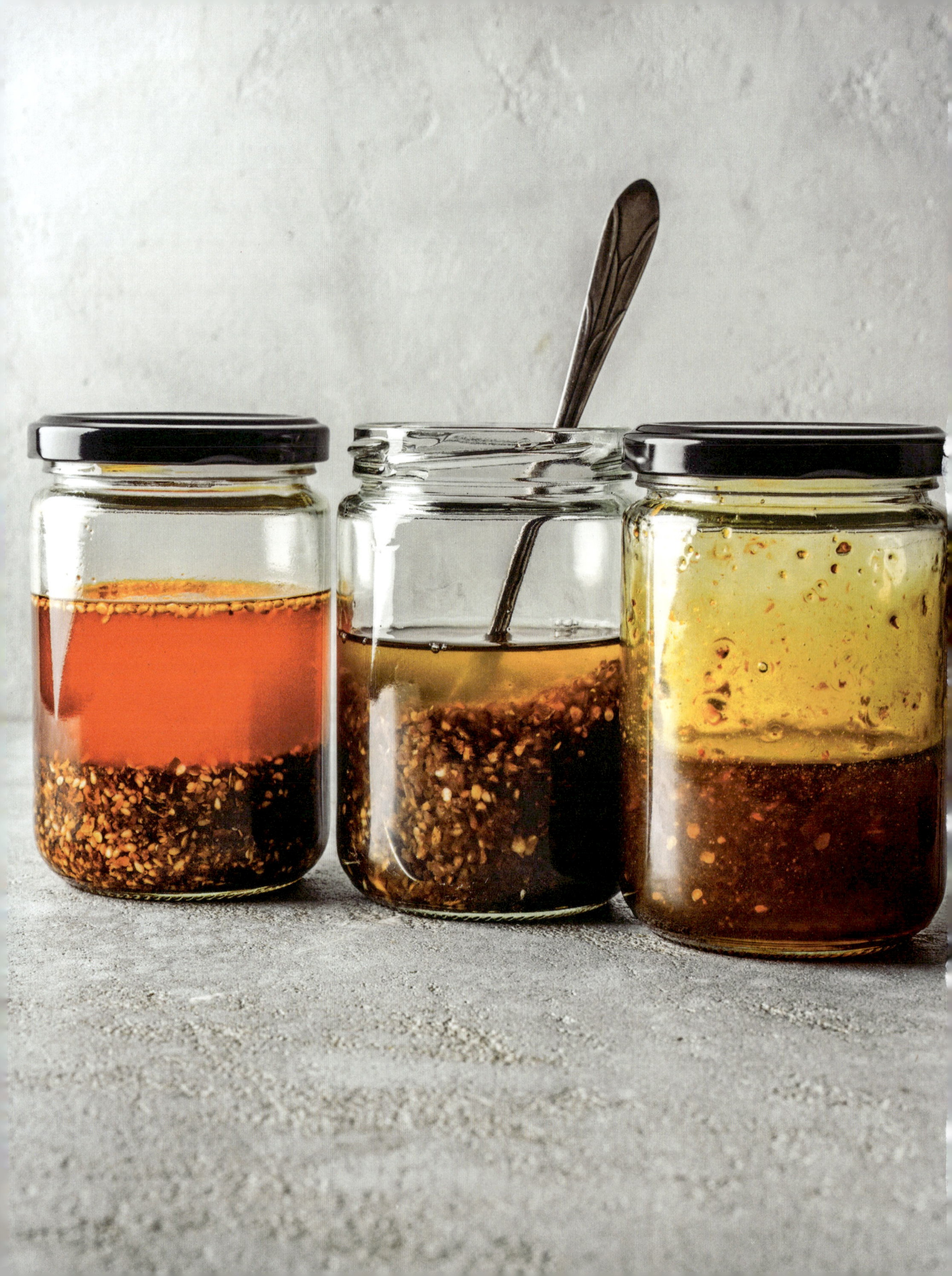

COOK LIKE A
KING

MELISSA KING
WITH JJ GOODE

COOK LIKE A
KING

RECIPES FROM MY CALIFORNIA CHINESE KITCHEN

RECIPE PHOTOGRAPHS BY ED ANDERSON
LIFESTYLE PHOTOGRAPHS BY ASHLEY BATZ

TEN SPEED PRESS
California | New York

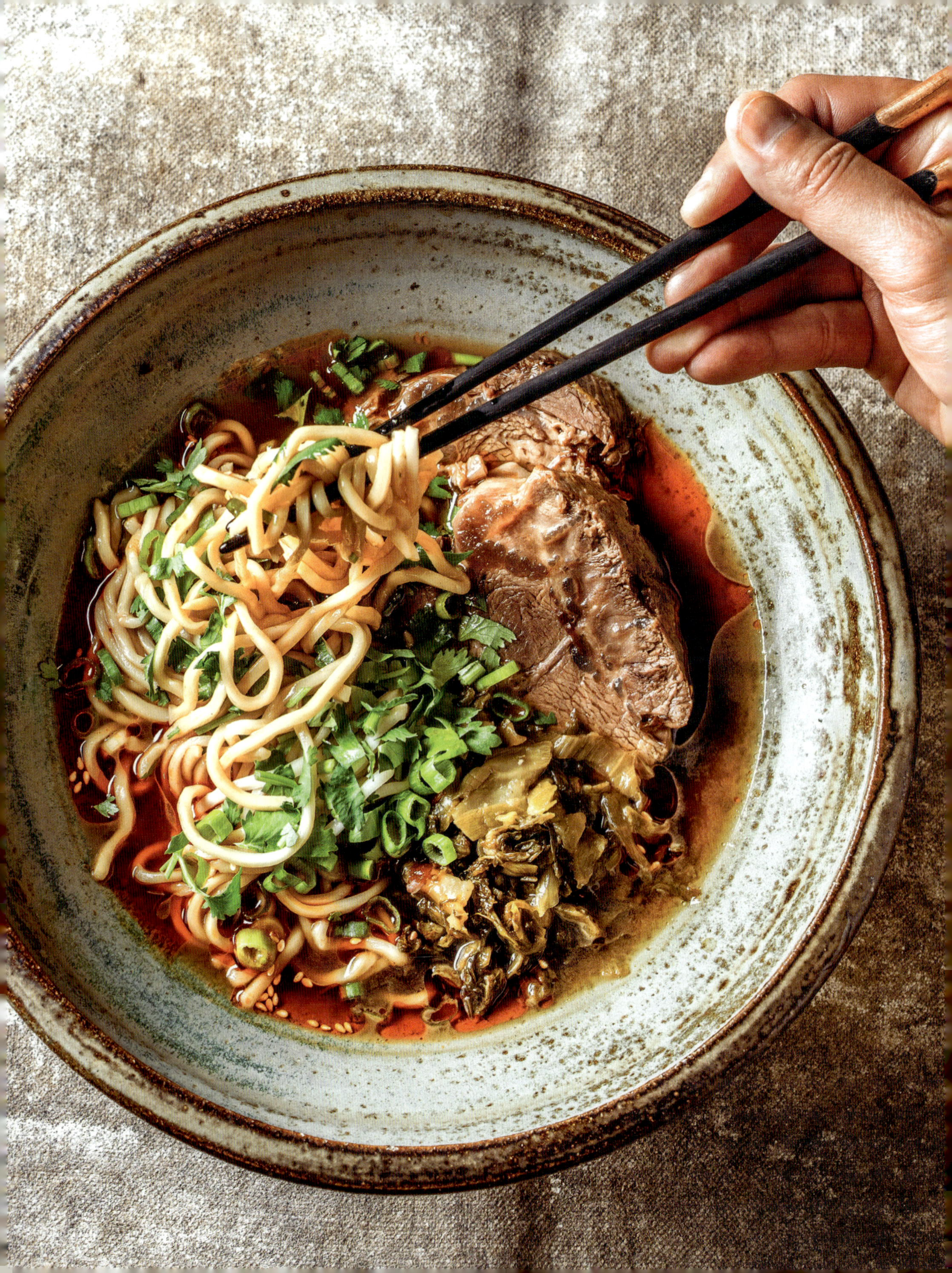

CONTENTS

Introduction   9
Pantry   14

1 SNACKS, APPS & DIPS   21

Smoky Tea Eggs   23
Miso Baba Ghanoush   24
Coconut Shrimp Toast   27
King's Guacamole   28
Sichuan Steak Tartare   31
Chili Crisp Labneh   32
Black Vinegar–Marinated Sweet Peppers   35
Tuna Tostadas with Avocado, Ginger, and Scallion   36
Yellowtail Crudo in Ginger-Citrus Broth   39
Sicilian-Style Crudo with Shoyu-Cured Salmon Roe   40
Grilled Oysters with Sichuan Chile–Bourbon Butter   43
King's Wings   44
Grilled Fish Sauce–Caramel Chicken Wings   47
Taiwanese Popcorn Chicken   48
Century Duck Eggs with Chilled Tofu   51
Lemongrass Shrimp Cocktail with Michelada Mayo   52
My Shanghainese Grandma's Fish   55
Pork Lettuce Wraps   56
Hot Honey–Cured Egg Yolks on Garlic Toast   59

2 SALADS   61

Chili-Lime Melon and Prosciutto   63
Fennel and Endive Salad with Asian Pear and Walnuts   64
Miso Caesar with Gai Lan and Chrysanthemum Greens   67
Classic Wedge with Shiso Ranch   68
Chilled Beef Shank Salad with Celery and Radish   71
Chicory Salad with Anchovy, Kumquats, and Smoked Cheese   72
Spiced Charred Peaches with Olives, Feta, and Orange Zest   75
Heirloom Tomatoes with Fish Sauce, Mint, and Fried Shallots   76
Jicama with Avocado, Macadamia Nuts, and Sesame-Lime Vinaigrette   79

3 BREADS & SANDWICHES   81

King's Focaccia   82
Milk Buns   86
Sheet Pan Pizza with Stracciatella, Pepperoni, and King's Hot Honey   89
Cheesy Scallion Pancakes   93
Al Pastor Bao   97
Ginger Scallion Lobster Rolls   98
Shanghainese Pork Belly Cubanos   100

4 NOODLES, DUMPLINGS & RICE   103

Dan Dan Mein   105

Taiwanese Beef Noodle Soup   106

Garlic Soy Sauce Noodles   109

Crispy Lace Dumplings Two Ways: Kimchi Beef & Pork and Salted Cabbage   110

Shiso Pea Pappardelle   115

Lobster Wontons in Yuzu Broth   116

Chinese Sticky Rice with Dried Seafood and Sausage   119

Chicken and Ginger Jook   122

5 VEGETABLES   124

Blistered Snap and Snow Peas with Cumin-Shiso Tzatziki   126

Street Corn Three Ways: Thai, Sichuan, and Italian   129

Salt and Pepper Maitake   133

Roasted Japanese Sweet Potato with Olives, Walnuts, and Miso-Tahini   134

Scallion Hash Browns with Crème Fraîche and Asian Pear   137

Shoyu Butter Mushrooms   138

Eggplant Caponata   141

Roasted Kabocha with Five Spice and Hot Honey   142

Really F***ing Crispy Potatoes with Raclette and Cornichons   144

Charred Cabbage with Burnt Lemon–Anchovy Vinaigrette   147

Corn Soup with Chili Crisp and Puffed Wild Rice   148

Pea Soup with Coconut Milk, Lap Cheong, and Green Oil   151

Green Beans with Pancetta and Caramelized Soy Sauce   152

Spiced Carrots with Pistachio and Labneh   155

6 SEAFOOD   157

Lemongrass Cioppino   159

Scallops with Creamed Corn and Prosciutto XO   160

Flounder with Yuzu Brown Butter and Capers   163

Grilled Fish Collars with Pickled Daikon and Ponzu   164

Steamed Clams with Burnt Lime–Cilantro Butter   167

Black Pepper–Garlic Lobster   168

Beer-Battered Fish with Apple Tartar Sauce   171

Salt-Baked Whole Fish   172

Mom's Steamed Egg Custard with Clams   175

Sichuan Chile Butter Shrimp   176

Swordfish au Poivre   179

Crispy Salmon with Summer Corn and Chanterelles   180

Char Siu Black Cod   183

7 POULTRY & MEAT   184

Grilled Lemongrass–Soy Sauce Chicken Thighs   187

Hainan Chicken with Chicken-Fat Rice and Ginger-Scallion Sauce   188

Five Spiced Duck à l'Orange   191

Grilled Quail with Sweet and Sour Plum Glaze   195

Rib Eye on the Bone with Black Garlic–Anchovy Butter   196

Lemongrass Beef Stew   199

Mala Lamb Skewers   200

Mama Mel's Meatballs   203

Pork Katsu with Snow Peas, Herbs, and Yuzu Vinaigrette   205

Black Vinegar Ribs   209

Chicken and Ginseng Bone Broth
with Goji Berries   210

Oxtail and Daikon Soup   213

Shanghainese "Lion's Head" Meatballs   214

Turmeric-Lemongrass Pork Belly Roast   217

8 SWEETS   221

Hong Kong Milk Tea Tiramisu   222

Torched Banana Pudding with Chinese
Almond Cookies   225

Almond Madeleines with
Citrus Marmalade   228

Dutch Pancake with Ricotta and
Strawberry-Ginger Jam   231

Salted Egg Yolk Basque Cheesecake   232

Vietnamese Coffee Flan   235

Hong Kong Stuffed French Toast   236

Chocolate Chunk Cookies   239

Yuzu–Coconut Olive Oil Cake with Berries   240

9 SAUCES, CONDIMENTS & OTHER FUN   242

Weekend Broth   244

Quick Pickles   245

Slow-Roasted Cherry Tomatoes with Garlic,
Fennel, and Coriander   245

Cured Duck Egg Yolks   247

Black Vinegar–Caramelized Onions   248

Charred Green Oil   248

Cipollini Onions Agrodolce   249

Sesame-Lime Vinaigrette   250

Fish Sauce Caramel   250

King's Hot Honey   251

Coconut Rice   251

Flavored Butters   252

Fried Shallots   254

Steamed Bao   254

Olive Oil–Fried Sourdough Croutons   255

Fried Bread Crumbs   256

Lap Cheong Crumble   256

Puffed Wild Rice   257

King's Chili Crisp   257

Citrus Marmalade   258

King's Ponzu   258

Pineapple-Habanero Hot Sauce   259

Hong Kong Milk Tea   259

Prosciutto XO   260

Chimichurri   261

Apple Tartar Sauce   261

Sweet Soy Sauce   262

Olive Tapenade   262

Ginger-Scallion Sauce   263

Black Vinegar–Chili Dipping Sauce   263

King's Mala Spice 263

Acknowledgments   264

About the Authors   267

Index   268

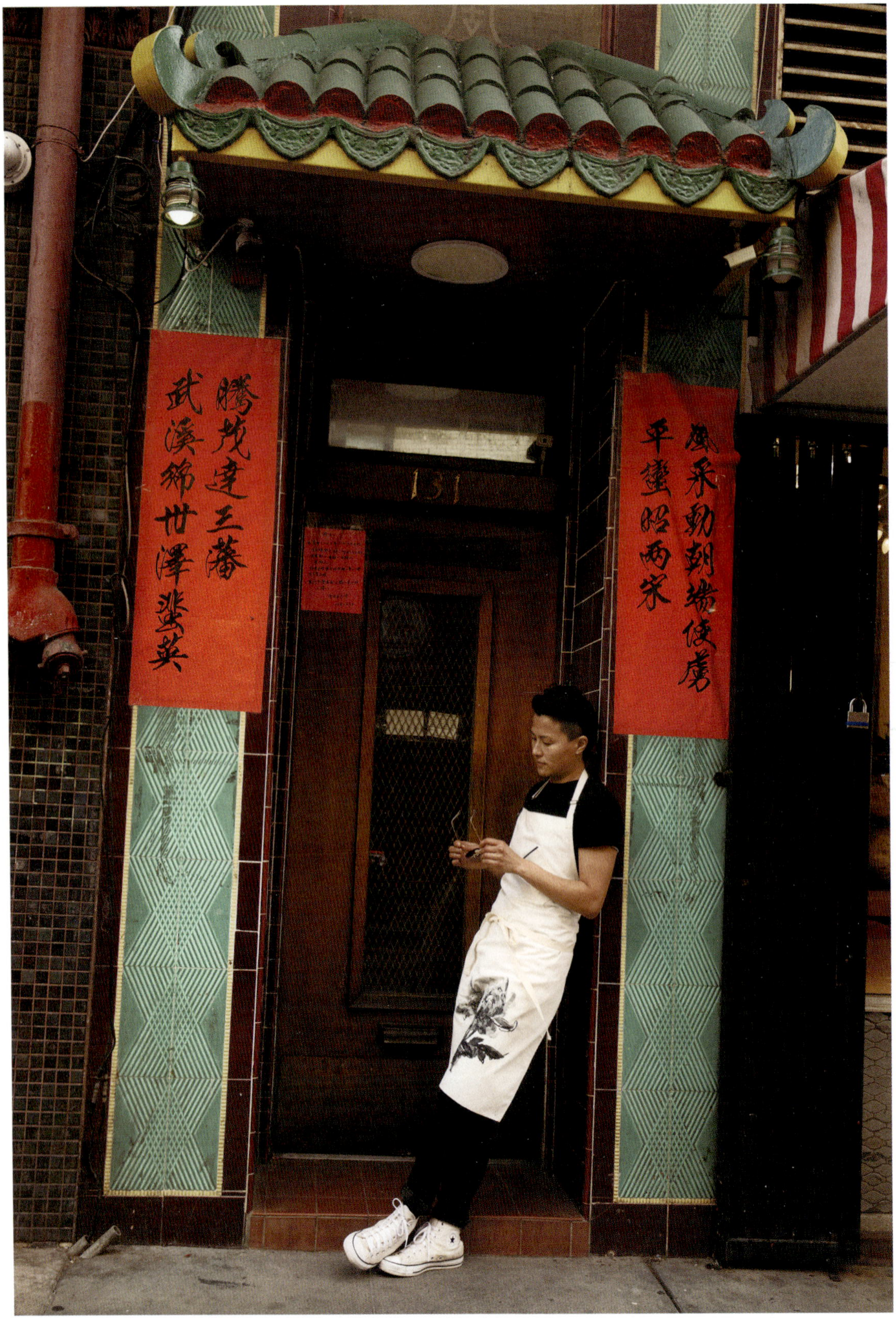
騰茂達三藩
武溪錦世澤斐英
131

INTRODUCTION

I had been trying to wow famed Italian butcher Dario Cecchini. I didn't mean to make him cry.

I was in Tuscany for the finale of *Top Chef: All-Stars*, contemplating the sweet ending to the four-course meal I would prepare for the judges. I didn't know it at the time but this meal would ultimately change my life. To honor where we were, I decided to make tiramisu, the iconic Italian dessert of espresso-soaked ladyfingers layered with mascarpone custard. I didn't want to fundamentally change the dish, but I did want to add a bit of me.

I thought of my childhood home. There was my mom and dad, both first-gen immigrants from Hong Kong and hard-working engineers, and my sister and me, who raced around the house wearing the Styrofoam sweaters that cradle Asian pears on our wrists as Wonder Woman cuffs. When we woke up, it wasn't to the smell of coffee but to that of lai cha (or Hong Kong milk tea), the strongly brewed black tea with sweetened condensed milk that my parents drank every morning.

If I traded the classic coffee element in tiramisu for lai cha, and if I tweaked the other elements just slightly, so the subtle, tannic qualities of the tea could shine through the richness, I might just bridge two culinary cultures I deeply admired. That's what, Dario explained, had moved him to tears. The idea that respect for tradition and openness to new ideas can coexist, and deliciously at that.

My ability to honor who I was, a seemingly simple ask, had actually been a lifetime in the making. And the winding path toward finding myself ran through the kitchen. So many of my childhood memories are of food. The beef shank simmered with rock sugar and soy sauce (page 71) that I'd snack on like deli meat from our fridge. The Thanksgiving feasts with sticky rice–stuffed roasted duck instead of turkey. The crispy pork belly, poached chickens, and red slabs of glistening char siu swinging in the window of our local Cantonese barbecue house in the San Gabriel Valley, and the taco trucks next door in East LA serving al pastor, another sort of red pork, this one carved from a vertical spit.

When we did have a homecooked meal, my mom was the cook (though not for long). My dad rarely entered the kitchen, but when he did, he'd make the only dish he knew: "lion's head" meatballs (page 214), a cozy Shanghainese dish of silky pork meatballs simmered in broth with cabbage and glass noodles that reminds him of his mom. I loved it for dinner, but not so much when it made its way into my school lunchbox, where it turned heads and scrunched up noses. My mom cooked simple homestyle Cantonese dishes: pork ribs braised in black vinegar, chicken wings glazed with soy sauce and sugar, steamed egg custard with clams, and whole fish with ginger and scallions. By the time I could see over the counter, I would help.

While my mom cooked, I watched from a wooden stool and we'd talk in our own seamless blend of Cantonese and English. I cherished this time with her, so I set out to make it more likely, rushing home from school to finish my homework and then chopping bok choy and washing rice in preparation for her arrival.

Soon, I graduated from being mom's tiny sous-chef to making meals myself. Because I wasn't yet old enough to use the stove, I'd assemble the whole fish and microwave it, just like mom occasionally did. If my parents were sick, I'd make them jook (rice porridge) in the rice cooker, propping open the lid with chopsticks, just like my mom taught me, to keep it from overflowing. When I was stove ready, I'd climb my stool after school and start a pot of bone broth with black Silkie chicken, ginger, and ginseng. I'd stir-fry bok choy and steam pork patties with salted duck egg. In an early experiment with fusion, I cooked jook with a stock made from smoked turkey legs I'd taken home from Disneyland.

Sometimes I'd forget the salt. Sometimes I'd add a handful instead of a pinch. But my family always ate what I'd made, usually without complaint. Feeding my parents was my way of taking care of them, or at least of thanking them for taking care of me. But I won't lie. I also loved the thrill of playing with fire and knives.

When I graduated high school, I knew I wanted to be a chef. My parents, however, weren't having it. Like many immigrants, they had sacrificed so much to give their children the life they wished they'd had. They wanted better for me than toiling in a kitchen. Yet the heart wants what it wants. While in college, I juggled entry-level kitchen work between semesters, dabbling in the world of pastries and banquet cooking. After college, I enrolled at the Culinary Institute of America, with my mom and dad's reluctant blessing, trading my Chinese meat cleaver (a gift from my mom for my eighth birthday) for a French chef's knife.

At first, I was slightly disoriented. When my instructors demonstrated how to cook duck breasts, slowly rendering the skin to crisp it and then cutting it into rosy red slices, I wondered: Why were we shooting for mid-rare when the roast duck I grew up eating was delicious cooked extremely well done? Yet I welcomed the new perspectives and flavors. I had my first taste of beets and parsnips, and my first experience with cheese that wasn't sold as slices individually wrapped in plastic. I learned to brown butter and deglaze with wine. I saw that carrots, celery, and onion were to French cooking what scallion, ginger, and garlic were to Cantonese. Most of all, culinary school revealed a path to being a great cook: discipline and repetition to tone the muscle of cooking.

After culinary school, my job search took me to the culinary boomtown that was San Francisco in the early 2000s. My focus was fine dining, and I landed in several Michelin-starred kitchens. I fell for the hustle and the pressure of perfectionism. Working as a saucier under chef Dominique Crenn, I practiced patience to unlock flavors in sauces and soups. I saw how attention to detail—the quality of ingredients, generosity with salt, the importance of developing a deeply browned crust on a rib eye—could transform a good dish to a great one.

After several years of making gelées and foams, I left to cook rustic Italian, applying the same level of care I'd devoted to molecular French cooking to simpler food. With some love, flour and water could become beautiful ribbons of tagliatelle or crusty, bubbly focaccia. The same layering of flavor that produced great bordelaise could also make fantastic marinara. I loved the purity of Italian cooking. Instead of twenty ingredients on each plate, there might be three, each thoughtfully selected and embellished with little more than good olive oil, citrus, and flaky salt. In many ways, the soulful flavors reminded me of the Cantonese food I made at home between shifts. I started to notice moments of overlap between the very different cuisines. As I formed ravioli at work, I thought of the dumplings I'd make with my Cantonese grandma, Sabrina PoPo. As I cooked risotto, I thought of the jook I cooked for my parents. Still, I kept this part of me separate from my work as a professional cook. Back then, Michelin stars were still the most important measures of success, and at the time you didn't win them by making wontons.

At the Ritz-Carlton Dining Room, chef Ron Siegel instilled in me an ethos of sustainability and a joy for cooking with ingredients at their seasonal peak. Without the sweetest summer corn or tender spring peas, your skill as a cook can only get you so far. As the restaurant's fish butcher, I also did battle against waste, finding delicious use for every snapper head and salmon collar, to prune food costs and show respect to the oceans that provided such bounty. At Luce, I was a butcher full-time, breaking down whole pigs and sides of beef. There, almost all the actual cooking I did was for family meal.

As much as I liked cooking for appreciative diners, I absolutely loved feeding my kitchen family, the line cooks, dishwashers, servers, and sous-chefs who worked so hard they barely had time to feed themselves. It's why they started to call me Mama Mel. Cooking for them, I felt a satisfaction familiar from those dinners I made for my birth family. I got something out of it, too. I had spent my career dutifully executing other people's food. I was beginning to make my own.

Grandma Sabrina and me

I'd raid the walk-in for vegetable trim and cuts of meat and fish not quite perfect enough to fetch tasting-menu prices. I'd turn lobster knuckles and fish tails into a sort of Thai-ish cioppino, San Francisco's iconic fish stew infused with lemongrass and lime leaves. I'd batter and fry odd pieces of halibut for tacos and make guacamole, which I'd learned from my Mexican colleagues over the years, who called me chinita and then, after I chopped off my hair, chinito. The part of my brain that linked risotto and jook went into overdrive. Suddenly, Italian porchetta reminded me of Filipino lechon liempo, just with different aromatics. Chinese orange chicken struck me as similar to French duck à l'orange. My culinary voice was starting to take shape.

By the time I competed on season 12 of *Top Chef*, I was dabbling in the food that would become my style today. But looking back on that season, I was mostly mimicking what I'd learned from my mentors. I was stuck in my head, overthinking, overanalyzing, doubting myself. Yet something changed when my mom showed up for one of the challenges. In a full-circle moment, she became my sous-chef for the day, helping me cook luxurious lobster-topped Japanese egg custard, a dish that reminded me of but was also so different from the egg custard with clams she cooked for our family. It was as if a switch had flipped. I stepped out of my head. I stopped worrying about what I should cook and embraced what I wanted to cook. It remains one of the most memorable moments of my life. Cooking side by side with my mom, I felt the comfort and freedom I did as a kid, but now I also had the skill and experience I'd worked so hard to build.

I was no longer cooking to please my culinary mentors or the judges. I was cooking food that told the story of my life—the full story, mom's egg custard, my dad's meatballs, and all. I spent the next few years curating events around the country and building a restaurant in Tokyo (which sadly didn't survive the pandemic). Then, because I love a challenge, I returned to *Top Chef* to compete on the All-Star season.

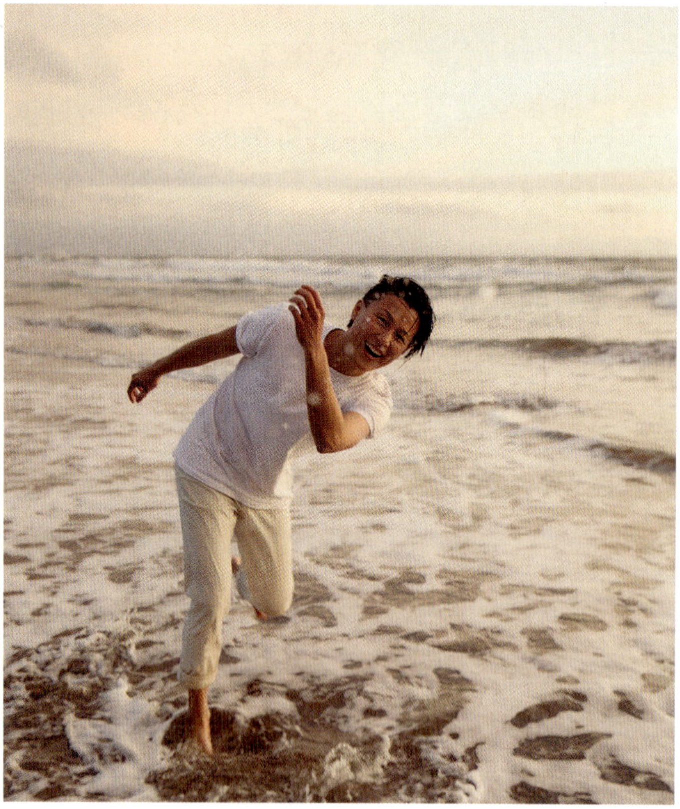

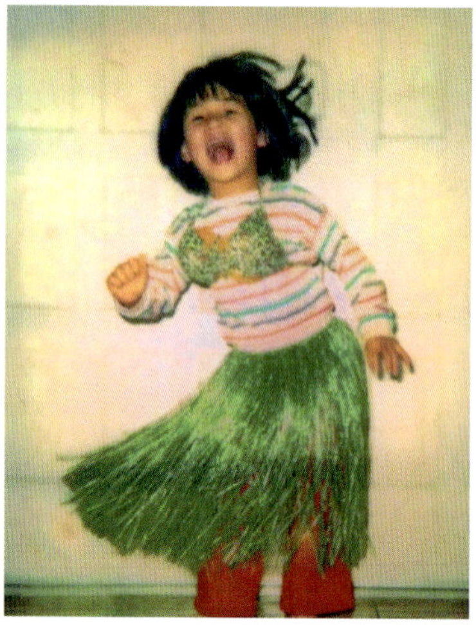

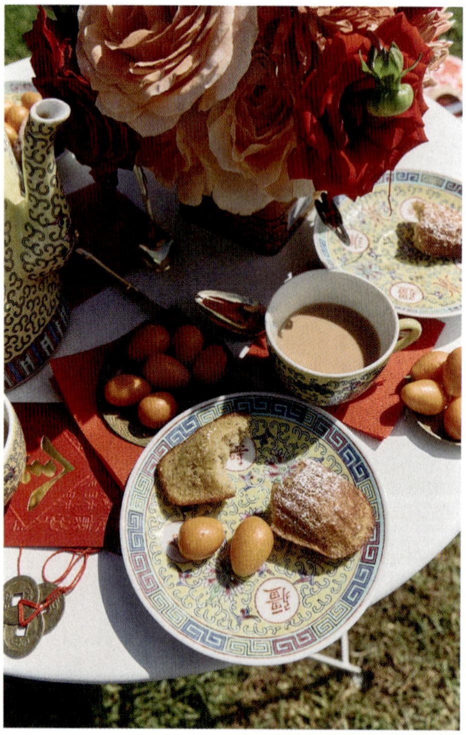

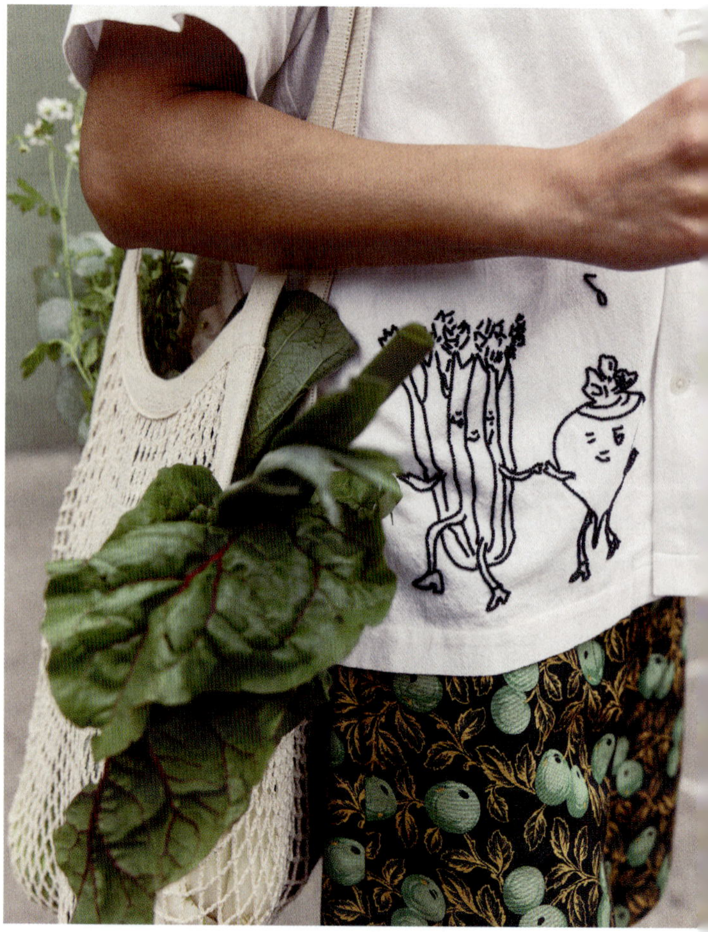

At last, I was ready to cook food that reflected all of me: the French-trained chef who led Michelin-starred kitchens. The cook who would love to do nothing else but make fresh pastas and simmer meatballs. The California girl who sneaks citrus from the trees in her sister's yard to make marmalade, who can't get enough of her favorite taco trucks. The Chinese American who grew up on Hainan chicken and head-on spot prawns poached in rice wine. The out queer woman who was finally comfortable with all of it.

I won the All-Star season of *Top Chef* by cooking unapologetically, by embracing my voice. I found moments when cultures and cuisines ran parallel, and then with intention and care, I made a few tweaks to build a bridge between them without sacrificing what makes each such a joy in the first place. To eat my food was to see me. To taste my lobster wontons was to understand the kid raised on shrimp wontons who grew up to cook lobster in fancy French kitchens. To taste my grilled quail with plum glaze was to get to know the chef who adores the roasted ducks and squabs at Cantonese barbecue houses in the San Gabriel Valley and fell for the dainty game bird and seasonal stone fruit in San Francisco. To take a spoonful of my Hong Kong milk tea tiramisu was to meet someone who respects tradition but isn't tied to it, to meet the girl who can make a grown butcher cry.

I've happily spent the years since traveling the country to cook for people. As a chef without a restaurant, I essentially curate dinner parties, large and small, touching people's lives through food. And when I'm not working, I throw them for my friends and family. That little girl who made jook for her parents grew into an adult whose joy comes from nurturing people through food. That's what this cookbook is about—it's a way to share my food, my love, and to help you cook like a king.

Cooking like a king doesn't just mean making the food of this particular King, though you'll find a collection of my absolute favorite dishes. Some are signatures from my time on *Top Chef*. Some are pulled from my dinner party repertoire. Some speak to my love of seasonal cooking, and their goal is simply to highlight produce or seafood at its peak, often with an element of surprise snuck in. And many are loving mash-ups, food that blurs lines in fun and delicious ways.

Cooking like a king also means expanding your pantry and learning fundamental techniques, so you feel confident enough in the kitchen to create dishes of your own. Above all, the goal of this book is to empower home cooks at any level, to show that you really can make Hainan chicken that would impress a Chinese grandma and lobster wontons that will impress your friends. I want you to feel the pride I feel when I feed my friends and see their faces light up, and the joy of watching them fight for the last bites.

I begin with a guide to the ingredients you'll want to have on hand in order to make my recipes and that I know will improve and inspire your own cooking. I hope you'll play, with restraint and respect, with the particular sources of fat and salt, acid and heat that, taken together, create flavors recognizable as Italian, French, Chinese, or Japanese. I want you to see how simply swapping yuzu for lemon or Chinese black vinegar for red wine vinegar can make a familiar dish feel new and exciting.

The recipes in this book have a little more detail than the typical cookbook. I want you to feel like I'm by your side in the kitchen, holding your hand through the important moments. The recipes also include ideas for either switching up components to encourage flexibility and creativity or ways to level-up for all the overachievers out there. There's something for everyone in this book—weeknight dinners that'll become your go-tos, showstopping dishes for gatherings, and everything in between.

PANTRY

If you want to improve your cooking, give your pantry a glow-up. Small changes can make a big impact on your food, even something as simple as upgrading your olive oil, vinegars, and salt. And just wait until you welcome my favorites into your pantry, including some of the bottles and jars you might have only eyed in Asian and Italian markets. With these ingredients in your everyday arsenal, the food you cook will improve no matter what you make. Virtually all of these products are available online, but I highly recommend exploring your local markets.

Bay leaves: I prefer fresh, not only because in California I often pick them wild while hiking, but because they're significantly more fragrant and you know they haven't been sitting on a store shelf forever. Dried bay leaves, however, are just fine and are preferred in one recipe: For King's Chili Crisp (page 257), adding dried bay leaves, rather than fresh, to hot oil prevents splatter.

Black garlic: This East Asian ingredient is made by keeping garlic in a warm, humid environment for weeks until the natural sugars slowly caramelize and the cloves turn soft and black. Flavorful without the harshness of raw garlic, the cloves are sweet, slightly molasses-y, and full of umami. To use, cut the heads in half horizontally and squeeze out the cloves.

Canned tomatoes: Just as high-quality olive oil will make your salads taste better, so will great canned tomatoes immeasurably improve your sauces and stews. My favorites are SMT and Bianco DiNapoli.

Canola oil: In this book, I call for canola oil when I want a neutral flavor and relatively high smoke point. Grapeseed, vegetable, and avocado oils work great, too.

Champagne vinegar: Standard white wine vinegars almost always leave me wanting more acidity and flavor, so I typically choose champagne and other sparkling wine vinegars for their fruity character and crisp acidity. The Katz Farm brand is my favorite. If I don't have sparkling wine vinegar, I'll use apple cider vinegar.

Chiles, dried and fresh: The heat of chiles is a vital component of many dishes in this book. Because everyone has their own preference for heat and because chiles often vary in spiciness, be sure to adjust amounts based on your own preference.

In this book, I call for whole dried Sichuan chiles and Sichuan chile flakes. There are several varieties of dried chiles common in Sichuan cooking, each with its own nuances. In my cooking, acquiring a specific variety isn't vital. Seeking out whole chiles and chile flakes labeled "Sichuan" will lead you toward chiles with fruity, nutty flavor and moderate heat. Korean gochugaru is a solid sub for Sichuan chile flakes.

For fresh chiles, I look to ripe (red) Fresno chiles for slightly fruity flavor and moderate heat. Jalapeños and serranos bring similar fire, but have a sharp, grassy flavor, with serranos offering an extra level of heat. Thai chiles, red or green, are even spicier. Habanero chiles are very hot with a distinctive fruity character and tropical notes, and Calabrian chiles, often packed in oil or sold crushed to an oily paste, have a bright, fruity flavor.

Chinese chili crisp: I include a relatively simple recipe for chili crisp (see page 257), an infused oil that's aromatic from spices and packed with crispy bits of chiles and sesame seeds. I hope you make it, but you're also free to use your favorite brand. Each has a slightly different flavor profile and crispness factor, so I encourage you to find the one you like best, whether it be Lao Gan Ma or Fly By Jing.

Chinese five spice powder: While the precise formula varies, this spice blend often features the fivesome of star anise, fennel seeds, cloves, cinnamon, and Sichuan peppercorns. It contributes warm, sweet, and sharp flavors to marinades, rubs, and sauces.

遺伝子組換大豆は使用していません
特選
醬道
原味芝麻醬
Maggi
Seasoning
Improves the taste
KIM
金蘭
Café

CORIANDER SEED
CUMIN SEED
FENNEL SEED
FIVE SPICE POWDER
STAR ANISE
RED SICHUAN
CHINESE CHILIS

Coconut milk: I frequently use naturally sweet, fragrant, and fatty coconut milk to add flavor and richness to soups. Look for cans or boxes of unsweetened, full-fat coconut milk made without guar gum. Because the fat often separates from the liquid, shake the container well before using.

Dried shiitake: These dried mushrooms have a deeper, more concentrated flavor than fresh shiitake and significantly more umami. Rehydrated in hot water, they take on a delightful chewy, meaty texture. They're also frequently simmered in broth and stocks to build flavor. Buy whole mushrooms (I generally prefer Japanese brands) and give them a quick rinse before using.

Dried shrimp and scallops: Prized for their concentrated seafood flavor and umami, these two products are common in the food of Hong Kong and regions throughout China. In this book, they're essential to lo mai fan (Chinese sticky rice) on page 119. At Chinese markets, they're often sold in heaps among other dried goods like ginseng. Let price be your guide to quality.

Fish sauce: The flavor of this bold, salty, umami-rich seasoning made from fermented, salted fish (often anchovies) varies by country and brand, just like that of soy sauce. When used in small amounts in this book, practically any type or brand will do. But for certain recipes, I insist on the well-rounded, delicately salty Three Crabs brand. In those cases, using a different fish sauce will result in dishes that are too salty.

Ginger: One of the ingredients I use most often, ginger and its warm spice notes show up in my cooking where you might expect and where you might not. Peel off the thick skin with a sharp knife, a vegetable peeler, or as my mom taught me, a spoon, which is especially useful for getting in the nooks.

Herbs: So much of my food relies on the brightness of fresh herbs. Many of these herbs need little introduction, so I'll only note my preference for using just the leaves of herbs like basil, mint, and parsley, while using the tender, flavorful stems of cilantro. There are a few herbs you'll encounter in my recipes that may not be as familiar: Thai basil has purple stems and a sweet, anise-like flavor. Fresh makrut lime leaves are incredibly fragrant. Both can be found at East and Southeast Asian markets and farmers' markets. Shiso has serrated leaves and an earthy, mintlike flavor. It comes fresh in both red and green varieties, but green is preferred in this book for its color and accessibility. Japanese markets are a reliable source. For the best flavor and to prevent discoloration, chop fresh herbs with a sharp knife right before you use them.

Katsuobushi: A major component of the essential Japanese stock known as dashi, katsuobushi is bonito fish that has been simmered, smoked, and dried before being shaved thin. It has a delicately smoky flavor and tons of umami. Price is a good guide to quality. Look for katsuobushi that's light in color and purchase large flakes rather than fine shavings. Store in the refrigerator or a cool, dark place.

Kombu: Kombu is a type of dried sea kelp rich in flavor and a major component of dashi. I purchase Japanese kombu and let the price serve as my guide to quality. Don't be tempted to rinse or wipe off the white powdery substance from the surface of dark green sheets—it's umami!

Lap cheong: There are many varieties of Chinese pork sausages, but in this book, I call for the Cantonese-style firm, sweet-savory links with a slightly floral quality from the addition of rose wine. I typically use the Kan Yen Jan brand.

Lemongrass: In this book, I use fresh stalks to infuse a citrusy flavor and fragrance into soups, stews, and marinades. Before using, cut off the bottom ½ inch and the woody top (leaving about 4 inches of stalk), then remove the outermost layer. Reserve any trim for another purpose, like Weekend Broth (page 244). Fresh lemongrass is readily available, but it's particularly affordable at Asian markets.

Maggi: A popular liquid seasoning from Mexico to Hong Kong, this product made from fermented wheat is similar to soy sauce and Worcestershire sauce in that it's pungent and full of umami.

Miso: This paste of fermented soybeans is full of umami. For this book, you'll want to stock shiro (white) miso, which is only briefly fermented and has a relatively mild flavor and slight sweetness. Yellow miso works well in its place.

Olive oil: Like wine, olive oil has a wide range of flavor profiles based on the types of olives used, where they were grown, and how they were made. There is a vast range of quality as well, and while it may be tempting to buy the cheapest bottle you can find, investing an extra $5 to $10 per bottle can make a world of a difference. Choose extra-virgin olive oil that tastes great on its own or drizzled over raw tomatoes with a little flaky salt. I prefer oils with buttery, fruity, and grassy notes and a light peppery finish. Cobram Estate California Select and Partanna are great options. To keep your olive oil tasting its best, store bottles in a cool, dark place. Besides pure olive oil, one of my secret ingredients is lemon olive oil, made by crushing whole lemons together with olives to extract the unbelievably fragrant oil. I swear by the Agrumato brand. It tastes entirely unlike others on the market.

Oyster sauce: Traditionally made from oysters slowly cooked in their liquor until thick and concentrated, this seasoning is packed with umami and rich sweetness. The particulars of oyster sauce, like those of fish sauce and soy sauce, vary by country, so for the right flavor for the dishes in this book, Chinese oyster sauce is what you want to stock. Lee Kum Kee Premium is what I've used since I was a kid, and it's exceptional.

Preserved mustard greens: There are many varieties of pickled and preserved mustard greens used in Chinese cooking, and the quirks of labeling and transliteration doesn't always help the shopper. In Cantonese, they're called shun choy, which translates to "sour vegetable" and English language labels describe them as "preserved," "pickled," or "sour" mustard greens or "mustard leaf." I like the Fish Well brand (look for the pink package). Choose either the spicy or mild variety, depending on your preference. Buy it shredded or whole, then cut it into thin strips yourself.

Rice wine: In this book, you'll see two kinds of rice wine: For dishes with Chinese inspiration, I use Shaoxing wine, which is dry with a slightly nutty, floral quality. For those with Japanese inspiration, I use mirin, which is sweet and floral, with a lower alcohol content than Shaoxing and mirin's cousin, sake. Aji-mirin, a product that mimics mirin's flavor without the traditional processes used to make it, works well for my recipes, though hon mirin (true mirin) will give you a more delicious result.

Rock sugar: Chinese grandmas swear by these white or golden translucent chunks of crystallized sugar, also labeled "rock candy," for their mellow sweetness and nuanced flavor and the glossiness they lend to stews and braises. Light brown sugar in equal amounts makes a fine substitute, because it mimics the slight maltiness of rock sugar.

Salt: Like olive oil, the salt you use makes a big difference in the flavor of your food. I like to keep two kinds on hand: flaky sea salt and kosher salt. Flaky sea salt contributes a delicate crunch and a pop of clean salinity, making it perfect for finishing a dish. Maldon or Jacobsen Salt Co. are both great brands. Kosher salt is your workhorse, the salt you use for everything else. I always use the Diamond Crystal brand, which has a clean flavor and dissolves more quickly than Morton, the other common brand, making it less likely that you'll oversalt food. Note that because of the shape and size of the grains, 1 tablespoon of Diamond Crystal contains roughly half the amount of salt as

1 tablespoon of Morton. So, if you must—and *only* if you must—use Morton for my recipes, please use about half the amount called for.

Sichuan peppercorns: Common in Sichuan cooking, these are the sun-dried berries of the prickly ash tree. They're beloved for their floral, citrusy qualities (the prickly ash is a member of the citrus family) as well as the numbing, tingling sensation they create in the mouth. Red Sichuan peppercorns are the easiest to find and work for all the recipes in this book, though if you care to make the effort, the even more floral green Sichuan peppercorns are fantastic in Taiwanese Beef Noodle Soup (page 106).

Sesame paste: I call for two kinds of sesame paste in this book: tahini, a Middle Eastern product made from lightly toasted seeds, and Chinese sesame paste, which is made from heavily toasted sesame seeds and has a rich dark color.

Soy sauce: When you enter an Asian market, you'll often see dozens of types of soy sauce brewed from fermented soybeans, each of them delicious in its own way. Each country that uses soy sauce—including Korea, Thailand, China, and Japan—has several varieties in its repertoire, and despite some similarities, they're not interchangeable. Recipes in this book that are inspired by Chinese cooking call for Chinese light soy sauce, which is salty and thin, and dark soy sauce, which is often aged and is thicker, less salty, and a little more complex. It's used to add color as much as flavor. I like the Kimlan, Lee Kum Kee, and Pearl River Bridge brands. Dishes inspired by Japanese cooking taste best made with Japanese soy sauce, both the familiar dark variety and white soy sauce (shiro shoyu), which has a lighter color and more delicate flavor.

Stock: All the recipes in this book can be made with the boxed stock you'll find on the grocery store shelf, but you can absolutely use stock from your local butcher shop or that you've made yourself. Either way, buy low-sodium or unsalted stock so you'll have control over the salt levels.

Toasted sesame oil: Not to be confused with clear sesame oil that's pressed from raw sesame seeds, this golden brown oil is pressed from sesame seeds after they've been toasted to bring out their nuttiness. I find that when you heat toasted sesame oil, you lose some of its delicate flavor, so I typically use it in dressings or as a finishing drizzle. Store bottles in the fridge or another cool, dark place. Use it (or replace it) often.

White pepper: White pepper is made from the ripe, red berries of a flowering vine (as opposed to black pepper, which is made from the unripe, green berries of the same plant). Before they're dried, the berries are soaked to remove the outer layer. White pepper isn't as harsh as black and has an earthy, floral, slightly gingery quality that's prevalent in Chinese cooking. It's used as a primary flavor in dishes like hot and sour soup (it's the "hot") or as an accent. Buy preground white pepper and use it (or replace it) often.

Wonton skins and dumpling wrappers: Even as someone who loves to make fresh pasta, I don't make my own wonton skins and don't always have the time or energy to make my own dumpling wrappers. Like puff pastry, some things are just better (and quicker) when left to the industrial pros. Keep in mind that square wonton skins are significantly thinner than round dumpling wrappers and therefore not interchangeable. Wonton skins are sold in white and yellow varieties. I prefer the yellow variety, which is popular in Hong Kong; it contains egg and has a little extra chew. Twin Marquis is a good brand for both wonton skins and dumpling wrappers. They are sold fresh or frozen and will keep well in your freezer. Thaw before using.

Yuzu: If Meyer lemon, Key lime, and grapefruit had a baby, it might be this tart citrus beloved in Japan for its incredibly fragrant, floral zest and juice. Fresh yuzu can be challenging to find in the United States—look online, in Japanese grocery stores, and at California farmers' markets. It's really special. While bottled juice isn't quite the same as freshly squeezed, products that contain 100 percent yuzu juice are great options.

Zhenjiang (Chinkiang) black vinegar: This Chinese aged vinegar made from glutinous rice has a deep brown color, rich almost malty flavor, and sharp acidity. Don't mistake it for Taiwanese black vinegar, which contains sugar, tomato paste, and orange juice and has a very different flavor profile.

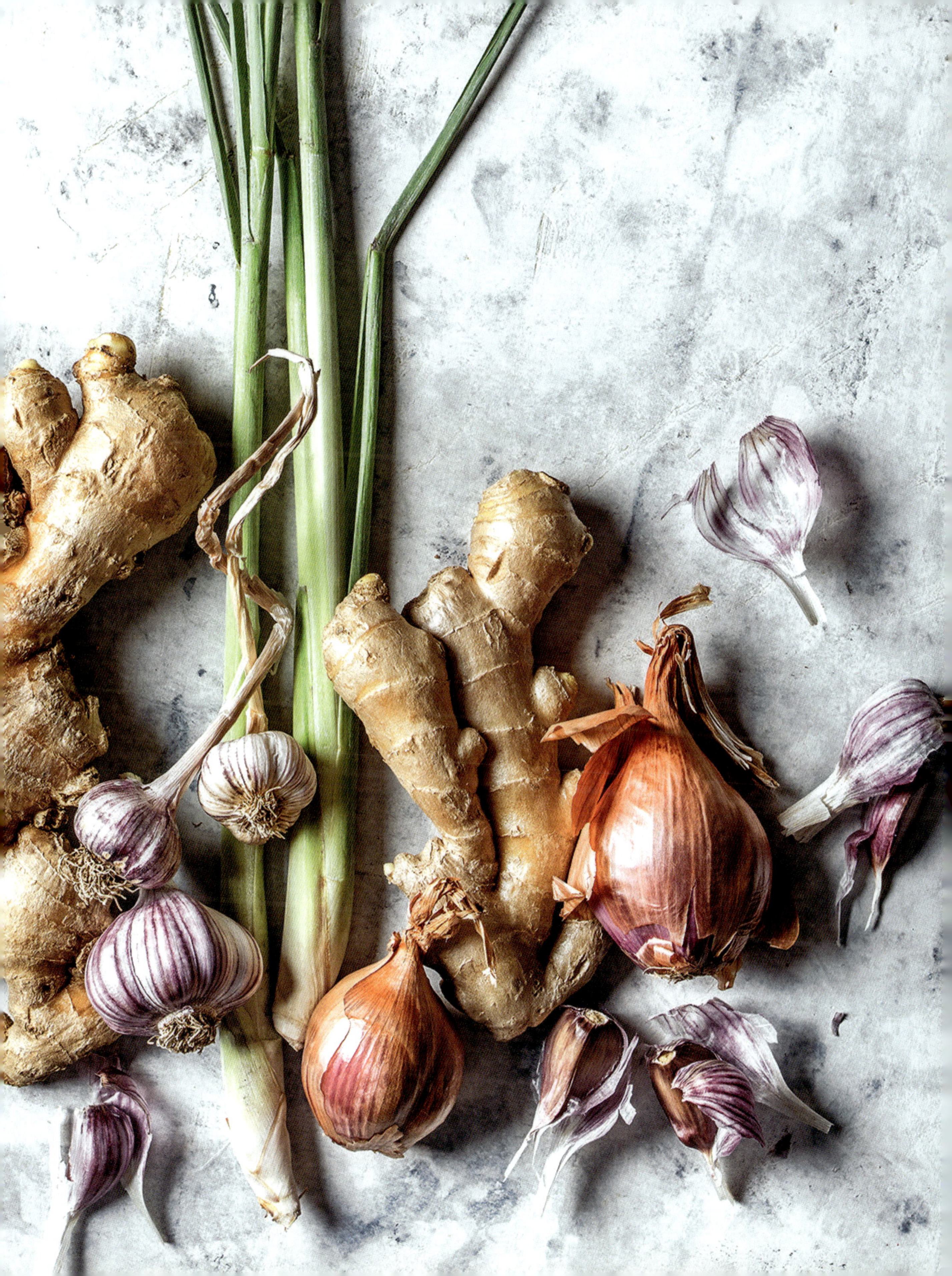

SNACKS,

APPS & DIPS

1

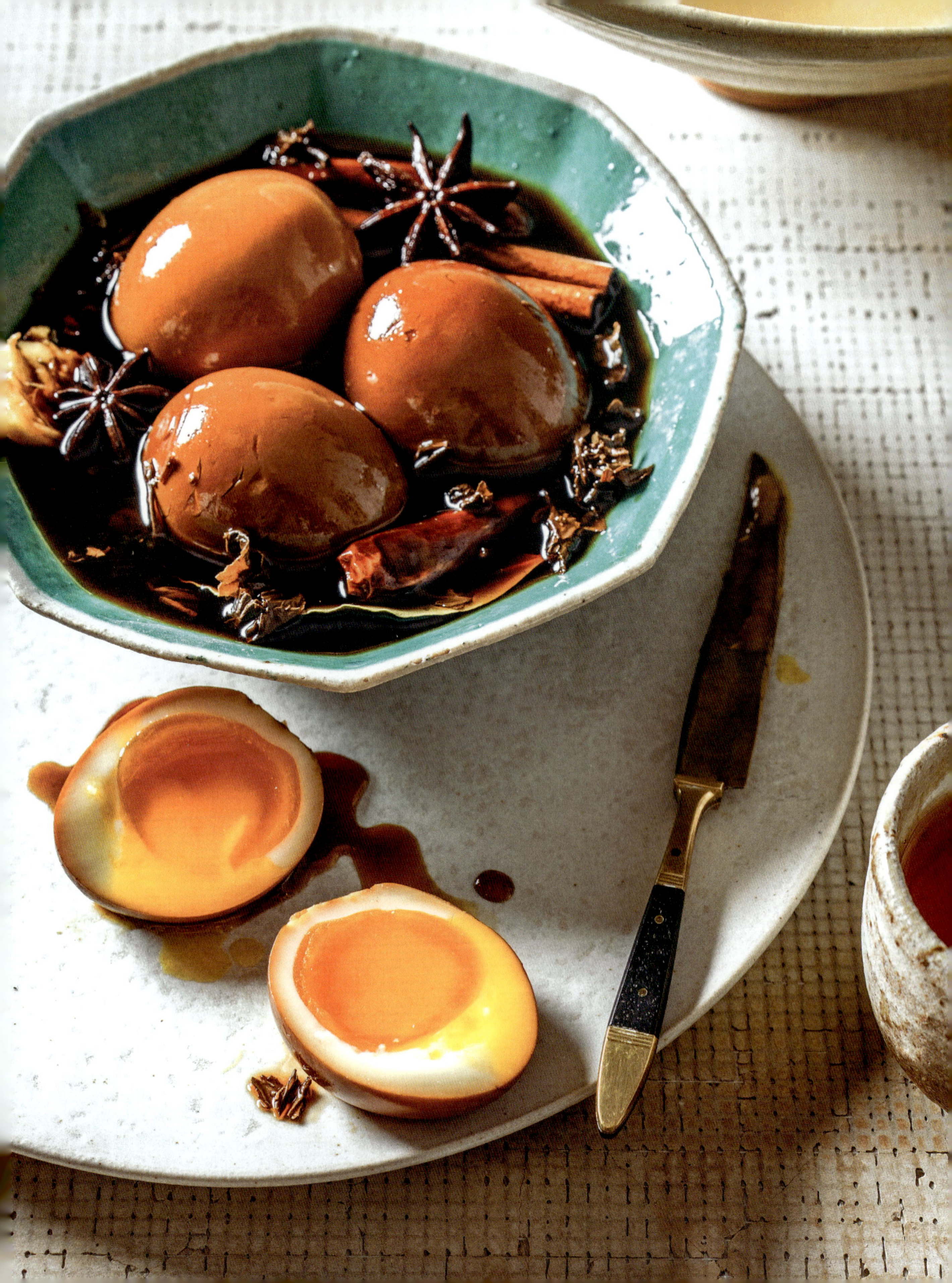

SMOKY TEA EGGS

One of my favorite after-school snacks were the marinated boiled eggs I used to sneak from my Cantonese grandma Sabrina PoPo's fridge. I boil mine just until the yolks are soft and jammy, then soak them in a sweet brine infused with warm spices like ginger and star anise and lapsang souchong tea, an earthy black tea dried over pinewood fire that gives the eggs a smoky flavor.

Twenty-four hours in the brine is the sweet spot, but if you're anything like me, I bet you'll eat them all before then. They're great on their own, but they're also delicious in ramen or jook (page 122) and over steamed rice along with Char Siu Black Cod (page 183) or Grilled Lemongrass–Soy Sauce Chicken Thighs (page 187).

MAKES 12

1½ cups Chinese light soy sauce

1 cup Chinese rock sugar or lightly packed light brown sugar

1 cup water

½ cup Chinese dark soy sauce

½ cup mirin

½ cup unseasoned rice vinegar

2 tablespoons lapsang souchong tea leaves

4 by 1-inch knob ginger, lightly smashed

4 whole dried Sichuan chiles (optional)

4 whole star anise

2 bay leaves

2 cinnamon sticks

¼ teaspoon ground white pepper

½ teaspoon red Sichuan peppercorns

12 large eggs

In a medium pot, combine all the ingredients except the eggs. Bring to a boil over high heat and cook, uncovered, stirring occasionally, until most of the sugar has dissolved, about 2 minutes. Remove from the heat and let the mixture cool to room temperature, at least 1 hour.

While the brine cools, in a covered 4- to 6-quart pot, bring 8 cups water to a full boil over high heat. Prepare a big bowl with half ice and half water.

Carefully but quickly lower the eggs (using a spider strainer helps) into the boiling water. Let the water return to a full boil, uncovered, then adjust the heat to cook at a steady simmer for 5 minutes (set a timer). When the timer goes off, turn off the heat and gently transfer the eggs to the ice water. Let them chill for at least 30 minutes. Remove the eggs, peel carefully, and rinse off any remaining bits of shell.

Put the eggs in one or more containers, then pour in the cooled brine to completely submerge the eggs. (They'll float in the brine, so either use a small weight to keep them submerged or rotate the eggs halfway through.) Cover and refrigerate for at least 12 hours or up to 48 hours (to me, 24 hours is the sweet spot).

After brining, you can drain the eggs (reserving the brine in the fridge for one more round) and store them in an airtight container in the refrigerator for up to 2 more days.

MISO BABA GHANOUSH

Baba ghanoush is simple and so damn good! After you roast whole eggplants over an open flame, the charred skins peel away to reveal creamy, smoky flesh. From there, I round out the flavor with tahini and olive oil for depth, and lemon and sherry vinegar for different notes of brightness to balance the richness.

Eating it reminds me of another elegantly simple dish that showcases the creamy texture of eggplant: Japanese nasu dengaku, where eggplant is split, slathered with miso, and broiled. The connection inspired this take on the Middle Eastern dip, where the umami of white miso and toasty fragrance of sesame oil bring delicious new dimension.

MAKES ABOUT 3½ CUPS

2 pounds Italian eggplants (about 4 medium)

¼ cup lemon juice, plus more as needed

2 teaspoons Diamond Crystal kosher salt, plus more as needed

Finely ground black pepper

2 medium garlic cloves, finely grated on a Microplane

¼ cup well-stirred tahini

2 tablespoons shiro (white) miso

¼ cup extra-virgin olive oil, plus more for serving

2 teaspoons toasted sesame oil

Splash of aged sherry vinegar (the older, the better)

FOR SERVING

Sichuan chile flakes or Aleppo chile flakes

Toasted sesame seeds

Mixed herbs, such as chives, dill, and flat-leaf parsley leaves

Flaky sea salt

Prepare a grill, preferably charcoal, to cook with high heat. (Alternatively, this can be done under the broiler.) Poke each eggplant all over with a paring knife, inserting the blade about 1 inch deep and making two dozen or so such cuts per eggplant.

Add the eggplants to the hot grill and cook, turning occasionally, until the skin is charred and brittle all over and the flesh is very soft, about 40 minutes. (Or broil the eggplants on a large [18 by 13-inch] foil-lined sheet pan 2 to 4 inches from the heat source, turning every 10 minutes or so, for about 40 minutes.) Set aside until cool enough to handle.

As you peel off and discard the charred skin of the eggplants, scoop the tender flesh into a fine-mesh sieve and set aside to drain for 10 minutes, discarding the liquid.

Meanwhile, in a medium bowl, combine the lemon juice, salt, several turns of pepper, and the garlic and whisk well. Add the tahini and miso and whisk until smooth.

Add the drained eggplant flesh to the bowl and mix and mash until creamy but slightly chunky. Then, while mixing, drizzle in the olive oil and sesame oil. Season to taste with the sherry vinegar and additional salt, pepper, and lemon juice.

To serve: Transfer the baba ghanoush to a shallow bowl. Use the bottom of a large spoon to make pretty divots in the mixture. Add a generous drizzle of olive oil. Sprinkle on chile flakes and sesame seeds, then herbs and flaky salt.

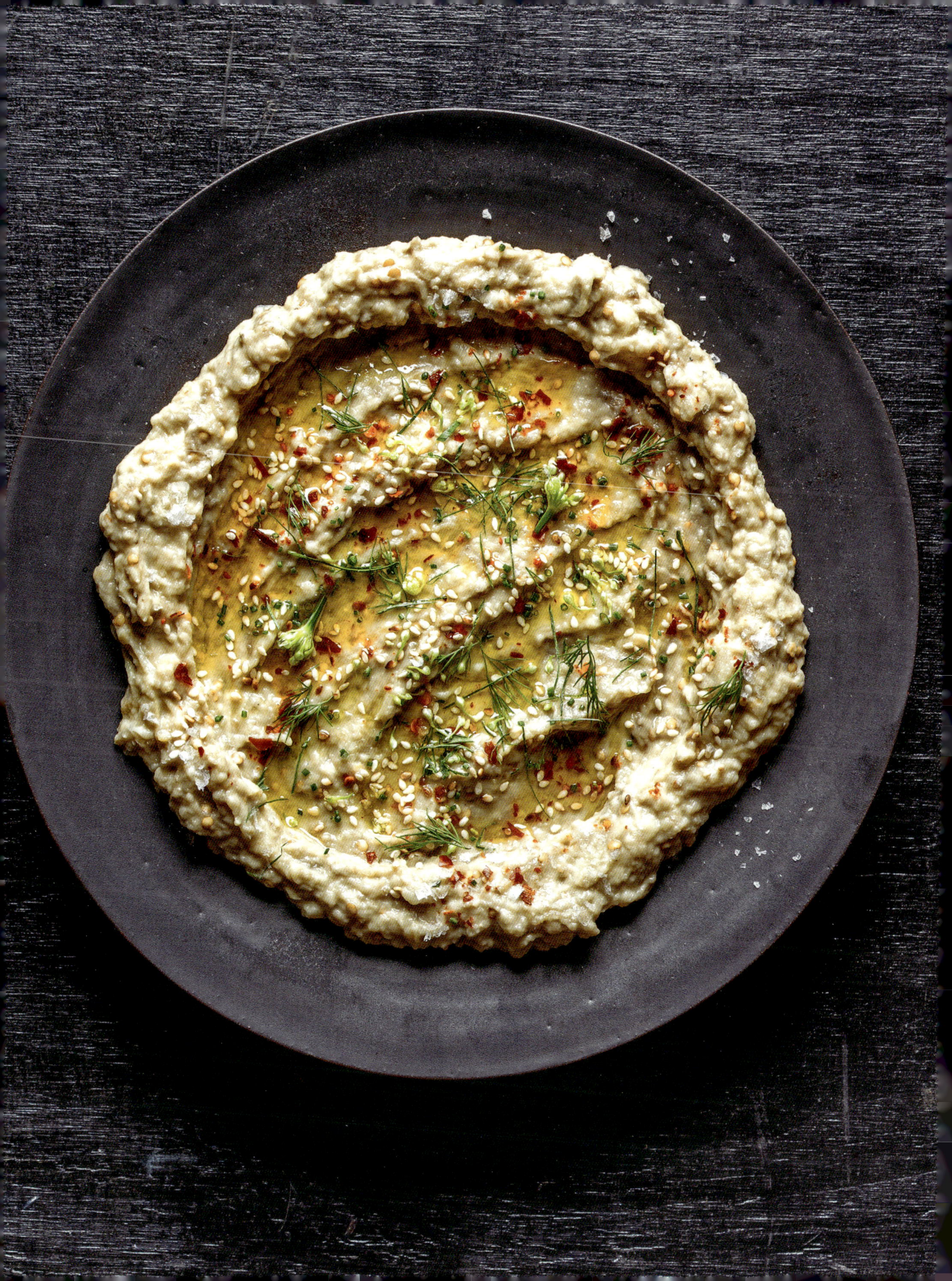

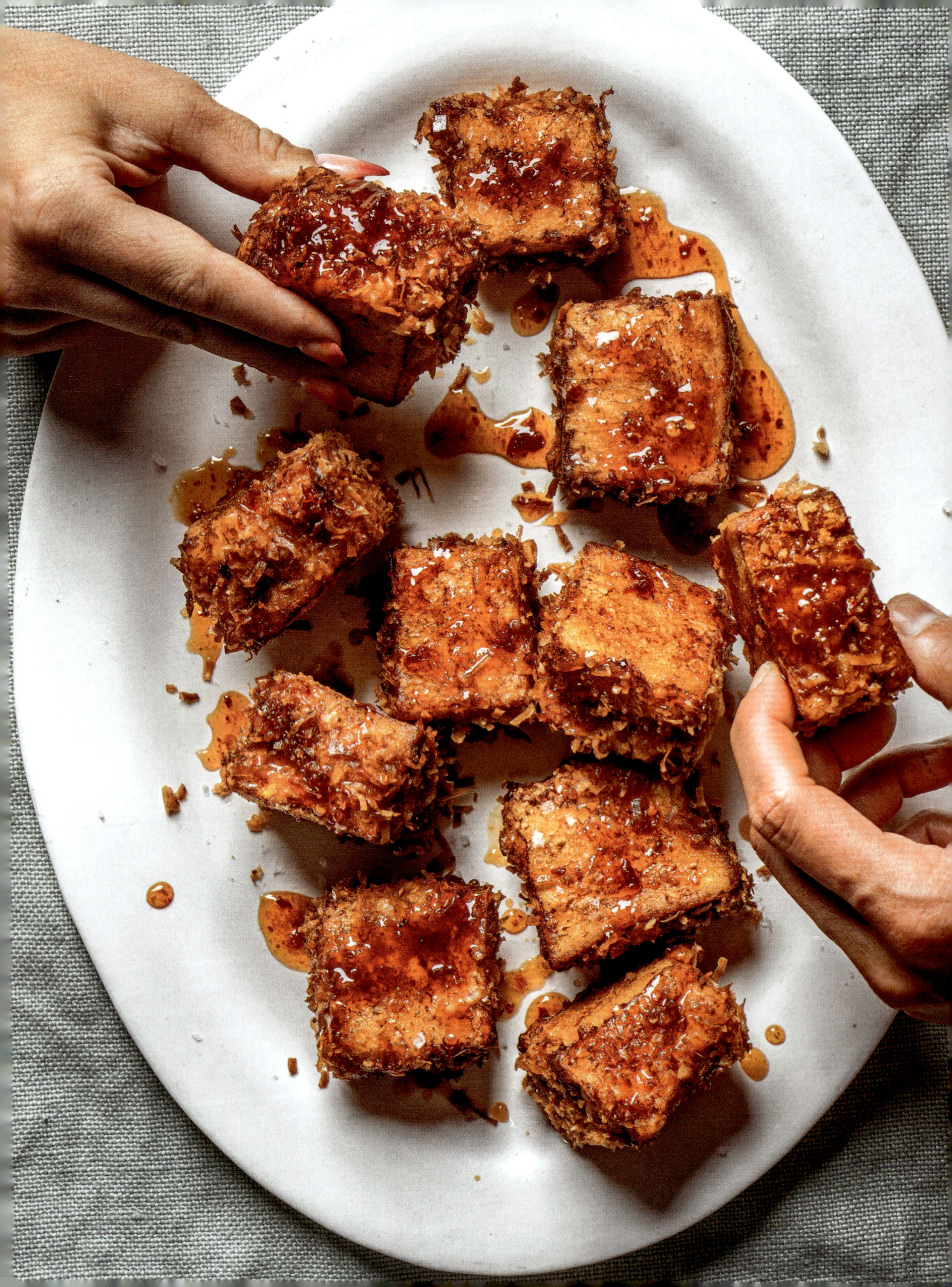

COCONUT SHRIMP TOAST

If two of my favorite snacks had a baby, you'd get this craveable appetizer. From Chinese shrimp toast, the dish gets the bouncy, pillowy texture (known in Cantonese as song) of cooked pureed shrimp and the crunch of fried bread. And from Hawaiian coconut shrimp, it gets slightly sweet, crispy coconut flakes and sweet chili dipping sauce. Serve these and watch how quickly they disappear.

MAKES 12 TOASTS

Equipment: Deep-fry thermometer

1 pound shrimp, peeled and deveined, roughly chopped

4 scallions, white and light green parts sliced, tops reserved for another day

2 egg whites

4 by 1-inch knob ginger, peeled and finely grated on a Microplane

1 large lemongrass stalk, trimmed (see page 16) and minced

1 tablespoon cornstarch

2 teaspoons Shaoxing wine

1 teaspoon Chinese light soy sauce

1 tablespoon cold water

2 teaspoons Diamond Crystal kosher salt

½ teaspoon white sugar

¼ teaspoon ground white pepper

ASSEMBLY

¼ cup well-stirred King's Hot Honey (page 251)

1 tablespoon lime juice

½ teaspoon fish sauce

6 slices (about ½ inch thick) milk bread or brioche

½ cup unsweetened coconut flakes

Canola oil (about 2 quarts), for deep-frying

In a food processor, combine the shrimp, scallions, egg whites, ginger, lemongrass, cornstarch, Shaoxing wine, light soy sauce, cold water, salt, sugar, and white pepper and process until mostly smooth and glossy, scraping down the sides as necessary, about 2 minutes. Transfer to a medium mixing bowl, cover, and chill for at least 15 minutes or up to 4 hours.

Meanwhile, when ready to assemble: Preheat the oven to 200°F. Set a wire rack on a large (18 by 13-inch) sheet pan.

In a small bowl, stir together the honey, lime juice, and fish sauce. Set aside. (The sauce keeps in an airtight container in the refrigerator for up to 2 days.)

Put the bread on the rack on the sheet pan and bake, flipping once, until the bread is brittle on the outside but soft in the middle, 15 to 20 minutes. This prevents the bread from absorbing too much oil during the frying process. Let it cool. Keep the rack and sheet pan handy for frying the shrimp toast.

Reserve about ½ cup of the shrimp mixture. Divide the rest evenly among 3 of the bread slices and spread to an even layer, all the way to the edges. Top with the remaining bread to make 3 sandwiches, pushing down gently to ensure the bread adheres to the filling. Use a large sharp knife to cut each sandwich into 4 squares.

Spread the coconut flakes on a medium plate. Spread a light layer of the reserved shrimp mixture onto the edges of each mini-sandwich (this helps the coconut stick), then dip the edges in the coconut flakes, gently pressing so they adhere.

Pour 2 inches of oil into a deep 5- to 6-quart pot and heat over medium-high heat until the oil registers 325°F on a deep-fry thermometer.

Working in two batches to avoid crowding the pan, fry the shrimp toast, flipping once, until golden brown and crispy all over, 3 to 4 minutes. Transfer to the rack to drain and immediately sprinkle with a little salt. Before frying the second batch, use a spider strainer to remove any stray bits from the oil and let the oil return to 325°F.

Serve the shrimp toasts hot and drizzled with the sauce.

KING'S GUACAMOLE

Born and raised in Southern California, I can't live without guacamole. My recipe has become a fan favorite among *Top Chef* friends, coworkers, and family. It's possibly my most requested dish from friends for potlucks and picnics and now you can make it, too.

The key to creaminess is to buy Hass avocados and wait until they're fully ripe. Then I use a mortar to bruise chiles, onion, and garlic (garlic is sacrilege to some but vital for me) and let it all marinate briefly with lime juice. (If you don't have a mortar, Microplane the garlic and chiles.) Marinating releases their flavor while also taming the sharpness of the onion and garlic. Once you mix in the avocado and mash to your preferred texture (I like mine creamy with some chunks), taste it with a chip, and let your palate guide you as you season to create the balance of lime, salt, and heat that's right for you.

Chips, tacos, and Al Pastor Bao (page 97) are obvious partners, but guacamole also makes great avocado toast, especially on thickly sliced bread fried in olive oil (page 59).

SWITCH IT UP

Try yuzu instead of lime for another dimension of acidity.

SERVES 6 TO 8

- 5 medium garlic cloves, peeled
- Diamond Crystal kosher salt
- ¼ cup finely diced red onion
- 1 medium jalapeño chile, seeded and finely diced
- 1 medium serrano chile, seeded and finely diced, plus more as needed
- ½ cup lime juice (about 5 juicy limes), plus more as needed
- 5 ripe large Hass avocados
- ½ cup finely chopped cilantro (leaves and stems)

In a large mortar, combine the garlic and a big pinch of salt and pound to a paste. Add the onion and both chiles and briefly pound, just to bruise them. Stir in the lime juice and let the mixture sit for at least 5 minutes.

Halve and pit the avocados. Use the tip of a sharp knife to cut through the avocado flesh in a crosshatch pattern, then use a spoon to scoop the flesh into a large mixing bowl. Add the lime mixture and start stirring and mashing with a fork to evenly distribute the ingredients and achieve a guacamole that's creamy but still nice and chunky. Add the cilantro and 1½ teaspoons of salt and mix gently but well.

Season to taste with more salt, chile, and lime. It's best served right away, but you can store guacamole for up to 24 hours in the refrigerator, if you drizzle on a thin layer of olive oil and cover with plastic wrap, pressing it against the surface to prevent oxidation.

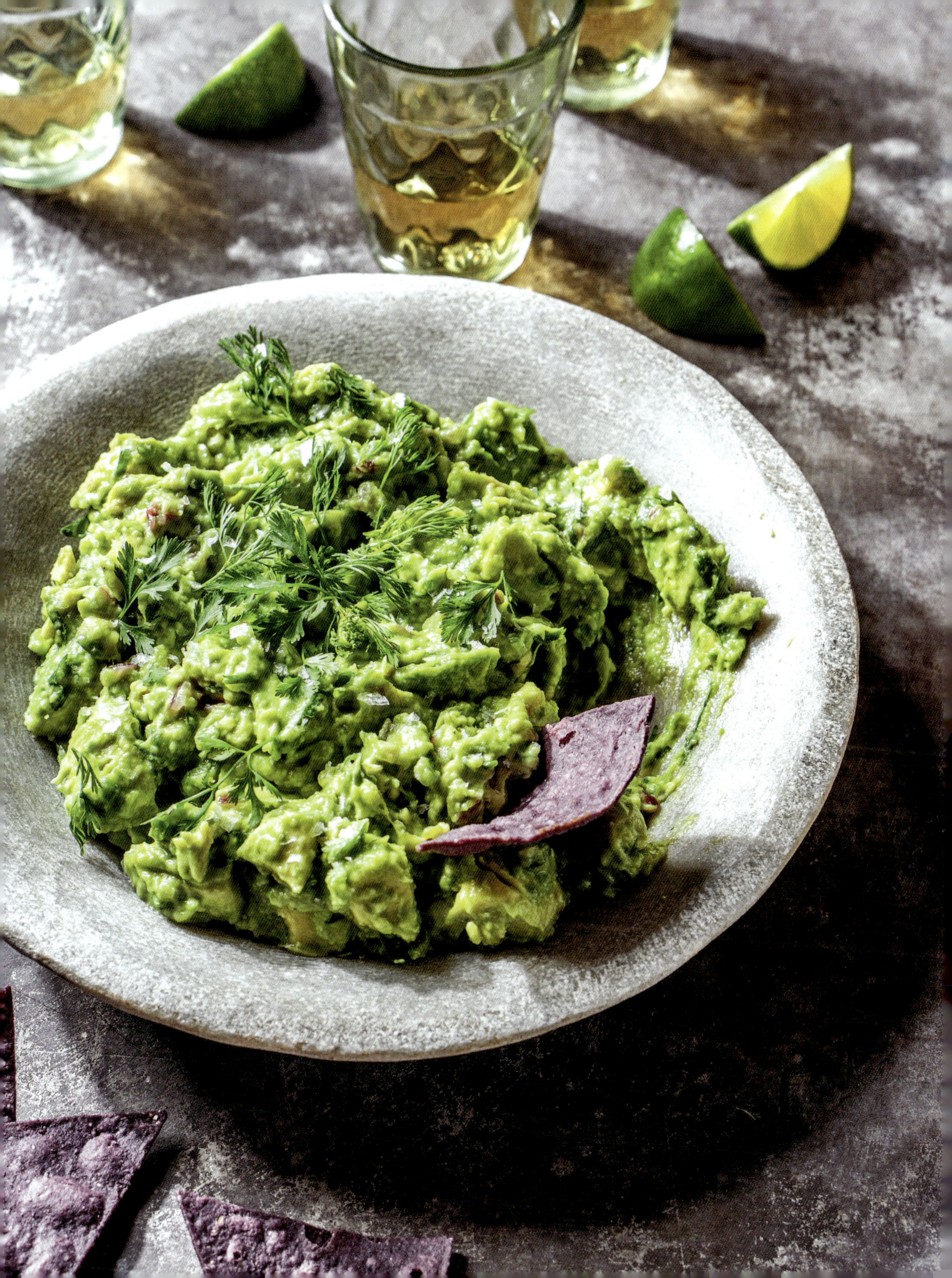

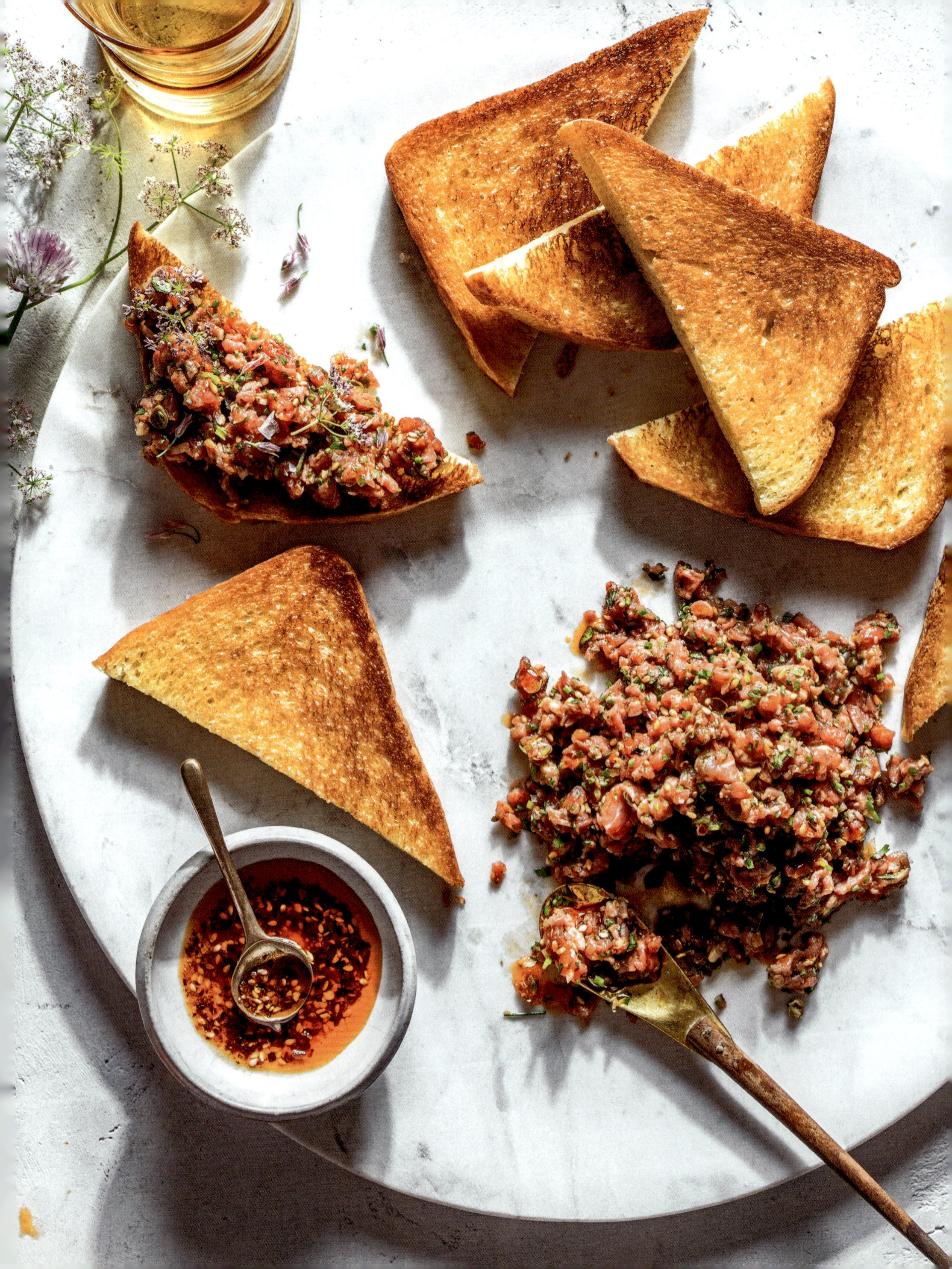

SICHUAN STEAK TARTARE

When I was thirteen, I went to Paris with my family. While sitting at a busy bistro trying to decipher the menu, I decided I wanted to order the steak tartare. I had some idea what it was since I'd read plenty of cookbooks and watched many episodes of Jacques Pépin. Still, once it arrived, I was . . . skeptical.

Until then, my experience with beef consisted of In-N-Out burgers and Chinese dishes where the meat was never even the slightest bit rare, let alone raw. Yet when I finally dug into those tiny glistening cubes of raw beef, my apprehension melted away. I loved the firm but delicate texture of the chilled meat enhanced by briny capers, sweet shallots, and sharp, tangy mustard. Nowadays, I can hardly resist beef tartare when I spot it on a menu.

After many years of eating and making this delicious dish, I wanted to tie in elements from my culinary upbringing—sesame oil and chili crisp standing in for the richness of traditional egg yolk, cilantro joining forces with the classic chives. Because it's so simple, I pay special attention to the details, buying high-quality beef, keeping it nice and cold, and using a sharp knife.

LEVEL IT UP

Top with finely grated Cured Duck Egg Yolks (page 247), or spoon on caviar.

SERVES 6 TO 8

½ pound beef tenderloin or skirt steak

2 tablespoons finely minced cornichons

2 tablespoons finely chopped cilantro

1 tablespoon finely minced drained capers

1 tablespoon thinly sliced chives

1 tablespoon Agrumato lemon oil or extra-virgin olive oil, plus more for drizzling

1 tablespoon King's Chili Crisp (page 257) or store-bought Chinese chili crisp

1 tablespoon finely minced Pickled Chiles (page 245), plus 1 teaspoon of the pickling liquid

1 tablespoon finely minced shallots

1 tablespoon toasted sesame oil

1 tablespoon toasted sesame seeds

¾ teaspoon Diamond Crystal kosher salt

Finely ground black pepper

A dash of ground white pepper

4 slices (about ¾ inch thick) milk bread or brioche

Flaky sea salt

Use a very sharp knife to trim off any external fat and sinew from the beef. Cut the beef into ¼- to ⅛-inch dice and give it all a rough chop. The result should look like very coarsely ground beef.

Transfer to a medium mixing bowl and refrigerate to keep it chilled as you gather the remaining ingredients.

Add the cornichons, cilantro, capers, chives, lemon oil, chili crisp, pickled chiles and pickling liquid, shallots, sesame oil, sesame seeds, salt, a few turns of black pepper, and white pepper to the bowl of meat and stir well. Refrigerate for 5 to 10 minutes to chill the beef and allow the flavors to absorb.

Toast the bread until golden brown and toasty, then slice in half on the diagonal.

Taste the tartare and adjust the seasonings—perhaps adding more salt, chili crisp, and pickled chiles. Stir, then spoon onto the toasts. Drizzle with additional lemon oil and sprinkle with flaky salt. Serve immediately.

CHILI CRISP LABNEH

I'm such a big fan of dips, and nothing tops a rich, velvety labneh. Common in Middle Eastern cooking, it's essentially tangy yogurt that's been drained until it's super thick. It's often served with a drizzle of good olive oil and maybe a sprinkle of za'atar or sumac.

During a Pride collaboration with my friend Edy Massih of the fantastic Lebanese mezze bar in Brooklyn called Edy's Grocer, I thought the creamy, cooling dip would play well with a generous drizzle of my lip-tingling chili crisp as well as some crispy fried shallots and toasted sesame seeds. The combination of tang, textures, and heat was a huge hit and it's a breeze to make for any get-together, whether you buy labneh or make it yourself from Greek yogurt.

Serve it with anything that benefits from creamy, spicy flavors—vegetable crudités, slow-roasted tomatoes (page 245), or roasted carrots (page 155); pita, scallion pancakes (page 93), or King's Focaccia (page 82); and roasted meat like kebabs, kofte, or Mala Lamb Skewers (page 200).

SERVES 4 TO 6

Equipment: Cheesecloth

LABNEH

One 16-ounce container 0% Greek yogurt

2 teaspoons lemon juice

1 teaspoon Diamond Crystal kosher salt

TO FINISH

1 tablespoon King's Chili Crisp (page 257) or store-bought Chinese chili crisp

Fried shallots, homemade (page 254) or store-bought, for garnish

Toasted sesame seeds, for garnish

Za'atar, for garnish

Chive blossoms, micro scallions, or thinly sliced chives, for garnish

Flaky sea salt

Make the labneh: In a medium mixing bowl, whisk together the yogurt, lemon juice, and kosher salt. Line a colander or sieve with cheesecloth so there's a few inches of overhang and set it over a separate bowl.

Spoon the yogurt mixture into the center of the cheesecloth, cover with the overhang, and let it drain over the bowl in the fridge for 8 hours. Remove the cheesecloth and discard any liquid that has collected in the bowl. The labneh keeps in an airtight container in the refrigerator for up to 2 weeks.

To finish: Stir the labneh well. Scoop the labneh onto a plate and use the bottom of a spoon to make some pretty divots. Drizzle with the chili crisp, then sprinkle generously with fried shallots, sesame seeds, and za'atar. Top with chive blossoms and a little flaky salt. Serve immediately.

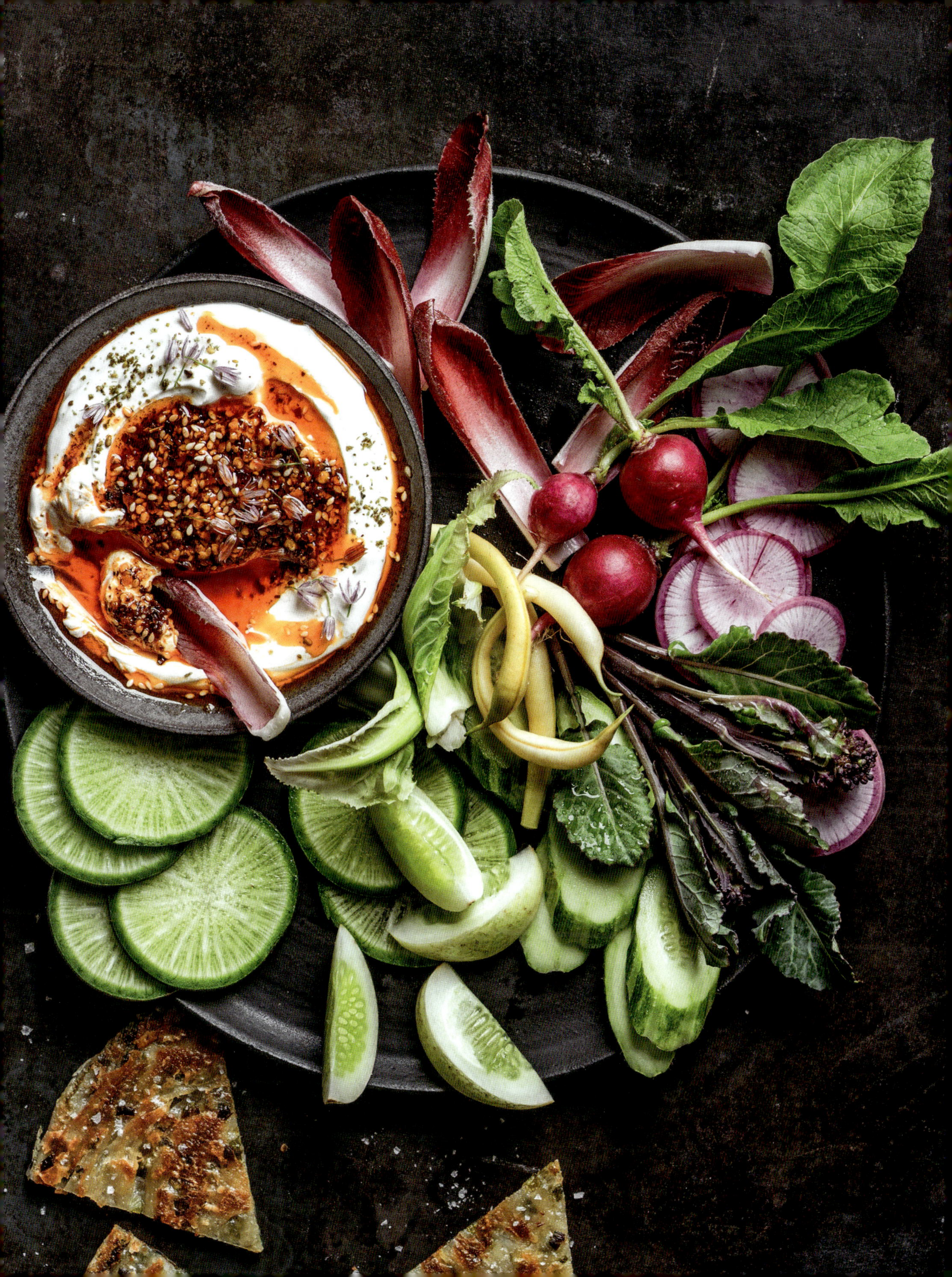

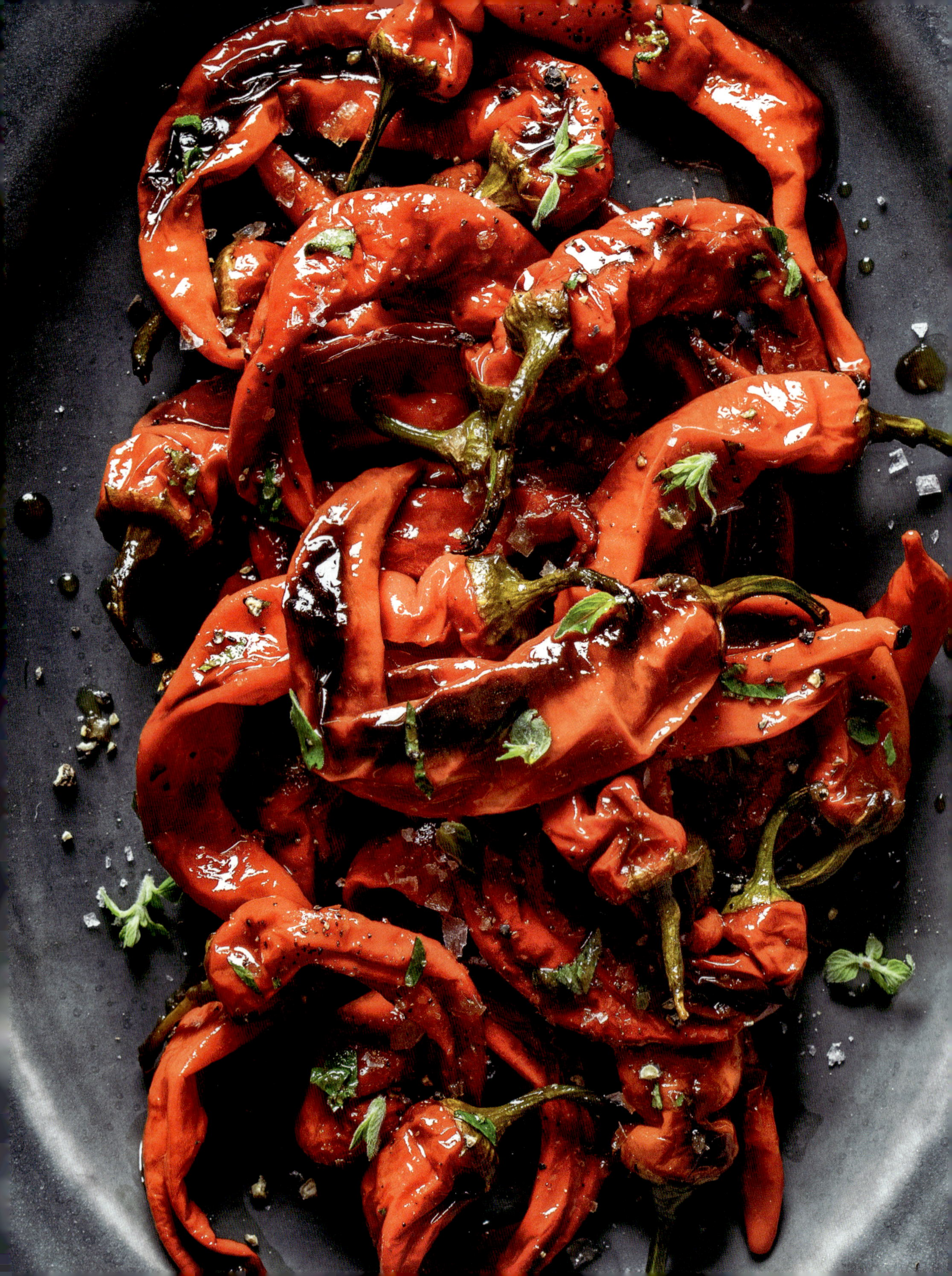

BLACK VINEGAR–MARINATED SWEET PEPPERS

Sweet Italian peppers need so little help. A hot oven (or grill) chars their skins, intensifies their flavor, and brings out their natural sweetness. A marinade of balsamic or sweet white wine vinegar, garlic, and olive oil adds acidity and a little fat. The result occasionally reminds me of a Sichuan preparation called hupi qingjiao, spicy green peppers seasoned with Chinese black vinegar, which gives them a sharp brightness and malty complexity. The name translates to "tiger skin peppers," a nod to the blistered stripes they get from a trip in a hot wok. My marinated peppers are a mix of both. They're more like kitten peppers—cute and full of sweetness with a sharp surprise. Serve them as a side for a rib eye (page 196), or crisp-skinned salmon (page 180), or on a charcuterie plate.

LEVEL IT UP

Serve over fresh burrata or labneh (page 32) and topped with Fried Bread Crumbs (page 256).

SERVES 4

MARINADE

6 tablespoons Zhenjiang black vinegar

2 tablespoons honey

4 garlic cloves, finely grated on a Microplane

1 teaspoon Diamond Crystal kosher salt

1 teaspoon chopped oregano leaves

Finely ground black pepper

¼ cup extra-virgin olive oil

PEPPERS

1 pound Jimmy Nardellos, shishito peppers, or sweet mini peppers

3 tablespoons extra-virgin olive oil, plus more for drizzling

1 teaspoon Diamond Crystal kosher salt

TO SERVE

Flaky sea salt

Finely ground black pepper

Make the marinade: In a medium mixing bowl, whisk together the vinegar, honey, garlic, salt, oregano, and pepper to taste. Slowly drizzle in the olive oil, whisking constantly, until thickened and emulsified. Set aside.

Cook the peppers: Preheat the oven to 450°F.

On a large (18 by 13-inch) sheet pan, toss together the peppers, oil, and salt.

Roast, turning the peppers occasionally, until blistered all over, browned in spots, and slightly deflated, 4 to 6 minutes for thin-walled peppers like Jimmy Nardellos and shishitos and 10 to 15 minutes for thick-walled peppers like sweet minis. (Alternatively, preheat a grill, toss the peppers in a bowl with 1 tablespoon of the oil and the salt, and char on the grates over high heat.)

Transfer the peppers directly to the bowl with the marinade and toss well. Cover and marinate in the refrigerator for at least 1 hour or up to 5 days.

To serve: Let the peppers come to room temperature. Arrange the peppers on a serving plate, then drizzle on some of the marinade and add a sprinkle of flaky salt and a few turns of pepper.

TUNA TOSTADAS WITH AVOCADO, GINGER, AND SCALLION

The perfect dinner party snack, this recipe is inspired by the tostadas de atún at the effortlessly cool Contramar, a restaurant in Mexico City. There, crunchy fried corn tortillas are topped with slices of pristine raw tuna, avocado, chipotle mayonnaise, and crispy leeks. In my rendition, tuna and avocado are drizzled with chili crisp for richness and heat. I also top it with ginger-scallion sauce, which I loved on a Hawaiian ahi poke I had on Oahu; it adds an unexpected dimension that at first bite reveals it's a natural fit.

LEVEL IT UP

Swap out the raw onion for Fried Shallots (page 254).

SWITCH IT UP

Sushi-grade scallops and hamachi make good substitutes for tuna.

MAKES 12 TOSTADAS

½ cup very thinly sliced (preferably on a mandoline) sweet white onion

Canola oil (about 2 cups), for shallow-frying

12 small (4- to 5-inch) corn tortillas

Diamond Crystal kosher salt

2 ripe medium Hass avocados, halved and pitted

2 teaspoons lime juice or bottled yuzu juice, plus more as needed

1 pound sushi-grade tuna, sliced ⅛ inch thick against the grain, chilled

Flaky sea salt

½ cup Ginger-Scallion Sauce (page 263)

King's Chili Crisp (page 257) or store-bought Chinese chili crisp, for drizzling

Cilantro flowers, micro cilantro, or cilantro leaves, for garnish

Put the onion in a medium bowl, fill it with cold water, and drain. Repeat several times, then drain well. This removes the onion's sharpness and gives it a crisp texture. Refrigerate until needed.

Line a large (18 by 13-inch) sheet pan with paper towels. Pour ½ inch of oil into a large skillet and heat over medium-high heat for about 2 minutes. To test when it's hot enough, dip the edge of a tortilla into the oil. When it bubbles immediately, fry 2 or 3 tortillas at a time, flipping once, until golden brown on both sides and completely crisp, about 1 minute per side. Transfer the tostadas to the paper towels in a single layer to drain and immediately season lightly on both sides with kosher salt.

Scoop the avocado flesh into a medium mixing bowl. Add the lime juice and a generous pinch of kosher salt, then use a fork to mix and mash until creamy but still a bit chunky. Season to taste with more salt and lime juice.

Spread the avocado mash onto the tostadas. Lay the tuna on the avocado mash. Lightly sprinkle each slice of fish with flaky salt, then add the ginger-scallion sauce (about 2 teaspoons per tostada) and a drizzle of the chili crisp. Top with the onions and cilantro, and serve immediately.

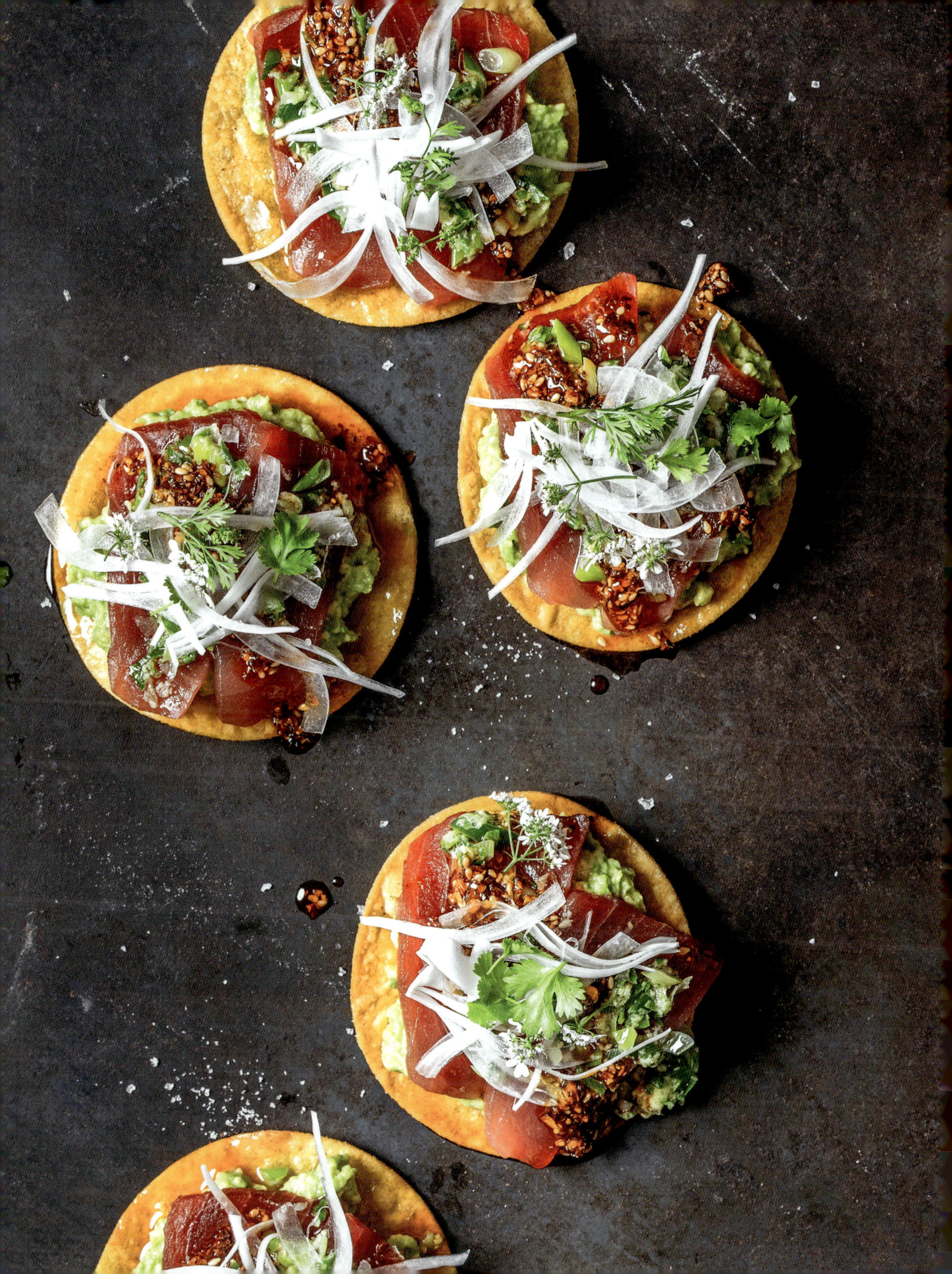

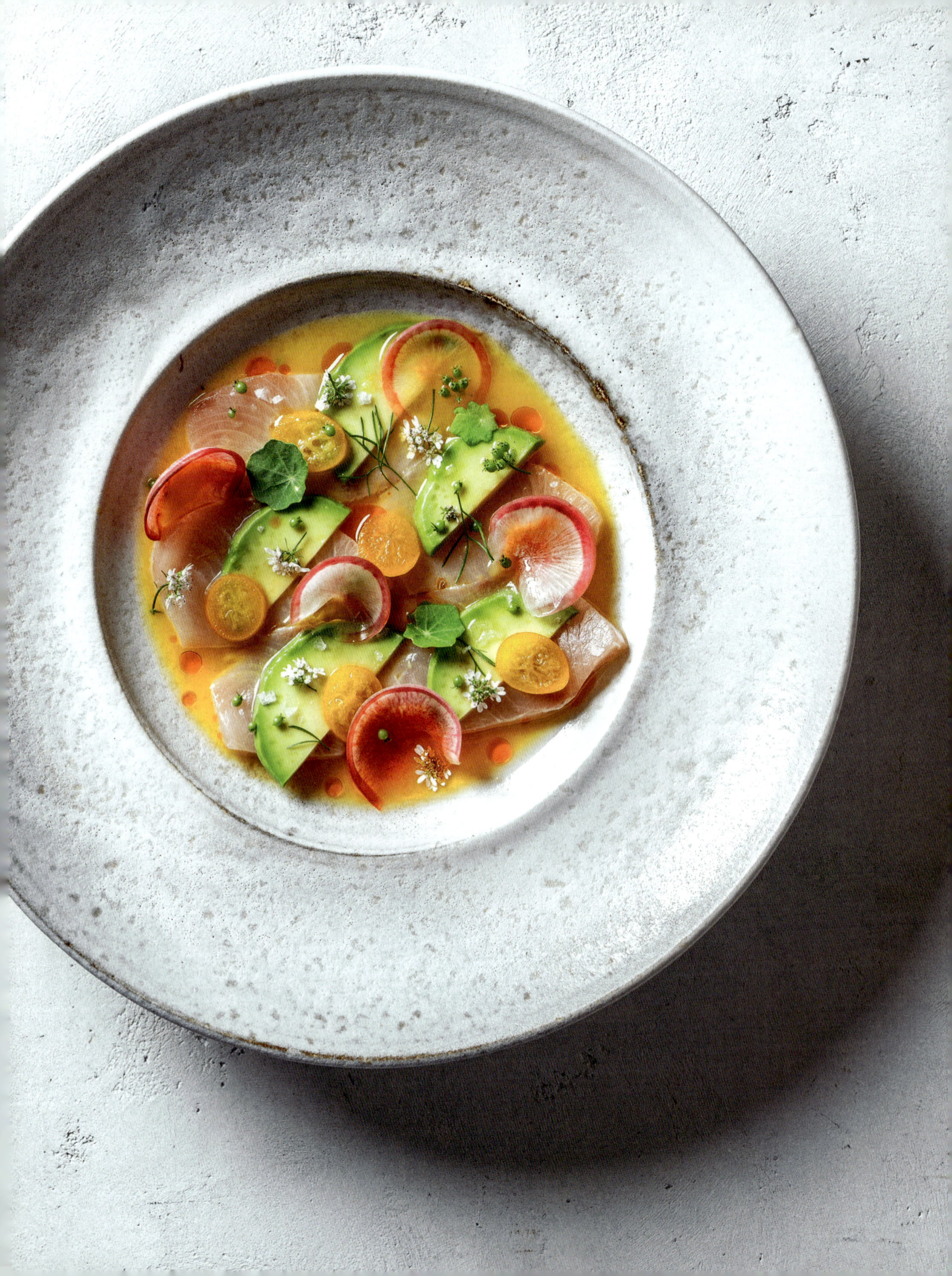

YELLOWTAIL CRUDO IN GINGER-CITRUS BROTH

This almost-too-pretty-to-eat crudo is in the style of a Japanese-Peruvian tiradito, where fish is prepared sashimi style and served in a chilled leche de tigre, a flavorful citrus-forward broth. Because crudo is so simple, paying attention to every little detail makes it shine. Make sure to chill the broth, fish, and even the serving bowls, so everything is cold and refreshing. Use a sharp knife to precisely cut slices of lush fish, creamy avocado, and crisp radish. And be sure to balance the acid with sweetness and heat, which I do with a medley of citrus, the warm touch of ginger, pickled kumquats for little sweet-tart hits of excitement, and Sichuan chili oil for an unexpected tingle.

LEVEL IT UP

Add Fried Shallots (page 254) or Puffed Wild Rice (page 257) as a garnish.

SWITCH IT UP

Swap the lime and lemon juice for pure passion fruit juice to make the Hawaiian-inspired crudo from my show *Tasting Wild*.

SERVES 4

GINGER-CITRUS BROTH

1 cup freshly squeezed orange juice (2 or 3 oranges)

¼ cup lime juice (2 or 3 limes), plus more as needed

¼ cup lemon juice (about 2 lemons), plus more as needed

¼ cup yuzu juice, bottled or fresh

½ orange bell pepper, roughly chopped

2 by 1-inch knob ginger, peeled and roughly chopped

1 large garlic clove, peeled

3 tablespoons white sugar, plus more as needed

¼ teaspoon Diamond Crystal kosher salt

CRUDO

½ pound sushi-grade yellowtail, ahi tuna, or scallops, chilled

1 ripe Hass avocado, thinly sliced

1 small radish, very thinly sliced and rinsed

Pickled Kumquats (page 245), for garnish

Micro cilantro, for garnish

Chili oil from King's Chili Crisp (page 257), for finishing

Agrumato lemon oil, for finishing

Flaky sea salt

Make the ginger-citrus broth: In a blender, combine all the ingredients and blend on high until smooth and frothy, 30 seconds to 1 minute. Season to taste with more sugar and lemon or lime juice. Pour the mixture through a fine-mesh sieve and into a container, discarding the solids and skimming off any froth. Cover and refrigerate until well chilled, at least 1 hour. (The broth can be made up to 4 hours ahead.)

Assemble the crudo: Working quickly so the seafood stays cold for serving, slice the fish against the grain into ¼-inch-thick slices or slice the scallops into ¼-inch-thick rounds.

Arrange the cold seafood in a single layer in four shallow serving bowls. Just before serving, skim the broth once more, then stir well. Pour in enough broth (directly into the bowl, not onto the fish) to reach just below the surface of the fish. Garnish with the avocado, radish, pickled kumquats, and micro cilantro. Drizzle lightly with the chili oil and lemon oil, and sprinkle each slice of seafood with a few flakes of sea salt. Serve immediately.

SICILIAN-STYLE CRUDO WITH SHOYU-CURED SALMON ROE

In many ways, this crudo is the most impressive recipe in this book and also the easiest. There's no cooking required. It's all in the assembly. My twin nieces love to help out, sprinkling the onion, gingerly placing the capers, and tapping the grater so lemon zest snowflakes onto the seafood. Yet like so much simple food, its success is in the details. Buy the best fish you can find—ask a trusted fishmonger what they'd eat raw—and slice it against the grain with a very sharp knife. Pick a good olive oil and use plenty of it. Serve it cold, cold, cold—chilled fish on a chilled plate. My little twist is the addition of ikura (salmon roe) that's briefly cured with shoyu (soy sauce) to add little pops of salt and umami.

LEVEL IT UP

Instead of lemon, use the zest and juice of one yuzu or sudachi, both truly special Japanese citrus fruits.

SERVES 4 TO 6

SALMON ROE

2 ounces salmon roe

2 teaspoons mirin

2 teaspoons Japanese soy sauce

CRUDO

1 pound assorted sushi-grade fish (such as tuna, yellowtail, and salmon) and scallops, chilled

1 to 2 tablespoons very finely diced red onion

1 tablespoon drained capers

1 lemon

Extra-virgin olive oil, for drizzling

Agrumato lemon oil, for drizzling

Coarsely ground black pepper

Thinly sliced chives, for sprinkling

Flaky sea salt

Cure the salmon roe: In a small bowl, combine the salmon roe, mirin, and soy sauce and mix gently. Cover and refrigerate for at least 1 hour or up to 24 hours.

For the crudo: Up to 1 hour before serving, use a sharp chef's knife and a swift, sure motion to cut the fish against the grain into ¼-inch-thick slices and the scallops into ¼-inch-thick rounds. Shingle the seafood (I like to group each variety) on a serving platter, cover, and refrigerate for at least 10 minutes or up to 1 hour. This dish tastes best chilled.

When ready to serve, evenly sprinkle on the red onion and capers. Use a Microplane to finely grate on the zest of the lemon. Halve the lemon and squeeze about 2 teaspoons of juice over the seafood, catching any seeds. Drizzle generously with olive oil, enough to coat the fish and pool at the edges of the platter. Lightly drizzle with lemon oil, then add several turns of black pepper and a sprinkling of chives. Sprinkle with the flaky salt, making sure each slice of seafood gets a few flakes. Spoon on the salmon roe and serve immediately.

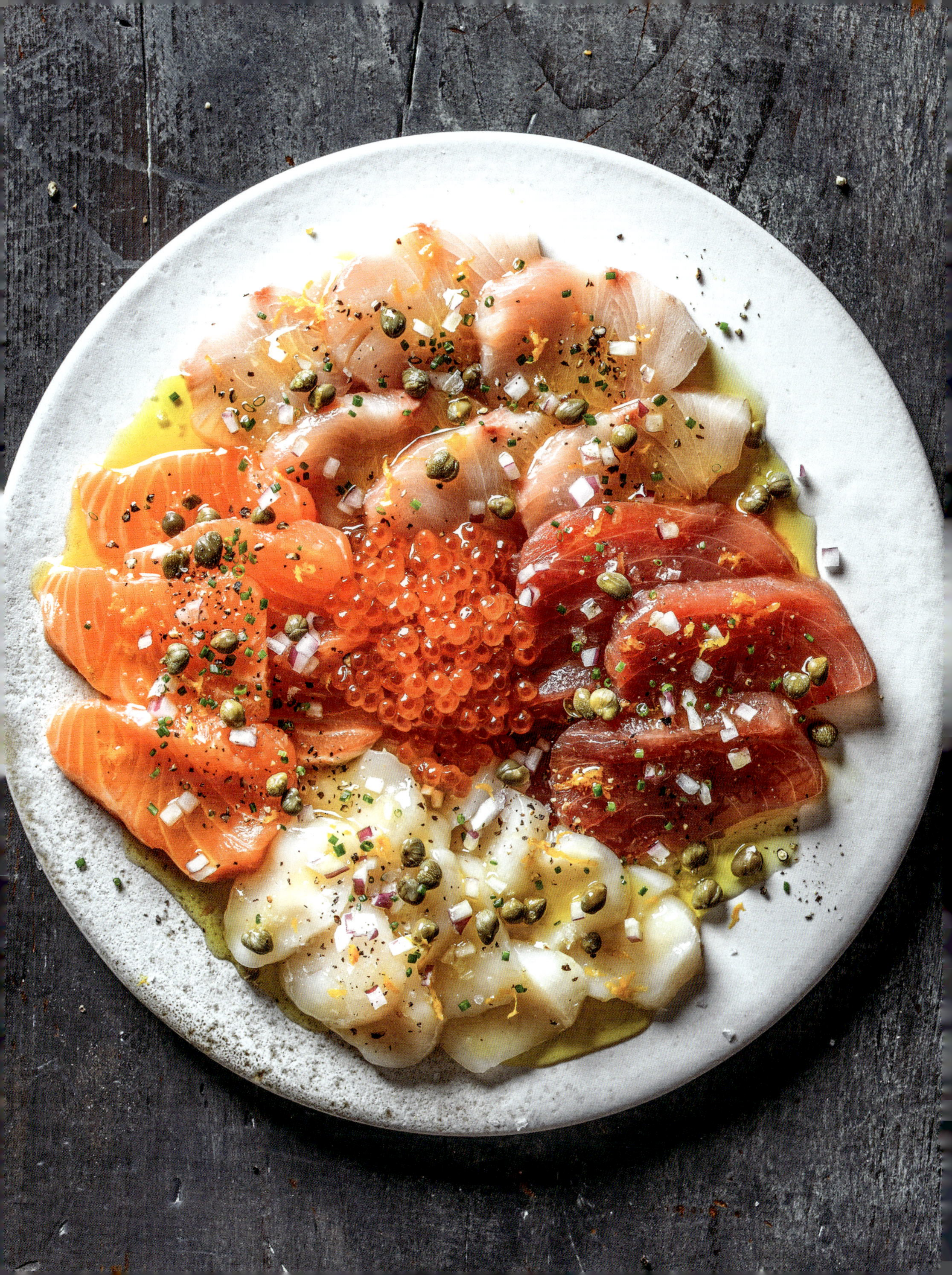

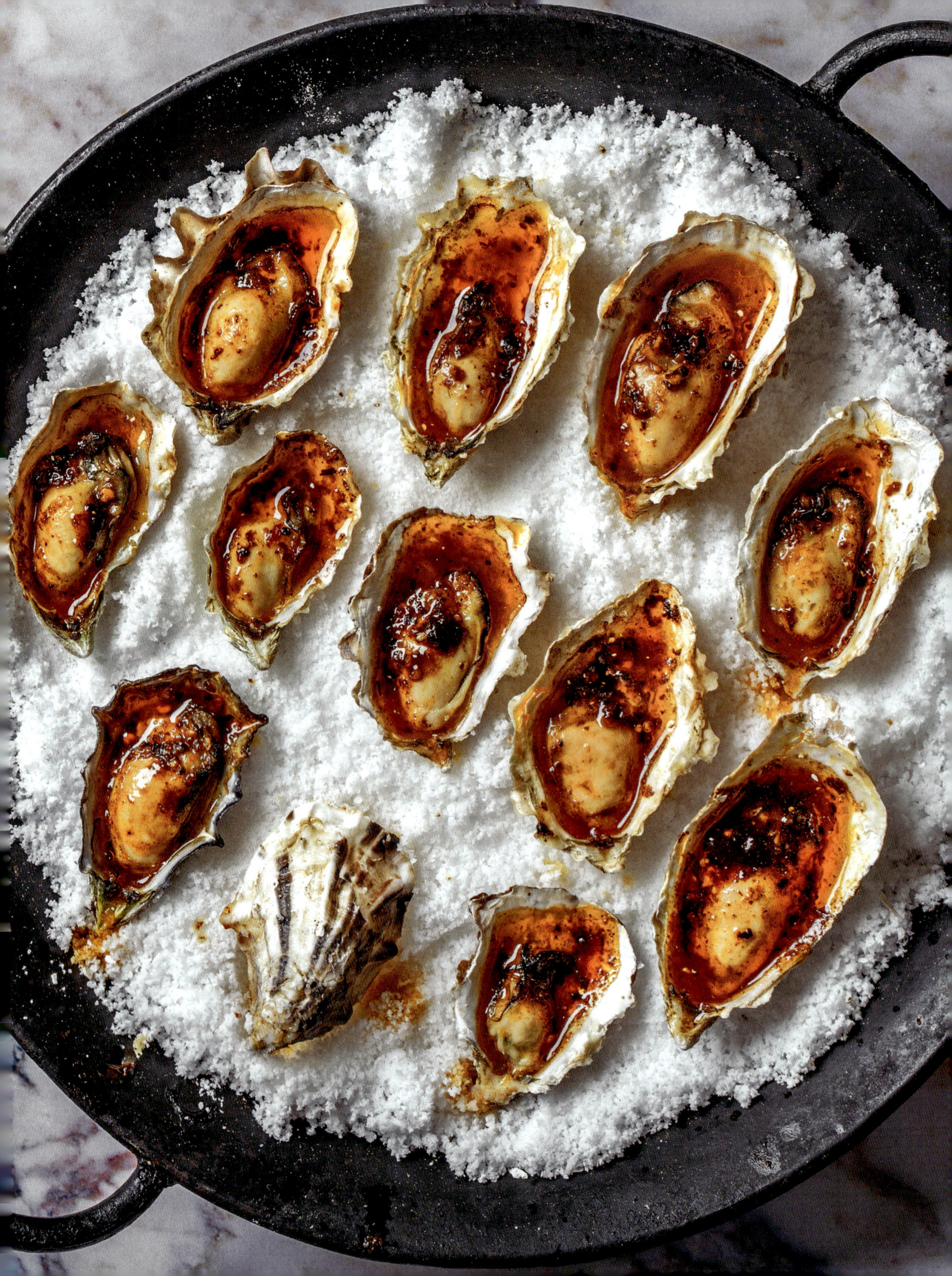

GRILLED OYSTERS WITH SICHUAN CHILE–BOURBON BUTTER

I'm a fan of all things oysters. Raw on the half shell? Yes, please. Battered and fried? Heck yeah. And don't forget about roasted oysters, which if you ask me deserve more love than they get. These are a thrilling gateway. Topped with a sweet and spicy butter spiked with bourbon, chili crisp, and garlic, the oysters cook quickly in their shells, so they're hot and charred but still pristine and plump. It's a great dinner party dish, in part because you can prep it up to 2 hours in advance, the oysters shucked and topped with little knobs of compound butter, just waiting in the fridge until friends arrive. Fair warning: They'll disappear the moment they come off the grill.

For this preparation, I prefer medium-size West Coast varieties for their deep shells and sweet creaminess. They're fantastic under the broiler or on a grill—if you dare, try nestling them directly on glowing hot coals. Find the sweet spot where the oysters are neither gently poaching in their shells nor catching fire but rather bubbling rapidly and charring at the edges within three minutes, max. (And don't be alarmed if you hear a pop as the delicate edges of the shells break off.) No matter how you cook them, eat them while they're hot and take care not to spill any of the precious spicy, buttery juices.

SWITCH IT UP

Experiment with other flavored butters (page 252) on your oysters!

MAKES 12

A dozen medium raw oysters, scrubbed and rinsed well

About ½ cup Sichuan Chile–Bourbon Butter (page 252), at room temperature

1 cup Diamond Crystal kosher salt, for serving or broiling

½ lemon

Shuck the oysters, being careful not to spill their liquor and removing any lingering bits of shell. Spoon a small dollop (1 generous teaspoon) of the butter onto each oyster.

Put the salt in a mixing bowl and gradually stir in water (about ¼ cup) until the salt is the texture of sandcastle sand.

To grill: Put the salt mixture in an even layer on a serving plate. This way, the oysters won't tip and spill when you serve them. Prepare a grill, preferably charcoal, to cook with very high heat. Use tongs to carefully arrange the oysters (be careful not to lose any of their delicious liquor) directly on the grill and cook, uncovered, until the oysters caramelize slightly at the edges, 2 to 3 minutes. Transfer them to the prepared serving plate.

To broil: Spread the salt mixture on a small (9 by 13-inch) sheet pan or in an ovenproof skillet wide enough to fit the oysters in a single layer. Position an oven rack about 3 inches from the heat source and preheat the broiler on high for 5 minutes. Carefully add the oysters to the prepared pan and broil, rotating the pan halfway through, until the oysters caramelize slightly at the edges, 3 to 4 minutes.

To serve: Squeeze on lemon juice to add brightness and serve hot.

KING'S WINGS

Sometimes you're in the mood for juicy, charred wings from the grill (see page 47), and sometimes you crave wings like these, double-fried like Korean fried chicken for exceptional crunch. They channel elements from some of my favorite fried chicken moments, fusing flavors from the orange chicken at Panda Express (a guilty pleasure) with the famous wings at San Francisco's San Tung. Like just about everyone else in the city, I can't get enough of their sticky-sweet, just-spicy-enough glaze.

SWITCH IT UP

Try this batter and glaze with white fish fillets, cauliflower, or mushrooms.

MAKES 24 WINGS

Equipment: Deep-fry thermometer

MARINATED WINGS

3 tablespoons Shaoxing wine

2 tablespoons Chinese light soy sauce

1 tablespoon cornstarch

1 teaspoon white sugar

1 teaspoon Diamond Crystal kosher salt

Dash of ground white pepper

1 by 1-inch knob ginger, peeled and finely grated on a Microplane

24 chicken wings (drumettes, flats, or a mix)

GLAZE

1 cup light brown sugar

½ cup corn syrup

½ cup freshly squeezed orange juice (2 oranges)

½ cup water

¼ cup Shaoxing wine

¼ cup Chinese light soy sauce

2 tablespoons Chinese dark soy sauce

2 teaspoons Zhenjiang black vinegar

2 teaspoons toasted sesame oil

4 garlic cloves, finely grated on a Microplane

4 by 1-inch knob ginger, peeled and finely grated on a Microplane

½ teaspoon ground ginger

½ teaspoon ground white pepper

5 whole dried Sichuan chiles, seeded and cut into ½-inch pieces

Marinate the wings: In a large resealable bag, combine the wine, soy sauce, cornstarch, sugar, salt, pepper, and ginger and mix well. Add the wings and seal the bag, pushing out as much air as you can. Massage the wings to coat them in the marinade and refrigerate for at least 4 hours or up to 24 hours.

Make the glaze: In a medium saucepan, combine the glaze ingredients and whisk well. Bring to a boil over high heat, then turn the heat down to cook at a steady simmer, whisking occasionally, until it thickens to a consistency a little looser than honey, about 30 minutes. Reduce the heat if it threatens to bubble up and overflow. To test if it's done, chill a plate, add a few drops of the glaze, and wait 15 seconds or so. If the drops hold their shape like honey, it's ready.

Set a fine-mesh sieve over a heatproof container and pour in the glaze, pressing on the solids to extract as much flavor as possible; discard the solids. (If making ahead, cool completely and store in an airtight container in the refrigerator for up to 4 days. Warm gently before using.)

To finish: In a medium mixing bowl, combine ½ cup of the sweet potato starch, ½ cup of the cornstarch, and the water and whisk until smooth. The batter will separate as it sits, so give it a stir occasionally. In a large mixing bowl, combine the remaining 1 cup sweet potato starch, 1 cup cornstarch, kosher salt, and white pepper.

Pour 2 inches of oil into a deep 5- to 6-quart pot over medium-high heat until the oil registers 350°F on a deep-fry thermometer. Line a sheet pan with a wire rack or several layers of paper towels and set near the stove.

While the oil is heating, transfer a few wings from the marinade to the wet batter, coat well, then transfer them to the dry starch mixture, tossing to coat well and gently pressing so plenty of clumps adhere. These clumps are your friends—they'll get extra crispy when you fry. Transfer to a plate or another sheet pan and repeat with the remaining wings.

CONTINUED

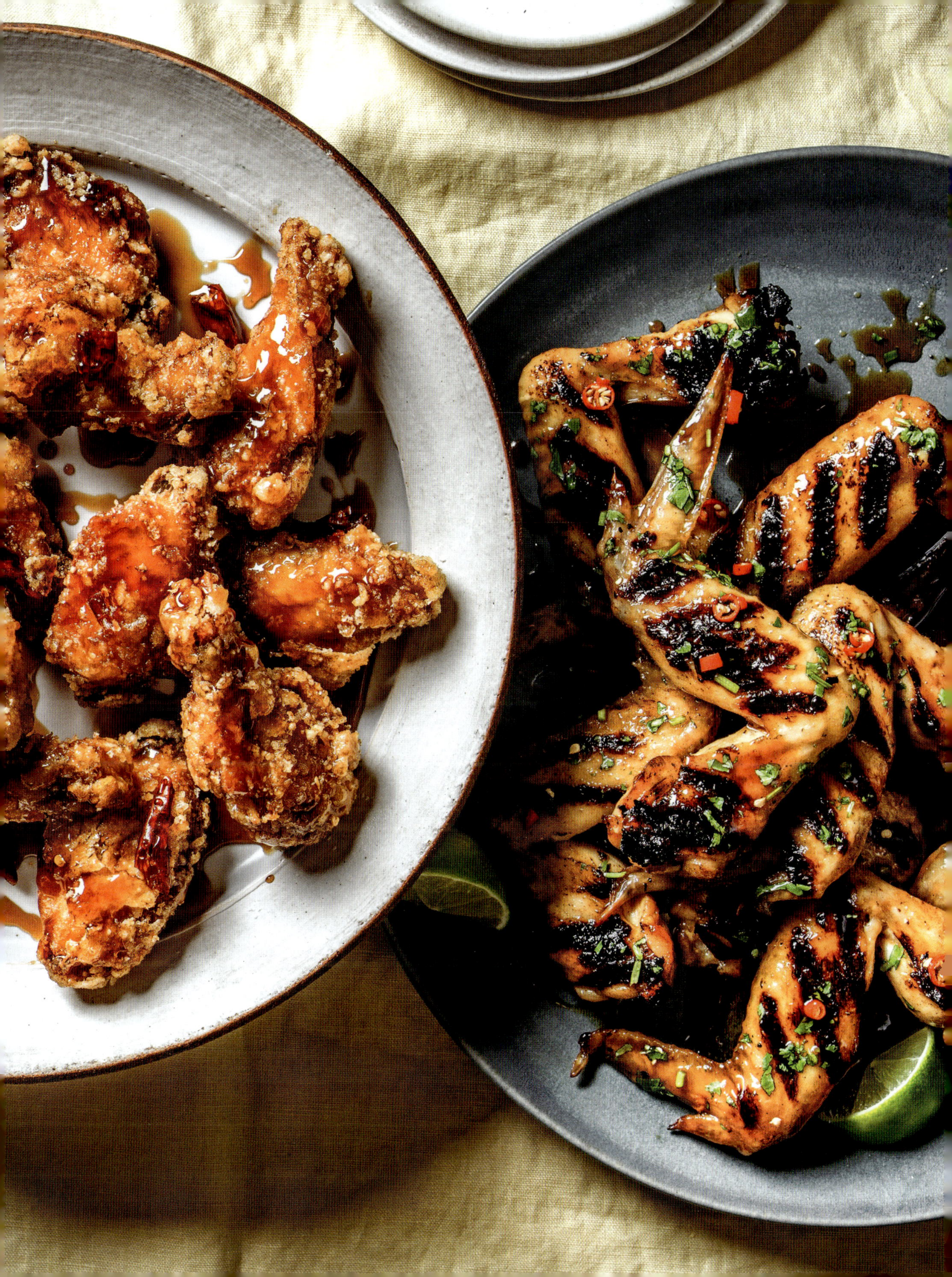

KING'S WINGS
CONTINUED

TO FINISH

1½ cups sweet potato starch (not "flour"), divided

1½ cups cornstarch, divided

1 cup water

1 teaspoon Diamond Crystal kosher salt

Dash of ground white pepper

Canola oil (about 2 quarts), for deep-frying

Working in three batches to avoid crowding, one by one carefully add 8 wings to the oil, leaving some space around each one. Fry until light golden and slightly crispy, stirring occasionally, about 4 minutes. Use a spider strainer to transfer the wings to the rack.

Between batches, use a spider strainer to remove any stray bits from the oil and let the oil temperature return to 350°F. This is the first fry.

For the second fry, let the oil temperature increase to 375°F and scoop out any stray bits. Cook, glaze, and serve 8 wings: Fry until golden brown and crunchy, about 3 minutes. Use the spider to remove the wings, let them drain well, then transfer to a large mixing bowl. Drizzle on enough of the warm glaze (about ½ cup) to generously coat and toss well.

Serve hot, then fry and glaze the remaining batches of wings just before eating.

GRILLED FISH SAUCE–CARAMEL CHICKEN WINGS

Sticky wings are my weakness, and these just might be my favorite. They take cues from the Vietnamese classic. The marinated wings pick up smoky char from the grill, then get a last-minute toss in sweet-salty fish sauce caramel (your new favorite pantry staple) along with fresh chiles, cilantro, and lime juice for balance. The recipe can be easily doubled or tripled, making them perfect for a party.

SERVES 4 TO 6

MARINATED WINGS

12 whole chicken wings

¼ cup plus 2 tablespoons fish sauce (Three Crabs is a must here)

¼ cup plus 2 tablespoons packed light brown sugar

6 medium garlic cloves, finely grated on a Microplane

2 teaspoons Diamond Crystal kosher salt

¼ teaspoon ground white pepper

TO COOK AND SERVE

½ teaspoon Diamond Crystal kosher salt

A few dashes of ground white pepper

½ cup Fish Sauce Caramel (page 250), gently warmed

1 or 2 fresh Thai chiles, thinly sliced

Handful of chopped cilantro (leaves and stems)

Limes wedges, for serving

Marinate the wings: Use kitchen shears to snip the flap of skin between the drumette and the flat, then gently pry open each wing. In a large resealable bag, combine the fish sauce, brown sugar, garlic, salt, and white pepper and mix well. Add the wings and seal the bag, pushing out as much air as you can. Massage the wings to coat them in the marinade and refrigerate for at least 8 hours or up to 24 hours.

To cook and serve: Prepare a grill, preferably charcoal, to cook with medium heat. Drain the wings, discarding the marinade, and season them on both sides with the salt and white pepper. Grill the wings, covered, flipping once, until charred on both sides, 5 to 8 minutes per side.

Transfer the wings to a large bowl, add the fish sauce caramel, and toss to coat well. Add the chiles and cilantro and toss again. Transfer to a serving plate, drizzle on any fish sauce caramel left behind in the bowl, and serve immediately with the lime wedges.

TAIWANESE POPCORN CHICKEN

After high school, my friends and I would jump in my hand-me-down Acura Integra, tricked out with rims and an obnoxious exhaust mod like we were in *The Fast and the Furious,* and hit up a boba shop in Hacienda Heights. With an iced milk tea in one hand, I'd snack on this popular Taiwanese street food from a paper bag with a bamboo skewer. Dusted in five spice and white pepper and tossed with crispy fried basil leaves, these chicken nuggets are my tribute to those happy days. Their coating of sweet potato starch (different, by the way, from sweet potato *flour*) gives them their distinctive crunch.

SERVES 4 TO 6

Equipment: Deep-fry thermometer

MARINATED CHICKEN

2 pounds boneless, skinless chicken thighs, cut into 1½-inch chunks

2 by 1-inch knob ginger, peeled and finely grated on a Microplane

2 large garlic cloves, finely grated on a Microplane

3 tablespoons Chinese light soy sauce

2 teaspoons Shaoxing wine

½ teaspoon Chinese five spice powder

2 teaspoons Diamond Crystal kosher salt

½ teaspoon ground white pepper

1 egg white

SPICE MIX

1 tablespoon Diamond Crystal kosher salt

½ teaspoon garlic powder

½ teaspoon ground white pepper

¼ teaspoon cayenne pepper (optional)

¼ teaspoon Chinese five spice powder

TO FINISH

2 cups sweet potato starch

2 tablespoons garlic powder

2 teaspoons Diamond Crystal kosher salt

Canola oil (about 3 quarts), for deep-frying

Large handful of Thai or Italian basil leaves, patted dry if necessary

Marinate the chicken: In a large mixing bowl, combine the chicken with the marinade ingredients, mix well, then cover and marinate in the refrigerator for at least 30 minutes or up to 12 hours.

Make the spice mix: In a small bowl, stir together all the ingredients and set aside.

To finish: In a large shallow bowl, stir together the sweet potato starch, garlic powder, and salt. Add about half the mixture to the bowl with the chicken and toss to evenly coat each piece, including the nooks and crevices. Set aside for 30 minutes.

When ready to fry, pour 3 inches of oil into a deep 5- to 6-quart pot and heat over medium-high heat until the oil registers 350°F on a deep-fry thermometer.

While the oil is heating, add the remaining sweet potato starch mixture to the bowl with the chicken and toss well. Small clumps of flour are your friends—they'll get extra crispy when you fry.

Fry and serve in batches to avoid crowding and because the chicken tastes best hot. Carefully add one-third of the chicken to the hot oil and stir to prevent sticking. Fry, stirring occasionally, until golden brown and crispy, 4 to 6 minutes.

Grab the pot lid (to protect against splatter), then add one-third of the basil to the oil and immediately cover with the lid. Wait 5 seconds, then remove the lid and fry, stirring with a spider strainer to submerge the leaves, until the basil turns bright green and translucent, 5 to 10 seconds more.

Use the spider strainer to remove the chicken and basil, letting it drain well in the strainer before transferring it to a large mixing bowl. Immediately and generously sprinkle with some spice mix as you toss to coat the chicken and break up the basil.

Serve hot, then fry and season the remaining chicken and basil the same way. Between batches, use a spider strainer to remove any stray bits from the oil and let the oil return to 350°F.

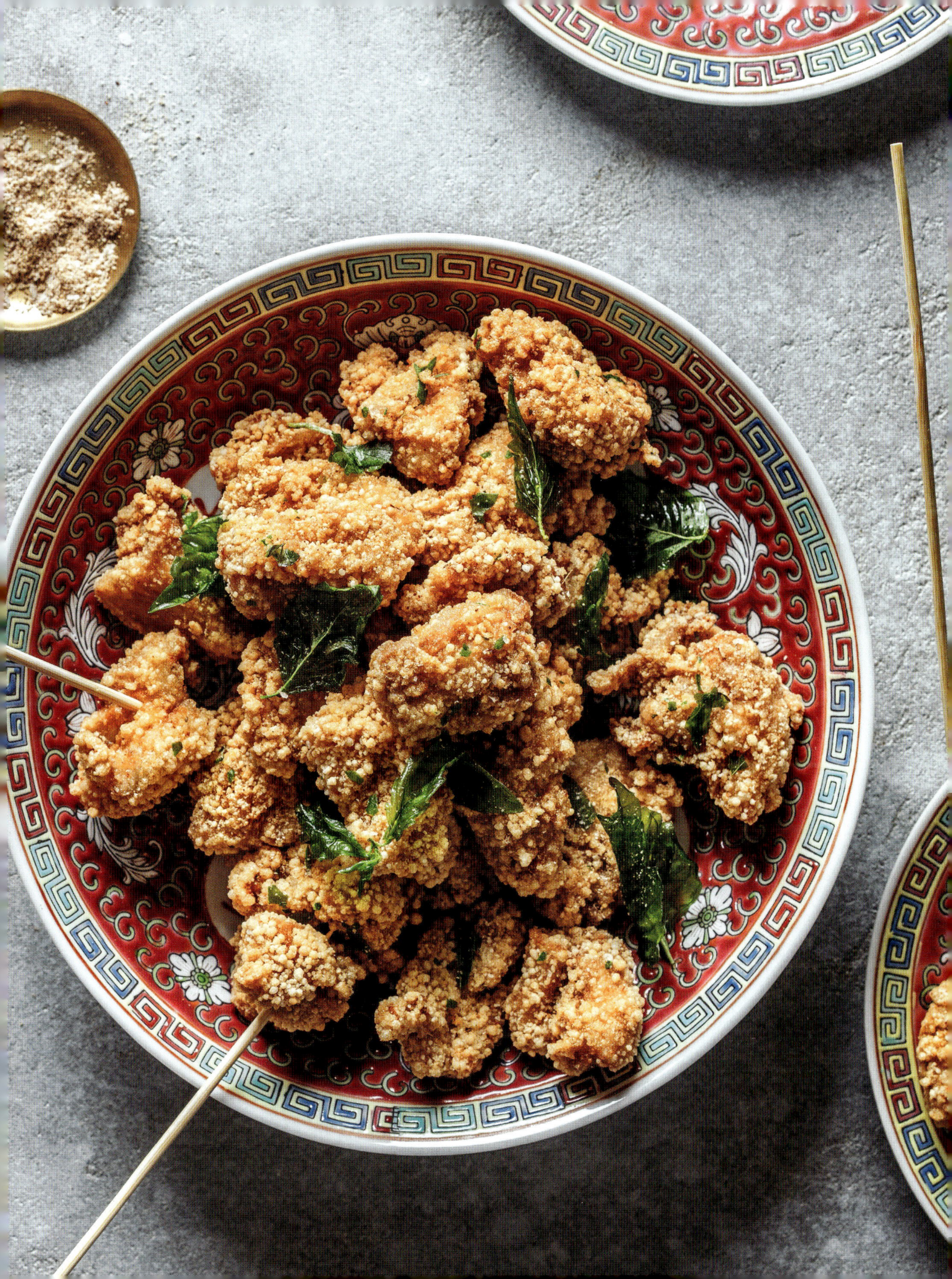

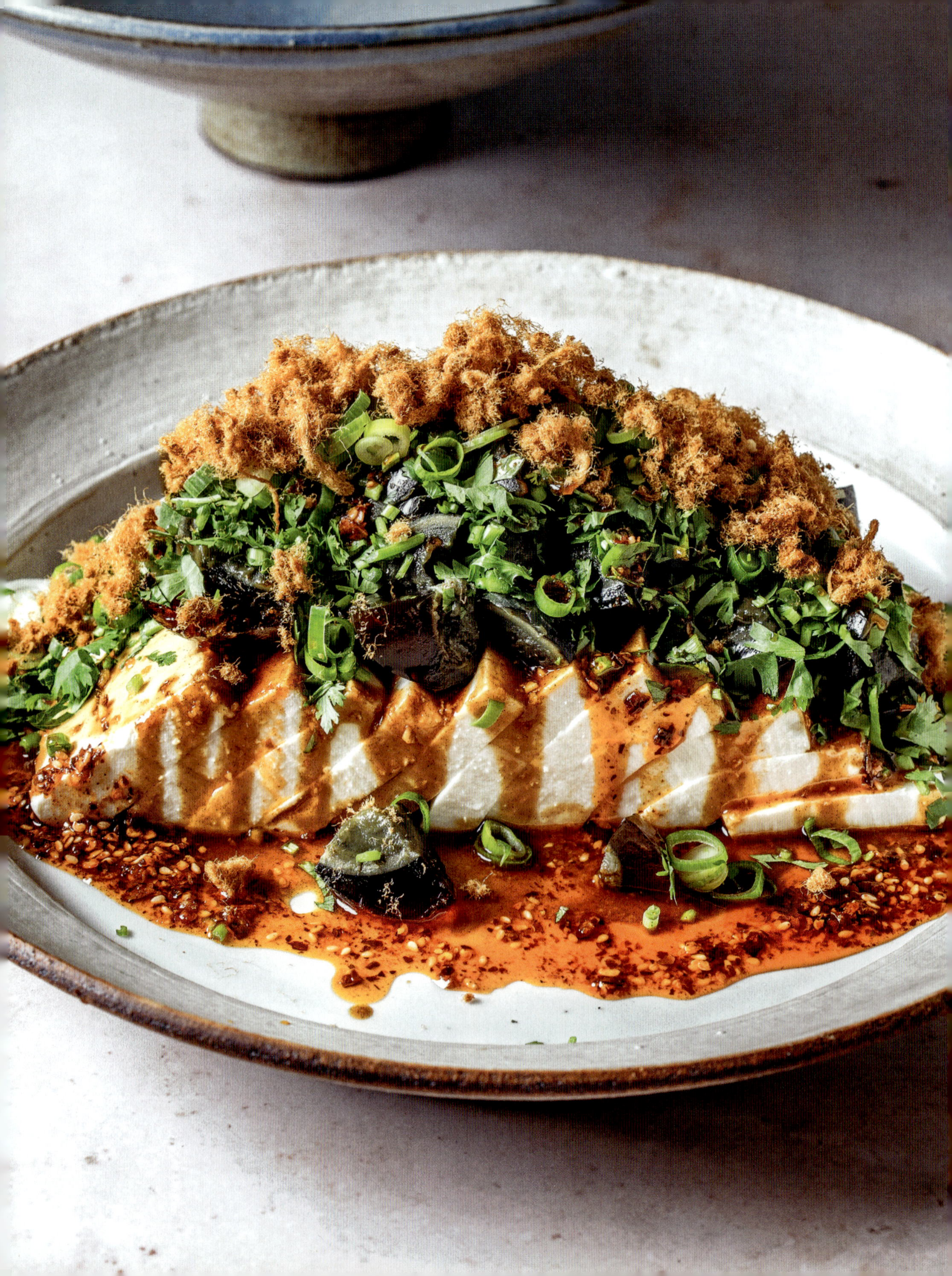

CENTURY DUCK EGGS WITH CHILLED TOFU

Often called century eggs or thousand-year-old eggs, the cured duck eggs that headline this dish do indeed look very, very old. Traditionally cured for weeks in a mixture of salt, quicklime, and ash, the whites develop a striking black translucence and firm texture while the yolks turn creamy. As a kid, I ate them often. I thought they looked like dinosaur eggs. I remember my confusion, and even my upset, when I saw them featured on the TV show *Fear Factor*. What about my culture was scary?

To the unfamiliar, they might seem intimidating, but I promise they're not. They require no cooking, just peeling, and their flavor is remarkable—bold and salty like fancy cheese. They're perfect for adding umami and deep, contrasting flavor to otherwise tame dishes, such as jook (rice porridge; see page 122). I particularly liked the way my mom served them: the eggs scattered on top of chilled tofu, then drizzled with a mixture of oyster sauce and ginger, and topped with scallions and cilantro. At the last minute, she'd pour hot oil over the herbs so they'd sizzle and release their fragrance right before we dug in.

SERVES 4 TO 6

One 16-ounce package silken tofu, drained and well chilled

3 preserved duck eggs (preferably made in Taiwan, Hong Kong, or Thailand), peeled and cut into ½-inch dice

¼ cup Chinese oyster sauce

2 tablespoons water

1 small garlic clove, minced

½ teaspoon grated ginger

Pinch of ground white pepper

Small handful of chopped cilantro (leaves and stems)

3 scallions, thinly sliced

3 tablespoons King's Chili Crisp (page 257) or store-bought Chinese chili crisp

3 tablespoons toasted sesame oil

¼ cup yuk sung (pork floss)

Flaky sea salt

Cut the tofu in half horizontally, then cut each half crosswise into ½-inch-thick slices. Use a thin metal spatula or the blade of a sharp knife to carefully transfer the pieces to a serving plate. Top with the eggs. As it sits, the tofu might exude a little water. If it does, dab it with a paper towel.

In a small bowl, combine the oyster sauce, water, garlic, ginger, and white pepper. Stir well and drizzle evenly onto the tofu and eggs. Top with the cilantro and scallions.

In a very small saucepan, combine the chili crisp and sesame oil, stir well, and set over medium-high heat just until it sizzles, about 30 seconds. Carefully pour the hot mixture directly over the cilantro and scallions.

Top with the yuk sung and a pinch of the flaky salt. Serve immediately.

LEMONGRASS SHRIMP COCKTAIL WITH MICHELADA MAYO

My mom's one request for this book was that it include my shrimp cocktail. A baking soda brine makes the shrimp plump and bouncy (a prized texture called song in Cantonese). Then I gently poach them in a white wine court bouillon—enhanced with fragrant lemongrass, ginger, and makrut lime leaves—until they're just cooked through. I even cool the shrimp in the same liquid to keep from diluting the flavor.

While I'm rather condiment-obsessed, I have to say that I can live without cocktail sauce. When coming up with a new dip, I remembered these amazing shrimp skewers I had in Mexico City that were shoved into an icy cold michelada (basically, beer meets Bloody Mary) and used the refreshing drink's seasonings—lime, chile, and Worcestershire—to rev up store-bought mayo.

SERVES 6 TO 8

MICHELADA MAYO

½ cup mayonnaise

¼ cup tomato paste

Finely grated zest of 2 limes

1 tablespoon lime juice, plus more as needed

2 teaspoons Worcestershire sauce

1 teaspoon Maggi seasoning

1 teaspoon Tabasco

½ teaspoon Tajín

½ teaspoon ground celery seed

2 medium garlic cloves, finely grated on a Microplane

Finely ground black pepper

Diamond Crystal kosher salt

POACHED SHRIMP

2 tablespoons plus 1 teaspoon Diamond Crystal kosher salt, divided

1 teaspoon baking soda

2 pounds colossal or jumbo shrimp

5 garlic cloves, lightly smashed and peeled

5 large makrut lime leaves (optional), bruised

2 lemongrass stalks, trimmed (see page 16) and smashed

1 celery stalk, roughly chopped

1 small yellow onion, quartered

3 by 1-inch knob ginger, sliced

2 cups dry white wine

Tajín, for serving

Lime wedges, for serving

Make the michelada mayo: In a bowl, combine the mayonnaise, tomato paste, lime zest, lime juice, Worcestershire sauce, Maggi, Tabasco, Tajín, celery seed, and garlic cloves. Stir until smooth. Season to taste with pepper and salt and additional lime. Cover and refrigerate until chilled, at least 30 minutes. (The mayo can be made up to 3 days ahead.)

Prepare the shrimp: In a medium bowl, stir together ¼ cup water, 1 teaspoon of the salt, and the baking soda until smooth. Add the shrimp and toss to coat well. Refrigerate for 30 minutes or up to 1 hour.

In a large pot, combine 10 cups water, the garlic, lime leaves (if using), lemongrass, celery, onion, ginger, and the remaining 2 tablespoons salt. Cover and bring to a boil over high heat, then turn the heat down to a gentle simmer and cook, uncovered, for 10 minutes to infuse the flavors. Use a spider strainer to scoop out and discard the aromatics.

Fill a large bowl about three-quarters of the way with ice. Add the wine to the poaching liquid in the pot and bring to a boil over high heat. Add the shrimp, discarding the marinade, then immediately turn off the heat. Stir, cover the pot, and let the shrimp gently poach until pink and firm, 2 to 4 minutes, depending on the size of the shrimp.

Transfer the shrimp to the bowl of ice, then carefully pour in enough of the poaching liquid to submerge the shrimp. Stir, then set aside until the shrimp are fully chilled, about 15 minutes.

Drain the shrimp, discarding the poaching liquid. (The shrimp keep in an airtight container in the refrigerator for up to 1 day.)

Transfer to a serving plate. Sprinkle with Tajín and serve chilled with the michelada mayo and lime wedges.

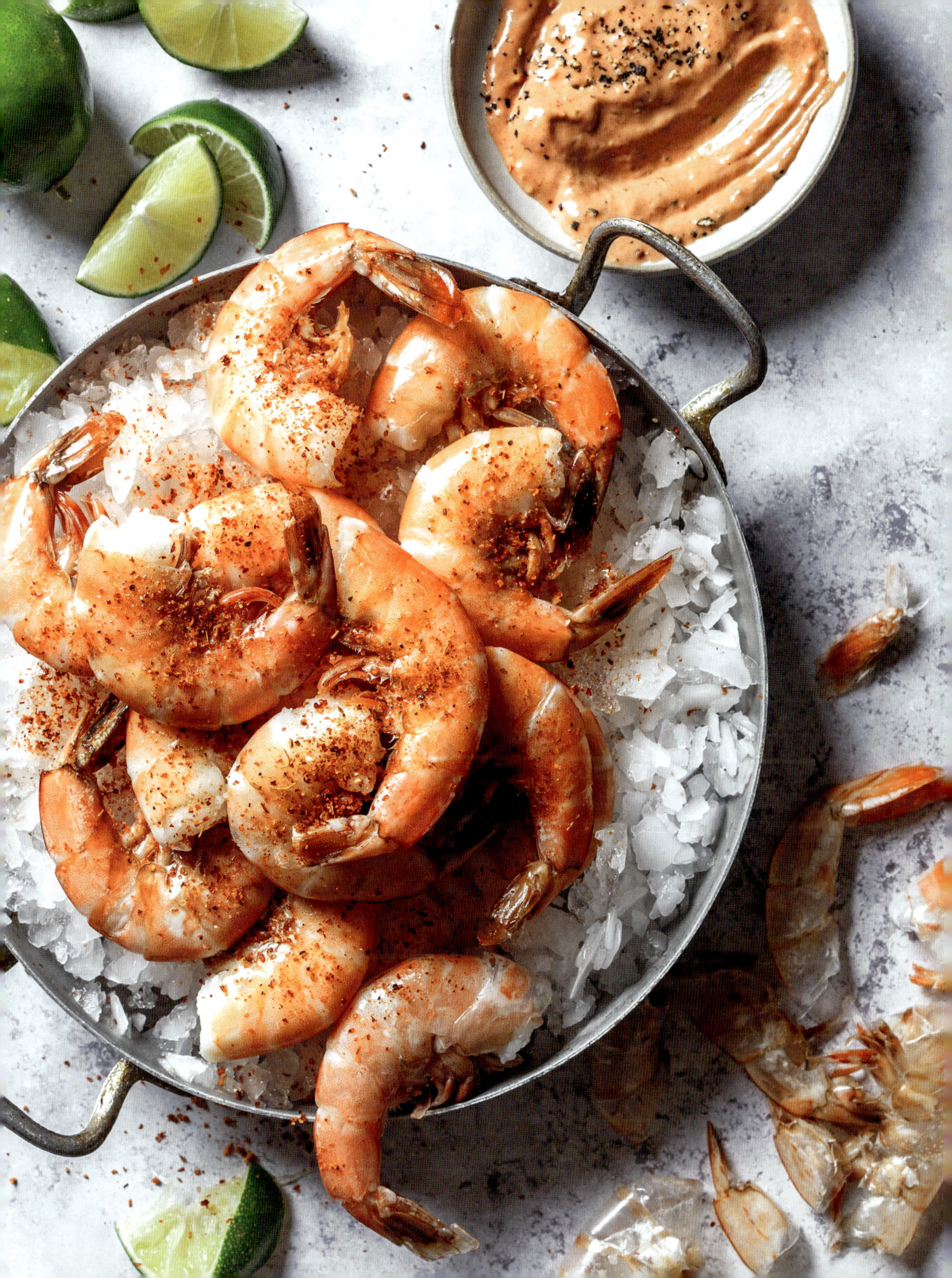

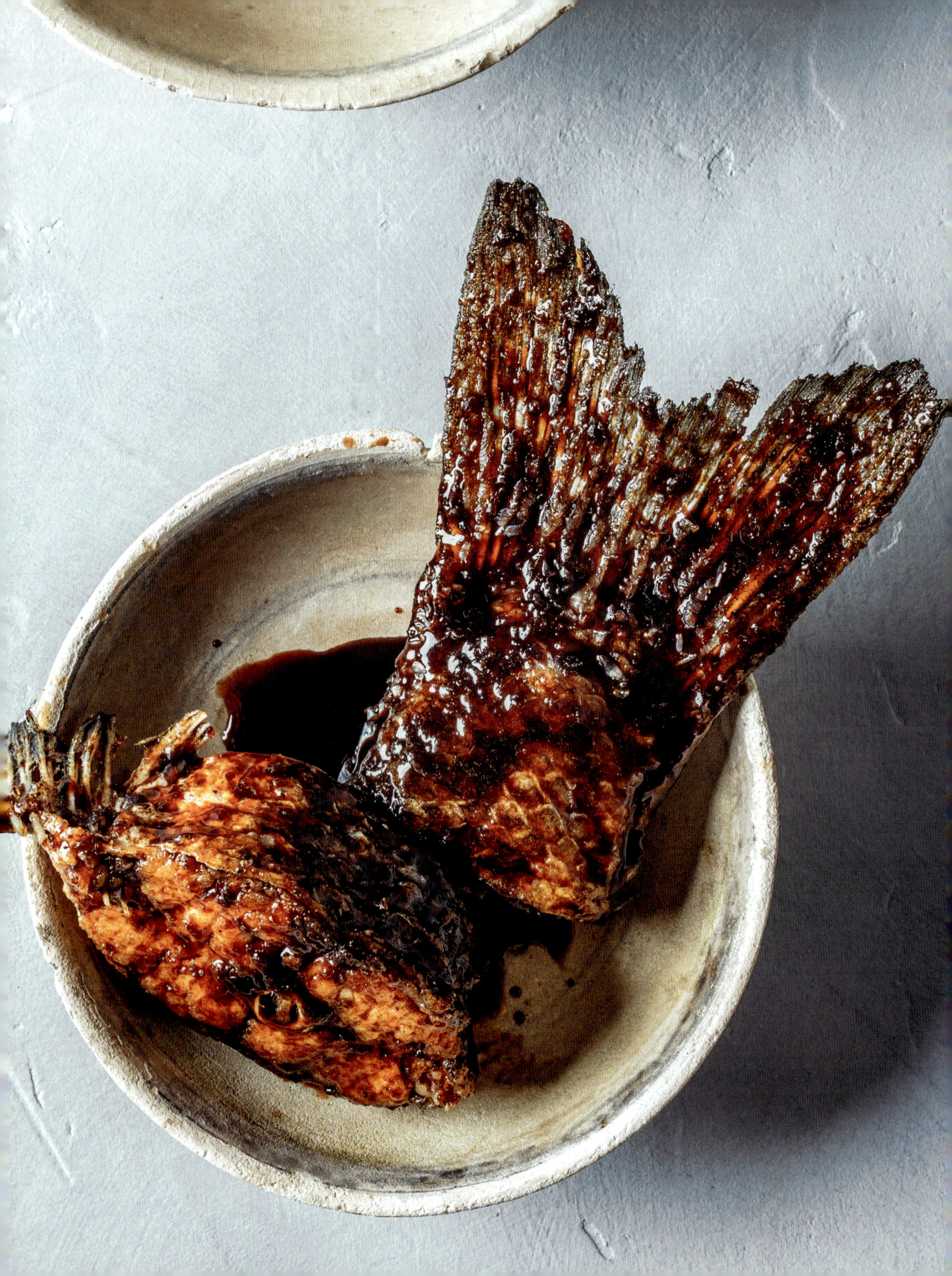

MY SHANGHAINESE GRANDMA'S FISH

In our family, Yang Yang, my Shanghainese grandma, was famous for her fun yu. She'd fry small steaks of firm, meaty white fish until golden and crisp, then soak them in a flavorful marinade overnight. To my current chef brain, the order of operations seemed backward, but that really doesn't matter when I'm gnawing at the bones. It's a bit like fish jerky, slightly chewy, sweet and sticky, and full of deep flavors like ginger and star anise. We ate it straight out of the fridge from my grandma's Tupperware.

SERVES 4 TO 6

MARINATED FISH

1 whole firm-fleshed white fish (1½ to 2 pounds), such as carp or pompano, scaled and gutted

¼ cup Shaoxing wine

2 by 1-inch knob ginger, peeled and finely grated on a Microplane

2 teaspoons Chinese light soy sauce

1 teaspoon Maggi seasoning

½ teaspoon ground white pepper

½ teaspoon Diamond Crystal kosher salt

SAUCE

2 cups water

1 cup Chinese rock sugar or light brown sugar

⅔ cup Chinese dark soy sauce

⅔ cup Shaoxing wine

½ cup Chinese light soy sauce

2 teaspoons Zhenjiang black vinegar

1 teaspoon Chinese five spice powder

1 teaspoon ground white pepper

4 by 1-inch knob ginger, peeled and finely grated on a Microplane

10 bay leaves

10 whole cloves

6 garlic cloves, lightly smashed and peeled

8 whole star anise

2 cinnamon sticks

TO FINISH

Canola oil, for shallow-frying (about 3 cups)

Steamed rice, for serving

Marinate the fish: Rinse the fish well inside and out, then pat it dry. Use scissors to trim the fins, then cut off the head, reserving it for stock, such as Weekend Broth (page 244). Use a sharp chef's knife to cut the fish into 1-inch-thick steaks. Kitchen shears help to cut through the spine.

In a large mixing bowl, combine the fish with the marinade ingredients and mix well. Let marinate in the refrigerator, tossing occasionally, for at least 30 minutes or up to 8 hours.

Make the sauce: In a medium saucepan, combine the sauce ingredients and bring to a boil over high heat. Turn the heat down to cook at a steady simmer until it has thickened to the consistency of warm maple syrup, about 20 minutes. Pour the spices and all, into a shallow heatproof dish that'll fit the fish in a snug single layer. Set aside.

To finish: Remove the fish from the marinade (discard this) and pat it dry with paper towels. Set the dish of sauce near the stove.

Pour ¾ inch of oil into a large wok or cast-iron skillet and heat it over high heat for 3 minutes. When the oil is ready, the end of a wooden chopstick or wooden spoon submerged in the oil will immediately release little bubbles. (Alternatively, cook in a deep-fryer at 350°F.)

Working in batches, gently add the fish pieces to the oil one at a time, leaving a little space around each one. Fry, undisturbed, until deep brown on the bottom, 5 to 6 minutes. Gently flip the fish and cook the same way until deep brown and crisp all over, 5 to 6 minutes more.

As they're fried, carefully transfer the fish directly to the sauce (it may splatter as you do) and gently turn to coat on all sides. Between batches, use a spider strainer to remove any stray bits from the oil and let the oil heat back up.

After all the fish is fried and coated in the sauce, cover and refrigerate for at least 4 hours or up to 12 hours, flipping the fish halfway through.

Enjoy chilled and on its own or with steamed rice and a drizzle of the sauce.

PORK LETTUCE WRAPS

I love Chinese lettuce wraps. If they're from P.F. Chang's, even better. Best of all, though, are my mom's. When she made them, it felt like a special occasion. I'd wash the lettuce while she laboriously peeled fresh water chestnuts with a paring knife and then stir-fried them with ground pork in a hoisin-forward sauce. Mine are modeled after hers and feature the same nostalgic combo of warm sweet-savory filling and chilled crisp lettuce, though here jicama offers the juicy crunch of water chestnuts without the work.

My mom used iceberg, though pretty red leaf or tender Bibb are also welcome. When I'm feeling fancy, I'll trim the floppy edges of each leaf to make perfectly round lettuce cups. Then I'll chop those edges and fold them into the meat mixture at the last minute so that no lettuce goes to waste.

SERVES 4 TO 6

GROUND PORK

1 pound ground pork (preferably 20% fat)

2 tablespoons Shaoxing wine

1 tablespoon Chinese light soy sauce

1 teaspoon Chinese dark soy sauce

1 tablespoon cornstarch

Dash of ground white pepper or a few turns of black pepper

SAUCE

3 tablespoons hoisin sauce

2 tablespoons Shaoxing wine

2 tablespoons Chinese oyster sauce

1 tablespoon Chinese dark soy sauce

1 tablespoon Chinese light soy sauce

2 teaspoons white sugar

1 teaspoon cornstarch

Dash of ground white pepper or a few turns of black pepper

ASSEMBLY

1 tablespoon canola oil

1 cup finely diced yellow onion

4 garlic cloves, minced

1 by 1-inch knob ginger, peeled and finely grated on a Microplane

1 cup finely diced fresh shiitake mushrooms

2 cups diced (¼-inch) peeled jicama

Handful of cilantro (leaves and stems), finely chopped

3 scallions, thinly sliced

1 head iceberg lettuce, cored, leaves separated, and chilled

Hoisin sauce, for drizzling

Prepare the ground pork: In a medium mixing bowl, combine all the ingredients and mix well. Set aside for 15 minutes to allow the pork to absorb the flavors.

Make the sauce: In a small mixing bowl, stir together the sauce ingredients until smooth. Set aside.

To assemble: Heat a large skillet or wok over high heat until it smokes lightly, about 2 minutes. Add the canola oil, swirl to coat the pan, and let the oil shimmer.

Add the ground pork mixture and cook, stirring occasionally and breaking up clumps with a wok spatula, until the meat is caramelized, 6 to 7 minutes.

Stir in the onion, garlic, and ginger and cook, stirring, for 1 minute. Stir in the mushrooms and cook until softened, about 2 minutes.

Add the jicama and the sauce and cook, stirring frequently, for 2 minutes, so the meat can absorb the sauce. Remove from the heat and stir in the cilantro and scallions (or serve them on the side).

Serve with the lettuce leaves for wrapping and more hoisin sauce for drizzling.

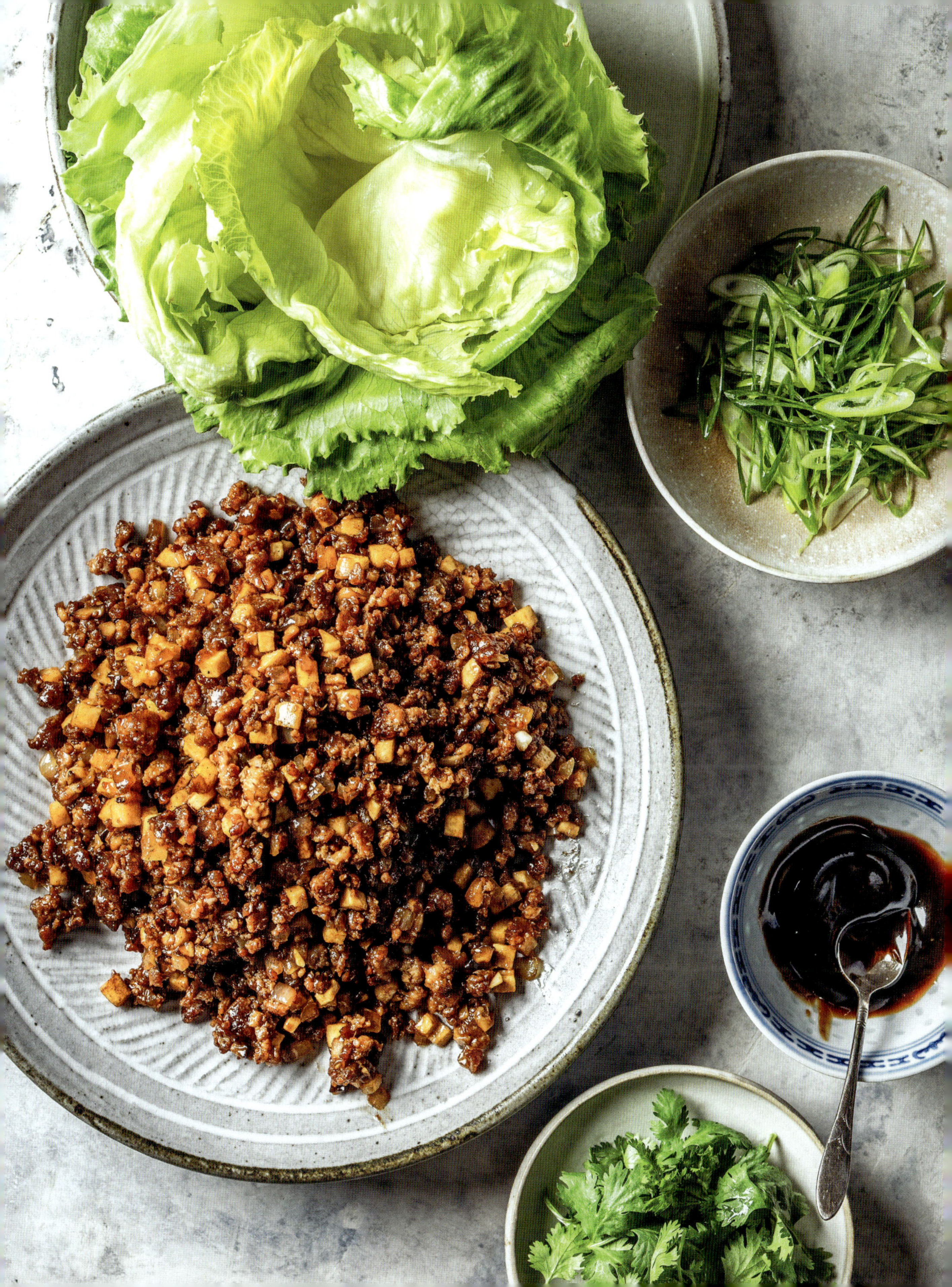

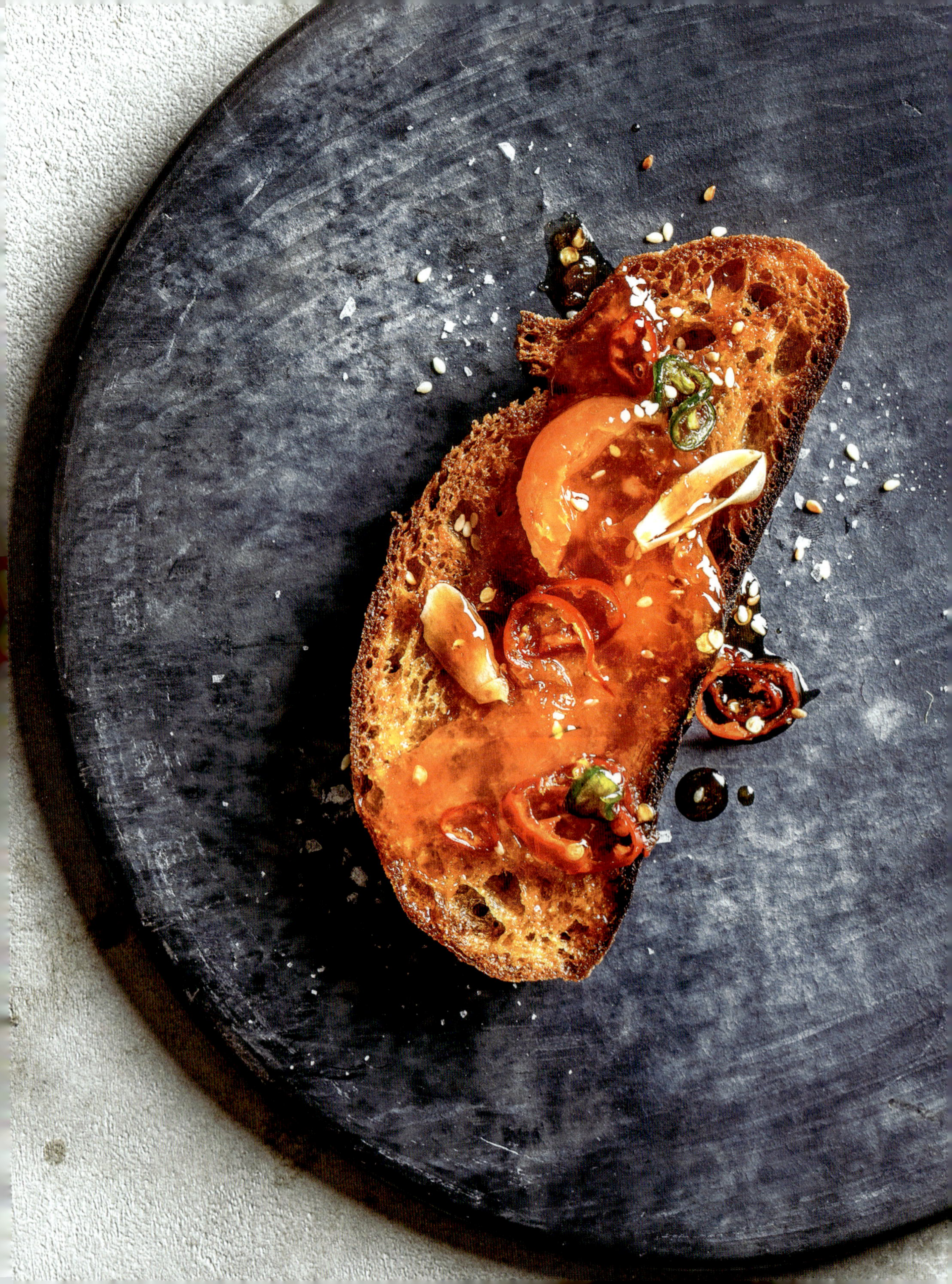

HOT HONEY–CURED EGG YOLKS ON GARLIC TOAST

Fans of jammy eggs will go wild for these. A mixture of honey, soy sauce, garlic, ginger, and chiles transforms these yolks into a luscious, deep-golden topping for steamed rice, focaccia (page 82), or steak tartare (page 31). I particularly love spreading them on garlic-rubbed toast, which I fry briefly in a pan with olive oil so the bread crisps but stays fluffy inside. I hope this toasting method becomes your go-to, no matter what you choose to serve on top.

LEVEL IT UP

Along with the yolks, top the toasts with fresh goat cheese and Black Vinegar–Marinated Sweet Peppers (page 35).

SERVES 4 TO 6

CURED YOLKS

1 cup honey
¼ cup Japanese soy sauce
¼ cup thinly sliced fresh chiles, such as Fresno, jalapeño, or serrano
4 large garlic cloves, thinly sliced
½ teaspoon finely grated ginger
8 egg yolks, unbroken

GARLIC TOAST

½ cup extra-virgin olive oil, divided
8 slices (about ¾ inch) crusty bread
1 large garlic clove, peeled
Diamond Crystal kosher salt
Flaky sea salt
Toasted sesame seeds, for garnish

Cure the yolks: In a small mixing bowl, whisk together the honey, soy sauce, chiles, garlic, and ginger. In a container large enough to hold the yolks in a single snug layer, gently add the yolks, then carefully pour on the honey mixture. Do not mix. Cover and cure in the refrigerator for at least 2 days, flipping the yolks once after 24 hours, or up to 4 days. The longer they cure, the firmer the yolks.

Make the garlic toast: Heat a large skillet over medium-high heat for 1 minute. Add ¼ cup of oil and swirl to coat the skillet. When the oil shimmers, add half of the bread in a single layer and then immediately flip to coat both sides with oil. Cook, flipping once more, until golden brown on both sides but still soft in the center, 2 to 3 minutes total. Transfer to a platter, and repeat with the remaining oil and bread.

To serve: Rub the garlic clove against one side of each bread slice. Sprinkle with a pinch of kosher salt. Remove the yolks from the honey mixture and spread one on each toast. Drizzle with some of the honey mixture, including some of the garlic and chiles, then sprinkle with flaky salt and sesame seeds. Serve right away.

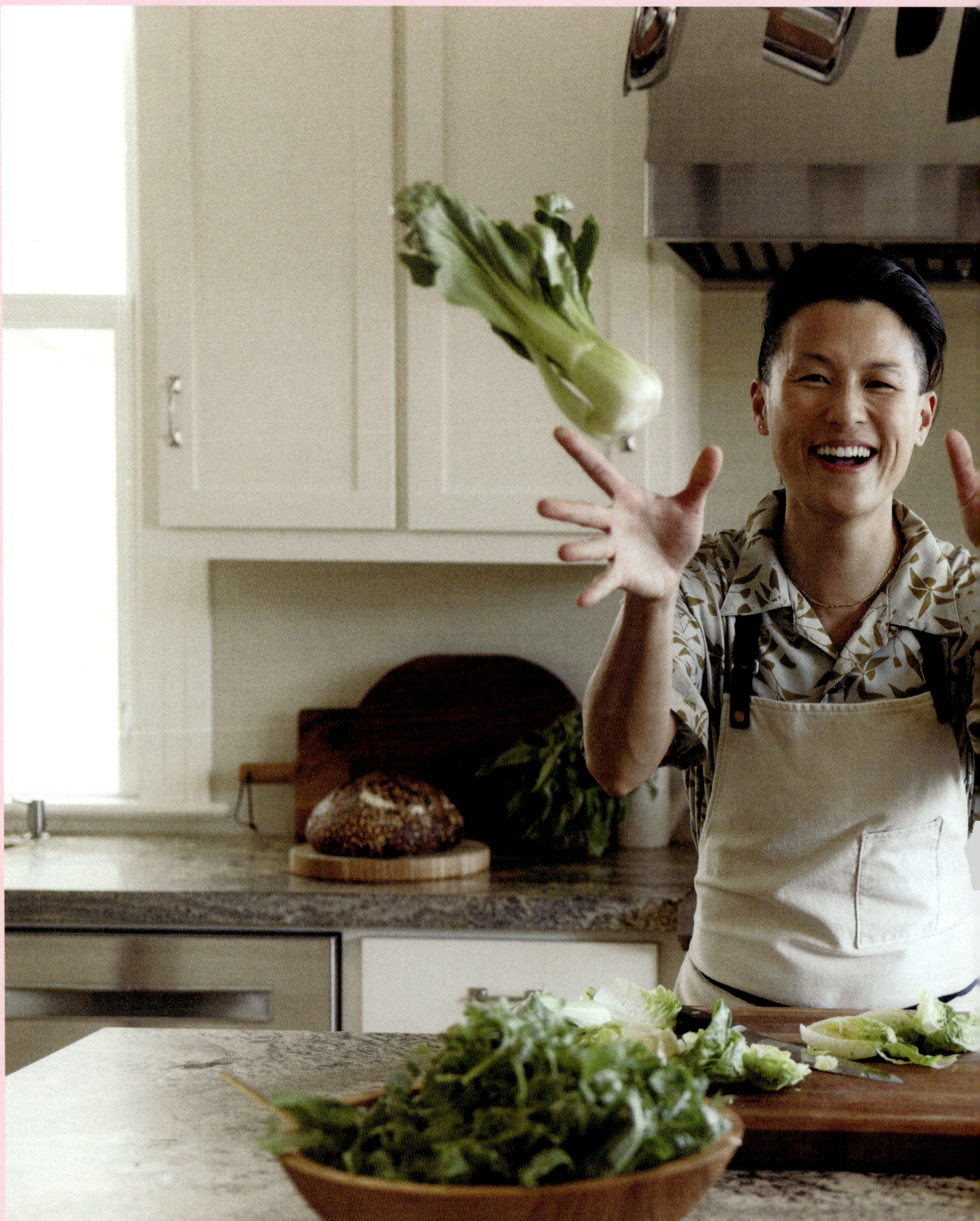

SALADS

2

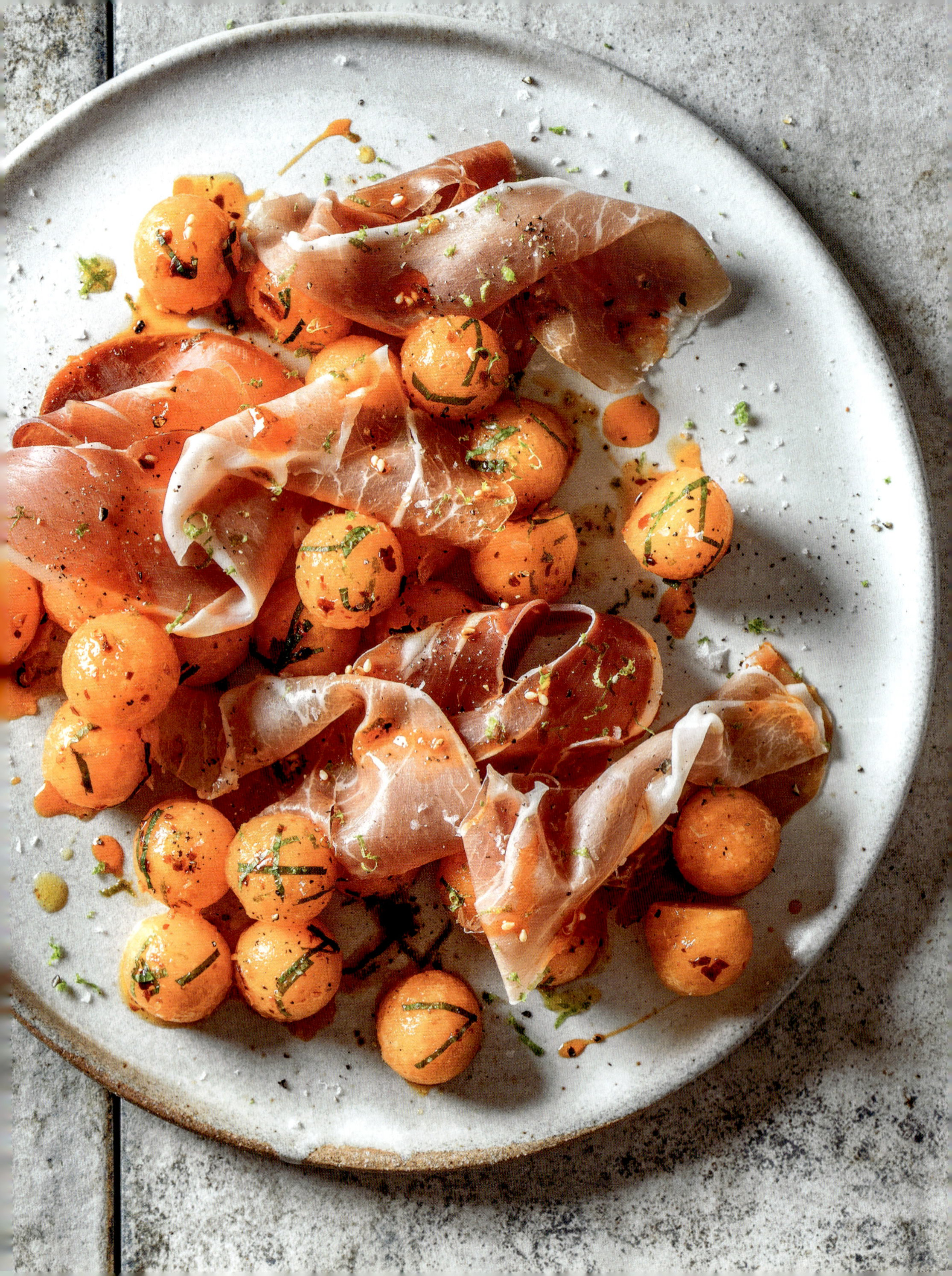

CHILI-LIME MELON AND PROSCIUTTO

Melon and prosciutto are a classic pairing for a reason. And really, if you have sweet, juicy summer melon and top-quality prosciutto, you don't have to do much more than arrange them on a plate. But why not have a little fun with it to take this iconic combination in a new direction? I tweak how the dish eats by balling the melon—cubes or wedges are fine, but come on, they aren't nearly as cute!—and adding flavors from Mexico via LA, where I grew up enjoying fruit doused with lime juice and Tajín. I swap them out in favor of lime zest and the lip-buzzing oil from my chili crisp.

LEVEL IT UP

Add room-temp stracciatella or burrata (I love the Di Stefano brand), shavings of Parmigiano-Reggiano, and/or Olive Oil–Fried Sourdough Croutons (page 255).

SERVES 4

Equipment: Melon baller

1 ripe melon (about 4 pounds), halved and seeded

1 tablespoon Agrumato lemon oil or extra-virgin olive oil, plus more for serving

1 teaspoon Sichuan chile flakes

¼ teaspoon Diamond Crystal kosher salt

Pinch of mint leaves or 1 shiso leaf, plus more for garnish

1 lime, for zesting

6 ounces very thinly sliced prosciutto

Chili oil from King's Chili Crisp (page 257) or store-bought Chinese chili oil, for serving

Flaky sea salt

Coarsely ground black pepper

Use a melon baller to scoop the flesh into balls (they don't have to be perfect) to yield about 4 cups. Transfer the melon to a medium mixing bowl and refrigerate for at least 20 minutes to chill.

Remove the bowl from the fridge. Add the lemon oil, chile flakes, and kosher salt and toss well. Thinly slice the mint or shiso, add to the bowl, and toss again.

Transfer the melon to a serving plate, use a Microplane to finely grate on the lime zest, then drape the prosciutto on and in between the melon.

Lightly drizzle with chili oil and additional lemon oil. Sprinkle with flaky salt, making sure each melon ball gets a few flakes, and add a few turns of black pepper. Top with additional sliced mint or shiso and serve.

FENNEL AND ENDIVE SALAD WITH ASIAN PEAR AND WALNUTS

Attention to detail elevates this otherwise classic, straightforward salad. Focusing on different textures and thoroughly chilling the ingredients keeps each bite interesting. There's fennel—one of my favorite vegetables and one so incredibly underrated—that's a little sweet and anise-y and thinly sliced to accentuate its refreshing crunch. There's endive, crisp and slightly bitter in the best way. I dress them lightly with lemon zest and juice and layer them in order to hide the treasures underneath—wispy fennel fronds; chopped walnuts left raw for a subtle, delicate nuttiness; and sweet, juicy Asian pear, the fall fruit of my childhood. Pecorino shaved on top brings sharp, salty balance. Mix it all together at the table in front of your guests for a fun reveal.

LEVEL IT UP

Finish with Fried Bread Crumbs (page 256) to add yet another fabulous texture.

SERVES 4

3 tablespoons champagne vinegar

1 tablespoon minced shallot

Diamond Crystal kosher salt

Coarsely ground black pepper

3 tablespoons extra-virgin olive oil, plus more for drizzling

1 medium fennel bulb (about 10 ounces), trimmed, stalks and fronds reserved

1 medium Asian pear, thinly sliced into half-moons

¼ cup walnuts, chopped

1 endive, bottom trimmed, halved lengthwise if large, leaves separated

Finely grated zest of 1 lemon

2 tablespoons lemon juice

A nice chunk of Pecorino Romano

In a small mixing bowl, combine the vinegar, shallot, ¼ teaspoon salt, and a few turns of black pepper and stir well. Let sit for 2 minutes to tame the shallot's sharp flavor. Slowly drizzle in the olive oil, whisking constantly, until thickened and emulsified.

Pick ½ cup of fennel fronds and thinly slice enough of the stalks to give you about ½ cup. In a large, wide salad bowl, combine the fronds, stalks, Asian pear, and walnuts. Whisk the dressing briefly, add to the bowl, and use your hands to toss gently but well.

Trim off any blemishes from the fennel bulb. Halve the bulb lengthwise, then shave the fennel (including the core) into ⅛-inch-thick slices (a mandoline helps).

In a large mixing bowl, combine the sliced fennel bulb, endive, lemon zest, lemon juice, ¼ teaspoon salt, and a few turns of black pepper and toss well.

Arrange the dressed fennel and endive prettily over everything in the salad bowl, generously drizzle with olive oil, then use a vegetable peeler to shave on a generous amount of pecorino. Add a few more turns of black pepper and mix well at the table just before serving.

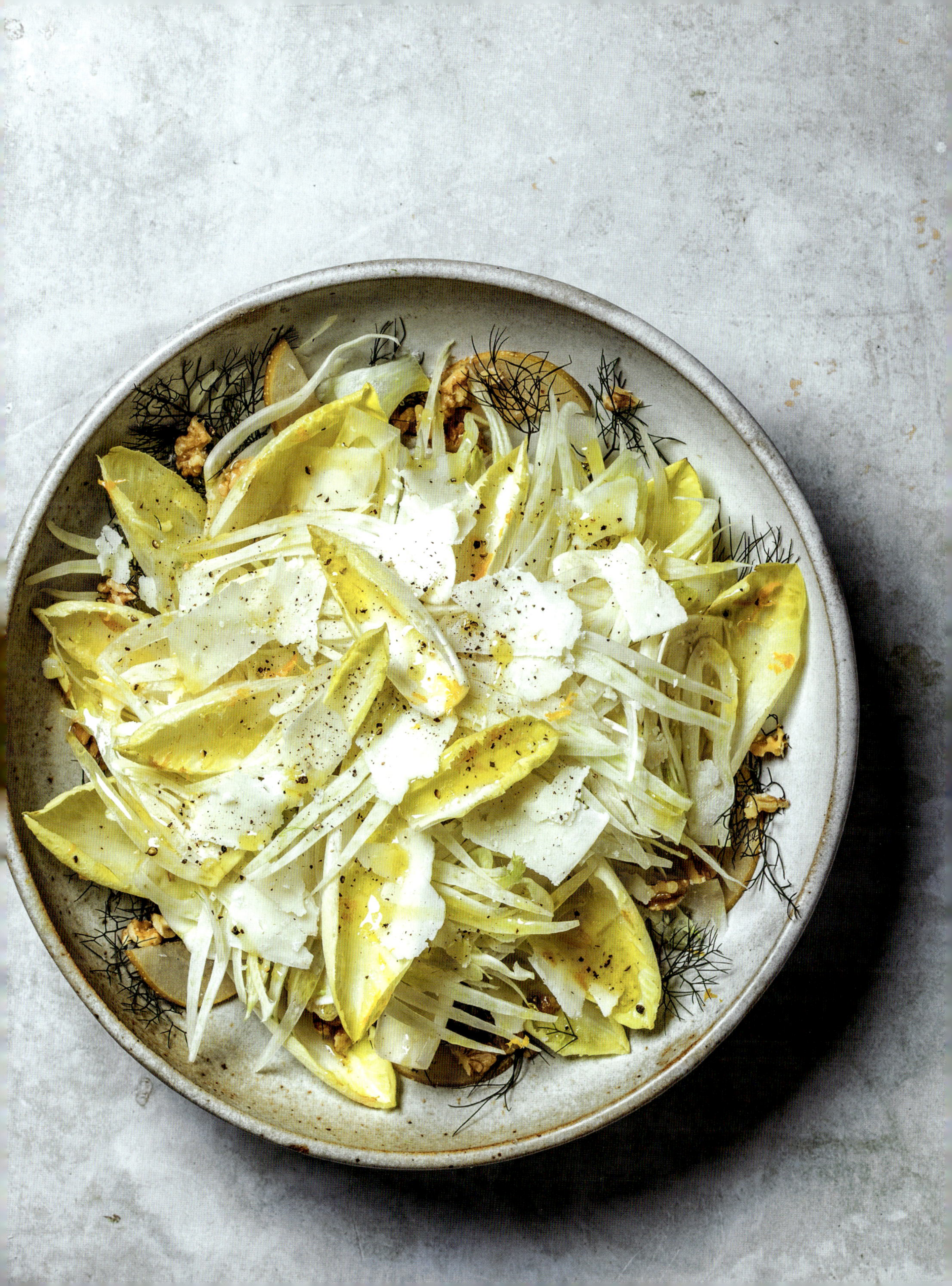

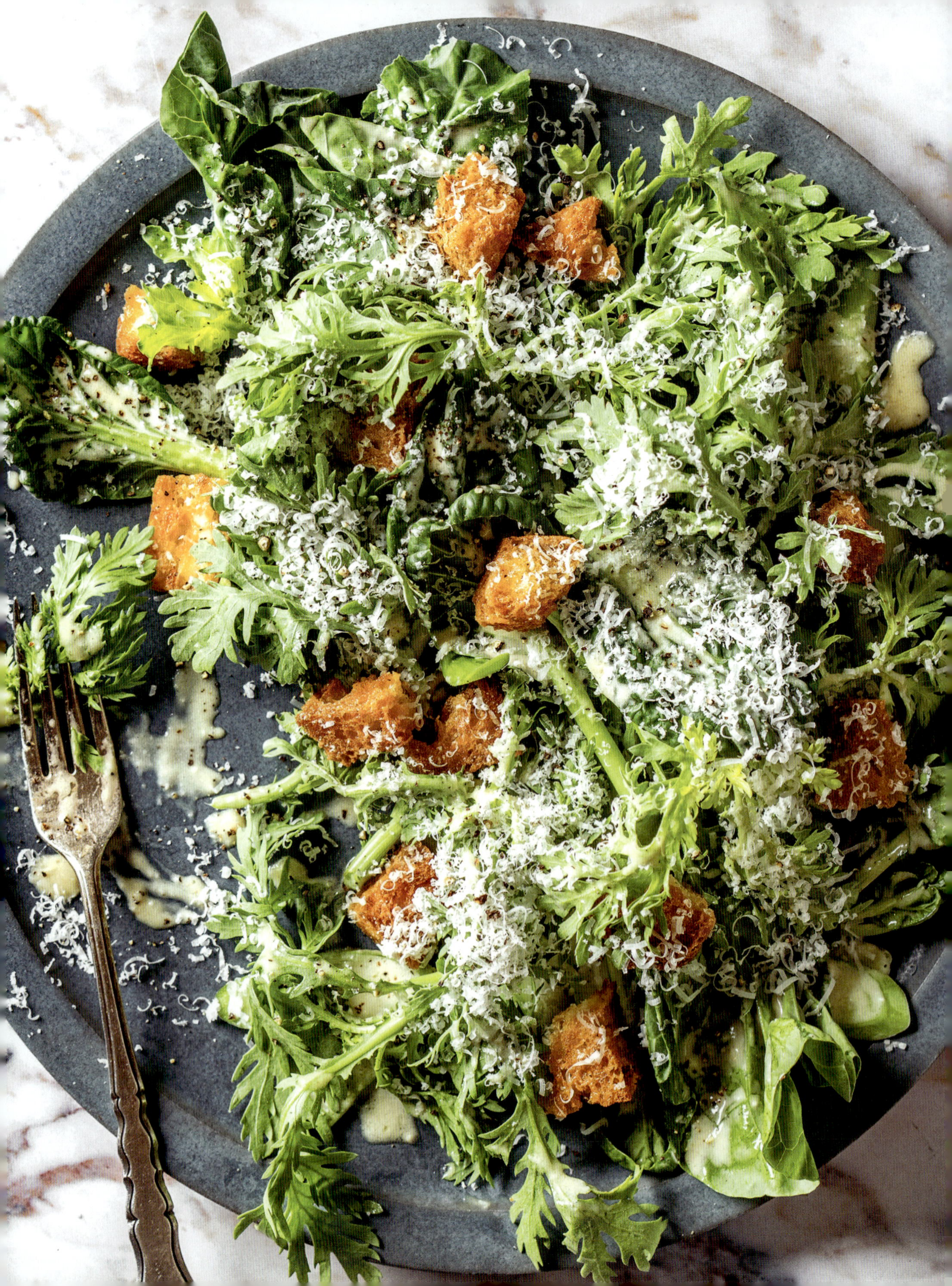

MISO CAESAR WITH GAI LAN AND CHRYSANTHEMUM GREENS

If I were a salad, I'd be a cold, slightly overdressed Caesar. Or more specifically, I'd be this Caesar, which has all the pleasures of the classic—crisp greens, crunchy bread, a little too much punchy dressing—but with a twist. In place of romaine, I look to a combination of tender Asian greens, like leafy, herbaceous chrysanthemum (tough stems removed), crunchy gai lan (Chinese broccoli, stems thinly sliced on the bias), and crisp baby bok choy (leaves torn, stems sliced). I take the time to chill them thoroughly, so they're especially refreshing. I also chill the dressing, already an umami powerhouse thanks to anchovies and Parmigiano-Reggiano even before I add just enough miso and soy sauce to bring extra depth and savoriness without detracting from the classic. Warm fried sourdough and a generous amount of grated Parmigiano-Reggiano complete the dish to make an exceptional Caesar turned not upside down but on its side.

LEVEL IT UP

Add Lap Cheong Crumble (page 256) or grate on bottarga or Cured Duck Egg Yolks (page 247) for an extra hit of flavor and umami.

SERVES 4 TO 6

DRESSING

¼ cup shiro (white) miso

3 tablespoons lemon juice

1 teaspoon Dijon mustard

1 teaspoon Chinese light soy sauce

10 oil-packed anchovy fillets

2 large garlic cloves, peeled

¼ teaspoon Diamond Crystal kosher salt

¼ teaspoon finely ground black pepper

1 large egg yolk

⅔ cup canola oil

1 ounce Parmigiano-Reggiano, finely grated

SALAD

12 cups mixed trimmed Asian greens

Kosher salt and coarsely ground black pepper

3 cups Olive Oil–Fried Sourdough Croutons (page 255), made just before serving

A nice chunk of Parmigiano-Reggiano

Make the dressing: In a small food processor, combine the miso, lemon juice, mustard, soy sauce, anchovy fillets, garlic, salt, and pepper and process, scraping down the sides as necessary, until smooth. Add the egg yolk and process until incorporated. With the machine running, slowly drizzle in the oil. The dressing will thicken and become glossy. Add the Parmigiano and pulse until incorporated.

Transfer the dressing to a container and season to taste with salt and pepper. Cover and refrigerate until slightly thickened and well chilled, at least 20 minutes or up to 3 days.

Make the salad: Wash the greens in a big bowl of very cold water, then drain and dry very well. Cover with a damp paper towel and chill the greens in the refrigerator for up to 4 hours.

In a large mixing bowl, drizzle the chilled greens with ¾ cup of the dressing. Use your hands to gently toss, making sure the leaves are evenly coated (including any nooks and crannies). Season with salt and pepper to taste and gradually add more dressing if you'd like.

Transfer to plates. Grind on some more black pepper, scatter on the croutons, and use a Microplane to grate on plenty of Parmigiano-Reggiano.

CLASSIC WEDGE WITH SHISO RANCH

A wedge salad rivals Caesar as my favorite salad—cold, refreshing, and creamy. Mine stays close to the classic with tomato and bacon (I prefer my bacon thick and cooked to a nice balance of crispy and chewy, but you do you). But I'm a ranch kinda gal, whether I'm dipping pizza; King's Wings (page 44), and crispy potatoes (page 144); or slathering crisp hunks of iceberg. (Don't worry, there's still blue cheese crumbled on top!)

When I make ranch, I keep it pretty classic, except for the fresh shiso leaves. They add a minty, herbal punch, though the dressing is equally delicious without them.

LEVEL IT UP

Swap out the bacon for Lap Cheong Crumble (page 256) and/or add Puffed Wild Rice (page 257) for crunch.

SERVES 4

- 1 head iceberg lettuce (about 1 pound), bottom trimmed
- Shiso Ranch (recipe follows)
- 8 slices thick-cut bacon, cooked to your liking, drained, and roughly chopped
- 1 cup Sungold or cherry tomatoes, halved
- ½ cup crumbled mild blue cheese, such as Point Reyes or Gorgonzola
- Handful of thinly sliced chives
- Coarsely ground black pepper
- Flaky sea salt

Remove any bruised leaves from the lettuce. Cut the head into quarters through the core, so each section remains intact. Rinse under running water, shake off excess water, and put cut-side down on a plate lined with paper towels. Refrigerate for at least 15 minutes or up to 4 hours to drain well and thoroughly chill so the lettuce gets crisp.

Transfer the lettuce cut-sides up to a platter or plates. Generously slather the cut sides of each wedge with ¼ cup of the dressing, so it has the chance to get in between the layers, then spoon another ¼ cup or so over each one.

Top with the bacon, tomatoes, blue cheese, chives, a few turns of pepper, and flaky salt. Serve immediately.

SHISO RANCH

MAKES 2½ CUPS

- 16 ounces full-fat sour cream
- ¼ cup lemon juice, plus more as needed
- 1 tablespoon Dijon mustard
- 2 teaspoons Diamond Crystal kosher salt, plus more as needed
- 20 green shiso leaves, roughly chopped
- 2 medium garlic cloves, peeled
- Handful of mixed flat-leaf parsley leaves, dill, and/or chives
- ¼ teaspoon coarsely ground black pepper

In a food processor, combine all the ingredients except the pepper and process, stirring and scraping down the sides once, until smooth, 30 seconds to 1 minute. Stir in the pepper. Season to taste with additional lemon and salt. Transfer the dressing to an airtight container and refrigerate for at least 30 minutes or up to 3 days.

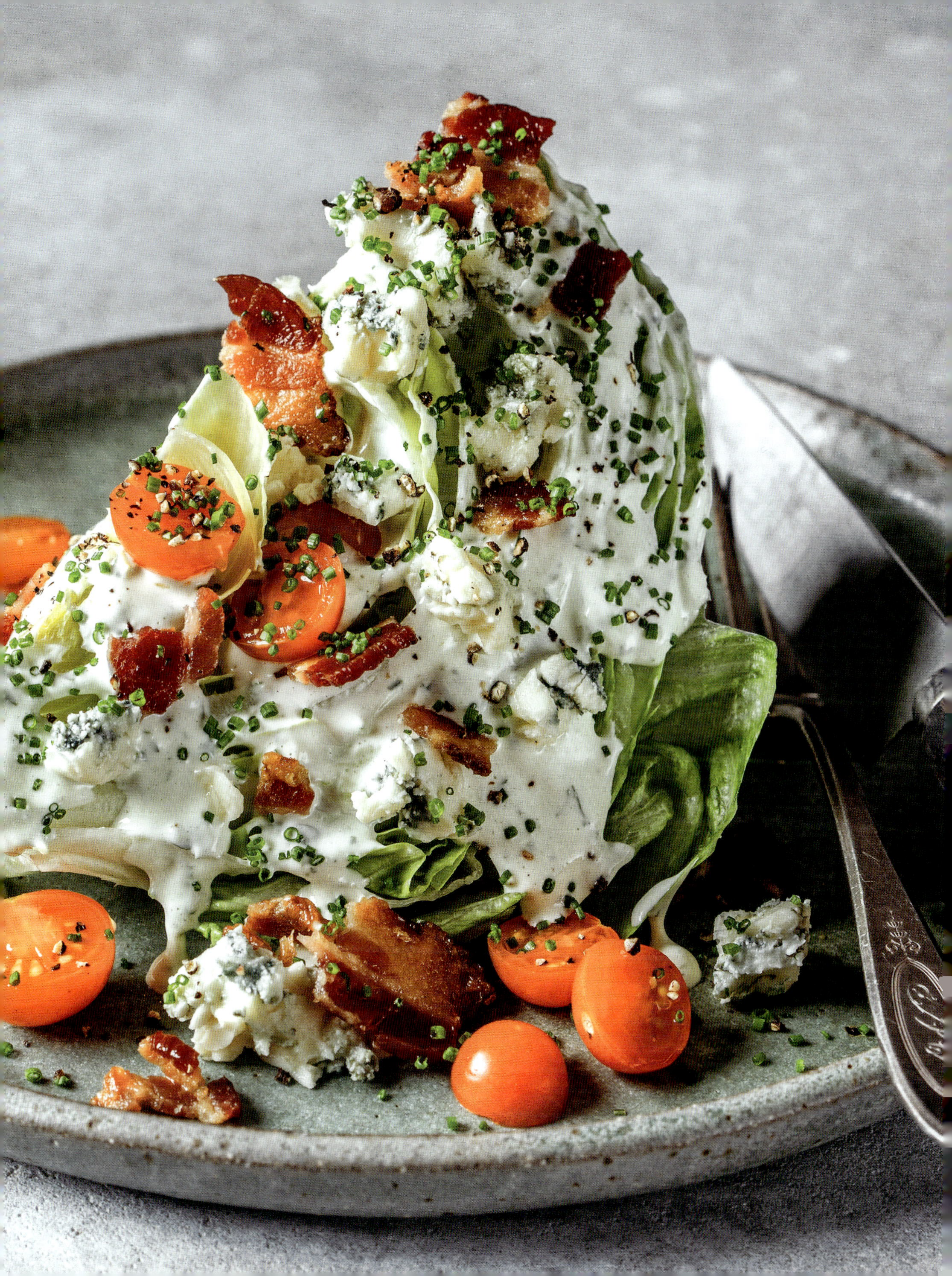

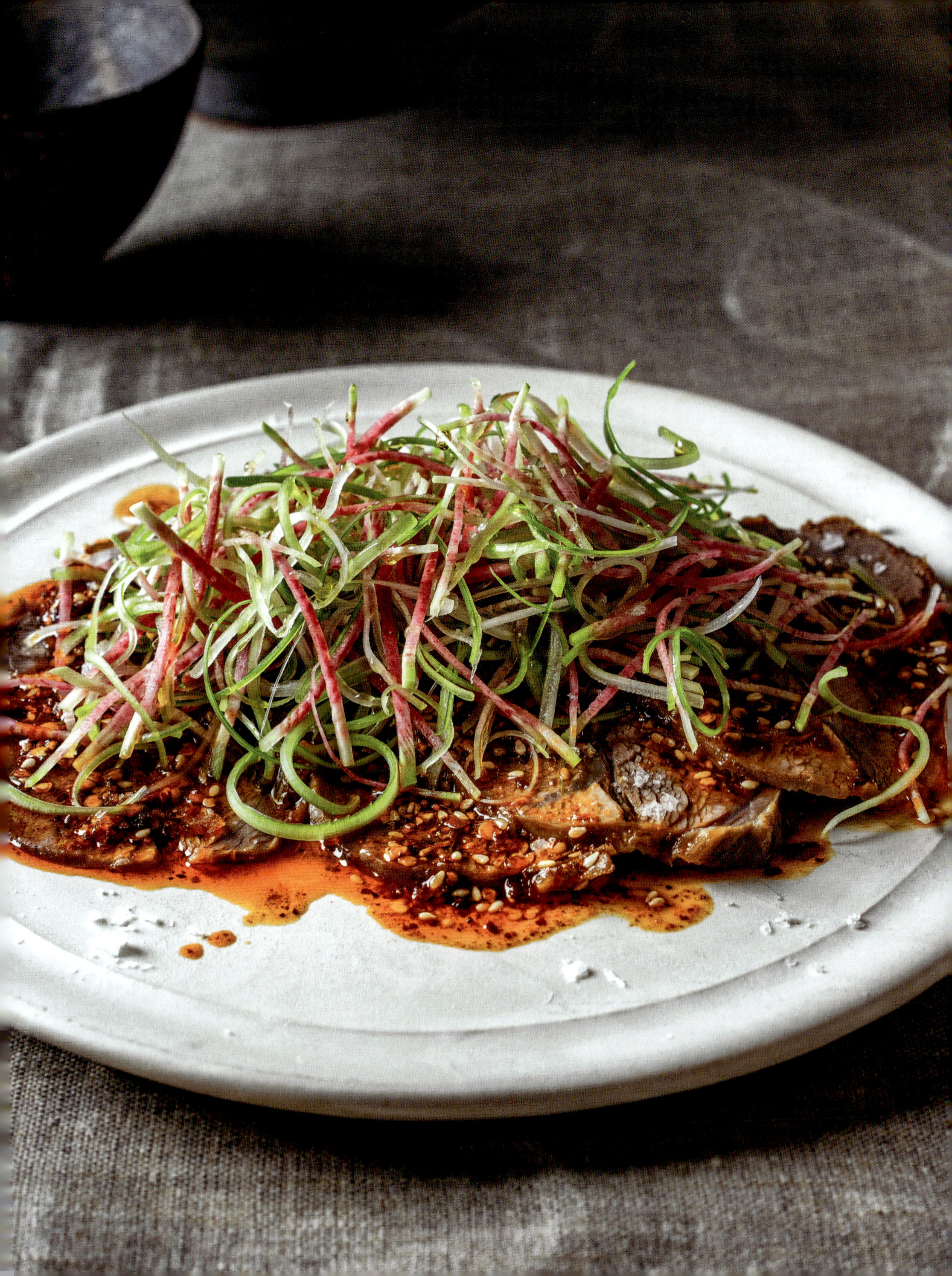

CHILLED BEEF SHANK SALAD WITH CELERY AND RADISH

One of my early memories is watching my mom make Cantonese-style beef shank. She'd simmer a shank with rock sugar, soy sauce, cinnamon, and star anise just long enough to soften the tendons that streak the flesh and achieve a delightful gelatinous bite—a bit different from the "fall off the bone" tenderness prized in the professional kitchens I'd go on to cook in.

She'd chill the shank overnight, and the next day, we would race downstairs to taste it. Throughout the week, our family would snack on flavorful slices straight from the fridge like deli meat. Occasionally, my mom would serve them as a simple salad that I upgrade with the heat of chili crisp and the refreshing crunch of celery and radish.

SERVES 8 TO 10

BEEF SHANK

2 pounds boneless beef shank (aka banana shank)

4 whole star anise

5 whole cloves

2 cinnamon sticks

2 whole dried Sichuan chiles

½ teaspoon red Sichuan peppercorns

1 teaspoon fennel seeds

¾ teaspoon ground white pepper

3 by 1-inch knob ginger, smashed

½ cup Chinese dark soy sauce

¼ cup Chinese light soy sauce

2 tablespoons Shaoxing wine

2 tablespoons Chinese rock sugar or packed light brown sugar

8 cups cold water

SALAD

¾ cup julienned watermelon radish

¼ cup julienned celery

Small handful of julienned scallions

¾ cup King's Chili Crisp (page 257), or store-bought Chinese chili crisp

¼ cup Zhenjiang black vinegar

Two dashes of ground white pepper

Flaky sea salt

Large handful of chopped cilantro (leaves and stems)

1 tablespoon toasted sesame seeds

2 teaspoons Agrumato lemon oil

¼ teaspoon Diamond Crystal kosher salt

Lemon wedges, for serving

Cook and chill the beef shank: In a large pot, combine all the ingredients, cover, and bring to a boil over high heat. Turn the heat down to cook at a very gentle simmer (with just a few bubbles breaking the surface) for 1½ hours. The shank will shrink and take on the color of the cooking liquid, but note that it won't be fork-tender.

Remove from the heat, uncover, and let the beef cool in the cooking liquid. Cover the pot and refrigerate for at least 5 hours or up to 12 hours.

Transfer the shank to a cutting board, discarding what's left in the pot. Cut the shank in half crosswise. Store one half in an airtight container in the fridge for snacking, up to 5 days. Very thinly slice the remaining shank against the grain. Shingle the slices on a serving platter.

Assemble the salad: Fill a medium mixing bowl with half ice and half water. Rinse the radish, celery, and scallions in a mesh sieve, then transfer to the ice water. This gives the vegetables a lovely crisp texture.

In a mixing bowl, stir together the chili crisp, vinegar, and pepper, then pour it over and around the beef slices. Lightly season with flaky salt, then sprinkle on the cilantro.

Drain the radish mixture and pat dry. In a medium mixing bowl, use your hands to gently toss together the radish, celery, scallions, sesame seeds, lemon oil, and kosher salt. Scatter it onto the beef and serve with the lemon wedges.

CHICORY SALAD WITH ANCHOVY, KUMQUATS, AND SMOKED CHEESE

This salad highlights the beauty of chicories. Lemony anchovy dressing and curls of salty, smoky cheese temper chicory's soft bitterness. Juicy segments of orange provide contrast, and sliced kumquats, which my grandma Sabrina PoPo used to snack on whole, bring their own delicious sweet-tart dimension.

LEVEL IT UP

Sprinkle on Fried Bread Crumbs (page 256) or Olive Oil–Fried Sourdough Croutons (page 255).

SWITCH IT UP

In the fall, sub in Fuyu persimmons, apples, pears, or pomegranate seeds for the oranges.

SERVES 4 TO 6

- 1¼ pounds chicories (preferably a mix; see Note)
- 1 small garlic clove, peeled
- Diamond Crystal kosher salt
- 4 oil-packed anchovy fillets
- 2 tablespoons lemon juice
- 2 tablespoons freshly squeezed orange juice
- 1 tablespoon minced shallot
- Coarsely ground black pepper
- 2 Cara Cara, blood, or mandarin oranges
- ¼ cup extra-virgin olive oil
- 6 kumquats, thinly sliced, seeds removed
- 6 ounces firm smoky cheese, such as Idiazabal or smoked Manchego

> **NOTE**
>
> The firm heads of purple radicchio at the supermarket work well, but I love to seek out pink radicchio rosa, colorful speckled Castelfranco, and striking curled Tardivo.

Trim the base of each head of chicory, then separate the leaves and tear them into large bite-size pieces. You should have a generous 5 quarts. Fill a large bowl with half ice and half water, submerge the chicories, and set aside while you prepare the rest of the salad. This makes the leaves especially crisp and tempers their bitterness.

In a medium-size mortar, pound the garlic with a pinch of kosher salt to a paste, about 1 minute. Add the anchovy fillets and pound to a paste. (Alternatively, you can mince and mash the ingredients on a cutting board, then scrape it into a bowl.) Add the lemon juice, orange juice, shallot, ¼ teaspoon salt, and a few turns of pepper and whisk well. Let the shallots marinate for a few minutes.

Use a Microplane to finely grate 2 teaspoons of zest from the oranges into the mortar. Slowly drizzle in the olive oil, whisking constantly, until thickened and emulsified. Carve off the remaining peel and pith from the oranges, halve them top to bottom, then slice crosswise into ¼-inch half-moons. Set aside.

Drain the chicories well. In an especially large mixing bowl, combine the chicories, kumquats, and reserved orange segments. Whisk the dressing again, then drizzle it into the bowl and add 2 heavy pinches of salt and another few turns of pepper. Use your hands to gently toss the salad, massaging the dressing onto the leaves without bruising them. Take some time to make sure the leaves are all coated.

Arrange the dressed salad on a plate. Use a vegetable peeler to shave the cheese over the salad, top with additional black pepper, and serve immediately.

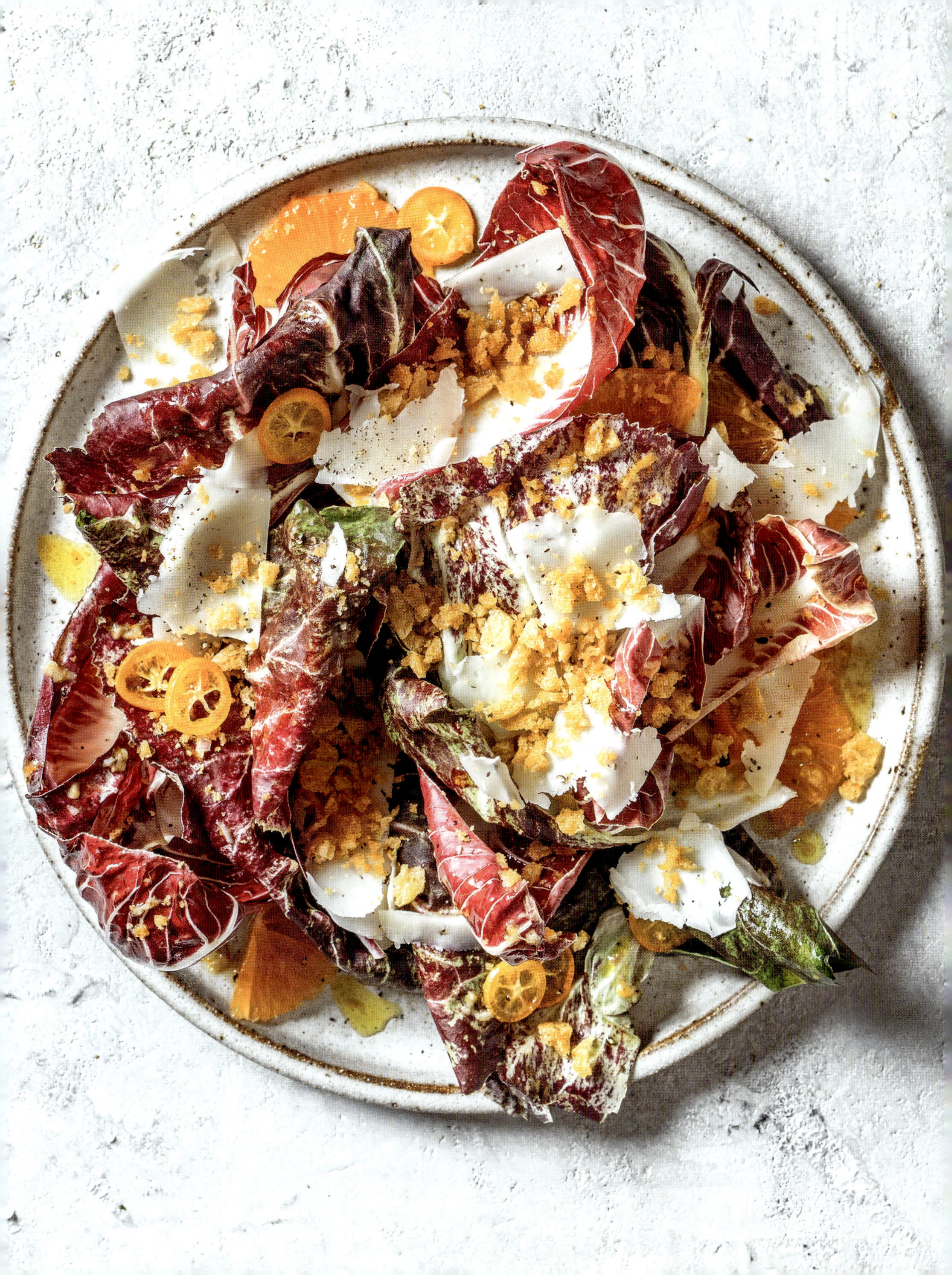

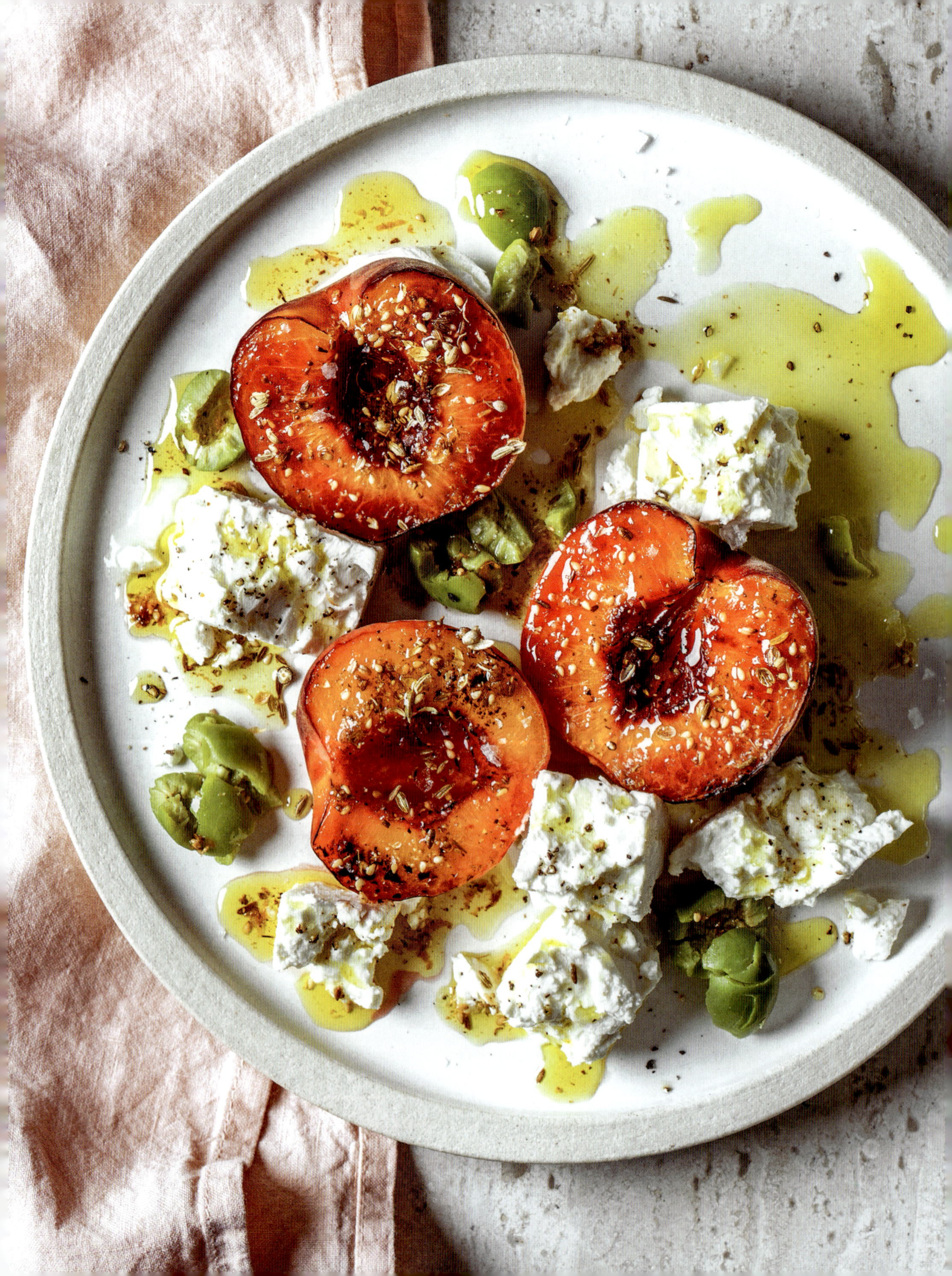

SPICED CHARRED PEACHES WITH OLIVES, FETA, AND ORANGE ZEST

When friends swing by at the last minute, I'll throw together Castelvetrano olives spiced with cumin seeds and orange zest—one of my favorite flavor combinations. With it, I'll serve a block of feta topped with toasted spices and nice olive oil. In the summer, I'll merge the two into one simple yet playful take on a fruit-and-cheese plate along with peaches or, really, any ripe stone fruit, like nectarines, plums, pluots, or apricots. Serving them fresh is great, but there's something special that happens when they're briefly charred on a grill (or under the broiler), caramelizing their sugars and concentrating their flavor.

SERVES 4 TO 6

½ teaspoon cumin seeds

½ teaspoon fennel seeds

¼ teaspoon coriander seeds

½ cup drained Castelvetrano olives, lightly smashed and pitted

3 tablespoons extra-virgin olive oil, plus more for cooking and drizzling

1 teaspoon finely grated orange zest

½ teaspoon toasted sesame seeds

2 ripe peaches or nectarines, halved and pitted

⅛ teaspoon Diamond Crystal kosher salt, plus more as needed

Coarsely ground black pepper

One 7-ounce block feta, drained and broken into large chunks

Flaky sea salt

In a small dry skillet, toast the cumin, fennel, and coriander seeds over medium heat, shaking the pan frequently, until fragrant and a shade darker, about 2 minutes. Transfer to a mortar or spice grinder and briefly pound or coarsely grind the spices.

In a medium mixing bowl, combine the spices, olives, olive oil, orange zest, and sesame seeds. Stir well and set aside.

Prepare a grill, preferably charcoal, to cook with high heat. (Alternatively, position an oven rack roughly 2 to 4 inches from the heat source and preheat the broiler. Line a small [9 by 13-inch] sheet pan with aluminum foil.)

Rub the cut side of each peach very lightly with olive oil and sprinkle with the kosher salt. Grill the peaches cut-sides down (or broil on the prepared sheet pan cut-sides up) until charred with some dark spots but still firm, 2 to 3 minutes. Leave them as is or cut into smaller pieces.

Transfer the peaches to the bowl with the spice mixture, season lightly with kosher salt and pepper, and toss gently to coat.

Arrange the peaches on a plate in a single layer, add the feta, then scatter on the olives and spoon on the spice mixture left in the bowl. Drizzle generously with additional olive oil, then sprinkle with flaky salt and black pepper to taste. Serve right away.

HEIRLOOM TOMATOES WITH FISH SAUCE, MINT, AND FRIED SHALLOTS

Few things beat a perfect, juicy summer tomato at the peak of its ripeness. Slice a few of these colorful beauties and you have an easy meal with a drizzle of good olive oil, a splash of vinegar, and a sprinkling of flaky sea salt to draw out their pure flavors. Or you can shake it up a little, giving the tomatoes some papaya salad vibes with fish sauce and lime juice. Cilantro, mint, and Thai basil freshen things up, and peanuts and sweet crispy shallots add fun, satisfying textures.

LEVEL IT UP

Add Fried Bread Crumbs (page 256) for crunch and/or julienned makrut lime leaves for their wonderful aroma.

SERVES 4

FISH SAUCE VINAIGRETTE

¼ cup lime juice (2 or 3 juicy limes)

2 teaspoons finely chopped garlic

1 teaspoon finely chopped shallot

2 tablespoons fish sauce (Three Crabs is a must here)

2 tablespoons white sugar or honey

¼ teaspoon Diamond Crystal kosher salt

Finely ground black pepper

1 to 2 fresh Thai chiles (optional), thinly sliced

2 tablespoons extra-virgin olive oil

SALAD

2 pounds ripe heirloom tomatoes, cored and cut into pretty pieces

Handful of mint or shiso leaves

Handful of cilantro (leaves and stems) or Thai basil leaves, finely chopped

Diamond Crystal kosher salt and coarsely ground black pepper

Extra-virgin olive oil, for drizzling

Flaky sea salt

¼ cup chopped unsalted roasted peanuts

¼ cup Fried Shallots, homemade (page 254) or store-bought

Make the fish sauce vinaigrette: In a large mixing bowl, combine the lime juice, garlic, and shallot, stir well, and let sit for 2 minutes to tame their sharp flavor. Stir in the fish sauce, sugar, salt, a few turns of pepper, and chiles (if using). Slowly drizzle in the olive oil, whisking constantly, until thickened and emulsified. (The vinaigrette keeps in an airtight container in the refrigerator for up to 1 week.)

Make the salad: Add the tomatoes to the large mixing bowl. Finely chop the mint and cilantro and add them to the bowl. Season with a generous pinch of kosher salt and a few turns of pepper and toss gently but well.

Arrange the tomatoes on a plate in an even layer and pour on the vinaigrette left in the bowl. Generously drizzle with olive oil and sprinkle a little flaky salt onto each tomato. Sprinkle on the peanuts and shallots and serve.

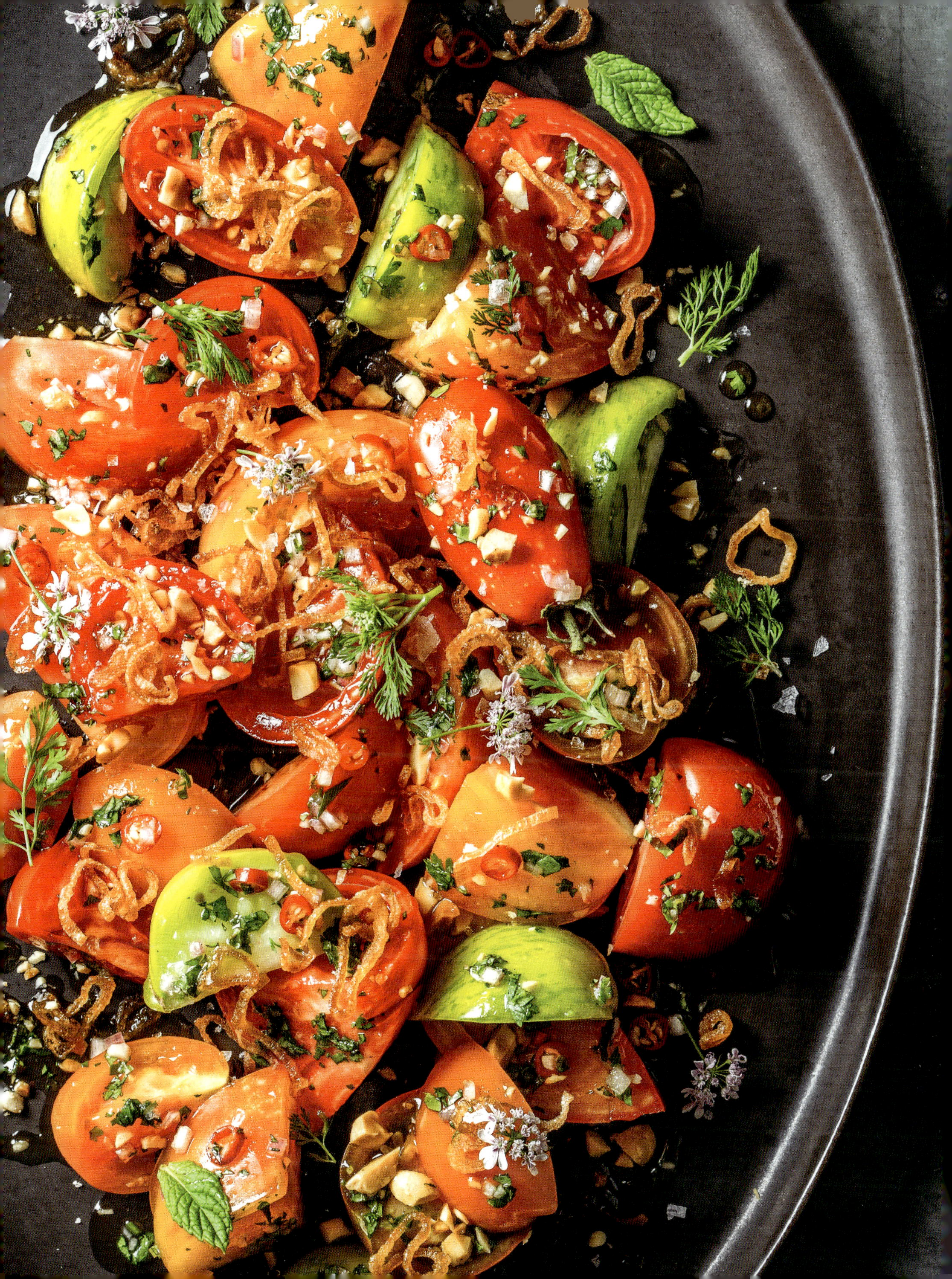

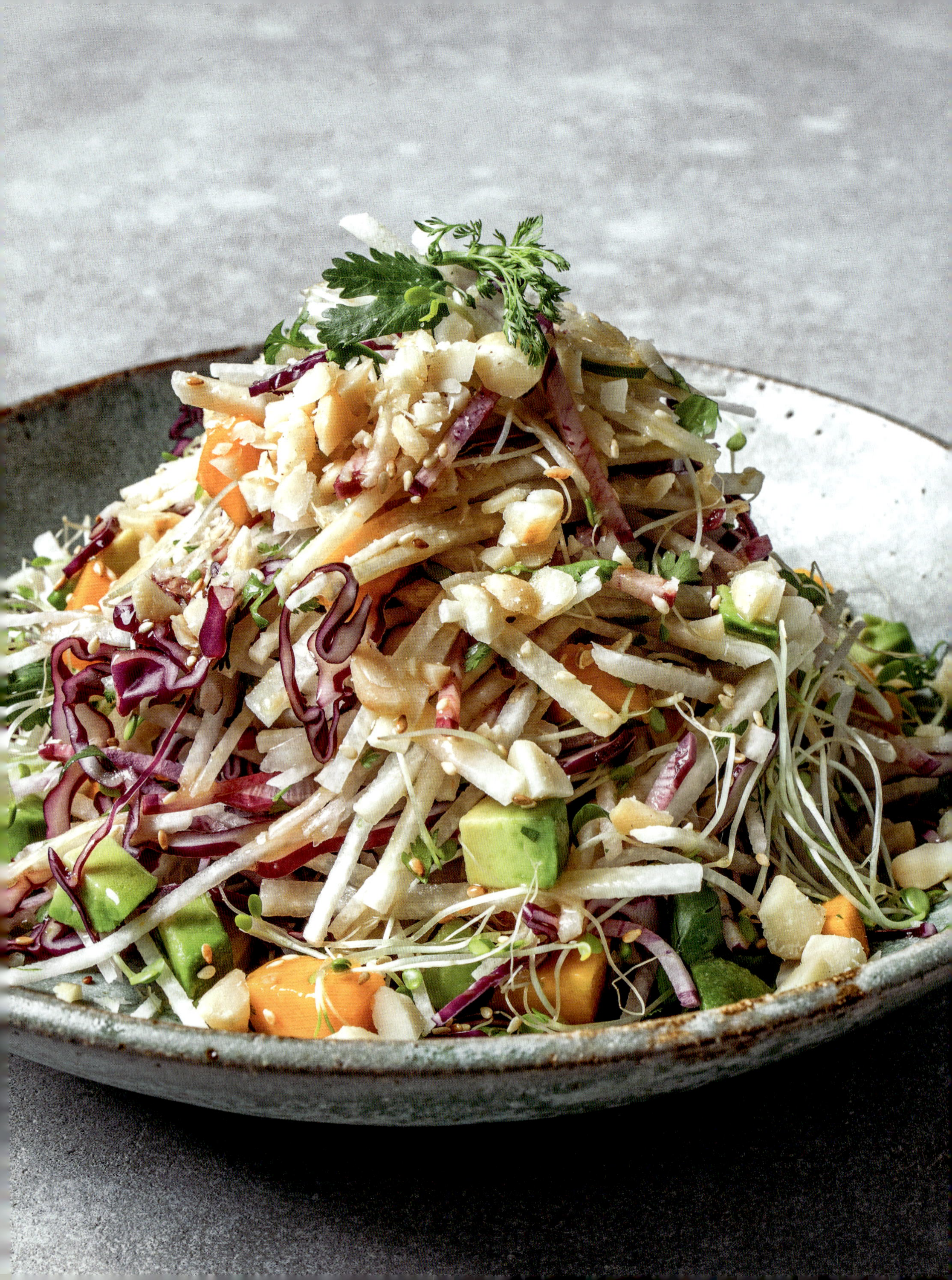

JICAMA WITH AVOCADO, MACADAMIA NUTS, AND SESAME-LIME VINAIGRETTE

Jicama is wildly underrated. Juicy, crunchy, and slightly sweet, it's super refreshing especially when chilled. I like to snack on it raw or serve with dips like Chili Crisp Labneh (page 32), Miso Baba Ghanoush (page 24), or Cumin-Shiso Tzatziki (page 128). But perhaps my favorite way to enjoy it is in this slaw-like salad with sweet ripe mango, creamy avocado, and crushed macadamia nuts for textural variety and tropical vibes. A great pairing for rich meat, the salad is just the thing to serve with Turmeric-Lemongrass Pork Belly Roast (page 217).

SWITCH IT UP

Trade out the macadamias for candied walnuts or Fried Shallots (page 254), jicama for daikon radish or green papaya, and mango for orange segments.

SERVES 4

- 2 cups matchsticks (2 by ⅛-inch) peeled jicama
- 1 cup cubed (about ½-inch) ripe mango
- 1 cup thinly shaved red cabbage
- ½ cup purple or red radish matchsticks
- Handful of sprouts, such as alfalfa, clover, or sunflower
- Handful of mint leaves, plus more for garnish
- Handful of cilantro (leaves and stems), plus more for garnish
- 1 ripe large Hass avocado, cut into ½-inch pieces
- ¾ cup Sesame-Lime Vinaigrette (page 250), whisked well, or more as needed
- ½ teaspoon Diamond Crystal kosher salt
- Finely ground black pepper
- ½ cup salted roasted macadamia nuts, chopped

In a large mixing bowl, combine the jicama, mango, cabbage, radishes, and sprouts and refrigerate for at least 10 minutes or up to 1 hour to chill.

Finely chop the herbs and add to the bowl along with the avocado, dressing, salt, and a few turns of black pepper and use your hands to toss gently but well.

Plate the salad in a pretty mound, then top with the nuts and additional herbs and serve immediately.

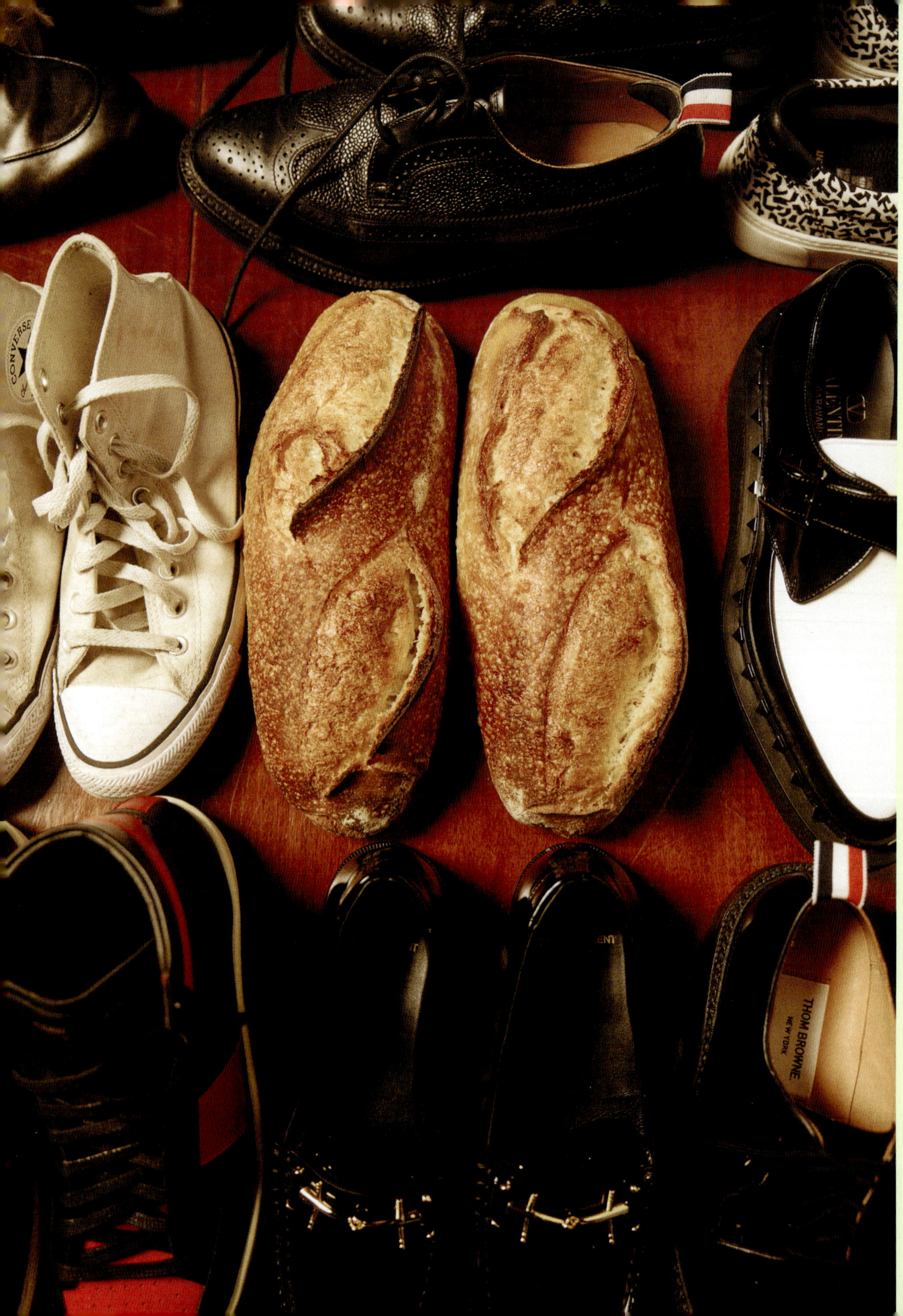
CONVERSE
THOM BROWNE.
NEW YORK

3
BREADS & SANDWICHES

KING'S FOCACCIA

I'm pumped to show you how to make my focaccia at home, transforming a handful of ingredients into this pillowy bread with a crisp exterior. Believe me, I know breadmaking can seem intimidating—I used to avoid attempting recipes that involved yeast. So here I provide detailed instructions—the length of the recipe does not reflect its difficulty—to ensure it works for everyone. Providing gram measurements here, and for all of my baking recipes, adds another layer of insurance against the quirks of baking. Caramelized onions laced with malty Chinese black vinegar are just one of endless delicious options for topping.

SWITCH IT UP

Try toppings like Slow-Roasted Cherry Tomatoes (page 245), Cipollini Onions Agrodolce (page 249), or sliced Shoyu Butter Mushrooms (page 138) along with sliced scallions and grated pecorino.

MAKES ONE 9 BY 13-INCH FOCACCIA

DOUGH

1¼ cups / 300g lukewarm water (70° to 90°F)

1 teaspoon / 3g active dry yeast

1 teaspoon honey

Extra-virgin olive oil, plus more for drizzling

2¾ cups / 425g bread flour

2½ teaspoons / 7g Diamond Crystal kosher salt

2 tablespoons / 30g cold water

TOPPINGS

Diamond Crystal kosher salt

1 cup Black Vinegar–Caramelized Onions (page 248)

2 tablespoons toasted white sesame seeds

1 tablespoon black sesame seeds

Extra-virgin olive oil, for drizzling

Flaky sea salt, for garnish

Make the dough: In a medium mixing bowl, whisk together the water, yeast, and honey until the honey dissolves. Let it sit for 10 minutes to activate the yeast. Stir in 2 tablespoons of olive oil.

Put the flour in a large mixing bowl and add the yeast mixture. Stir with a spoon until it comes together, then start mixing and kneading with wet hands to make a sticky, shaggy dough with no visible pockets of flour, about 1 minute. Cover with a kitchen towel and let sit at room temperature for 30 minutes to allow the flour to fully hydrate.

Sprinkle on the salt and cold water and use wet hands to squeeze the dough to incorporate the salt and water, about 1 minute. Cover with a kitchen towel and let the dough rest at room temperature for 30 minutes to let the gluten relax.

Coil-fold the dough: Using wet hands, gently release the edges of the dough from the bowl. Slide your fingers under the middle of the dough and lift it, letting gravity pull the ends (see photo on page 83), then set it back into the bowl so that one of the ends tucks underneath. This is known as a coil fold. It helps to develop the gluten structure. Repeat, giving the bowl a quarter-turn between folds, for a total of 8 coil folds. The more you fold, the tighter the dough will feel. Cover with a kitchen towel and set aside to rest at room temperature for 30 minutes.

Use wet hands to do another set of 8 coil folds, then cover and set aside for 30 minutes.

Finally, do 4 more coil folds. Lightly drizzle the dough with oil and rub to coat the top. Cover with plastic wrap and refrigerate in the bowl for 12 to 16 hours (it will double in size). This is called cold fermentation. It allows the dough to rise slowly while developing flavor and gluten structure, so it's especially chewy and crispy after baking.

Stretch the dough: Pour ¼ cup of olive oil into a 9 by 13 by 2-inch metal baking pan (preferably nonstick) or an 8- to 10-inch cast-iron skillet, rubbing

To coil-fold   *To stretch*

to coat the corners and sides as well as the bottom. Tip the dough into the baking pan. With two hands, lift the dough from the ends, allowing gravity to stretch it. Repeat three times, rotating the pan a quarter turn between lifts. Be tender to avoid deflating the dough. The dough should be roughly the shape of the baking pan and reach ½ inch or so from the edges.

Cover and leave in a place in your kitchen where it's slightly warmer than room temperature until doubled in size, 2 to 3 hours.

Top and bake the focaccia: Position a rack in the center of the oven and preheat the oven to 475°F. Sprinkle the dough lightly with kosher salt. Scatter on the onions in a single layer, then sprinkle on both sesame seeds. Add a heavy drizzle of olive oil. Finally, dimple the dough: Wet your hands, gently sink your fingertips into the dough, then lift them out (see page 84). Repeat in four or five places. This creates big bubbles on the surface. Don't be too rough or pop the bubbles—they give the focaccia its distinctive look.

Bake until the edges are crispy and the top is evenly golden brown, about 25 minutes, rotating the pan halfway through.

Lightly drizzle with olive oil and lightly sprinkle with flaky salt. Carefully transfer the focaccia from the pan to a rack to cool for at least 15 minutes before cutting and eating. (Keep leftovers in an airtight container for up to a day. Reheat in a hot oven.)

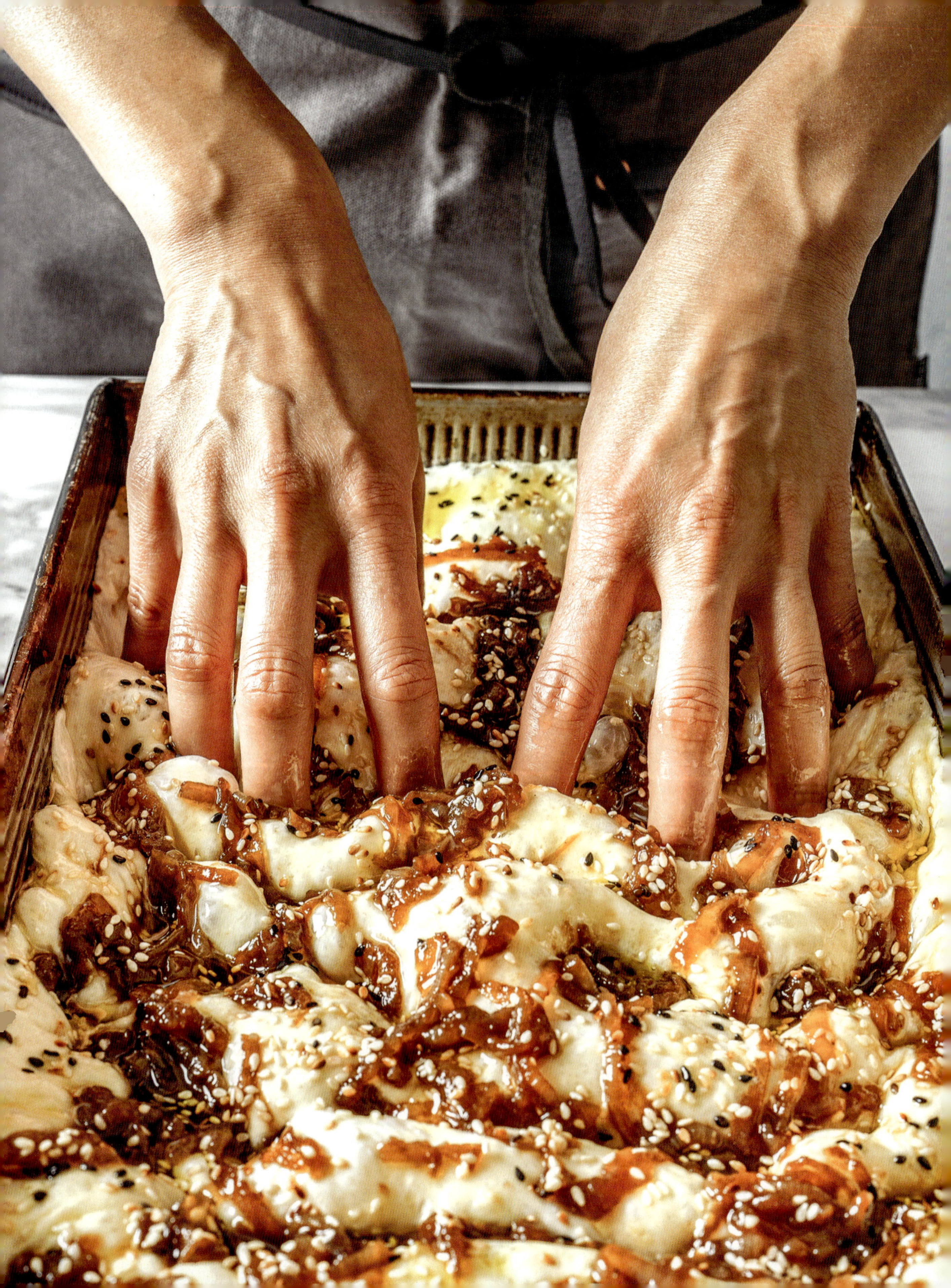

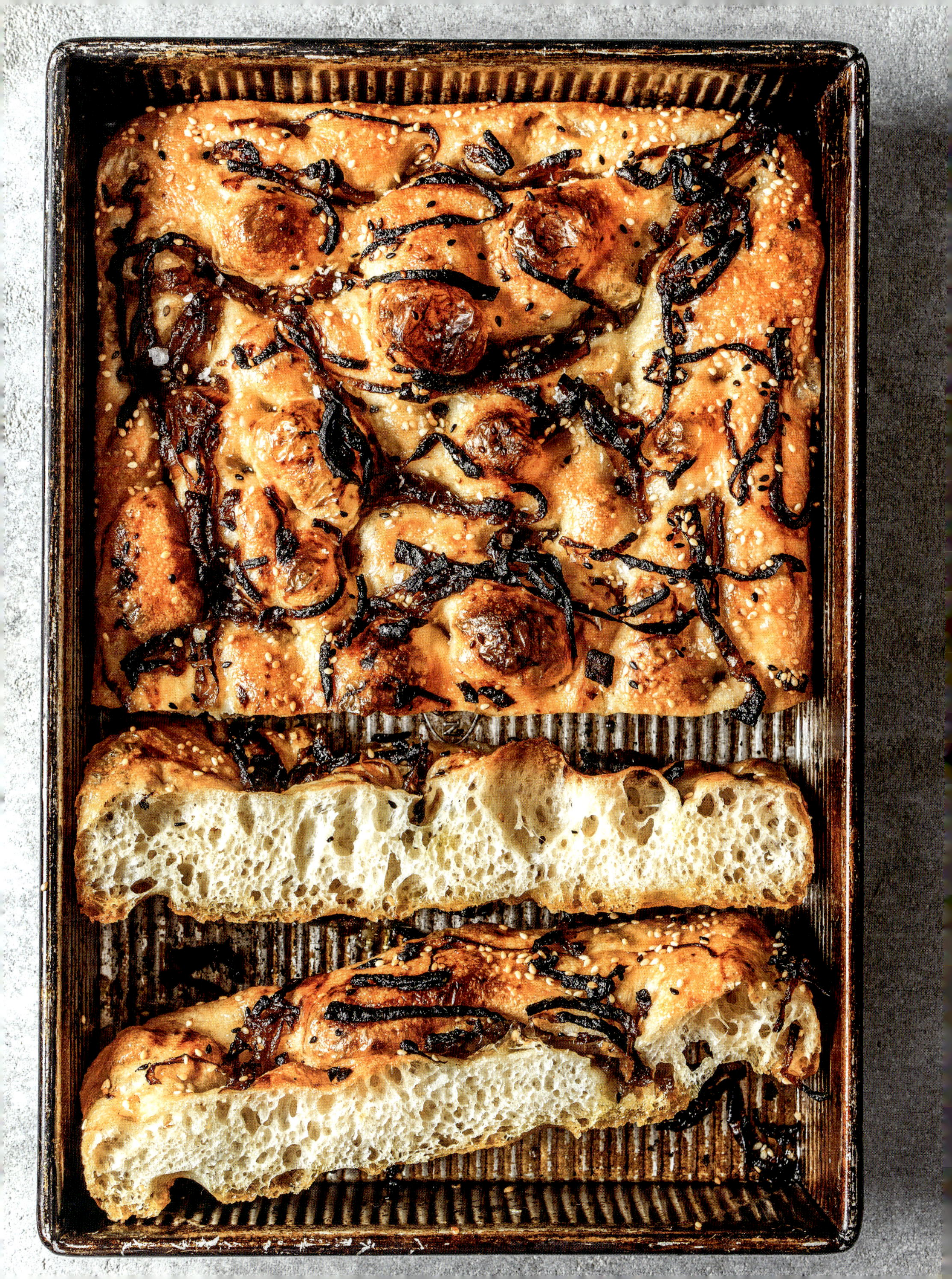

MILK BUNS

I love watching friends fight over these pillowy, buttery buns, pulled hot from the oven. They remind me of the ones my mom brought home each week from the Chinese bakery. The tangzhong, or water roux, is the secret to the fluffy, moist interior, and it's easy to execute, as is the rest of the mixing and proofing. So easy in fact that not only will you impress friends at your next dinner party, you'll also impress yourself.

LEVEL IT UP

Serve with soft butter sprinkled with flaky salt or any of the flavored butters on page 252.

MAKES 16 BUNS

Equipment: **Stand mixer**

TANGZHONG

4 tablespoons / 60g whole milk

2 tablespoons / 20g bread flour

2 tablespoons / 27g water

DOUGH

¼ cup / 54g lukewarm water (70° to 90°F)

1 tablespoon / 9g active dry yeast

¼ cup / 56g white sugar, plus a pinch

½ cup / 120g whole milk, at room temperature

1 large egg, at room temperature

2½ cups / 320g bread flour, plus more for dusting

¾ teaspoon / 3g Diamond Crystal kosher salt

3 tablespoons / 42g unsalted butter, at room temperature, plus more for greasing

Egg wash: 1 egg lightly beaten with 2 tablespoons milk

GARLIC BUTTER

2 large garlic cloves, finely chopped

4 tablespoons / 56g salted butter

Flaky sea salt, for sprinkling

Make the tangzhong: In a very small saucepan, stir together the tangzhong ingredients until fully incorporated. Set over medium heat, and cook, whisking constantly, until it thickens to a stiff paste, 2 to 3 minutes. Remove from the heat and let cool completely.

Make the dough: In a small bowl, whisk together the water, yeast, and the pinch of sugar. Let it sit for 10 minutes to activate the yeast. In another small mixing bowl, whisk together the milk and egg.

In a stand mixer fitted with the dough hook, combine the bread flour, the remaining ¼ cup sugar, and the salt. With the mixer on low speed, slowly add the milk/egg mixture to the flour mixture, then add the yeast mixture, and then the tangzhong. Increase the speed to medium-low and mix, scraping the sides occasionally, for 12 minutes.

Add the butter one-quarter at a time, waiting until each addition is incorporated before adding the next and occasionally scraping down the sides. Increase to medium and continue mixing until the butter is completely incorporated, 2 to 3 minutes.

Lightly grease a large mixing bowl with butter. Roll the dough on a work surface to shape it into a tight ball. Transfer to the bowl, cover the bowl with a damp kitchen towel, and let rise at room temperature until doubled in size, 1 to 2 hours.

Punch down the dough, then turn it onto a lightly floured work surface. Dust the dough very lightly with flour.

Lightly grease a 9 by 9-inch baking dish with butter. Cut the dough into 16 equal portions (about 48g each). Use a cupped hand to roll the pieces one by one on the work surface into smooth, tight balls. Transfer them seam-side down to the baking dish in rows of four with a little space between each one.

CONTINUED

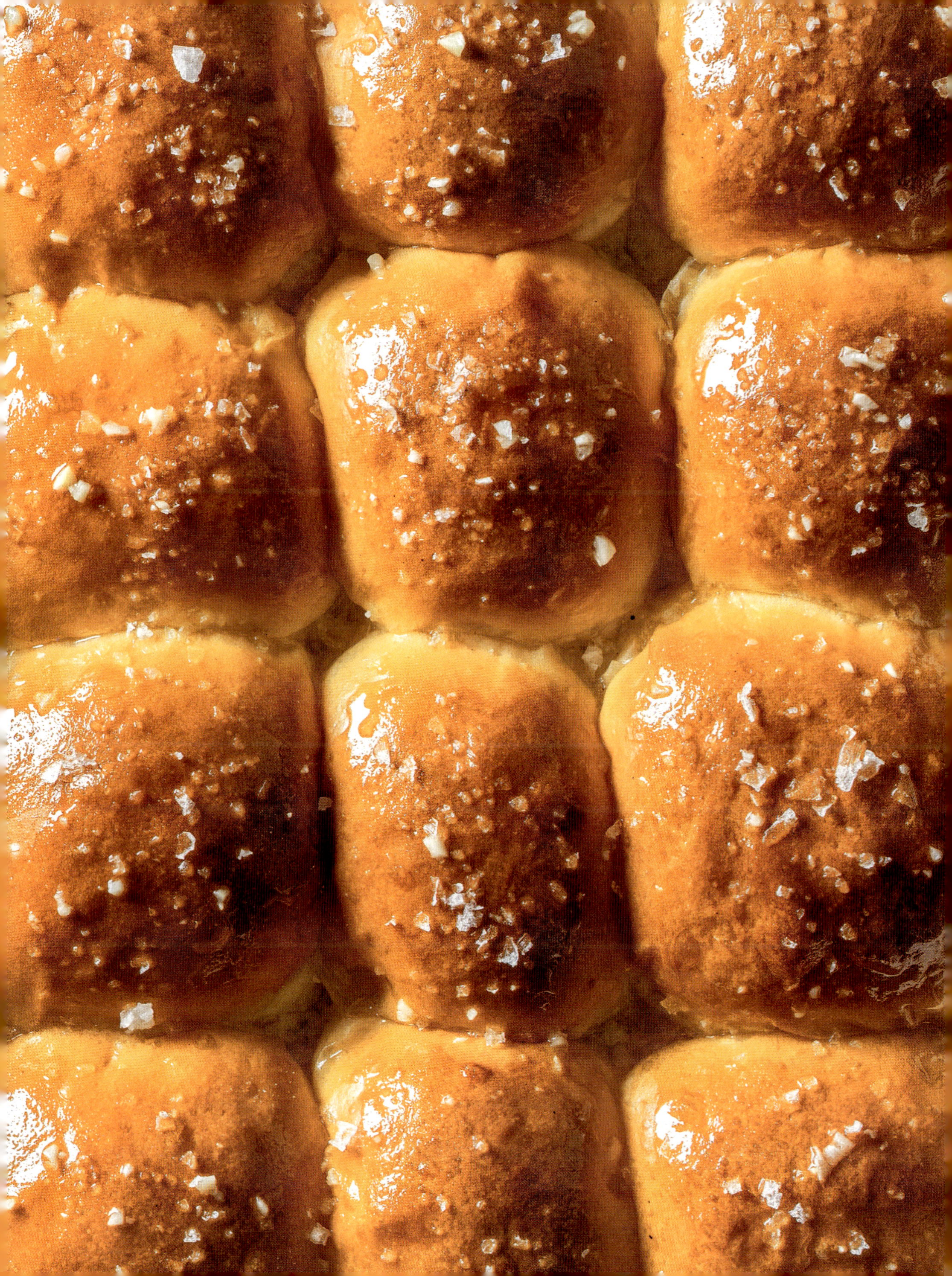

MILK BUNS
CONTINUED

Cover with a damp kitchen towel and let rise again at room temperature until the dough balls are touching, about 1 hour.

Position a rack in the center of the oven and preheat the oven to 350°F.

Gently brush the tops of the buns with the egg wash. Transfer the baking dish to the oven and bake until the tops are deep brown, about 20 minutes, rotating the dish halfway through.

Meanwhile, make the garlic butter: In a small saucepan, combine the garlic and butter and melt over medium heat. Let the butter bubble just until the garlic is fragrant, 30 seconds to 1 minute. Remove from the heat.

When the buns are ready, remove from the oven. Immediately brush generously with the garlic butter, and sprinkle on a generous pinch of flaky salt. Serve warm.

SHEET PAN PIZZA WITH STRACCIATELLA, PEPPERONI, AND KING'S HOT HONEY

When I was a line cook tasked with cooking staff meal to satisfy a big hungry crew, I'd often make this airy, crispy sheet pan pizza. Now I make it for family dinners, often recruiting my eight-year-old twin nieces to help with stretching and topping duties. The dough is little more than flour and water. The magic of time does most of the work for you.

I lay on the cheese first, Detroit-style, then spoon on the sauce and top with plenty of pepperoni. I especially love using pepperoni with natural casing and cut just under ¼ inch thick, so it curls in the oven to form little cups. After baking to a golden delight, I add blobs of creamy stracciatella or burrata. Hot honey, homemade if you please, adds a sweet and spicy kick.

MAKES ONE 18 BY 13-INCH PIZZA

Equipment: Stand mixer

DOUGH

1½ cups / 347g lukewarm water (70° to 90°F)

2 teaspoons / 7g active dry yeast

1½ teaspoons / 10g honey

2 tablespoons / 25g plus ½ cup / 100g extra-virgin olive oil, plus more for greasing and drizzling

4 cups / 600g bread flour

1 tablespoon / 10g Diamond Crystal kosher salt

TOPPINGS

One 28-ounce can crushed tomatoes

Handful of basil leaves

Pinch of red chile flakes

Diamond Crystal kosher salt and finely ground black pepper

One 8-ounce package sliced low-moisture mozzarella cheese

4 ounces sliced pepperoni

2 tablespoons thinly sliced Pickled Chiles (optional; page 245)

8 ounces stracciatella or burrata (I like the Di Stefano brand)

Extra-virgin olive oil, for drizzling

Flaky sea salt

King's Hot Honey (page 251), for drizzling

Make the dough: In the bowl of a stand mixer, combine the water, yeast, and honey and whisk until the honey dissolves. Set aside for 10 minutes to activate the yeast.

Attach the dough hook to the stand mixer. Add the 2 tablespoons olive oil, the bread flour, and salt and mix on low speed until a shaggy dough forms, about 1 minute. Increase the speed to medium to knead for 6 minutes, stopping to scrape the bottom after 1 minute. First the dough will wrap around the hook, then it will slap against the bowl, and after 6 minutes the dough will be smooth and taut.

Transfer the dough to a large, lightly oiled bowl, then lightly oil the top of the dough. Cover and refrigerate in the bowl for at least 18 hours or up to 24 hours (it will double in size). This is called cold fermentation. It allows the dough to rise slowly while developing flavor and gluten structure, so it's especially chewy and crispy after baking.

After the cold fermentation, pour the ½ cup olive oil into an 18 by 13-inch sheet pan, rubbing to coat the corners and sides as well as the bottom. Transfer the dough to the sheet pan by turning over the bowl and letting gravity do its thing. Lightly oil the top of the dough and let rest at room temperature for 15 minutes.

Use your fingertips to gently stretch the edges toward the sides of the sheet pan, popping any large bubbles in the dough during the process. Next, use two hands to lift the far edge of the dough and let gravity do the stretching, giving the baking sheet a quarter-turn between lifts, and continue until the dough is roughly the shape of the sheet pan. Don't worry, the dough will not reach the edges of the sheet pan just yet.

CONTINUED

SHEET PAN PIZZA WITH STRACCIATELLA, PEPPERONI, AND KING'S HOT HONEY
CONTINUED

As you stretch, you'll notice the dough will become more resistant to your efforts. When this happens, let the dough relax, covered, for 20 minutes and then resume stretching. Repeat the process (stretching and resting) until the dough reaches the edges of the sheet pan. Before baking, cover and rest for another 20 minutes.

Meanwhile, prepare the sauce: In a blender or food processor, combine the tomatoes, basil, chile flakes, ½ teaspoon kosher salt, and a few turns of pepper and pulse to a chunky puree. Pour into a medium saucepan and bring to a simmer over medium-high heat. Turn the heat down to cook at a gentle simmer, stirring occasionally, until reduced by about half, about 20 minutes. Set aside to cool slightly.

Top and bake: Position a rack in the bottom slot and preheat the oven to 500°F.

Lightly sprinkle the dough with kosher salt. Cover the dough, edge to edge, with a single layer of the mozzarella cheese. Add the sauce in three lengthwise stripes with a little space around each one. Scatter on the pepperoni and pickled chiles (if using).

Bake on the bottom rack until the cheese is melted and bubbling and the bottom of the crust is golden brown and crispy (use a spatula to peek underneath), 20 to 25 minutes, rotating the pan halfway through.

Remove from the oven. Top with dollops of the stracciatella, then drizzle a little olive oil and sprinkle flaky salt over the stracciatella. Cut the pizza into squares, drizzle generously with hot honey, and serve.

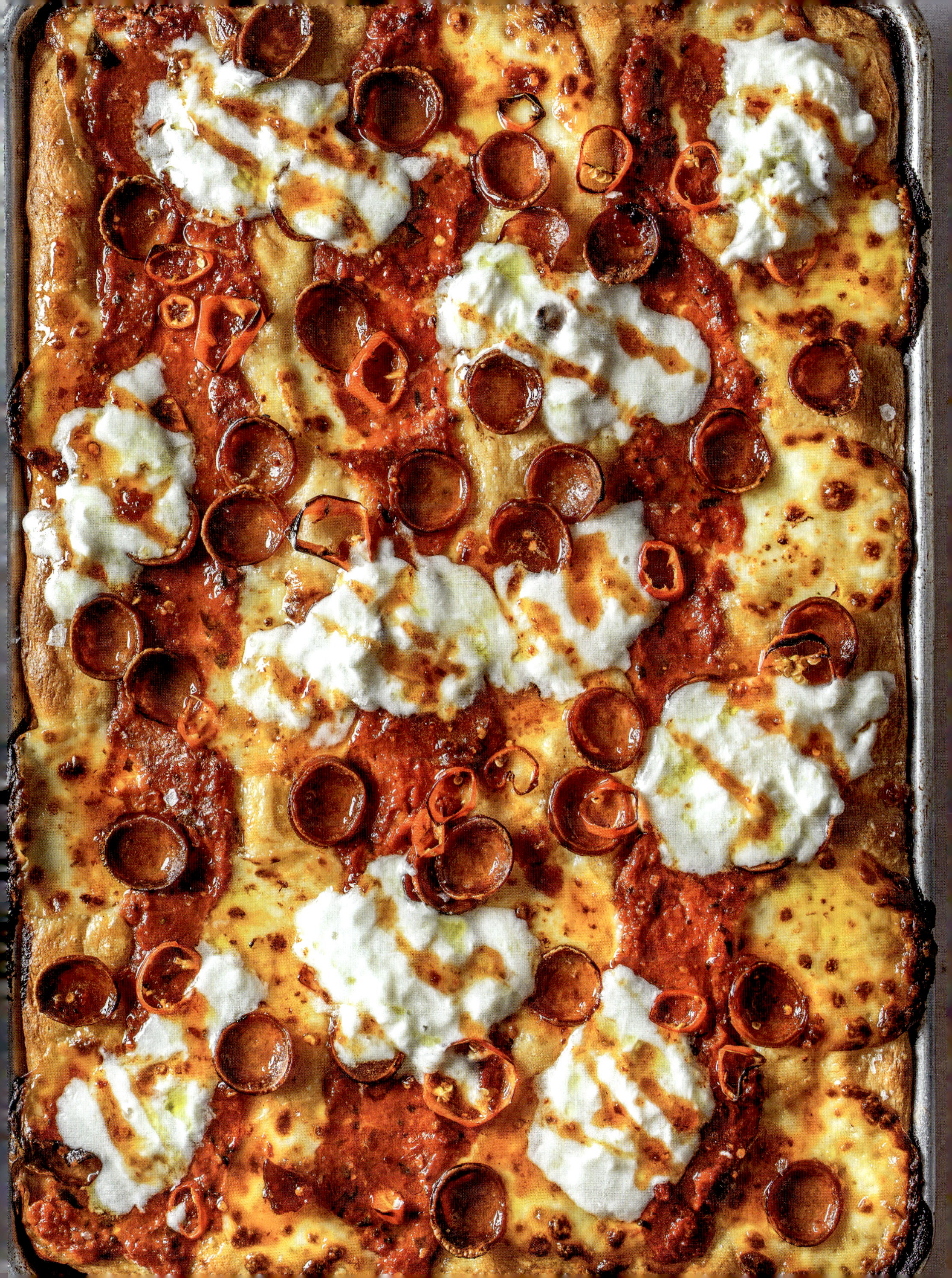

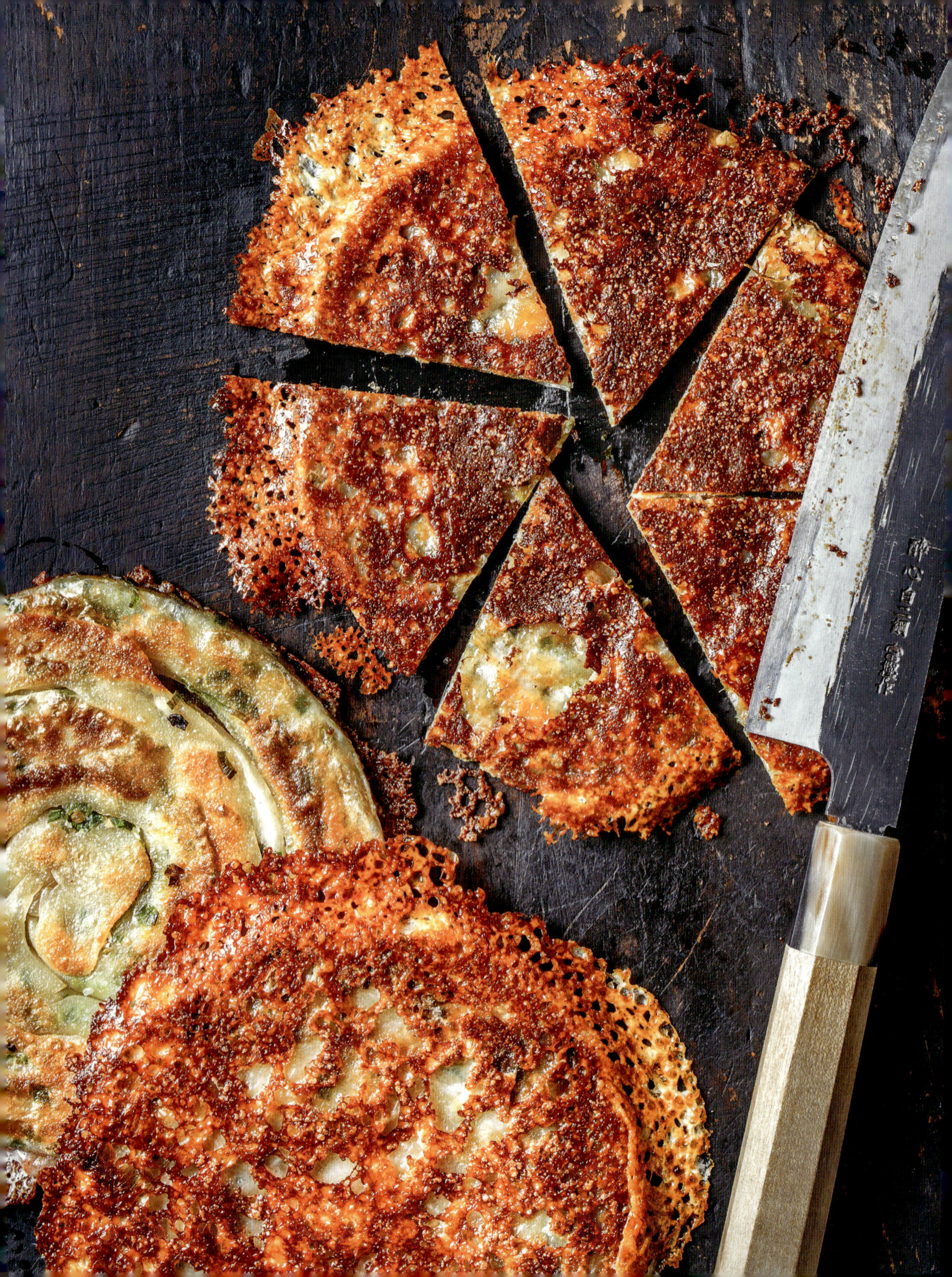

CHEESY SCALLION PANCAKES

Yang Yang, my grandmother on the Shanghainese side of my family, made awesome cong yow bang or "scallion pancakes." Essentially griddled flatbreads, they were crispy on the outside, flaky inside, and heavy on the scallion, just like I like it.

Eat them plain, serve them with Chili Crisp Labneh (page 32), or make a wrap with slices of chilled beef shank (see page 71), hoisin, cucumber, scallions, and cilantro. In this recipe, I griddle the cooked pancakes on a layer of shredded cheese until caramelized and crispy, like the cheese that sneaks out of the tortillas in quesabirria.

MAKES 8 SCALLION PANCAKES

Equipment: Sixteen 7- to 8-inch square pieces of parchment paper

DOUGH

2¼ cups / 316g all-purpose flour

½ teaspoon / 2g Diamond Crystal kosher salt

1 cup / 227g boiling water

1 tablespoon canola oil

ASSEMBLY

3⅔ cups thinly sliced scallions (4 bunches)

1½ teaspoons Diamond Crystal kosher salt, plus more for cooking

1 cup canola oil, plus more for rolling and cooking the pancakes

½ cup all-purpose flour

4 cups shredded Oaxaca cheese or low-moisture mozzarella (12 ounces)

Make the dough: In a large bowl, mix together the flour and salt. Carefully add the boiling water and mix with a rubber spatula until mostly incorporated. Set aside until cool enough to handle, about 5 minutes. Add the canola oil and mix with your hands, occasionally squeezing with your fingers to help the moisture absorb, until a shaggy dough forms, about 30 seconds.

Turn the dough onto a work surface and knead for about 3 minutes to ensure there are no dry patches and form the dough into a rough ball. Cover with a clean kitchen towel and set aside to rest at room temperature while you make the filling.

To assemble: While the dough rests, in a heatproof medium bowl, combine the scallions and salt. Make sure there's an inch or so between the scallion mixture and the rim of the bowl, because the hot oil added later will bubble up dramatically. Stir well and set aside.

In a small saucepan, heat the 1 cup oil over medium-high heat until it just starts to smoke, about 4 minutes. Pour it evenly and quickly over the scallion mixture and immediately stir well. Add the flour and stir well. (It will look clumpy and that's okay.) Set it aside to cool completely.

Form the dough into a log roughly 12 inches long, then cut into 8 equal portions. Cover the pieces with a clean kitchen towel. Lightly grease a clean work surface with canola oil. Work on one portion at a time throughout rolling, coiling, and transferring to the parchment paper before moving on to the next portion. Use a lightly greased rolling pin to roll out the dough into a very thin rectangle about 11 by 7 inches. (It doesn't have to be perfect.) Stir the scallion mixture, then spoon on about ¼ cup and spread to an even layer.

Starting with one of the long sides, roll the rough rectangle into a long, thin log. Next, coil the log to make a spiral shape (like a snail's shell). Tuck the open end underneath, then using your palm, gently press to flatten slightly. Transfer to a square of parchment paper, top with another square, and let rest while you repeat with the remaining dough and

CONTINUED

CHEESY SCALLION PANCAKES
CONTINUED

scallion mixture. Once you've made the final spiral, let it rest at least 5 minutes before proceeding to the next step.

Use a rolling pin to gently roll each spiral (still between the parchment paper) into a 6- to 7-inch round about ¼ inch thick. Some of the stuffing will squeeze out and that's okay!

Now, they're ready to cook. (Alternatively, you can freeze the pancakes, separated by parchment paper, in a resealable bag for up to 3 months. There's no need to thaw before cooking.)

Heat a large cast-iron or nonstick skillet or griddle pan over medium heat for 1 minute. Working in batches, add 1 tablespoon of canola oil per pancake and heat until it shimmers. Lightly season the top of the pancake with kosher salt, add salt-side down to the pan, and cook until the surface is crispy and deep golden brown in spots, 3 to 4 minutes (or 4 to 5 minutes if cooking from frozen). Lightly sprinkle the top side with salt, flip the pancake, and cook the second side the same way. As they're cooked, stack the pancakes on a plate.

For each pancake, sprinkle ½ cup of cheese into the skillet to make a round slightly larger than the pancakes. Top each cheese round with a pancake and cook, undisturbed, until the cheese at the edges is deep brown and crispy, 2 to 3 minutes.

Use a spatula to transfer the pancakes to a cutting board. Cut into triangles. Serve hot and cook the remaining pancakes just before eating.

BREADS & SANDWICHES

95

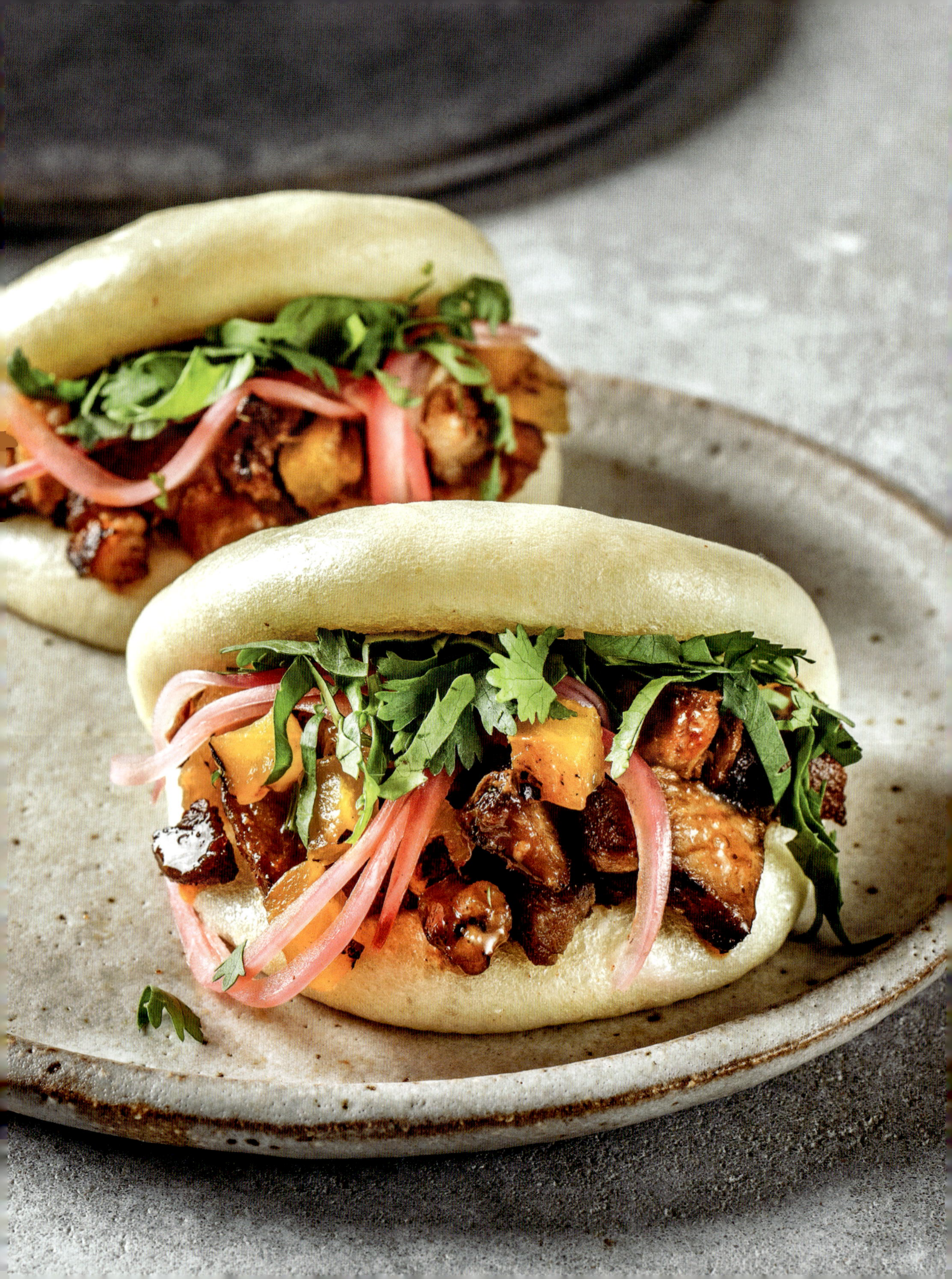

AL PASTOR BAO

Growing up on the eastside of LA, I ate a lot of street tacos, especially late at night from trucks and stands. Many feature al pastor, a hunk of pork rotating on a vertical spit and the delicious merging of Middle Eastern and Mexican flavors. Carved in charred, juicy slices, it's heaven on a corn tortilla with diced onions, cilantro, and a slice of sweet charred pineapple. But as a Chinese kid from LA, I'm tempted to capture everything al pastor has to offer inside a fluffy steamed Chinese bao.

LEVEL IT UP

Add Pineapple-Habanero Hot Sauce (page 259) and/or King's Guacamole (page 28).

MAKES 16 BUNS

AL PASTOR

6 dried guajillo chiles, stemmed, slit open, and seeded

1 dried ancho chile, stemmed, slit open, and seeded

½ cup roughly chopped white or yellow onion

¼ cup canned pineapple chunks, plus ¼ cup juice

2 tablespoons apple cider vinegar

1 tablespoon achiote paste

2 teaspoons dried oregano

1 teaspoon Diamond Crystal kosher salt

½ teaspoon ground cumin

¼ teaspoon ground black pepper

3 whole cloves

3 garlic cloves, peeled

2 canned chipotle peppers in adobo sauce, seeds removed

1 by 1-inch knob ginger, peeled and roughly chopped

One 3-pound piece boneless pork shoulder, cut against the grain into ½-inch steaks

TO FINISH

Six ½-inch-thick rings fresh pineapple

Diamond Crystal kosher salt and finely ground black pepper

16 Steamed Bao (page 254)

Big handful of chopped cilantro (leaves and stems)

¼ cup drained Pickled Red Onion or Pickled Daikon and Ginger (page 245)

Marinate the al pastor: Set a large skillet over high heat for 1 minute. Toast the guajillo and ancho chiles in the skillet, flipping occasionally, until fragrant, about 1 minute. Transfer to a medium mixing bowl, cover with hot tap water, and soak for 20 minutes to soften.

Reserving the soaking liquid, drain the chiles and transfer them to a blender. Add all the remaining al pastor ingredients except for the pork. Blend on high, adding some of the reserved soaking liquid if needed to get the blender going, until the mixture is completely smooth, 1 to 2 minutes.

Pour the marinade into a large resealable bag, add the pork, and seal the bag, pushing out as much air as you can. Massage to coat the pork in the marinade and refrigerate for at least 4 hours or up to 12 hours.

To finish: Prepare a grill, preferably charcoal, to cook with medium-high heat. (Alternatively, preheat the broiler and position an oven rack 2 to 4 inches from the heat source.)

Season the pineapple on both sides with salt. Grill (or broil), flipping once, until charred on both sides, 2 to 3 minutes. Cut into bite-size pieces.

Remove the pork from the bag (don't wipe off any of that marinade!) and season generously on both sides with salt and pepper. Grill (or broil) the pork, flipping once, until browned and charred on both sides, 5 to 6 minutes per side.

Transfer the pork to a cutting board to rest for 5 minutes. Thinly slice the pork, then give it a rough chop. If you're feeling extra, like me, caramelize and crisp the pork in a pan after chopping.

Serve with the steamed bao, cilantro, and pickled onions.

GINGER SCALLION LOBSTER ROLLS

My mom loves seafood with a shell, especially lobster. She loves it when I butter-poach it or use it to fill wontons (see page 116). She loves it wok-fried at her local San Gabriel Valley Cantonese restaurant or tucked in a buttery roll anytime we're strolling a pier in San Francisco or Santa Monica. This dish showcases the flavors of the wok-fried version—the ginger, garlic, scallion, and soy sauce—and of the buttery American classic. The best of both worlds in each bite.

LEVEL IT UP

Top with Fried Shallots (page 254) for a sweet crunch or trout roe to be fancy.

SWITCH IT UP

Skip the buns and spoon the lobster over Garlic Soy Sauce Noodles (page 109).

SERVES 4

Two 1¼- to 1½-pound live Maine lobsters (or 1 pound frozen cooked lobster meat, thawed)

2 tablespoons canola oil

5 medium garlic cloves, minced

2 tablespoons minced ginger

1 bunch scallions, thinly sliced

1 tablespoon Shaoxing wine

1 teaspoon Chinese light soy sauce

½ teaspoon white sugar

1 stick (4 ounces) unsalted butter, cut into cubes, plus 2 tablespoons room-temperature for the buns

Finely ground black pepper

4 brioche hot dog buns

Flaky sea salt

Lemon wedges, for squeezing

If using live lobsters, bring a very large pot of water to a boil. Add the lobsters so they're submerged, then cover the pot and turn off the heat. Set a timer for 7 minutes. Meanwhile, prepare a very large bowl of half ice and half water. When the timer goes off, transfer the lobsters to the ice water and set aside for 15 minutes to cool. Drain well.

Use a heavy knife and kitchen shears to extract the meat from the shells, keeping the meat intact as best you can. Devein the tail and cut the meat into 1-inch dice. Reserve the shells for another purpose, such as Weekend Broth (page 244).

Heat a large wok or skillet over medium-high heat for 1 minute. Add the oil and swirl to coat the pot. When it begins to smoke, add the garlic, ginger, and scallions and cook, stirring frequently with a wok spatula, until the scallions are softened with a touch of color, about 1 minute.

Add the Shaoxing wine and stir for 10 seconds. Add the soy sauce and sugar and cook, stirring, for another 10 seconds. Add the cubes of butter and a few turns of pepper and let the butter melt and foam. Add the lobster, stir gently to coat, and cook just until the lobster is warmed through, 15 to 30 seconds. Remove from the heat and set aside while you toast the buns.

Heat a griddle or clean large skillet over medium-high heat for 1 minute. Spread the softened butter on the sides of the buns and cook, flipping once, until both sides are golden brown and toasty, about 45 seconds per side. Transfer to plates.

Give the lobster a final toss in the butter, then spoon the lobster into the buns. Drizzle on a little of the butter remaining in the wok, sprinkle with flaky salt, and serve with lemon wedges on the side.

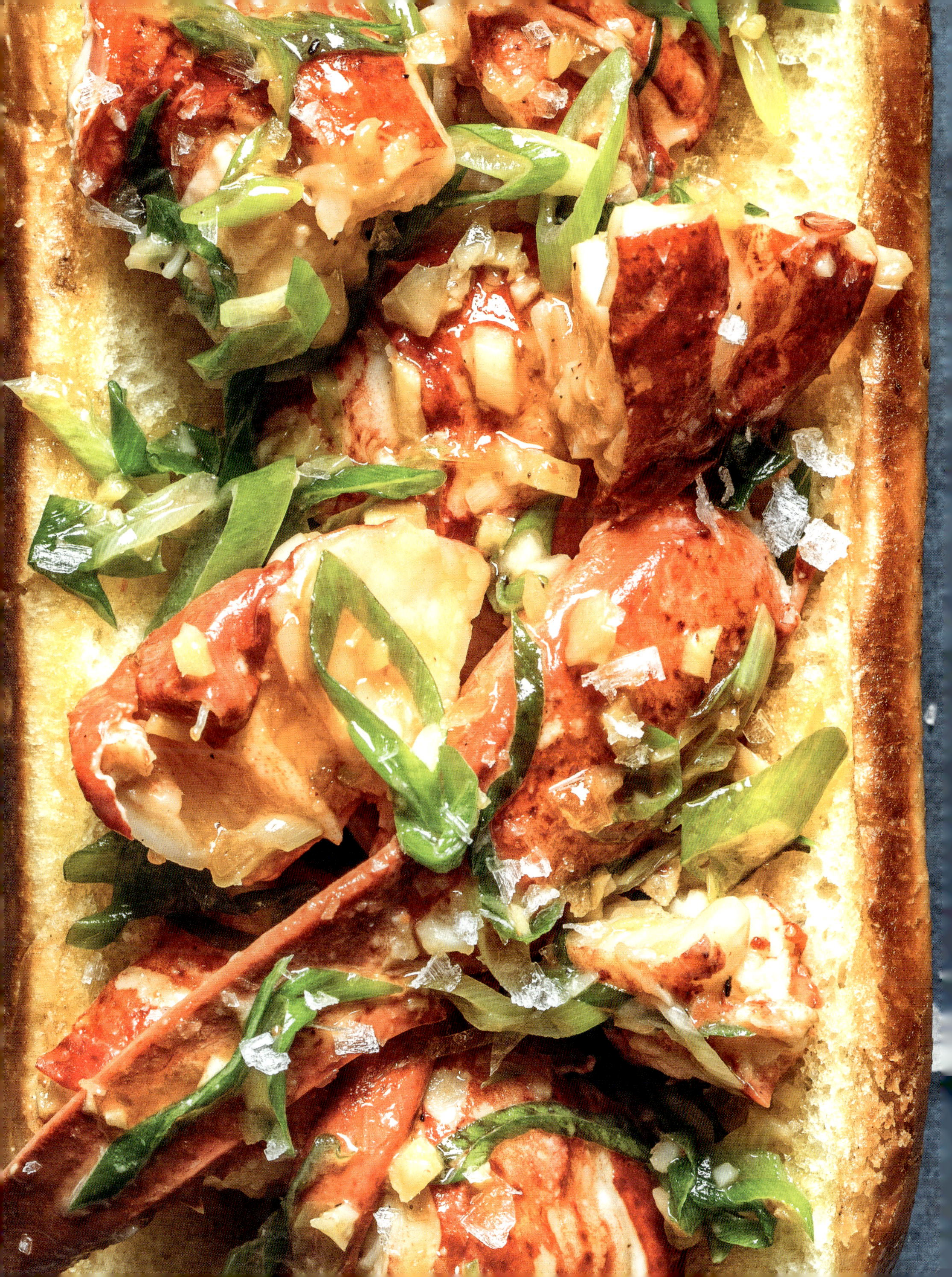

SHANGHAINESE PORK BELLY CUBANOS

My family eats hong sew yuk, a home-style Shanghainese dish of sweet, tender pork belly simmered with soy sauce and star anise, over steamed rice. But it's also pretty awesome tucked between bread in this toasty Cubano that borrows fresh herbs and daikon pickles from Vietnamese banh mi.

SWITCH IT UP

Tuck the belly in Steamed Bao (page 254) with preserved mustard greens, pickled daikon, and cilantro.

MAKES 2 SANDWICHES, PLUS EXTRA PORK BELLY

HONG SEW YUK

One 2-pound piece skin-on pork belly, cut lengthwise into 3-inch-wide slabs

1 tablespoon canola oil

6 medium garlic cloves, lightly smashed and peeled

3 large shallots, thinly sliced

Two 3 by 1-inch knobs ginger, peeled and lightly smashed

3 whole star anise

1 cinnamon stick

2 teaspoons Chinese five spice powder

½ teaspoon ground white pepper

1 cup Chinese rock sugar or light brown sugar

¼ cup Chinese dark soy sauce

½ cup Chinese light soy sauce

1 cup Shaoxing wine

2 cups water

CUBANOS

¼ cup mayonnaise

2 teaspoons toasted sesame oil

Small squeeze of lemon juice

Pinch of Diamond Crystal kosher salt

Two 6-inch sections Cuban bread or soft Italian bread, halved horizontally

⅓ cup Black Vinegar–Caramelized Onions (page 248)

Flaky sea salt

⅔ cup drained Pickled Daikon and Ginger (page 245)

Small handful of cilantro sprigs

Small handful of thinly sliced scallions

Several slices provolone cheese

2 tablespoons Chinese hot mustard

2 tablespoons (1 ounce) unsalted butter

Make the hong sew yuk: Bring a large wide pot of water to a rolling boil. Add the pork belly, boil for a few minutes, then drain and rinse under cold water. Cut the slabs crosswise into ½-inch pieces.

Clean the pot and set over high heat for 1 minute. Add the oil, then add the garlic, shallots, and ginger and cook, stirring, until fragrant, about 30 seconds. Add the pork belly and cook, stirring occasionally, until lightly colored, about 5 minutes. Add the star anise, cinnamon stick, five spice, and white pepper and stir frequently until fragrant, about 1 minute.

Stir in the rock sugar and let it melt completely, about 5 minutes. Add the dark soy sauce, light soy sauce, Shaoxing wine, and water. Bring to a strong simmer, then turn the heat down to cook at a gentle simmer, uncovered and stirring occasionally, until you can poke a chopstick through the top layer of fat with no resistance, about 1½ hours.

Remove from the heat. (To store, cool in the pot and refrigerate for up to 3 days. Gently reheat the pork in the sauce before using.)

Make the cubanos: In a small bowl, stir together the mayonnaise, sesame oil, lemon juice, and salt.

Spread a layer of the mayonnaise mixture on the bottom halves of the bread. Add the caramelized onions, a layer of pork belly, flaky salt, and pickles. Top with the cilantro and scallions and then with the provolone. Spread the mustard on the top halves of the bread and close the sandwiches.

Set a large cast-iron skillet over medium-low heat for 3 minutes. Add 1 tablespoon of the butter, let it froth, then add the sandwiches. Put a clean, heavy pan on top and press down to compress the sandwiches slightly. Cook with the pan in place until the bottoms are toasty and golden brown, about 4 minutes.

Remove the pot, lift the sandwiches, and add the remaining butter to the pan. Flip the sandwiches over into the pan, then press and cook until melty, about 4 minutes more. Slice in half on the diagonal, and serve immediately.

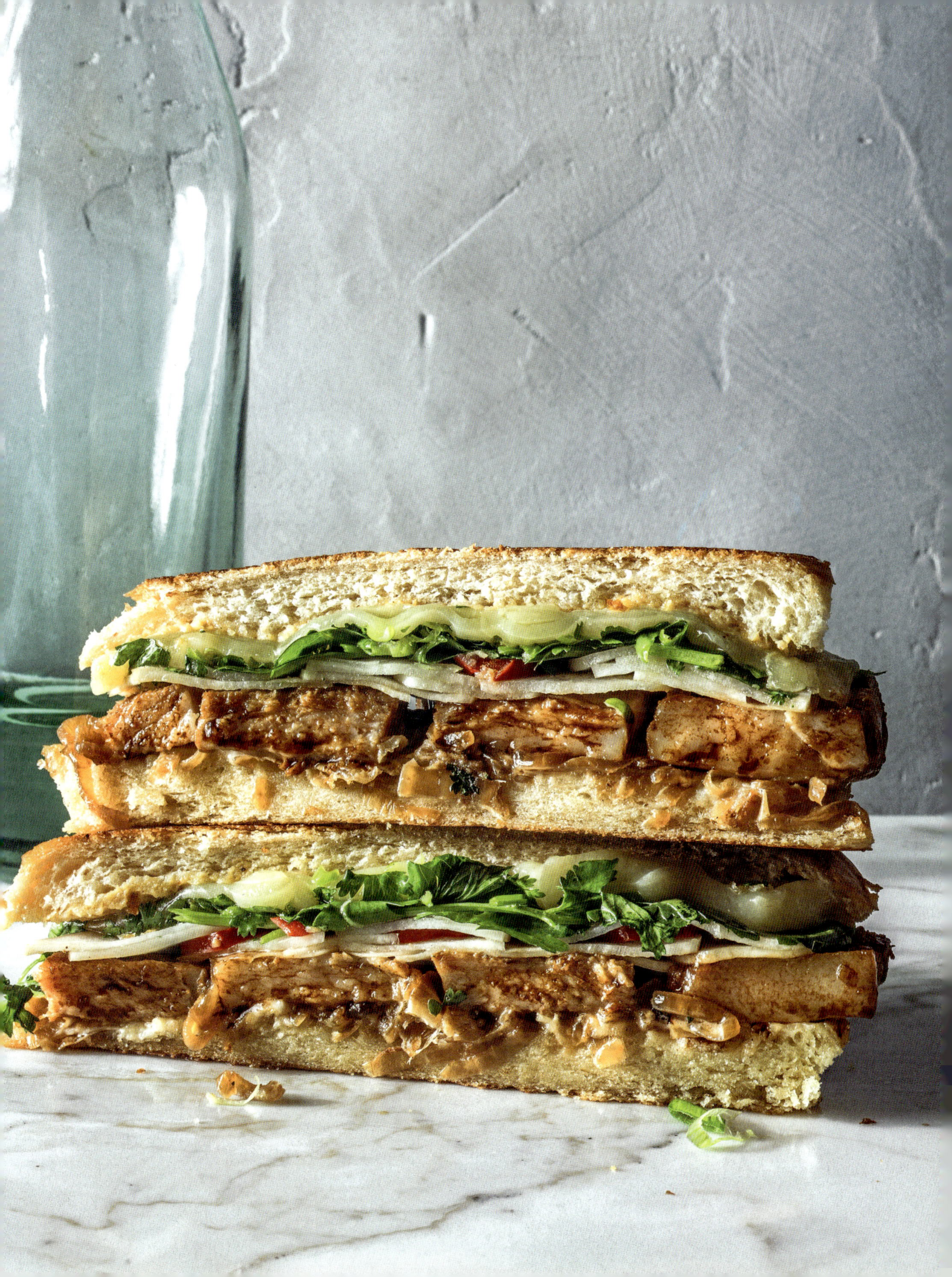

NOODLES, DUM

PLINGS & RICE

4

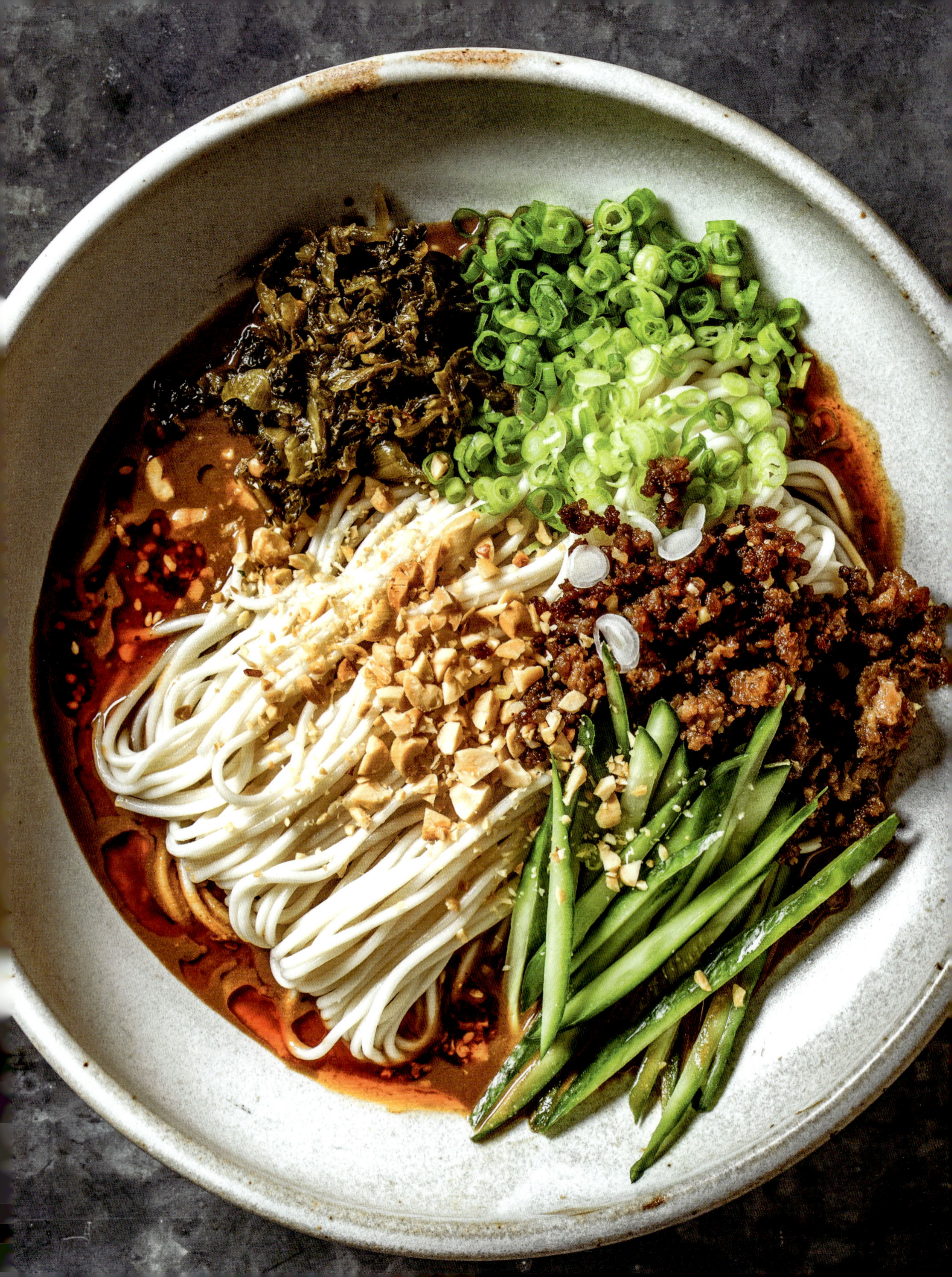

DAN DAN MEIN

SAUCE

- ⅓ cup Chinese sesame paste or any peanut butter
- ⅓ cup unsalted chicken stock
- 2 tablespoons Zhenjiang black vinegar
- 2 tablespoons Chinese light soy sauce
- 2 tablespoons honey
- 1 tablespoon plus 1 teaspoon finely chopped garlic
- 1 tablespoon toasted sesame oil
- 2 teaspoons Chinese dark soy sauce
- 1 teaspoon Diamond Crystal kosher salt
- ½ teaspoon red Sichuan peppercorns (optional), finely ground
- ¼ teaspoon Chinese five spice powder
- ¼ teaspoon ground white pepper

PORK

- 1 pound fatty ground pork (20% fat)
- 3 tablespoons Shaoxing wine
- 1 tablespoon Chinese light soy sauce
- 1 tablespoon Chinese dark soy sauce
- 1 tablespoon white sugar
- 2 teaspoons cornstarch
- ½ teaspoon Diamond Crystal kosher salt
- ¼ teaspoon Chinese five spice powder
- ¼ teaspoon ground white pepper
- 2 tablespoons canola oil
- 3 garlic cloves, finely chopped
- 2 by 1-inch knob ginger, peeled and minced

DAN DAN MEIN

- 4 tablespoons King's Chili Crisp (page 257), plus more as needed
- 1 pound fresh Chinese wheat noodles
- 1 cup julienned cucumbers, chilled
- ½ cup chopped unsalted roasted peanuts
- ½ cup shredded preserved mustard greens (see page 17)
- ½ cup thinly sliced scallions
- About 1 cup unsalted chicken stock, hot

I've eaten so many variations of dan dan mein, the famous street-style noodles from Sichuan province. Sometimes the nutty sauce is made with dark-roasted Chinese sesame paste and sometimes with peanut butter. Some are served hot, others cold. When my Shanghainese family made dan dan, it was never spicy, while the Sichuan versions I've had often have a red sheen of chili oil. I like mine spicy, saucy, and heavy on the sesame and raw garlic with crisp cucumbers, preserved greens, and crushed peanuts for texture. I serve these noodles like they do on the street, with all the components in the bowl to be mixed just before eating.

SWITCH IT UP

Fresh thin wheat noodles are my pick, but any variety works well, from wide noodles to ramen to fresh pasta. Dried noodles are fine, too.

SERVES 4

Make the sauce: In a medium mixing bowl, combine the sauce ingredients, then whisk gently until smooth. Set aside.

Prepare the pork: In a separate medium bowl, combine the ground pork, Shaoxing wine, light soy sauce, dark soy sauce, sugar, cornstarch, salt, five spice, and white pepper and mix well. Set aside for 10 minutes to allow the pork to absorb the flavors.

Heat a large wok or skillet over high heat for 1 minute. Add the canola oil, swirl to coat the pan, and let the oil shimmer. Add the ground pork mixture and cook, stirring occasionally and breaking up any clumps, until the meat is caramelized, 5 to 6 minutes. Stir in the garlic and ginger, cook for 1 minute more, and keep warm off the heat.

Assemble the dan dan mein: Bring a large pot of water to a boil. Meanwhile, give the sauce a good stir, then divide it among four bowls. Add 1 tablespoon of the chili crisp per bowl. Set aside.

When the water boils, add the noodles and cook, stirring occasionally, until just tender, according to the package instructions. Drain well. Divide the noodles among the bowls.

Among the bowls, evenly divide the pork, cucumbers, peanuts, mustard greens, and scallions. Add a splash of hot chicken stock (about ¼ cup) to each bowl, and serve. Have everyone mix very well and drizzle with more chili crisp to taste.

TAIWANESE BEEF NOODLE SOUP

BROTH

2½ pounds boneless beef shank (aka banana shank), cut crosswise into 1¼-inch slabs, patted dry

2 teaspoons Diamond Crystal kosher salt

3 tablespoons canola oil

1 medium yellow onion, quartered

8 medium garlic cloves, lightly smashed and peeled

Three 3 by 1-inch knobs ginger, peeled and smashed

2 medium shallots, halved

6 scallions (white and pale green parts)

3 whole star anise

3 whole dried Sichuan chiles

1 cinnamon stick

1 teaspoon whole cloves

1 teaspoon fennel seeds

1 teaspoon coriander seeds

½ teaspoon green or red Sichuan peppercorns

¼ teaspoon ground white pepper

2 tablespoons rock sugar or packed light brown sugar

3 tablespoons Chinese dark soy sauce

2 tablespoons Shaoxing wine

1 tablespoon Chinese light soy sauce

1 medium bunch cilantro (stems only)

4 cups low-sodium beef stock

4 cups water

BOWLS

1 pound fresh Chinese wheat noodles

8 teaspoons Zhenjiang black vinegar

Ground white pepper

1 medium bunch cilantro (leafy tops only), roughly chopped

6 scallions (dark green parts), thinly sliced

½ cup shredded preserved mustard greens (see page 17)

King's Chili Crisp (page 257) or store-bought Chinese chili crisp

My first memories of this homey, rich noodle soup came from my Shanghainese grandmother Yang Yang's pot. But it wasn't until I was sixteen and took a trip to Taiwan that I really fell in love with it. The Taiwanese version packs a deeper punch. The flavorful broth was infused with warm spices like ginger, star anise, and clove, similar to the one my grandma made, but the dish also had fiery chili oil, Sichuan peppercorns, and pickled mustard greens. I came home obsessed with trying every version in the San Gabriel Valley to unlock its secrets, and now those secrets are yours. Switch the pot for a pressure cooker and the broth takes just 30 minutes.

SERVES 4

Make the broth: Heat a large wok or heavy skillet over high heat for 1 minute. Season the beef on both sides with the salt. Add the oil, swirl to coat, and let shimmer. Sear the beef in batches until deeply browned, 3 to 4 minutes per side. Transfer the beef to a plate.

Add the onion, garlic, ginger, shallots, and scallions to the wok and cook, stirring occasionally with a wok spatula, until fragrant, about 1 minute. Add the star anise, dried chiles, cinnamon stick, cloves, fennel seeds, coriander seeds, Sichuan peppercorns, and white pepper and cook, stirring frequently, until they're fragrant, about 1 minute.

Stir in the sugar and let it melt and bubble, 1 to 2 minutes. Add the dark soy sauce, Shaoxing wine, and light soy sauce and cook, scraping the wok, for 15 seconds. Turn off the heat.

Transfer the mixture to a 5- to 7-quart pot. Add the beef, cilantro stems, stock, and water, stir well, and bring to a boil. Reduce the heat to cook at a gentle simmer, partially covered, until the meat is fork-tender but not falling apart, 1 to 1½ hours.

Make the bowls: Carefully transfer the beef shank to a clean medium pot. Strain the broth through a fine-mesh sieve into the pot, discarding the solids, and skim off the fat. Cover and keep warm over very low heat.

Bring a large pot of water to a boil. Add the noodles and cook, stirring occasionally, until just tender, according to the package instructions. Drain well.

To each of four bowls, add 2 teaspoons vinegar and a dash of white pepper. Divide the noodles and beef among the four bowls. Ladle on the hot broth, then use chopsticks to loosen the noodles. Garnish generously with chopped cilantro, sliced scallions, preserved mustard greens, and chili crisp. Serve immediately.

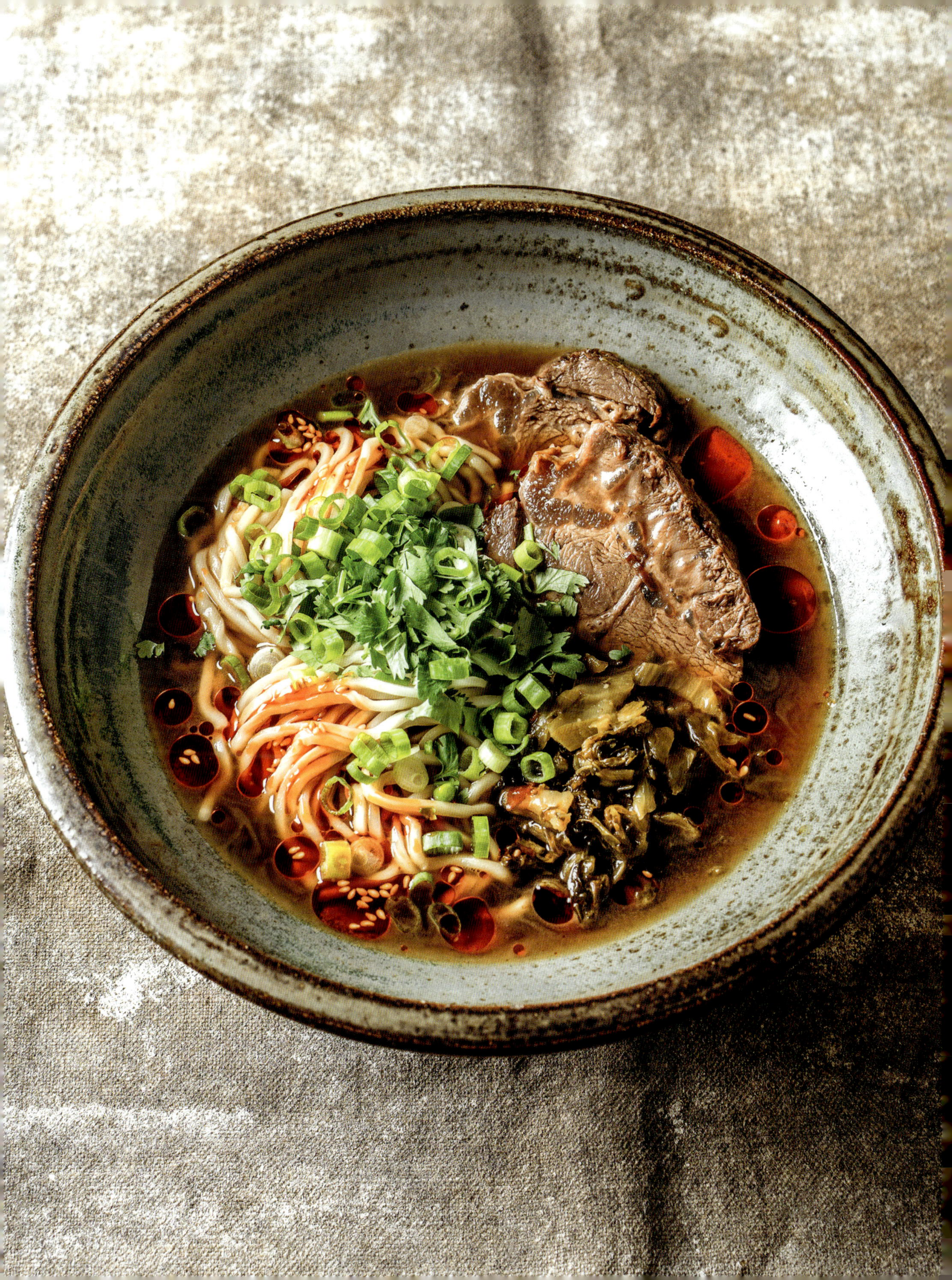

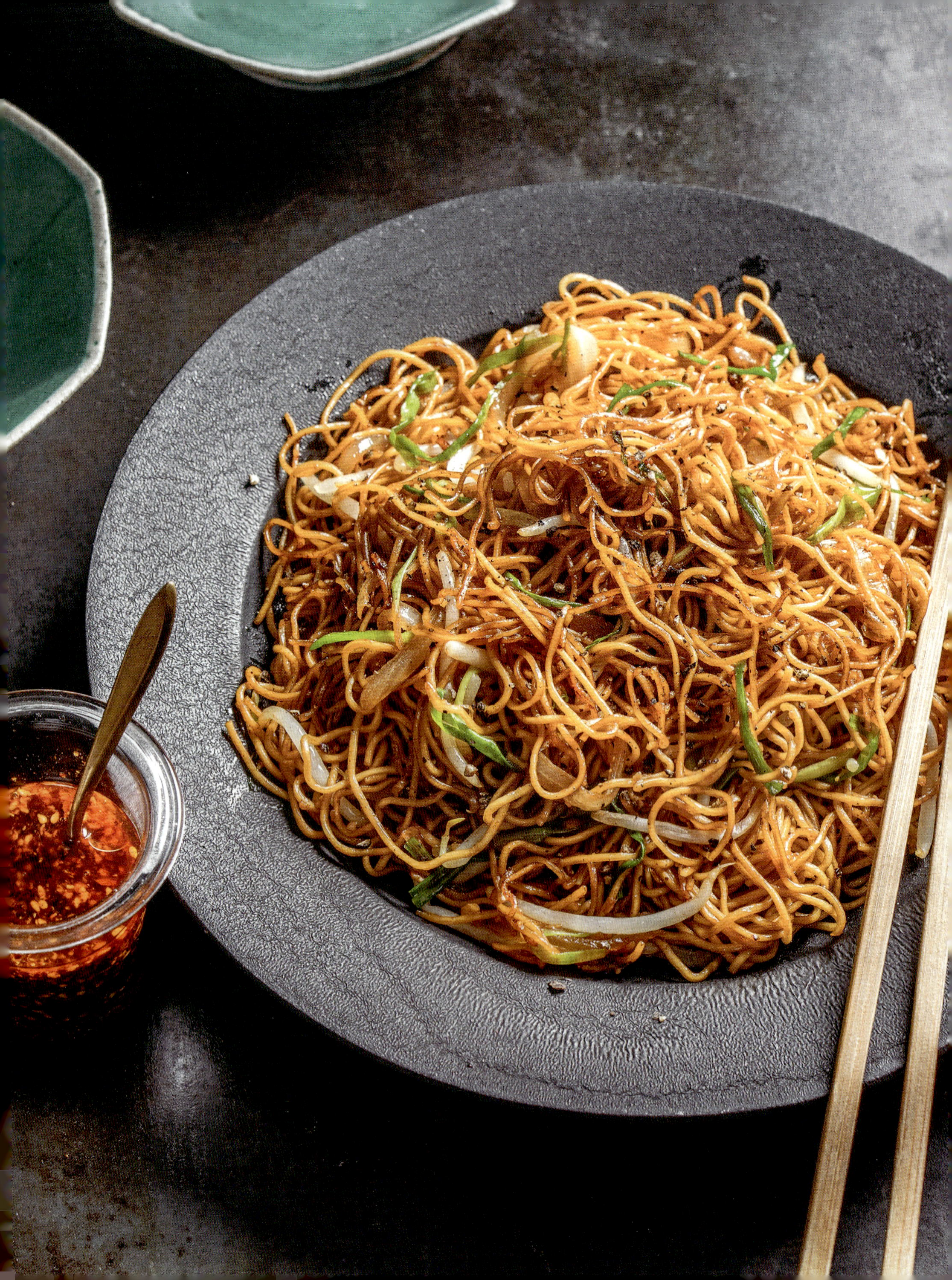

GARLIC SOY SAUCE NOODLES

I have a hard time serving Chinese-style shellfish without these noodles. They just go so well together. This particular version is a hybrid of the garlicky, buttery, Maggi-laced noodles that accompany whole Dungeness crab feasts at some of my favorite Vietnamese restaurants in San Francisco and the Cantonese street-style see yow mein my family ate at Hong Kong–style cafés in LA. It's the perfect partner for both Black Pepper–Garlic Lobster (page 168) and Sichuan Chile Butter Shrimp (page 176).

SWITCH IT UP

Virtually any fresh noodle will be delicious in this dish: thicker Shanghai noodles, Japanese ramen or udon, or even a long, thin Italian pasta. Substitute in the butter from Shoyu Butter Mushrooms (page 138) to kick up the umami, or Sichuan Chile–Bourbon Butter (page 252) for extra heat.

SERVES 4

SAUCE

2 tablespoons Chinese oyster sauce

1 tablespoon Chinese dark soy sauce

1 tablespoon Chinese light soy sauce

1 teaspoon fish sauce

1 teaspoon Maggi seasoning

1 tablespoon white sugar

1 tablespoon toasted sesame oil

¼ teaspoon coarsely ground black pepper

NOODLES

½ pound fresh thin Chinese egg noodles

2 tablespoons canola oil

½ cup thinly sliced yellow onion

2 by 1-inch knob ginger, peeled and minced

4 large garlic cloves, minced

4 tablespoons (2 ounces) unsalted butter, cut into several pieces

1 cup mung bean sprouts

2 scallions, cut into 2-inch julienne

King's Chili Crisp (page 257) or store-bought Chinese chili crisp, for serving

Make the sauce: In a small bowl, stir together the sauce ingredients.

Prepare the noodles: Bring a large pot of water to a boil. Add the noodles and cook to a springy al dente texture, 1 to 2 minutes. Drain, rinse well under cold water, then drain again. Transfer them to a clean kitchen towel and pat dry—this helps the noodles crisp when stir-fried. Set aside.

Heat a large wok or skillet over high heat for 1 minute. Add the canola oil, swirl the pan, and let it smoke lightly. Add the onion and stir-fry with a wok spatula until golden at the edges, about 1 minute. Add the ginger and garlic and cook, stirring frequently, until fragrant and lightly golden, about 20 seconds. Add the sauce and cook about 20 seconds, stirring, until slightly reduced. Add the butter and stir until it bubbles.

Add the noodles and toss to coat well, gently separating any that clump together. Spread the noodles into an even layer and let them sizzle, undisturbed, for 1 minute. Toss well, spread out again, and cook for 1 minute, then repeat until the noodles crisp slightly at the edges, 1 to 2 minutes more.

Add the bean sprouts and scallions and stir-fry for 30 seconds. Serve hot with a drizzle of chili crisp.

CRISPY LACE DUMPLINGS TWO WAYS: KIMCHI BEEF & PORK AND SALTED CABBAGE

Dumplings hold a very special place in my heart and in my belly. Every Lunar New Year, one of my aunties would put a big bowl of ground pork and salted cabbage on the dining table and recruit family members for hours of wrapping dumplings. With a lot of hands and a lot of love, we'd have hundreds of them, ranging from Sabrina PoPo's perfectly pleated beauties to my and my little cousins' unidentifiable blobs. But that's the beauty of dumplings. They're a labor of love, and pretty or not, they make everyone happy.

Dumpling making is a tradition I carry on with my twin nieces. I even had the best day ever on *Sesame Street* teaching my sous-chef Cookie Monster how to make pleats that would've made PoPo proud. Here, I share two fillings: my family's pork and salted cabbage and another with beef and kimchi, which takes its cues from kimchi mandu, flavorful Korean dumplings with spicy fermented cabbage inside. I also share a technique for creating dumpling lace, a crispy tuile-like crown that's sure to impress your friends.

Cook as many as you'd like (in batches of 6) and freeze the rest for another day. To make them without the lace, omit the flour mixture and use ¾ cup of water per batch.

SWITCH IT UP

Instead of pan-frying, boil or deep-fry dumplings, freshly made or straight from the freezer.

MAKES ABOUT 70 DUMPLINGS FOR EACH FILLING

KIMCHI-BEEF FILLING

- 1 pound ground beef (preferably 20% fat)
- 1 cup finely chopped drained cabbage kimchi
- 5 scallions, thinly sliced
- 2 tablespoons Chinese light soy sauce
- 1 tablespoon cornstarch
- 1 tablespoon finely grated ginger
- 1 tablespoon toasted sesame oil
- 1 teaspoon white sugar
- 1 teaspoon Diamond Crystal kosher salt
- ½ teaspoon ground white pepper
- 2 egg whites

PORK AND SALTED CABBAGE FILLING

- 3 cups thinly shredded then roughly chopped napa cabbage
- 3½ teaspoons Diamond Crystal kosher salt

Make the kimchi-beef filling: In a medium mixing bowl, combine all the ingredients and mix well with your hands just until everything is evenly distributed.

Make the pork and salted cabbage filling: In a medium mixing bowl, combine the napa cabbage and 2 teaspoons of the salt and use your hands to toss and scrunch well. Set the mixture aside for 20 minutes so the cabbage softens and releases liquid.

Squeeze out and discard the liquid from the cabbage and transfer to a large mixing bowl. Add the remaining 1½ teaspoons salt and the rest of the filling ingredients. Mix well with your hands just until everything is evenly distributed.

For either dumpling filling, test the seasoning of the filling by cooking a teaspoon or two in a small pan with a little oil. Season the filling with additional salt and pepper to taste. (To store, cover and refrigerate for up to 1 day.)

Form the dumplings: Set up a small bowl of water, two large (18 by 13-inch) sheet pans generously dusted with cornstarch to prevent sticking, and kitchen towels to cover the wrappers and the dumplings as you form them, so they don't dry out.

CONTINUED

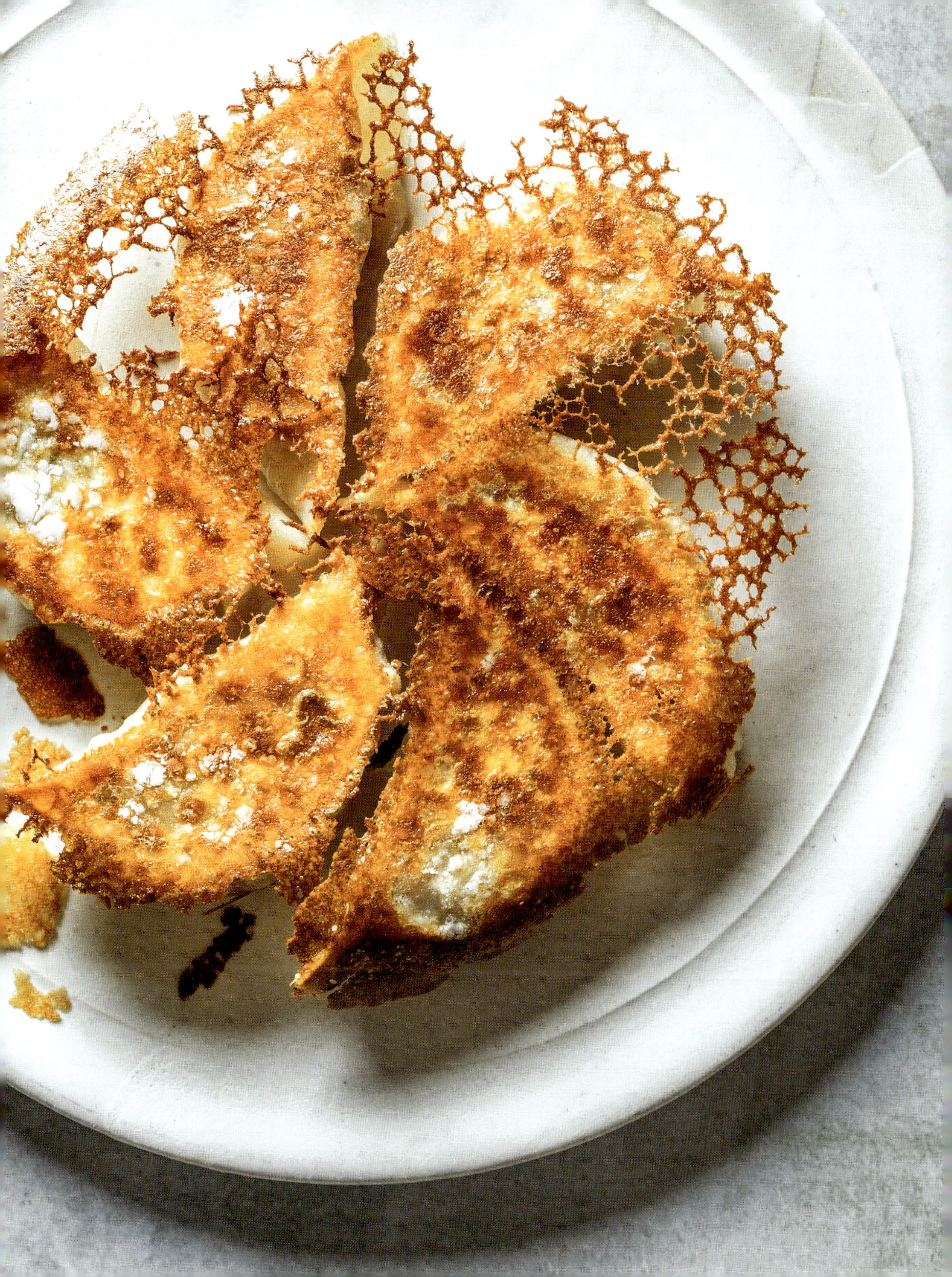

CRISPY LACE DUMPLINGS TWO WAYS: KIMCHI BEEF & PORK AND SALTED CABBAGE
CONTINUED

1 pound ground pork (preferably 20% fat)

¼ cup Shaoxing wine

2 tablespoons Chinese light soy sauce

1 tablespoon cornstarch

2 tablespoons finely grated ginger

1½ tablespoons toasted sesame oil

½ teaspoon ground white pepper

5 scallions, thinly sliced

2 egg whites

1 tablespoon water

DUMPLINGS

Cornstarch, for dusting

70 round dumpling wrappers

2 teaspoons vegetable oil, per batch of 6 dumplings

Lace mixture: 2 teaspoons all-purpose flour stirred into ¾ cup cold water, per batch of 6 dumplings

Black Vinegar–Chili Dipping Sauce (page 263), for serving

To make each dumpling, hold a wrapper in one hand and scoop 1 generous teaspoon of the filling into the center of the wrapper. Dip a fingertip into the water and use it to lightly moisten the edges of the wrapper. Fold the wrapper over the filling like a taco, then make pleats (ideally 5 to 7) and press to seal the edges, ensuring there are no air pockets. Put the dumplings on the sheet pans, leaving a little space around each one and covering with the towel. Now, they're ready to cook or store. (To store, wrap the sheet pans tightly with plastic wrap and freeze overnight. Transfer the dumplings to resealable bags and freeze for up to 2 months. Do not thaw before cooking.)

Cook the dumplings: Heat a 6- to 8-inch nonstick skillet over medium for 30 seconds. Swirl in the oil and heat until it shimmers. Arrange 6 dumplings in a circular pattern in the skillet (flat-sides down, pleats facing in the same direction, and with a little space around each one).

In a small bowl, use a fork to remix the lace mixture until smooth. Pour the mixture directly into the skillet and immediately cover with a lid. Cook until most of the liquid has evaporated and the dumpling skins are slightly translucent, 6 to 8 minutes. Remove the lid and let the flour mixture on the skillet's surface cook until it becomes a crispy, deep golden brown lace, about 2 minutes. Turn off the heat.

To help the lace release from the skillet without breaking it, give the pan a shake, then use chopsticks to gently lift a few of the dumplings by the pleats.

Invert a large serving plate onto the skillet, flip both, and remove the skillet. Serve immediately with dipping sauce.

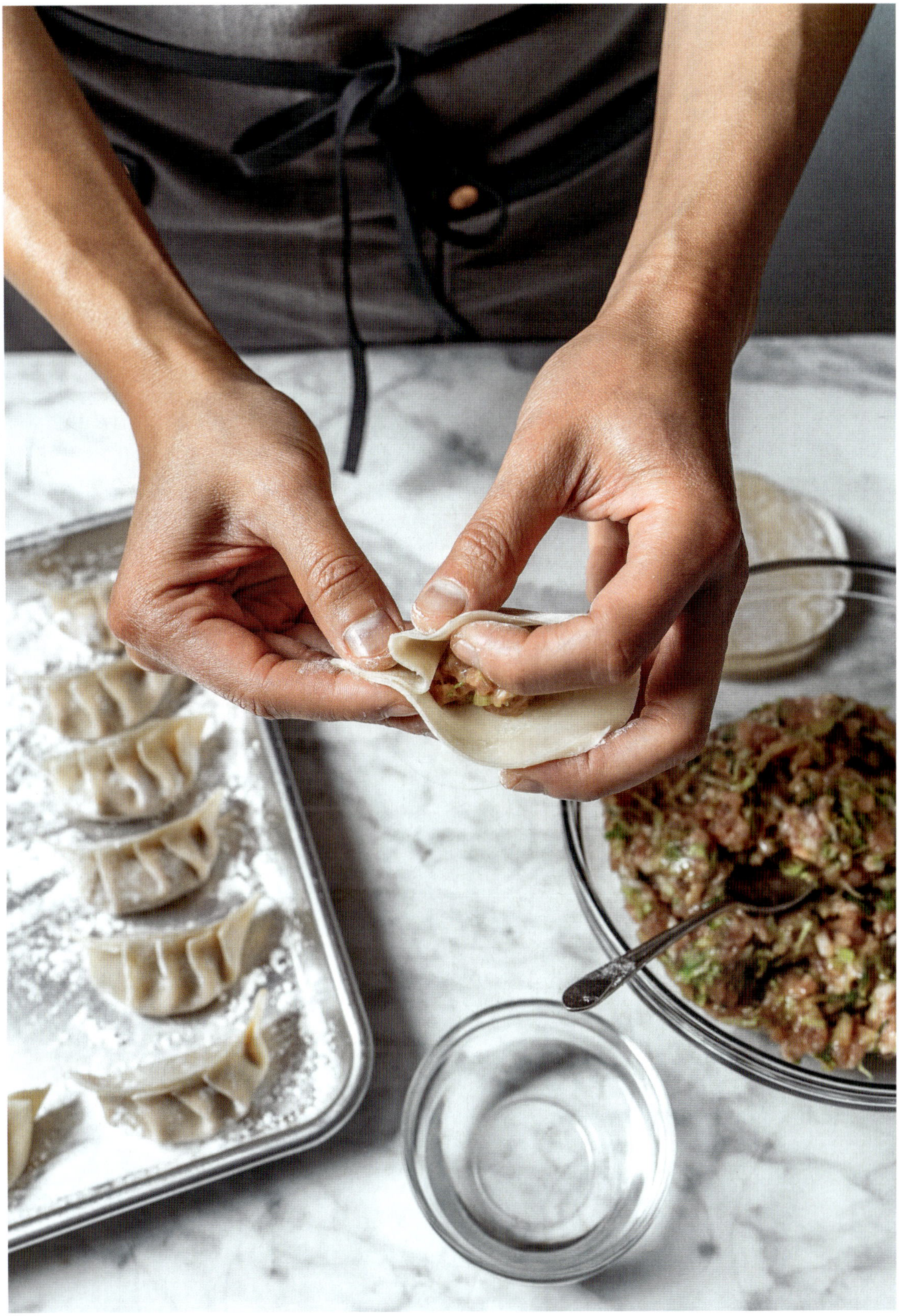

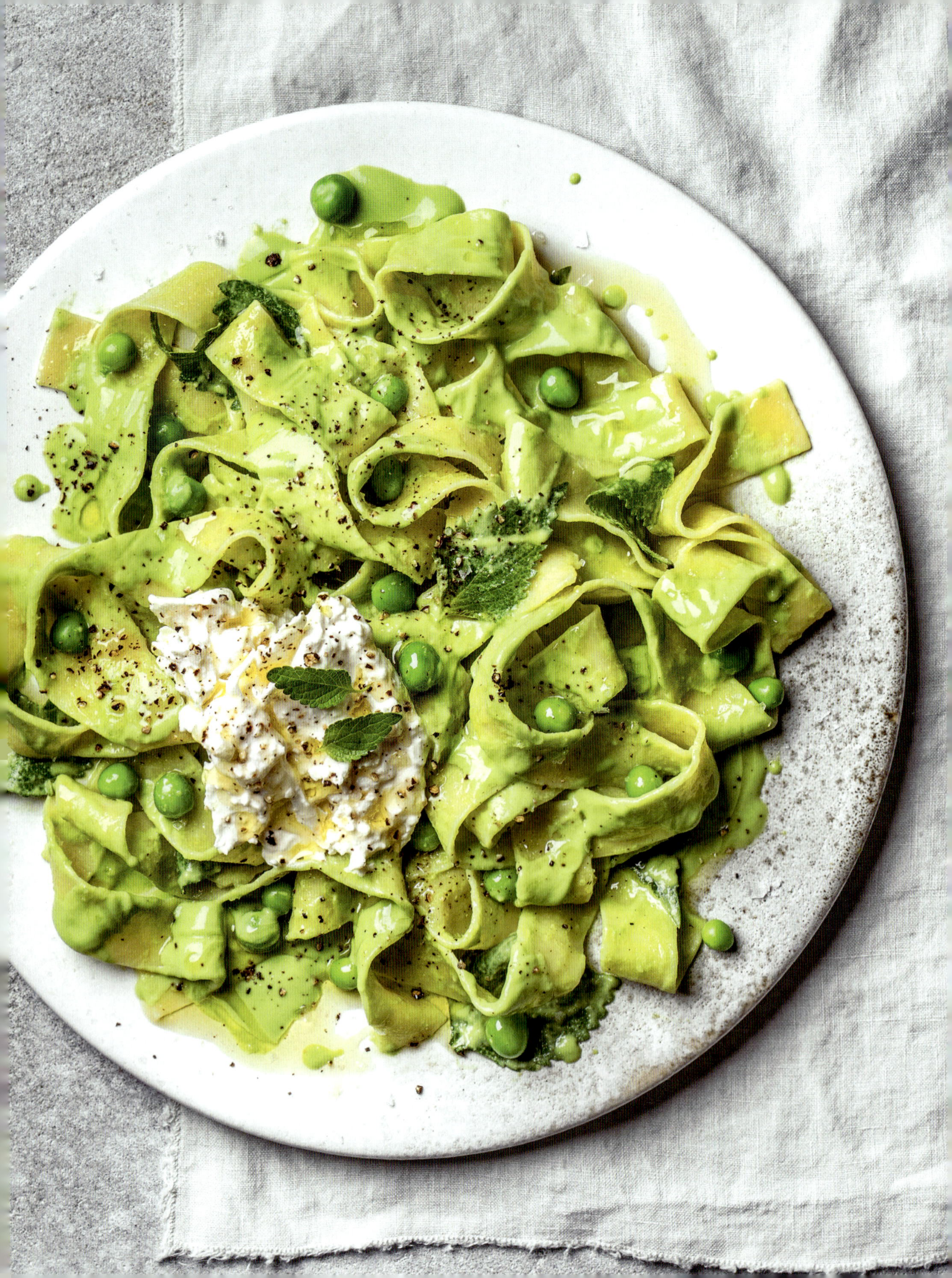

SHISO PEA PAPPARDELLE

Like my pea soup (page 151), this bright, rich vegetarian pasta takes full advantage of the beautiful culinary hack that is frozen peas. No tedious shucking required, just a quick blanch to lock in their vibrant color and a buzz in the blender turn them into a puree full of springtime sweetness. I like to feature Japanese shiso for a play on the classic pairing of peas and mint, then finish it with lemon, butter, and creamy dollops of burrata. Enjoy leftover pea puree as a dip for vegetable crudités, spread on toast with ricotta or burrata, or in place of the lobster filling for the wontons on page 116.

SERVES 2

PEA PUREE

3 tablespoons plus 2 teaspoons Diamond Crystal kosher salt, divided

One 16-ounce bag frozen peas (3⅓ cups)

¼ cup Agrumato lemon oil or extra-virgin olive oil

A small handful of shiso or mint leaves

1 medium garlic clove, peeled

PASTA

Diamond Crystal kosher salt

8 ounces fresh pappardelle pasta

3 tablespoons (1½ ounces) unsalted butter, cut into pieces

Coarsely ground black pepper

Finely grated zest of 1 lemon

Big pinch of shiso or mint leaves

Small squeeze of lemon juice

One 8-ounce ball burrata (I like the Di Stefano brand), at room temperature

Agrumato lemon oil, for drizzling

Flaky sea salt

Make the pea puree: In a medium pot, bring 8 cups water and 3 tablespoons of the salt to a boil. Meanwhile, fill a large bowl with half ice and half water. Grab a sieve that can hold all the peas comfortably and can fit in the bowl.

Add the peas to the boiling water and cook, stirring occasionally, until tender all the way through but still vibrant green, 2 to 3 minutes. Drain the peas in the sieve, then transfer the sieve to the bowl of ice water. Briefly stir the peas in the sieve, then let them sit in the ice water for 10 minutes to lock in their vibrant green color. Lift the sieve to drain them well.

Reserve ½ cup of the peas. Transfer the remaining peas to a blender and add the lemon oil, shiso, garlic, and remaining 2 teaspoons salt. Start blending on low speed, gradually increasing the speed to high, and blend, scraping down the sides occasionally, to a smooth puree, about 1 minute. Measure out ¾ cup of the pea puree for the pasta. (Store the rest in an airtight container in the fridge for up to 2 days.)

Make the pasta: Bring a large pot of water to a boil and stir in a generous pinch of kosher salt. Add the pasta and cook, stirring occasionally, until partially cooked (the pasta will still have a slight bite), about 1 minute less than the package instructions advise.

Meanwhile, add the butter, ¼ teaspoon kosher salt, several turns of pepper, and ¾ cup of pea puree to a large pan. When the pasta is ready, gently use tongs to transfer it to the skillet along with ½ cup of the pasta water, reserving the rest. Bring to a simmer over high heat, and cook, stirring gently and frequently, until the sauce has tightened slightly, 30 seconds to 1 minute.

Add the reserved peas, lemon zest, and shiso (tear as you add them) and cook, stirring frequently and adding splashes of pasta water as necessary to keep it slightly saucy, until the pasta is al dente and the sauce coats the pasta, about 1 minute more. Add lemon juice for brightness, toss well, and turn off the heat.

Serve the pasta dolloped with the burrata. Drizzle the burrata with additional lemon oil and sprinkle it with more pepper and flaky salt.

LOBSTER WONTONS IN YUZU BROTH

YUZU BROTH

8 cups water

6 large dried shiitake mushrooms

5 makrut lime leaves, roughly torn

2 large lemongrass stalks, trimmed (see page 16) and smashed

6 by 2 inches kombu (dried kelp), broken into a few pieces

2 by 1-inch knob ginger, peeled and lightly smashed

3 lightly packed cups / 20g katsuobushi (bonito flakes)

3 tablespoons bottled yuzu juice, plus more as needed

3 tablespoons mirin

2 tablespoons Japanese white soy sauce (shiro shoyu) or standard soy sauce

1½ teaspoons Diamond Crystal kosher salt, plus more as needed

1 stick (4 ounces) unsalted butter, cubed

WONTONS

1 pound raw lobster meat (thawed if frozen), cut into ½-inch dice

¼ cup Agrumato lemon oil

2 tablespoons water

1 tablespoon Shaoxing wine

1 tablespoon Diamond Crystal kosher salt

2 teaspoons finely grated ginger

1 teaspoon cornstarch, plus more for dusting

¼ teaspoon ground white pepper

5 makrut lime leaves, center stems removed, finely minced

Finely grated zest of 2 lemons

50 yellow wonton (square) wrappers

FOR SERVING

Charred Green Oil (page 248), for garnish

If I have a signature dish, it's probably this play on the Hong Kong–style shrimp wontons I grew up on. They're elegant and impressive, but still have the soul and ease of the ones I'd make with my mom. I fill them with lobster and, when I'm feeling extra, top them with caviar. I float my fancy-girl wontons in a special broth. At its core, the broth is Japanese dashi, layered with the flavors of bonito, kombu, and shiitake, but I infuse it with Southeast Asian aromatics like lemongrass and lime leaves and brighten it up with fragrant yuzu juice. Finally, I finish the delicate broth with butter, to draw out the smoky notes of the bonito, and a last-minute drizzle of a savory jade-green oil.

LEVEL IT UP

Top each wonton with caviar.

SWITCH IT UP

Feel free to use shrimp instead of lobster or pipe in pea puree (from Shiso Pea Pappardelle, page 115) as the filling.

SERVES 8 TO 10

Make the broth: In a medium pot, combine the water, mushrooms, lime leaves, lemongrass, kombu, and ginger and bring to a boil over high heat. Turn the heat down to cook at a gentle simmer, partially covered, for 30 minutes.

Remove from the heat, then add the katsuobushi, cover, and steep like tea for 15 minutes.

Set a fine-mesh sieve over a clean pot. Strain the broth, discarding the solids. Stir in the yuzu, mirin, soy sauce, and salt. Return the broth to a gentle simmer. Whisk in the butter a few pieces at a time. Season to taste with additional yuzu juice and salt. Cover to keep warm while you make the wontons.

Make the wontons: In a bowl, combine the lobster, lemon oil, water, Shaoxing wine, salt, ginger, cornstarch, white pepper, lime leaves, and lemon zest and mix well, about 30 seconds. I taste the raw mixture and season to taste with additional salt.

Set up a small bowl of water, a large (18 by 13-inch) sheet pan generously dusted with cornstarch to prevent sticking, and kitchen towels to cover the wrappers and the wontons as you form them, so they don't dry out.

To make each wonton, hold a wrapper in one hand and scoop 1 generous teaspoon of the filling into the center of the wrapper. Dip a fingertip

CONTINUED

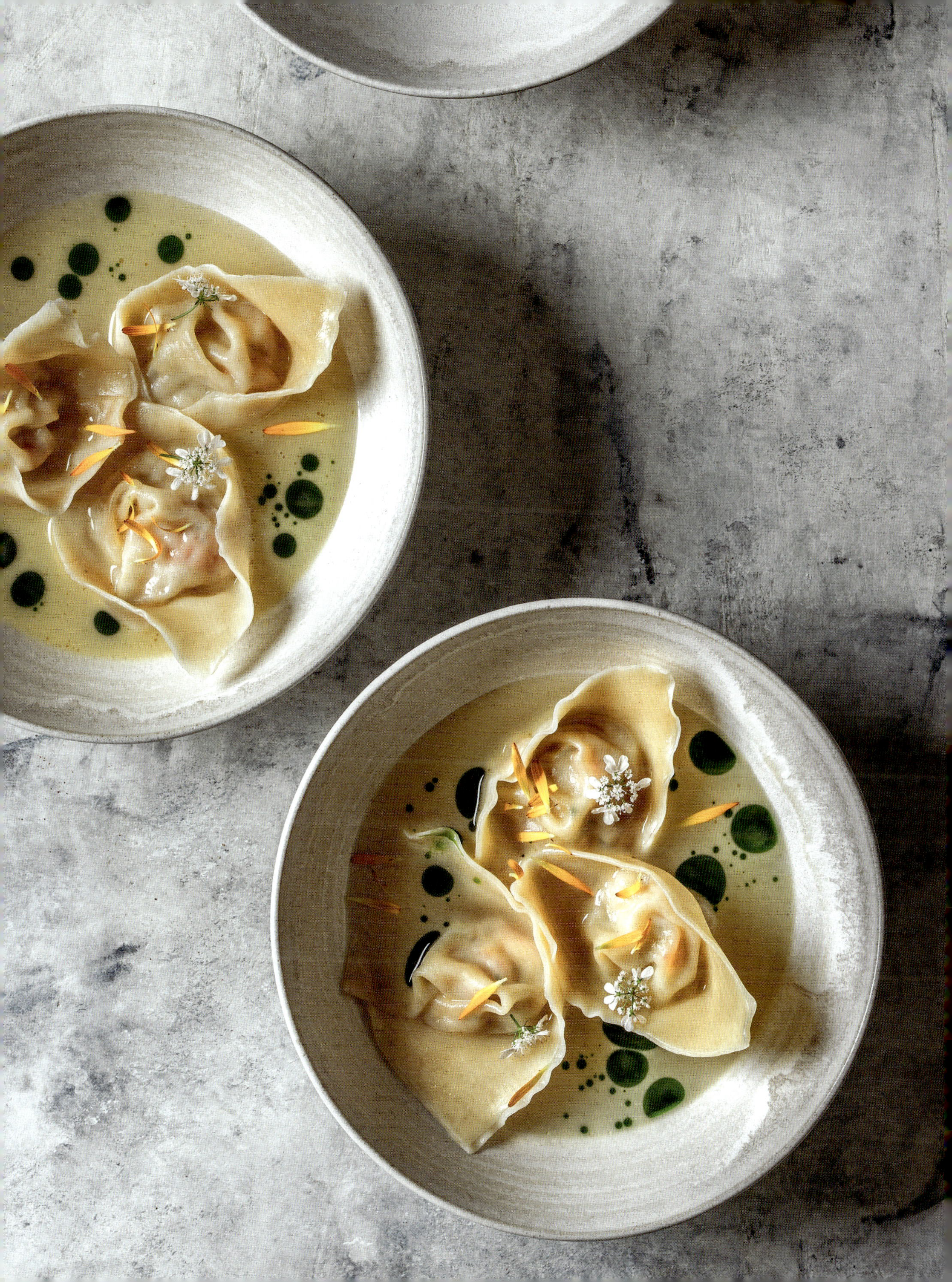

LOBSTER WONTONS IN YUZU BROTH
CONTINUED

into the water and use it to moisten the edges of the wrapper. Fold the wrapper in half over the filling to make a rectangle, then press the edges to seal, ensuring there are no air pockets. Hold the rectangle long-seam-side up, moisten the bottom right corner, and cover with the bottom left corner as pictured below, pinching so they adhere.

Put the wontons on the sheet pan, leaving a little space around each one and covering with a kitchen towel. Now they're ready to cook or store. (To store, wrap the sheet pan tightly with plastic wrap and freeze overnight. Transfer the wontons to an airtight container and freeze for up to 2 months. Do not thaw before cooking.)

Serve the dish: Bring a large pot of water to a boil. Bring the broth to a very gentle simmer. Working in batches to cook the wontons, carefully add them to the boiling water, gently stirring to prevent sticking, and cook until they float to the surface and the filling is fully cooked (try one!), about 2 minutes (or 3 minutes if frozen).

Use a spider strainer to remove the wontons, then transfer them to bowls. Whisk the broth well, then ladle as much as you'd like over the wontons. Drizzle with the green oil. Serve the bowls, then cook and serve the remaining wontons the same way.

CHINESE STICKY RICE WITH DRIED SEAFOOD AND SAUSAGE

I made my first turkey when I was thirteen, and ruined Thanksgiving for my entire family. I'm only half joking. And it wasn't just because my turkey was dry, but also because they were used to a different whole bird at the center of our table: stuffed roast duck that we'd pick up from our local Cantonese barbecue house.

To me, the star was the stuffing: lo mai fan, steamed sticky rice wok-fried with dried scallops, dried shrimp, shiitake, and lap cheong. It's super savory, full of umami, and delicious on its own. It's become a must on my holiday table. My family still makes a little fuss when I insist on making turkey, but as long as there's lo mai fan next to the mashed potatoes, it's all gravy. Tip: Make it up to 6 hours ahead and keep in a rice cooker on the "warm setting."

SERVES 6 TO 8

Equipment: 12-inch bamboo steamer, cheesecloth

2 cups short-grain sweet (glutinous) rice

20 medium dried shiitake mushrooms, rinsed

½ cup dried shrimp, rinsed

¼ cup dried scallops, rinsed

2 tablespoons canola oil

6 lap cheong (Chinese pork sausage), chopped into ½-inch dice

8 large garlic cloves, finely minced

1 by 1-inch knob ginger, peeled and finely minced

5 tablespoons toasted sesame oil

¼ cup Chinese oyster sauce, plus more as needed

1 tablespoon Chinese dark soy sauce

1 tablespoon Chinese light soy sauce, plus more as needed

3 scallions, thinly sliced

Forty-eight hours in advance, put the rice in a large mixing bowl, cover with cold water, agitate the rice with your hands, then pour out the water. Repeat until the water is just barely cloudy, at least 5 times. This is important: Sweet rice is especially starchy and sufficiently washing the surface of the grains prevents the rice from steaming into a gummy clump.

In the mixing bowl, combine the rice and enough fresh water to cover by 4 inches. Cover and soak in the fridge for 48 hours. In three separate containers, soak the dried mushrooms, shrimp, and scallops in water in the fridge for at least 24 hours or up to 48 hours.

When ready to cook, bring 2 inches of water to a boil in a wok (my preference) or pot that'll hold a 12-inch bamboo steamer without the bottom touching the water.

Line the steamer with damp cheesecloth. Drain the rice through a fine-mesh sieve. Add the rice to the lined steamer, spread to an even layer, then cover the steamer.

Reduce the heat to maintain a moderate simmer, then carefully set the steamer in the wok or pot. Steam, covered, until the grains are fully cooked but still chewy, about 45 minutes.

Meanwhile, drain the mushrooms, shrimp, and scallops, discarding the liquid. Finely chop the shrimp, chop the mushrooms into ¼-inch pieces, and use your hands to finely shred the scallops.

CONTINUED

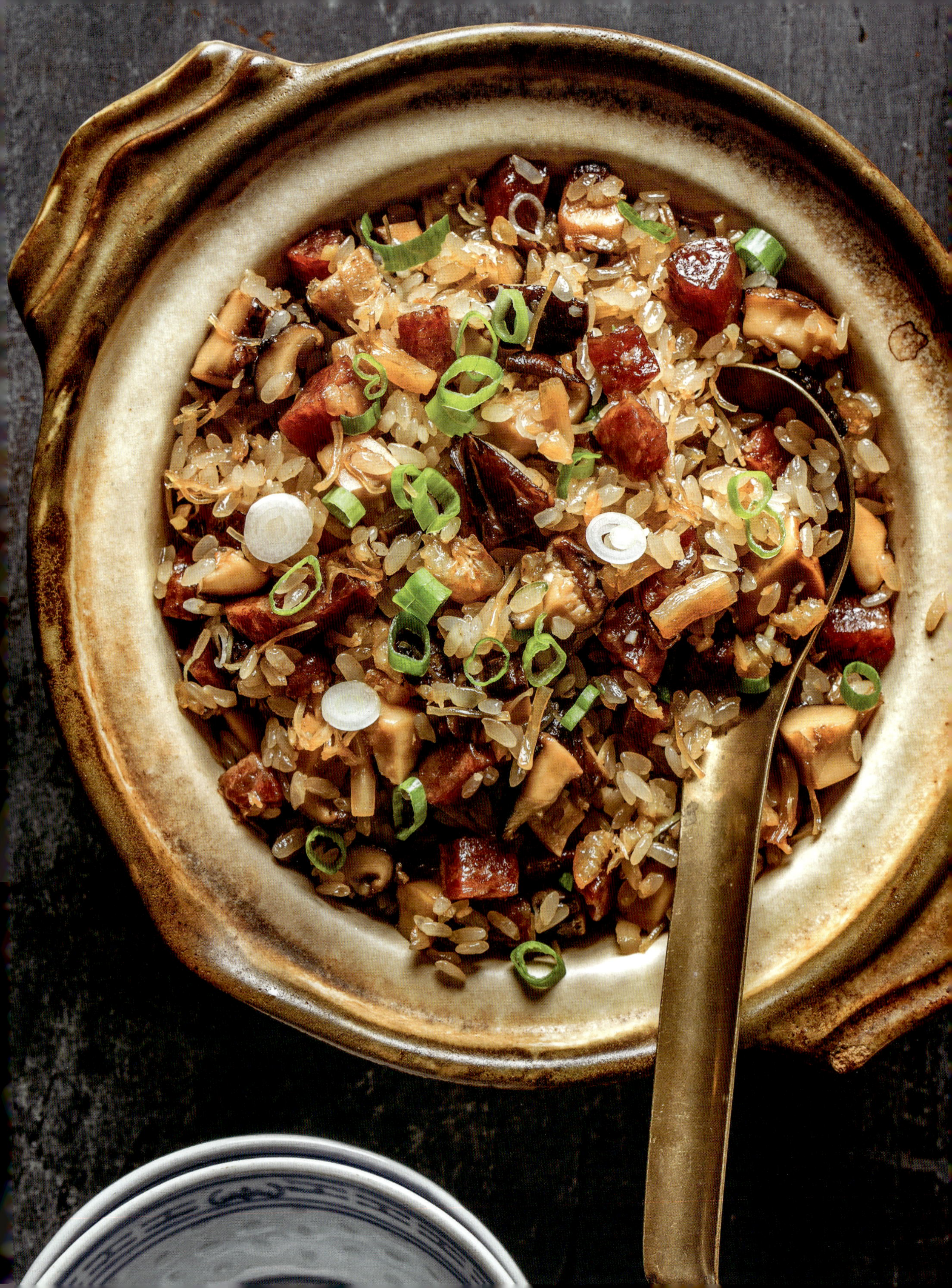

CHINESE STICKY RICE WITH DRIED SEAFOOD AND SAUSAGE
CONTINUED

Transfer the cooked sticky rice (some will inevitably stick to the cheesecloth) to a medium mixing bowl.

Heat a wok or large sauté pan over high heat until it just begins to smoke, about 1 minute. Add the canola oil and swirl the pan to coat the surface. Add the sausage and cook for about 2 minutes, stirring with a wok spatula, until the sausage picks up some color. Add the garlic, ginger, mushrooms, scallops, and shrimp and cook, stirring occasionally, until they turn golden, about 4 minutes.

Add the rice to the wok, toss well, and stir-fry for 1 minute more. Add the sesame oil, oyster sauce, dark soy sauce, and light soy sauce and stir-fry, breaking up clumps, so the rice takes on the color of the sauces without any remaining patches of white, about 3 minutes.

Stir in the scallions and season to taste with more oyster sauce and/or light soy sauce. Transfer to a serving bowl and serve hot.

CHICKEN AND GINGER JOOK

Jook, also called congee, was my breakfast before school and what my mom made for me when I was sick. And at eight, before I was old enough to use the stove, I was cooking it in the rice cooker for my parents when *they* were sick. Our jook was just rice and water cooked until the grains broke down into a cozy, creamy porridge. Choosing the toppings was the best part. Sometimes that was a splash of soy sauce and a big pinch of yuk sung (pork floss)—a sort of jerky, sweet-savory and shredded so fine it resembles cotton candy. I liked Sabrina PoPo's picks best. She'd add diced century eggs, shredded duck from the local Cantonese barbecue shop, and shredded iceberg lettuce.

When I make jook today, I briefly toast the rice with ginger and garlic, and use flavorful stock instead of water. (This is a great moment for homemade stock—I love making jook the day after Thanksgiving with simmered turkey bones—but boxed is just fine.) The garnishes are also key to elevating your jook, so choose among these options or go rogue and find your own faves.

LEVEL IT UP

Choose 3 to 5 of the following garnishes:

- Chopped scallions
- Chopped cilantro
- Crushed peanuts
- Fried garlic
- Fried Shallots (page 254)
- Century eggs
- King's Chili Crisp (page 257)
- Ground white pepper
- Grated ginger
- Yuk sung (pork floss)
- Shredded iceberg lettuce
- Sliced radishes
- Puffed Wild Rice (page 257)

SERVES 4

1 pound boneless, skinless chicken thighs, cut into ½-inch pieces

2 tablespoons Shaoxing wine

1 tablespoon Chinese light soy sauce

½ teaspoon cornstarch

¼ teaspoon white sugar

Diamond Crystal kosher salt

Ground white pepper

2 tablespoons canola oil

1 cup finely diced yellow onion

4 garlic cloves, minced

2 tablespoons minced ginger, plus one 2 by 1-inch knob, peeled and julienned

½ cup short-grain white rice, rinsed until the water runs clear and drained

8 cups low-sodium chicken stock

1 tablespoon fish sauce (preferably Three Crabs brand)

In a medium mixing bowl, combine the chicken, wine, soy sauce, cornstarch, sugar, a pinch of salt, and a dash of white pepper and toss well. Set aside in the refrigerator while the jook cooks.

Heat a 4- to 6-quart medium pot over medium-high heat for 1 minute. Add the oil and heat until it shimmers. Add the onion, garlic, minced ginger, and 1 teaspoon salt and cook, stirring occasionally, until the onion is translucent but not colored, about 2 minutes. Add the rice and cook, stirring frequently, for 30 seconds to lightly toast the grains.

Add the stock and let it come to a boil, stirring frequently. Turn the heat down to cook at a gentle simmer, partially covered, stirring occasionally, until the rice grains break apart and the liquid looks starchy and thickens slightly, about 45 minutes.

Stir in the chicken and julienned ginger. Let the mixture return to a steady simmer and cook, partially covered and stirring frequently to prevent scorching, until the jook looks like a velvety porridge, rather than broken rice in liquid, 25 to 35 minutes more. If it's thick like oatmeal, gradually add additional water or stock to adjust the consistency.

Stir in the fish sauce and ¼ teaspoon ground white pepper and season to taste with additional salt and white pepper. Serve with optional garnishes.

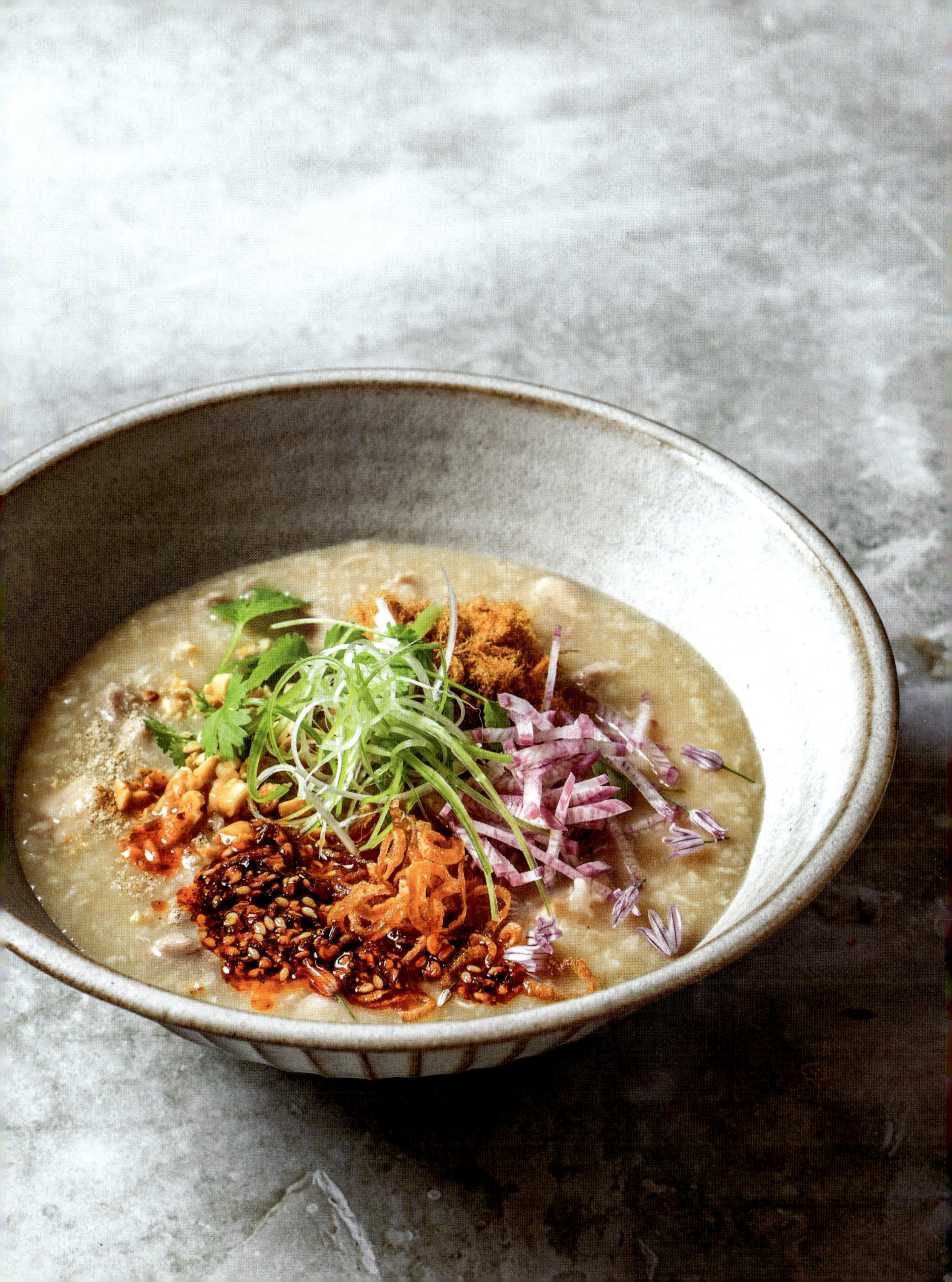

VEGETABLES

5

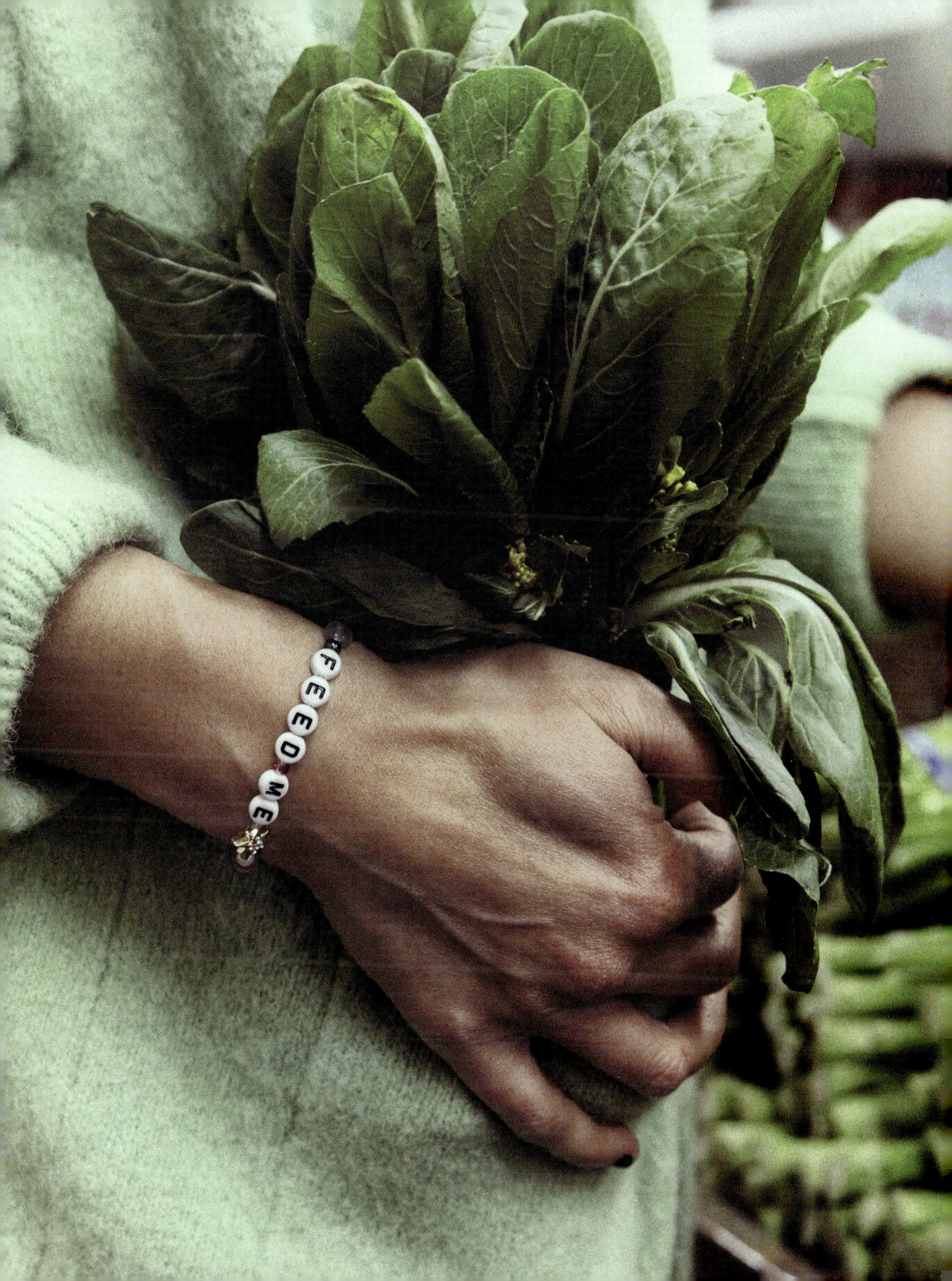
FEED ME

BLISTERED SNAP AND SNOW PEAS WITH CUMIN-SHISO TZATZIKI

Just a minute over hot coals takes the raw off this medley of spring peapods and also adds a touch of smokiness. The hot-cold, sweet-tangy, crisp-creamy contrasts of the peas with the zippy yogurt dip make this a real treat.

LEVEL IT UP

Add a sprinkle of Puffed Wild Rice (page 257) or Fried Shallots (page 254) for crunch.

SERVES 4

Equipment: A heavy-duty grill grid

1 pound mixed snap peas and snow peas, trimmed

2 teaspoons extra-virgin olive oil

Diamond Crystal kosher salt

1 lemon, for zesting and juicing

Agrumato lemon oil or extra-virgin olive oil

Cumin-Shiso Tzatziki (page 128)

Flaky sea salt and coarsely ground black pepper

Shiso or mint leaves, for serving

Prepare a grill, preferably charcoal, to cook with high heat. Set a grill grid on the grill and let it get hot. This way, the peas can pick up that smoky flavor from the grill but won't fall through the grates.

In a medium mixing bowl, combine the snap and snow peas, olive oil, and ½ teaspoon kosher salt and toss to coat well. Add the peas in a single layer to the grill and cook, flipping them once, until they're blistered and charred on both sides but still crisp and vibrant in color, 30 seconds to 1 minute. Transfer them back to the mixing bowl.

Use a Microplane to finely grate on the lemon zest and squeeze in just enough lemon juice to add brightness. Add a pinch of kosher salt and a generous drizzle of the lemon oil. Toss well.

Scoop the tzatziki onto a plate and use the bottom of a spoon to make some pretty divots. Arrange the charred peas on top, then drizzle with a little more lemon oil, sprinkle on some flaky salt, and add a few turns of black pepper. Tear and sprinkle with the shiso and serve immediately.

CONTINUED

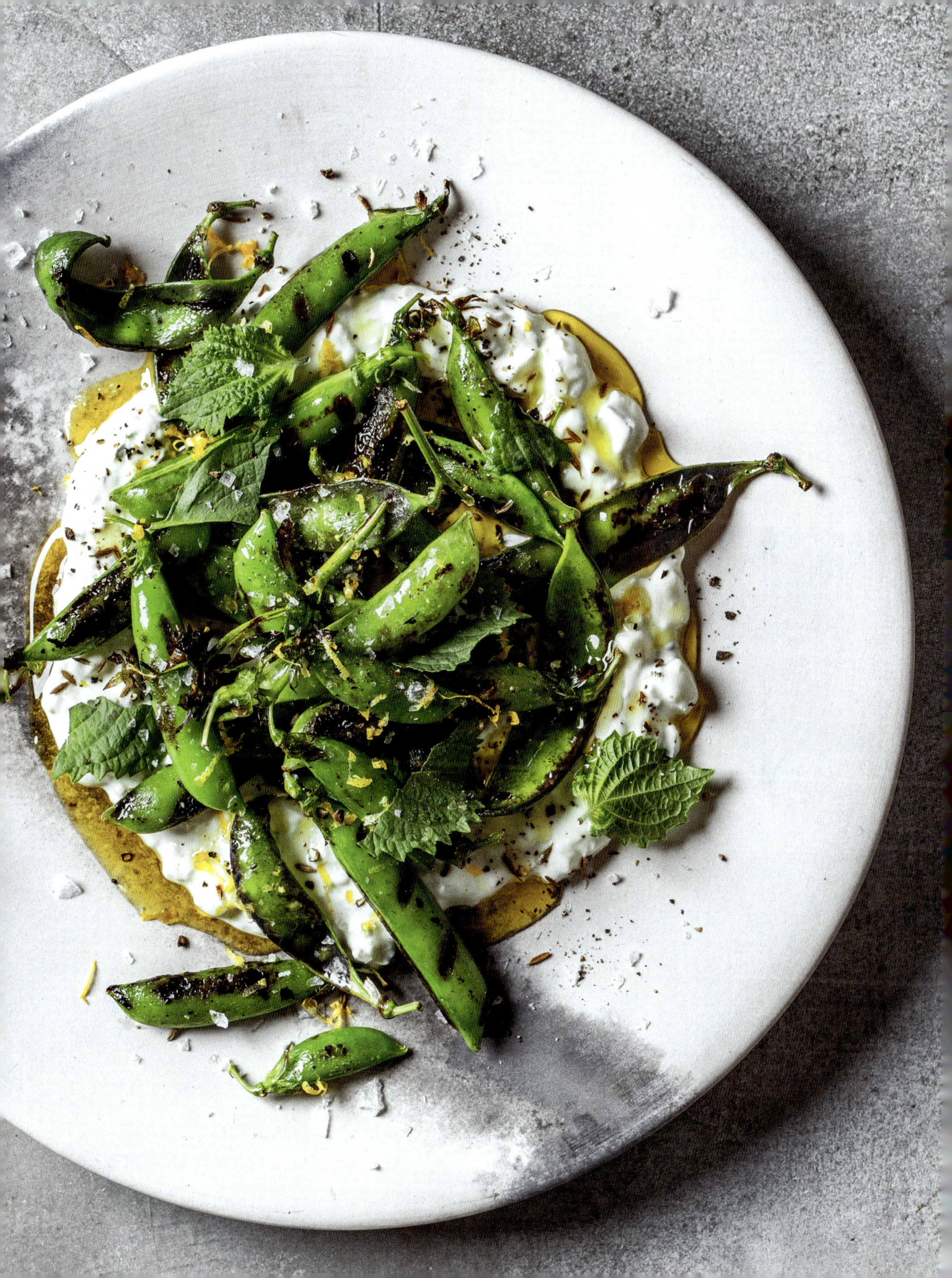

BLISTERED SNAP AND SNOW PEAS WITH CUMIN-SHISO TZATZIKI

CONTINUED

½ teaspoon cumin seeds

1 cup plain whole-milk Greek yogurt

1 tablespoon lemon juice

2 tablespoons coarsely grated seeded cucumber

2 tablespoons finely diced seeded cucumber

1 by ½-inch knob ginger, peeled and finely grated on a Microplane

1 medium garlic clove, finely grated on a Microplane

Small handful of cilantro (leaves and stems), finely chopped

Small handful of shiso or mint, finely chopped

2 teaspoons extra-virgin olive oil

½ teaspoon Diamond Crystal kosher salt

Coarsely ground black pepper

CUMIN-SHISO TZATZIKI

Your friends will battle over the last traces of this cucumber-spiked yogurt dip that clocks in somewhere between garlicky Greek tzatziki and South Asian raita, with my beloved shiso standing in for mint. I particularly enjoy it with the blistered pea pods on the previous page, but it's equally tasty with raw vegetables, grilled lamb chops, or Cheesy Scallion Pancakes (page 93).

MAKES ABOUT 1 CUP

In a small dry skillet, toast the cumin seeds over medium-low heat, shaking the pan occasionally, until fragrant, 2 to 3 minutes.

In a medium mixing bowl, combine the toasted cumin seeds, yogurt, lemon juice, grated cucumber, diced cucumber, ginger, garlic, cilantro, shiso, olive oil, salt, and a few turns of black pepper and stir well.

Chill in the fridge for at least 15 minutes or up to 4 hours.

STREET CORN THREE WAYS: THAI, SICHUAN, AND ITALIAN

I can't stress enough how much I love elote, the grilled corn on the cob popular on the streets of Mexico and my hometown of LA. It's slathered with mayo, dusted with Tajín, rolled in salty Cotija cheese, and served, sometimes, with a wedge of lime. It's become my go-to way to serve summer corn straight off the grill. The corn's natural sweetness combined with creaminess and heat, salt, and acidity, is hard to resist.

I especially love using those basic elements as an inspiration to take the dish in different directions. Sometimes I veer toward Italy with Parmigiano-Reggiano and a bright mayo spiked with fruity Calabrian chiles. Other times, I look to the Sichuan province with black vinegar mayo and chili crisp or to Thailand with creamy peanut sauce and fried shallots. Pick one path for 6 ears of corn. For a party, triple the corn and make all three.

SERVES 4 TO 6

GRILLED CORN

6 large ears corn, shucked

PEANUT SAUCE

½ cup creamy peanut butter

¼ cup well-shaken full-fat coconut milk

1 tablespoon plus 1 teaspoon honey or sugar

1 tablespoon plus 1 teaspoon fish sauce (Three Crabs is a must here)

1 tablespoon plus 1 teaspoon lime juice

2 teaspoons store-bought Thai red curry paste

3 garlic cloves, finely grated on a Microplane

GARNISH

Flaky sea salt

3 tablespoons Fried Shallots, homemade (page 254) or store-bought

Handful of Thai basil leaves, torn at the last minute

½ cup chopped unsalted roasted peanuts

Lime wedges, for serving

CORN

Prepare a grill, preferably charcoal, to cook with high heat. Grill the corn, turning occasionally, until slightly charred all over, 3 to 5 minutes.

THAI

In a medium bowl, whisk together the peanut butter, coconut milk, honey, fish sauce, lime juice, curry paste, and garlic until smooth.

Slather the grilled corn generously with the peanut sauce. Sprinkle on flaky salt, then the fried shallots, Thai basil, and peanuts, turning to coat all sides. Serve immediately with the lime wedges.

CONTINUED

STREET CORN THREE WAYS: THAI, SICHUAN, AND ITALIAN
CONTINUED

BLACK VINEGAR MAYO

¾ cup mayonnaise

3 medium black garlic cloves, peeled and minced

2½ teaspoons Zhenjiang black vinegar

¼ teaspoon Diamond Crystal kosher salt

Finely ground black pepper

GARNISH

3 tablespoons store-bought fried garlic

Flaky sea salt

Handful of cilantro (leaves and stems), finely chopped

King's Chili Crisp (page 257) or store-bought Chinese chili crisp

CALABRIAN CHILE MAYO

¾ cup mayonnaise

1½ tablespoons crushed Calabrian chiles

1½ teaspoons Agrumato lemon oil or extra-virgin olive oil

¼ teaspoon Diamond Crystal kosher salt

Finely ground black pepper

1 large garlic clove, finely grated on a Microplane

Finely grated zest of 1 lemon

1½ tablespoons lemon juice

GARNISH

Flaky sea salt

1 cup Fried Bread Crumbs (page 256)

½ cup finely grated Parmigiano-Reggiano

Handful of basil leaves, torn at the last minute

SICHUAN

In a medium bowl, whisk together the mayonnaise, black garlic, vinegar, salt, and several turns of pepper.

Slather the grilled corn generously with the vinegar mayo. Sprinkle on the fried garlic, flaky salt, and cilantro, turning to coat all sides. Drizzle with chili crisp and serve immediately.

ITALIAN

In a medium bowl, whisk together the mayonnaise, chiles, lemon oil, salt, several turns of pepper, garlic, lemon zest, and lemon juice until smooth.

Slather the grilled corn generously with the chile mayo. Sprinkle with the flaky salt, bread crumbs, and Parmigiano-Reggiano, turning to coat all sides. Top with the basil and serve immediately.

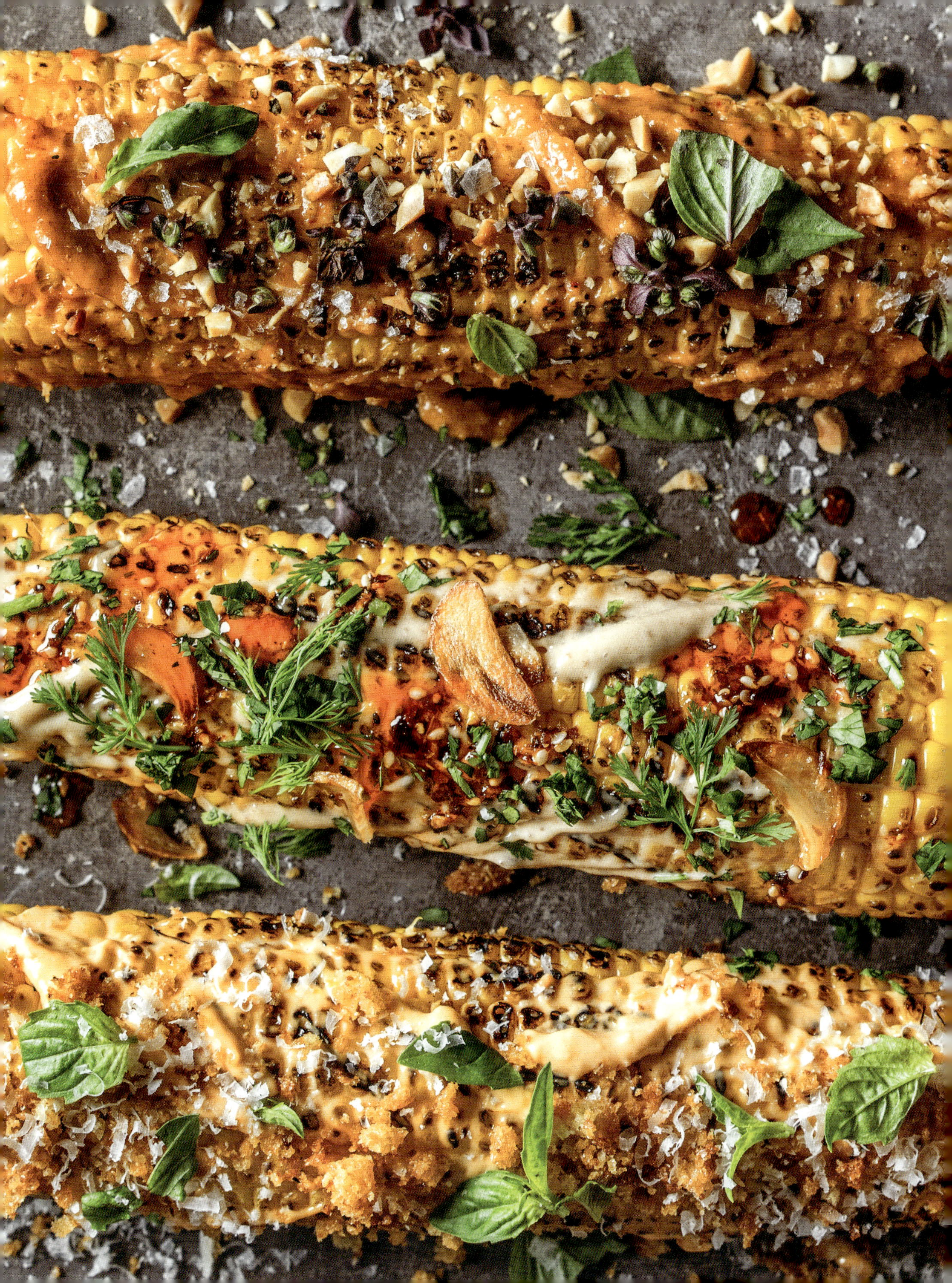

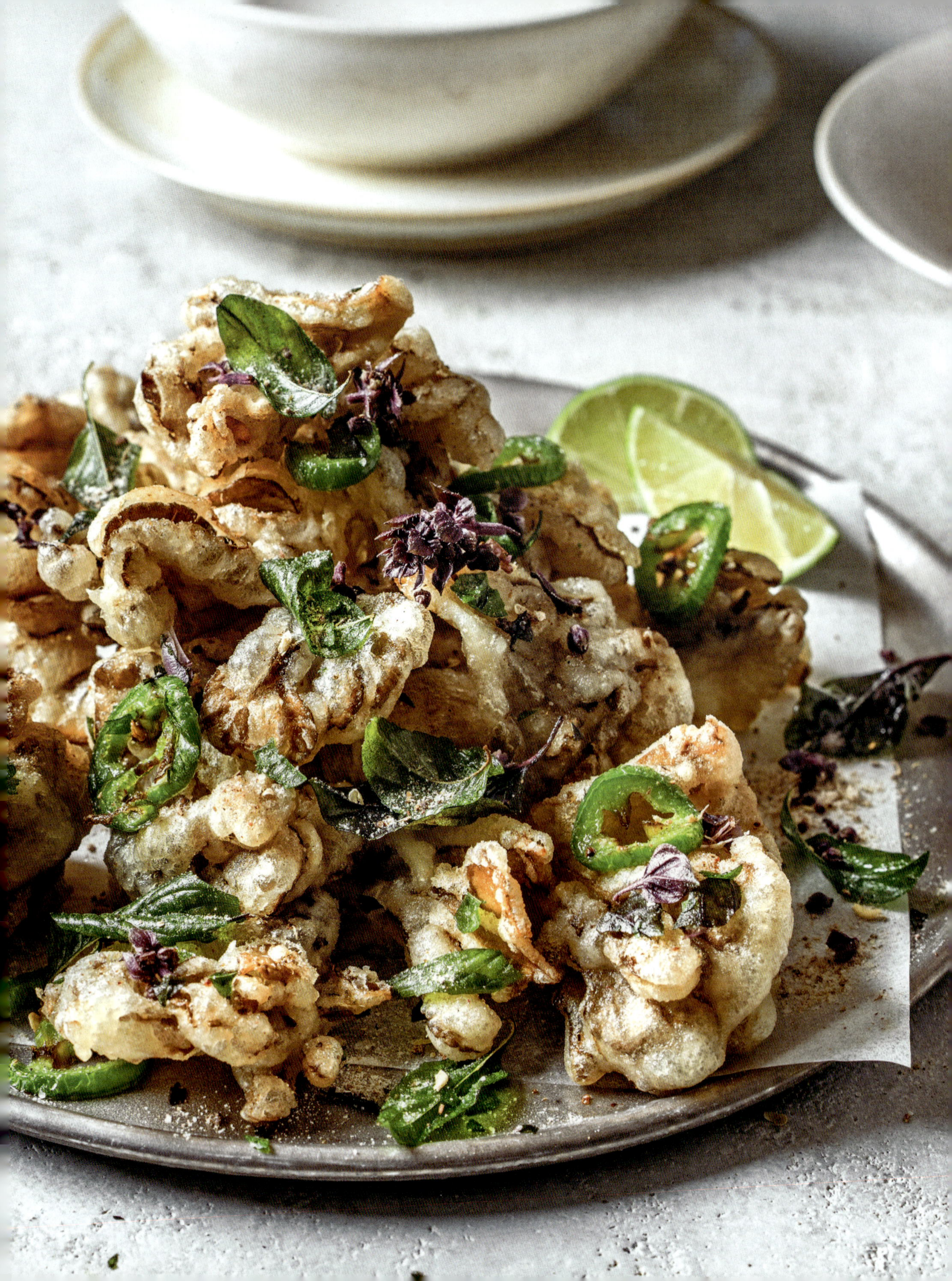

SALT AND PEPPER MAITAKE

My childhood was full of shrimp, frog legs, and oyster mushrooms cooked in the Cantonese "salt and pepper" style—a light dredge that fries crisp followed by a toss with a salty, peppery spice mixture. Those flavors go so well with another fantastic fried food: the airy, crispy battered tempura I spent six months straight making at a Japanese restaurant with deep-fryers so big I could've climbed in. Practically anything can be tempura-ed and salt-and-pepper-ed, so feel free to sub in shrimp, squid, zucchini, or asparagus.

LEVEL IT UP

Dunk the fried maitake in a fluffy, creamy mixture of 1 cup of crème fraîche, a teaspoon of lemon juice, and ¼ teaspoon salt whipped to soft peaks, then topped with a drizzle of Charred Green Oil (page 248).

SERVES 4 TO 6

Equipment: Deep-fry thermometer

SPICE MIX

1½ teaspoons Diamond Crystal kosher salt

⅛ teaspoon finely ground red Sichuan peppercorns

⅛ teaspoon ground white pepper

⅛ teaspoon ground ginger

MAITAKE

1 pound maitake (also called hen of the woods), base trimmed

Canola oil (about 2 quarts), for deep-frying

2 cups all-purpose flour

2 teaspoons cornstarch

½ teaspoon Diamond Crystal kosher salt

2 cups sparkling water, cold

About 5 ice cubes

1 small jalapeño, thinly sliced

1 cup lightly packed Thai basil leaves

Lime wedges, for serving

Make the spice mix: In a small bowl, mix together the salt, Sichuan peppercorns, white pepper, and ginger. Set aside.

Make the maitake: Gently pull apart the maitake into small clusters attached by the stem. Shoot for two-bite pieces.

Pour 2 inches of oil into a deep 5- to 6-quart pot and set it over medium-high heat until the oil registers 350°F on a deep-fry thermometer.

While the oil heats up, in a medium mixing bowl, stir together the flour, cornstarch, and salt. In a separate container, combine the sparkling water and ice cubes and stir until very cold. In a thin, steady stream, pour the cold sparkling water into the flour mixture, whisking gently, just until smooth.

The maitake taste best hot, so fry in three batches to avoid crowding and serve each batch as it's ready. One maitake cluster at a time, dip one-third of the mushrooms into the batter, coating all sides and shaking off excess, then immediately and carefully add them to the hot oil. Fry, stirring occasionally, until crispy on all sides, flipping if necessary, 2 to 3 minutes.

Before removing the mushrooms, ready a pot lid, add one-third of the sliced jalapeño and one-third of the basil, and immediately cover with a lid to protect you from any splatter. Wait 5 seconds, then remove the lid and fry, stirring with a spider strainer, until the basil turns bright green and translucent, 10 to 15 seconds.

Use the spider strainer to remove the mushrooms, jalapeño, and basil, draining well in the spider before transferring to a large mixing bowl. Immediately and generously sprinkle on some of the spice mix while tossing to coat the mushrooms and break up the basil.

Serve hot along with lime wedges. Between batches, let the oil return to 350°F.

ROASTED JAPANESE SWEET POTATO WITH OLIVES, WALNUTS, AND MISO-TAHINI

The Japanese sweet potato is my top tuber and is pretty perfect on its own. Street vendors around Japan and Hong Kong simply roast them over hot coals to celebrate their fluffy, sugary interiors. At home, I bake them until completely tender and the skins are a bit crisp. Then I slather them with a creamy, nutty miso-tahini, brûlée them under the broiler until bubbling and caramelized, and top them with briny Kalamata olives and crunchy walnuts.

SERVES 4

4 Japanese sweet potatoes (about 8 ounces each), scrubbed and washed well

4 teaspoons extra-virgin olive oil, plus more for drizzling

Diamond Crystal kosher salt and finely ground black pepper

½ cup well-stirred tahini

¼ cup shiro (white) miso

2 teaspoons honey or maple syrup

¼ cup water

½ cup pitted Kalamata olives, roughly chopped

1 cup toasted walnuts, chopped

Toasted sesame seeds, for garnish

Flaky sea salt

Preheat the oven to 400°F.

Use a fork to prick the skin about 8 times all around each potato. Put the potatoes on a large piece of foil, rub each potato with 1 teaspoon of the oil, and season generously with salt and pepper. Cover with another piece of foil and wrap the potatoes tightly in a package.

Transfer to a sheet pan and bake for 35 minutes. Remove the top piece of foil, flip the potatoes, and continue to bake until the skins brown and crisp slightly and you can insert and remove a sharp knife with no resistance, 30 to 40 minutes more. Remove from the oven.

Preheat the broiler with a rack 2 to 4 inches from the heat source. In a medium bowl, whisk together the tahini, miso, honey, water, and a pinch of salt until it's smooth.

Split the potatoes lengthwise, return them to the foil-lined sheet pan cut-sides up, then slather on the miso-tahini. Broil until bubbling and charred in spots, 2 to 3 minutes.

Serve topped with the olives and walnuts, sprinkled with sesame seeds, flaky salt, and black pepper, and drizzled with olive oil.

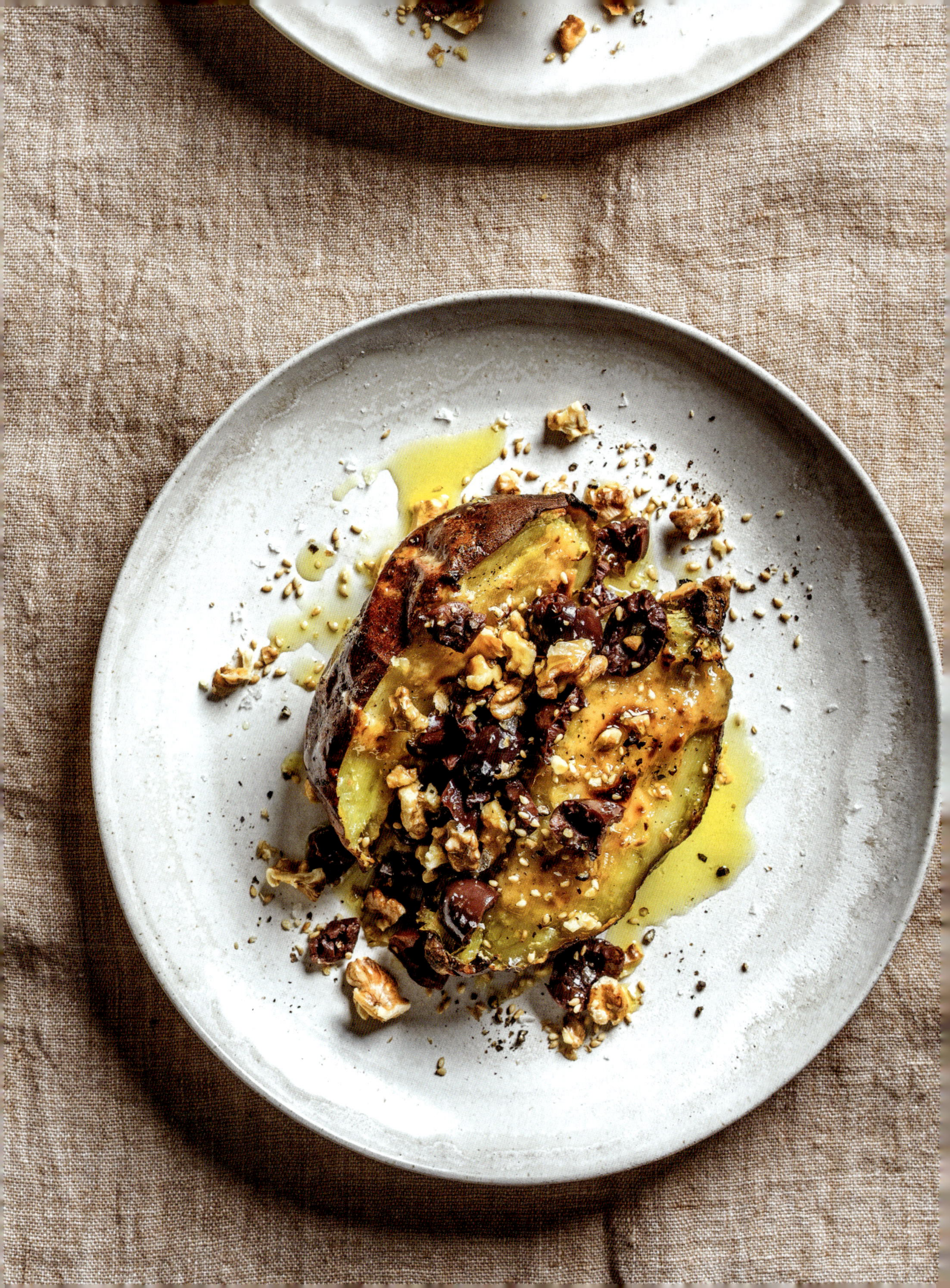

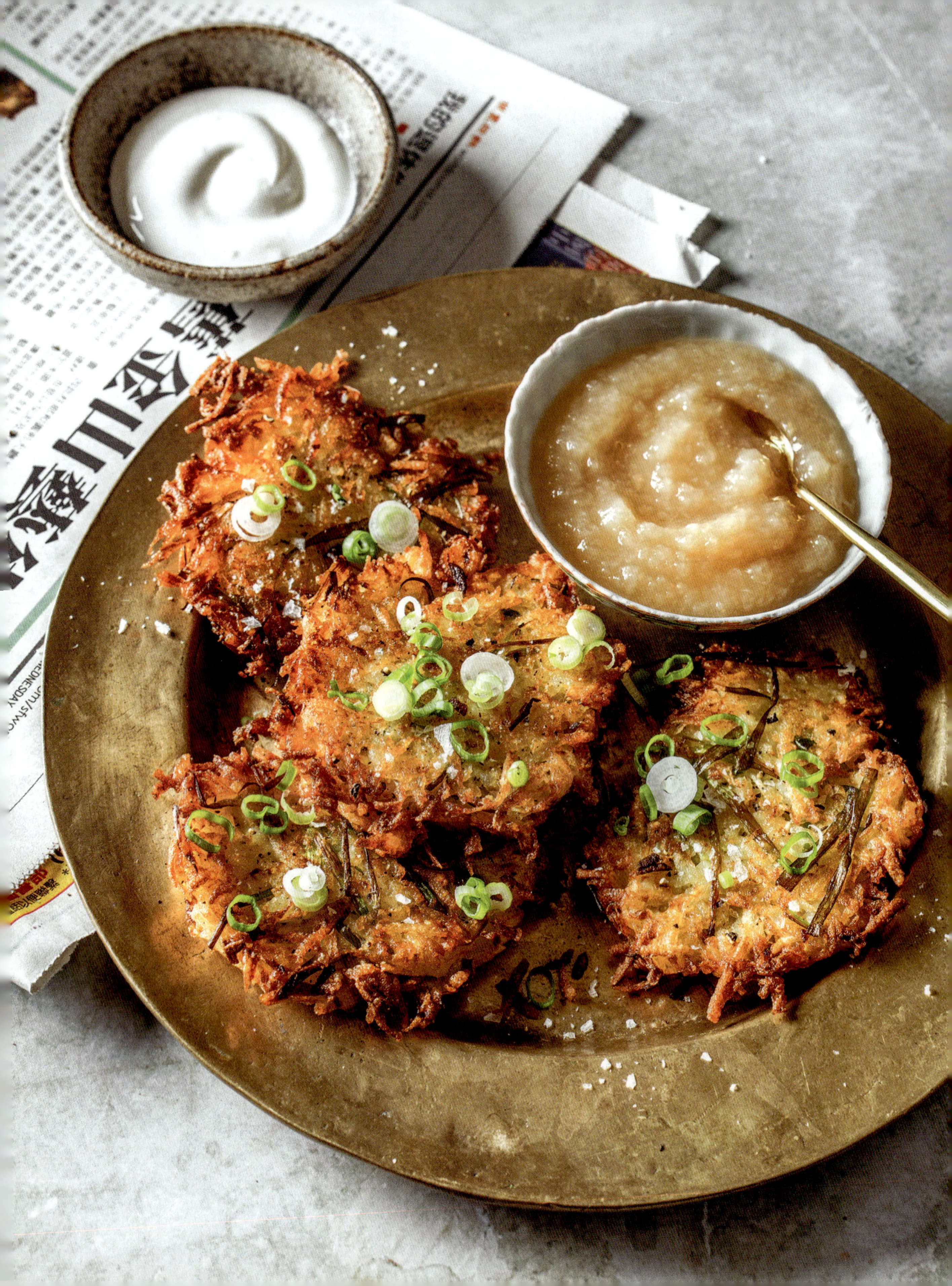

SCALLION HASH BROWNS WITH CRÈME FRAÎCHE AND ASIAN PEAR

Nothing's better than golden, crispy hash browns. I like mine with cold crème fraîche and sweet-tart Asian pear sauce. I've picked up a few techniques from making latkes with Jewish friends during Hanukkah that I use to maximize crunch, including squeezing the moisture out of shredded russet potatoes and onions and binding them with egg and potato starch. If you'd like, add a dollop of beef tallow to the frying oil—while it might not be kosher, it makes them extra crispy.

SERVES 4 TO 6

Equipment: Cheesecloth

ASIAN PEAR SAUCE

2 pounds Asian pears (about 2), peeled, cored, and sliced

1 pound Fuji or Gala apples (about 2), peeled, cored, and sliced

¼ cup white sugar

Pinch of Diamond Crystal kosher salt

½ cup water

1 teaspoon lemon juice

SCALLION HASH BROWNS

2 pounds russet potatoes (about 4)

1 small yellow onion, halved lengthwise and peeled

6 scallions, cut into 2-inch julienne

1 large egg

2 tablespoons potato starch

1 teaspoon Diamond Crystal kosher salt, plus more for sprinkling

¼ teaspoon finely ground black pepper, plus more for sprinkling

Canola oil (about 2 cups), for shallow-frying

Flaky sea salt

Thinly sliced scallions, for garnish

Crème fraîche, for serving

Make the Asian pear sauce: In a medium pot, combine the pears, apples, sugar, salt, and water and bring to a boil over high heat. Reduce the heat to cook at a gentle simmer, covered, stirring occasionally, until the fruit is very soft, about 30 minutes. Uncover, increase the heat, and simmer, stirring frequently, until most of the liquid has evaporated, 15 to 20 minutes.

Transfer to a blender, add the lemon juice, and blend on low, gradually increasing the speed to medium-high, until smooth, 10 to 20 seconds.

Cool completely, then refrigerate until chilled, at least 30 minutes or up to 1 week.

Make the hash browns: Peel the potatoes and keep them submerged in water to prevent discoloration.

Line a large bowl with two layers of cheesecloth. Using the large holes of a box grater (or the grating disc of a food processor), grate the onion into the cheesecloth-lined bowl. Grate the potatoes into the bowl as well.

Gather the cheesecloth around the potatoes and onion, then squeeze out and discard as much liquid as possible. Return the potatoes and onion to the large bowl and add the scallions, egg, potato starch, salt, and pepper and toss well.

Line a large sheet pan with paper towels. Pour ½ inch oil into a large skillet and heat over medium-high heat for about 2 minutes. When the oil is ready, the end of a wooden chopstick or wooden spoon submerged in the oil will immediately release little bubbles.

Working in batches, spoon a scant ¼ cup of the potato mixture per hash brown into the oil and gently flatten to a 3-inch round, leaving a little space around each one. Fry, flipping once, until deep golden brown and crispy on both sides, 4 to 5 minutes total. Transfer to the rack, and immediately sprinkle lightly with kosher salt and black pepper. Between batches, scoop out and discard any bits remaining in the oil, and let the oil heat back up.

Serve warm, sprinkled with flaky salt and the sliced scallions, alongside the Asian pear sauce and crème fraîche.

SHOYU BUTTER MUSHROOMS

The flavor of Japanese shoyu butter mushrooms joins forces with the French technique of confit, and the pairing makes your kitchen smell amazing. Meaty king trumpets, like little flavor sponges, absorb the pleasures of butter, shoyu (soy sauce), ginger, and garlic. (So do fresh porcinis and portobellos, so feel free to play around!) Once they're cooked, halve and sear the mushrooms for a side dish or put slices on toast, pizza, and focaccia (page 82). Cooking these mushrooms also leaves you with sweet, spreadable cloves of garlic and a bounty of aromatic butter super-charged with umami that's fantastic on steak, garlic noodles (page 109), grilled corn on the cob, and crusty bread.

MAKES ABOUT 10 MUSHROOMS, 2 HEADS OF GARLIC, AND 3 CUPS BUTTER

1 pound small king trumpet mushrooms (about 10)

8 sticks (2 pounds) unsalted butter

2 heads garlic, bases trimmed, tops cut off to expose the cloves

1 small bunch thyme

3 tablespoons Japanese soy sauce

2 tablespoons mirin

1 teaspoon white sugar

8 by 3 inches kombu (dried kelp)

2 by 1-inch knob ginger, peeled and smashed

Preheat the oven to 275°F.

Trim off ¼ inch from the base of each mushroom, reserving the trim for stock, like Weekend Broth (page 244). If the mushrooms are thicker than 1½ inches in diameter, halve them lengthwise.

In a 4- to 6-quart ovenproof pot, combine the butter, garlic, and thyme and set over medium-high heat. Let the butter melt completely, about 8 minutes. Add the mushrooms, soy sauce, mirin, sugar, kombu, and ginger, stir gently, and let the liquid bubble. It's fine if the mushrooms aren't fully submerged.

Cover the pot, transfer it to the oven, and cook, stirring occasionally and reducing the oven temperature if necessary to keep the butter at a moderate bubble, until the garlic cloves are soft, 1 to 1¼ hours. The mushrooms will have shrunken and they'll be knife-tender and darker from having absorbed the soy sauce. Remove from the oven and let sit, covered, for 30 minutes.

Discard the thyme, ginger, and kombu. Transfer the mushrooms and garlic to separate containers. Strain the butter into a different heatproof container. (The mushrooms and garlic keep in airtight containers in the refrigerator for up to 5 days. The butter keeps frozen for up to 3 months.)

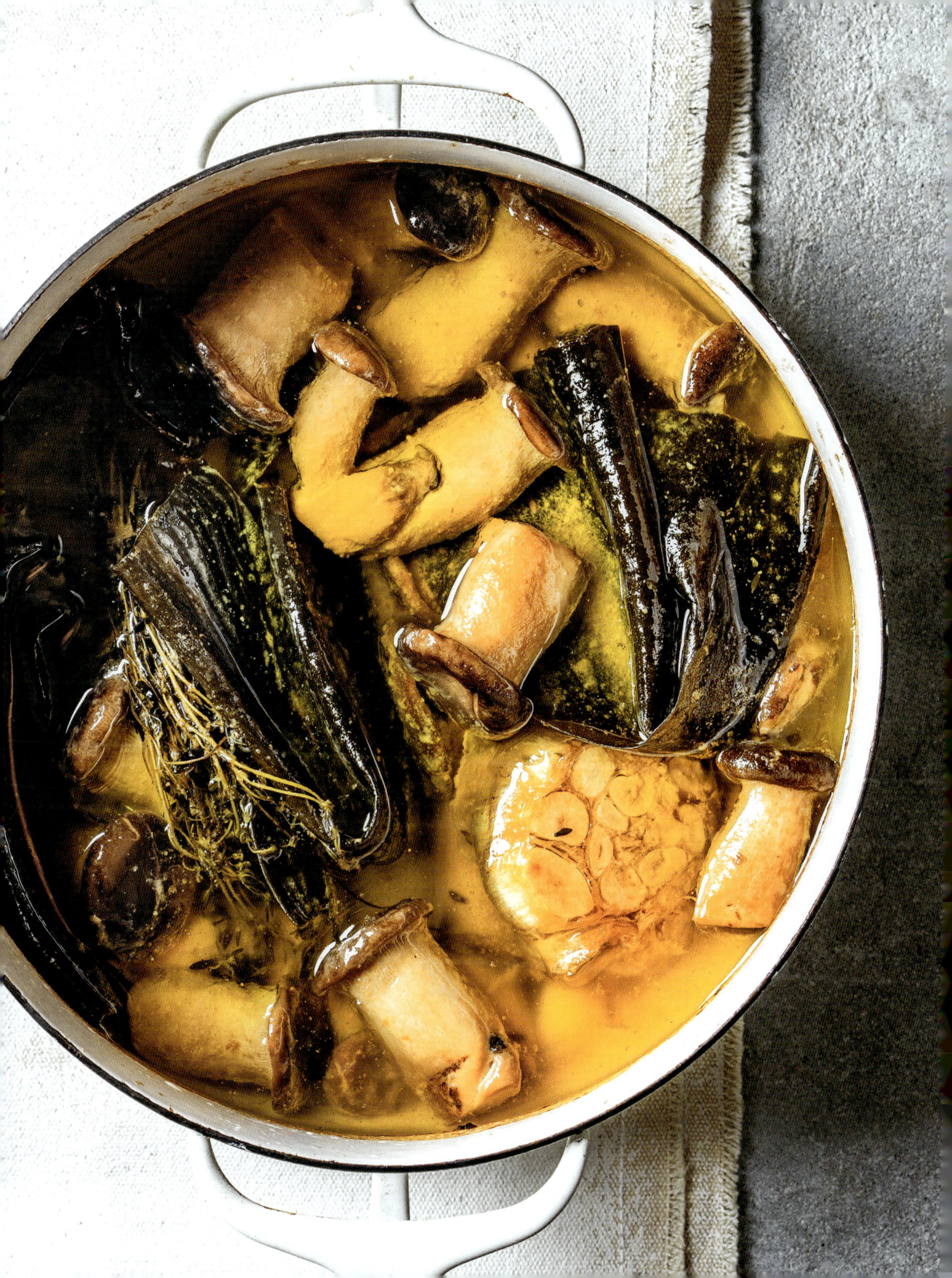

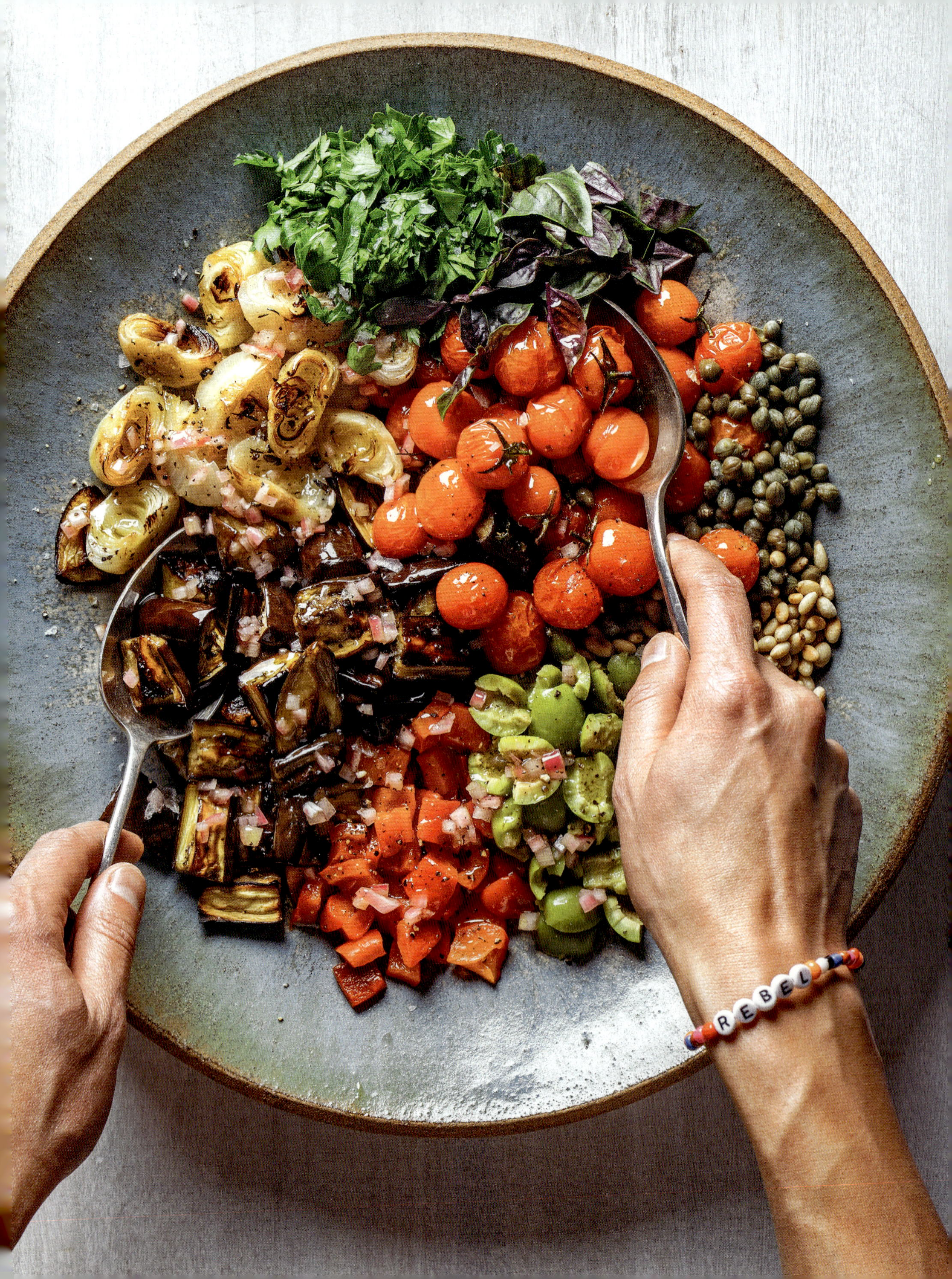
REBEL

EGGPLANT CAPONATA

Caponata is a celebration of summer in a bowl. While many delicious renditions of the Italian dish eat like braised vegetables, mine is closer to a bright salad. I dress caramelized cubes of creamy eggplant, smoky roasted peppers, and sweet cherry tomatoes in a sharp red wine vinaigrette and toss in briny capers and olives, toasted pine nuts, and handfuls of fresh herbs. It goes great with fried garlic toast (page 59), rib eye steak (page 196), crispy-skinned salmon (page 180), and Salt-Baked Whole Fish (page 172).

LEVEL IT UP

Toss in Olive Oil–Fried Sourdough Croutons (page 255) for panzanella vibes.

SERVES 4 TO 6

6 cups 1-inch cubes Italian or globe eggplant

Diamond Crystal kosher salt

1 red bell pepper

6 medium garlic cloves, lightly smashed and peeled, divided

Extra-virgin olive oil

1 pint cherry tomatoes

Finely ground black pepper

3 tablespoons red wine vinegar, plus more as needed

1 small shallot, minced

1 cup Cipollini Onions Agrodolce (page 249)

¼ cup pitted Castelvetrano olives, roughly chopped

2 tablespoons drained capers

2 tablespoons toasted pine nuts

Large handful of basil leaves, roughly chopped at the last minute

Large handful of flat-leaf parsley leaves, roughly chopped

Position racks in the upper third and lower third of the oven and preheat the oven to 400°F.

In a large bowl, toss the eggplant with 2 teaspoons salt and let sit for 10 minutes to release moisture and season the eggplant. Discard any liquid that collects in the bowl.

Transfer the eggplant to a large (18 by 13-inch) sheet pan. Add the whole bell pepper and 3 of the garlic cloves, drizzle on ½ cup oil, and toss to coat well, spreading out the eggplant in a single layer with a little space around the pieces. On a small (9 by 13-inch) sheet pan, toss together the tomatoes, the remaining garlic cloves, 2 tablespoons oil, ½ teaspoon salt, and several turns of pepper, arranging it all in a single layer.

Slide the small sheet pan onto the upper rack and roast the tomatoes until their skins split, about 10 minutes. At the same time, slide the larger sheet pan onto the lower rack and roast, turning the bell pepper occasionally and stirring the eggplant halfway through, until the pepper is tender, blistered, and browned and the eggplant is deep brown and crispy, 25 to 30 minutes.

Let the vegetables cool slightly in the sheet pans. Stem the bell pepper, remove the seeds and veins, and pull off any loose skin (it's okay if some remains). Cut the pepper into roughly ¾-inch dice.

In a small bowl, combine the vinegar, shallot, and a pinch of salt, stir well, and let sit for 2 minutes to tame the shallot's sharpness. Slowly drizzle in 3 tablespoons oil, whisking constantly, until thickened and emulsified.

In a large serving bowl, arrange the eggplant, bell pepper, tomatoes (and any juices), garlic, cipollini onions, olives, capers, pine nuts, and herbs. At the table, add a big pinch of salt, several turns of pepper, and the vinaigrette. Toss well and serve warm or at room temperature. It's best served the day you make it.

ROASTED KABOCHA WITH FIVE SPICE AND HOT HONEY

If you ask me, everyone needs a solid roasted winter squash recipe in their repertoire, and this one is low effort with big flavor. Kabocha squash (also called Japanese pumpkin) is a variety known for its fluffy, tender interior, chestnut-like flavor, and exceptional sweetness. Once the tough outer skin is cooked, it's completely edible. The warm notes of Chinese five spice complement the squash's natural sweetness. Apple cider vinegar brings a little brightness. And a good drizzle of my hot honey contributes sweet heat.

LEVEL IT UP

Serve the squash on a creamy bed of labneh, store-bought or homemade (page 32).

SWITCH IT UP

Play around with other winter squashes, like butternut or the super-cute and flavorful Honeynut.

SERVES 4 TO 6

- One 3-pound kabocha squash, trimmed, seeded, and cut into 2-inch-thick wedges
- ¼ cup plus 1 tablespoon extra-virgin olive oil
- 2 tablespoons plus 1½ teaspoons apple cider vinegar
- 2 teaspoons Diamond Crystal kosher salt
- ½ teaspoon Chinese five spice powder
- Finely ground black pepper
- 3 large garlic cloves, lightly smashed and peeled
- Small handful of thyme sprigs
- 3 tablespoons well-stirred King's Hot Honey (page 251)
- Flaky sea salt

Position a rack in the bottom slot of the oven and preheat the oven to 400°F.

In a large mixing bowl, combine the squash, ¼ cup of the olive oil, 2 tablespoons of the vinegar, the kosher salt, five spice, a few turns of pepper, garlic, and thyme sprigs and toss well.

Transfer to a large (18 by 13-inch) sheet pan and arrange the squash, cut-sides down and with some space around the wedges. Roast on the bottom rack, flipping once halfway through, until a knife inserted into the flesh meets no resistance and the squash is caramelized and slightly charred at the edges, 30 to 35 minutes.

Transfer the squash, garlic, and thyme to a serving platter. In a small bowl, combine the honey, remaining 1 tablespoon olive oil, and remaining 1½ teaspoons vinegar and stir well. Drizzle on the honey mixture, sprinkle on a little flaky salt, and serve.

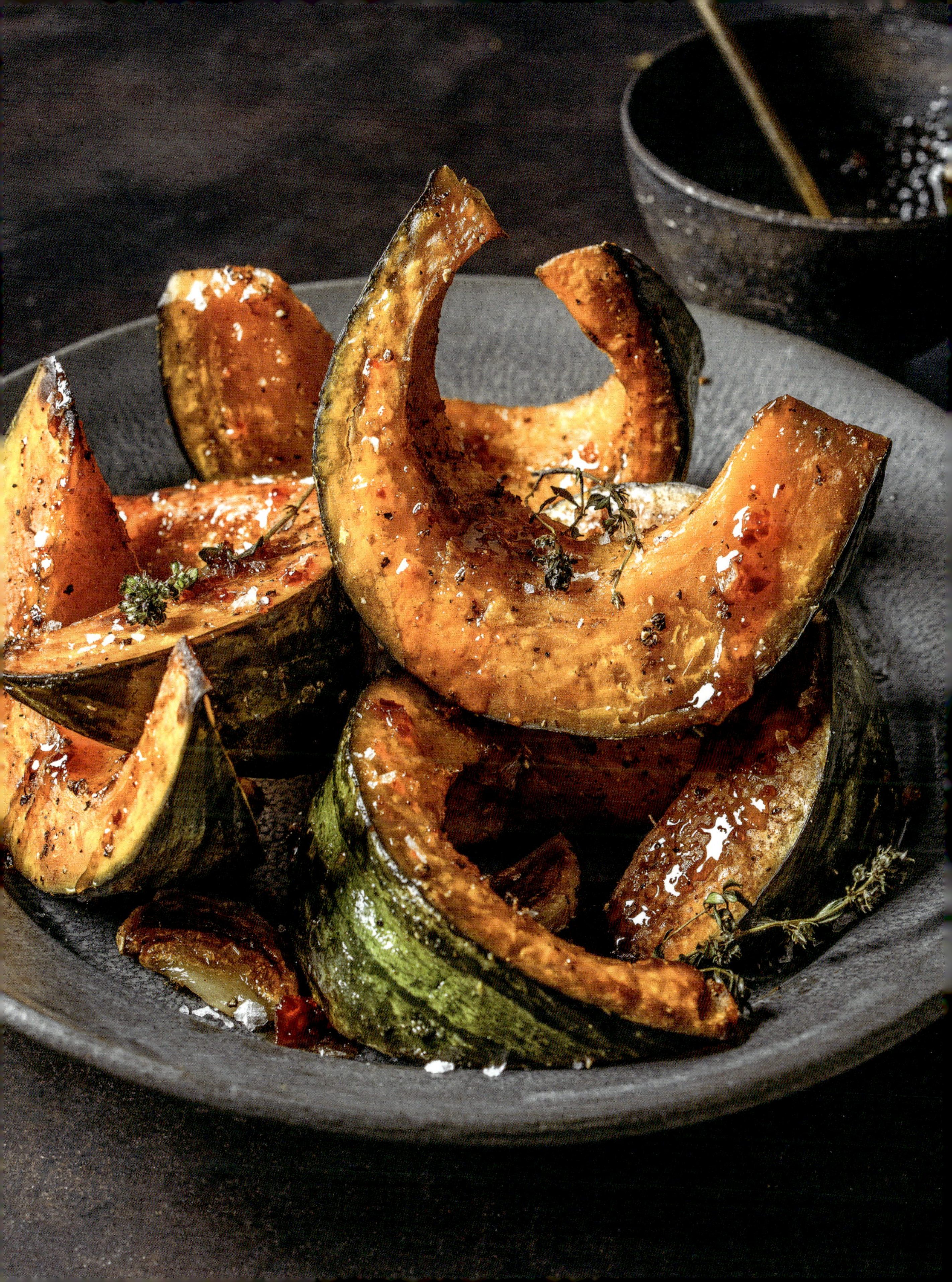

REALLY F***ING CRISPY POTATOES WITH RACLETTE AND CORNICHONS

CRISPY POTATOES

1½ pounds baby yellow or fingerling potatoes, scrubbed

1 cup Diamond Crystal kosher salt, plus more for seasoning

6 medium garlic cloves, lightly smashed and peeled, divided

5 sprigs rosemary, divided

¾ cup extra-virgin olive oil

¼ cup beef tallow, warmed

Finely ground black pepper

RACLETTE MORNAY

1 tablespoon unsalted butter

1 tablespoon all-purpose flour

½ cup whole milk, warmed

1 small garlic clove, finely grated on a Microplane

1 cup coarsely grated raclette cheese (about 3½ ounces)

¼ teaspoon Diamond Crystal kosher salt

Coarsely ground black pepper

Pinch of ground nutmeg

TO SERVE

Flaky sea salt

Coarsely ground black pepper

Small handful of thinly sliced chives

¼ cup cornichons, thinly sliced

In London's Borough Market, I was wowed by a simple plate of boiled potatoes with melty raclette cheese, lots of cracked black pepper, and crisp, briny cornichons. It inspired this fun version that I came up with for "Restaurant Wars" during *Top Chef: All-Stars*. You can absolutely roast with all olive oil, though a little beef tallow is the secret to really f***ing crispy potatoes.

SWITCH IT UP

Make the raclette mornay for steamed asparagus or mac and cheese. Serve the crispy potatoes with Cumin-Shiso Tzatziki (page 128).

SERVES 4 TO 6

Make the crispy potatoes: In a medium pot, combine the potatoes, 8 cups water, the salt, 3 of the garlic cloves, and 2 of the rosemary sprigs. If necessary, add more water to cover the potatoes by at least ½ inch. Bring to a boil over high heat. Turn the heat down to cook at a gentle simmer just until tender, 25 to 30 minutes.

Remove from the heat and let the potatoes sit in the water for 5 minutes, to let them gently finish cooking. Drain well, discard the garlic and rosemary, and set aside until cool enough to handle. (The potatoes keep in the refrigerator for up to 3 days.)

Position a rack in the center of the oven and preheat the oven to 450°F.

Put the potatoes on a large (18 by 13-inch) sheet pan and press to slightly flatten each one. Add the remaining 3 garlic cloves, remaining 3 rosemary sprigs, olive oil, and beef tallow. Lightly season with salt and pepper, and toss to coat well, arranging the potatoes in a single layer with a little space around each one. Roast, flipping once, until golden brown and crispy, 30 to 40 minutes.

Meanwhile, make the mornay: In a small saucepan, melt the butter over medium heat. Add the flour and whisk for 30 seconds. While whisking, pour in the milk in a steady stream until completely smooth. Whisk in the garlic. Simmer, whisking, until thick enough to coat the back of a spoon, about 2 minutes. Remove from the heat and whisk in the raclette, salt, a few turns of pepper, and nutmeg until the cheese melts completely, about 1 minute. Remove from the heat and cover to keep warm.

Serve: Plate the crispy potatoes (leaving the fat behind) and sprinkle with flaky salt, pepper, and chives. Serve alongside the mornay and cornichons.

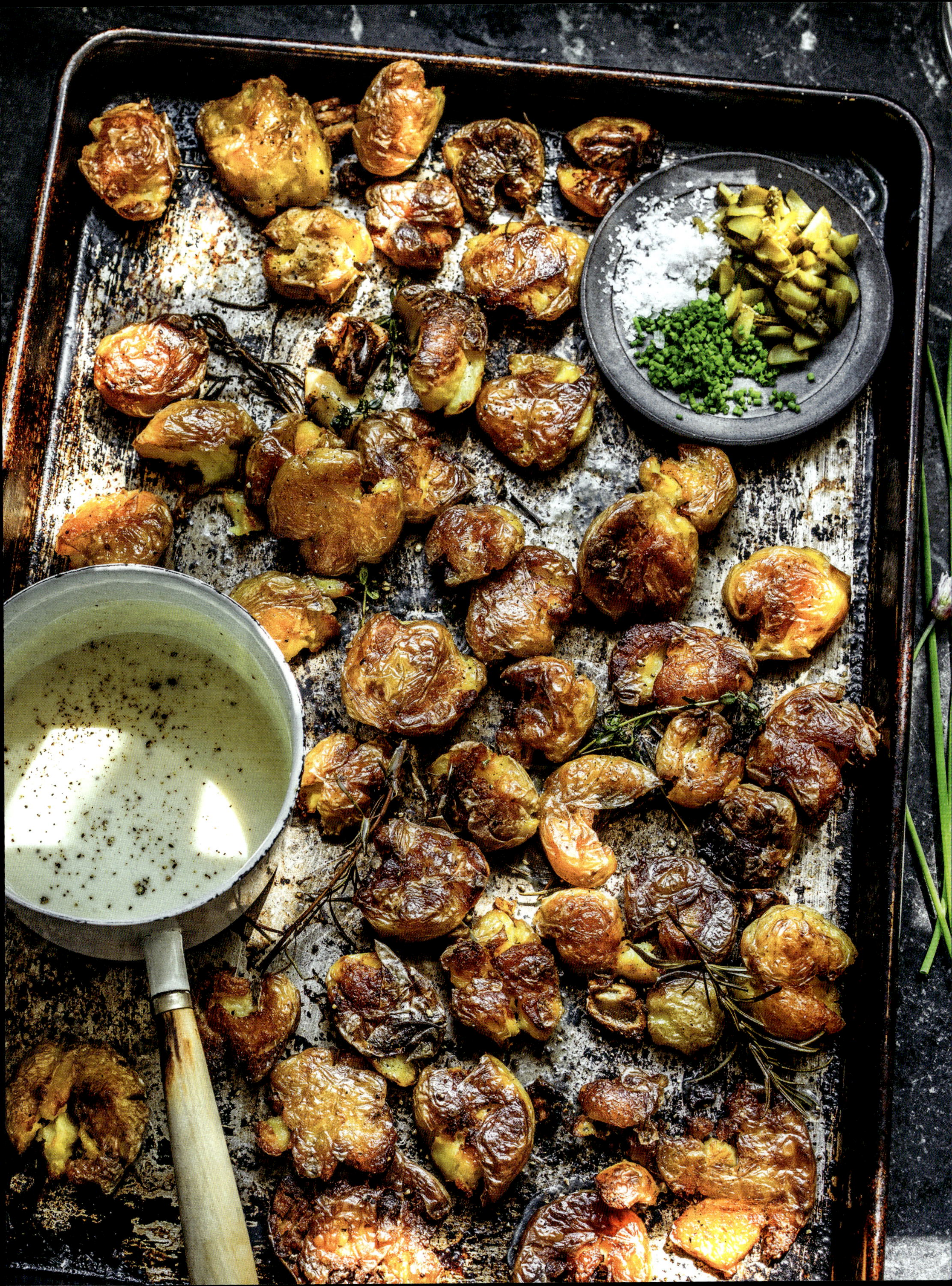

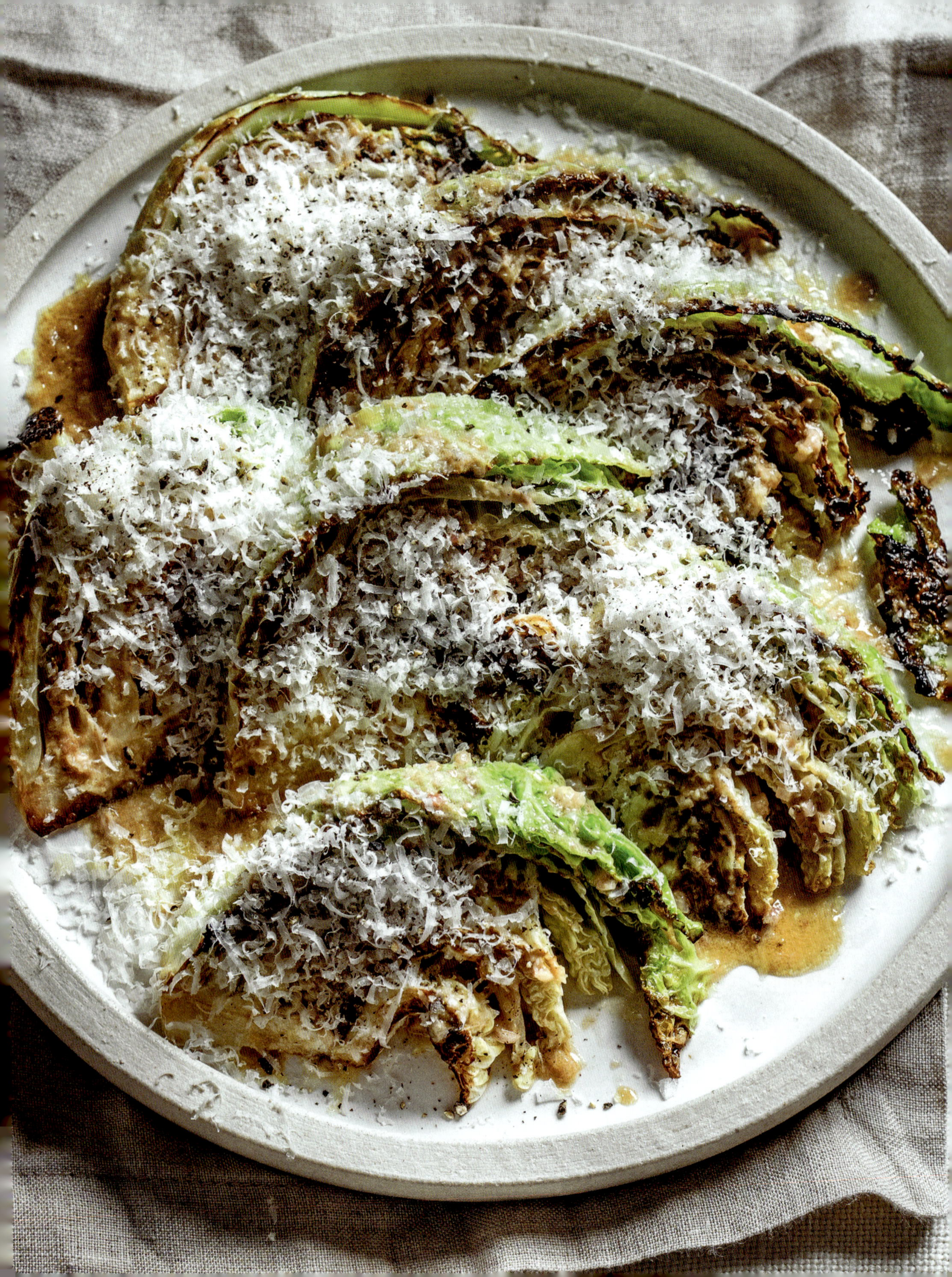

CHARRED CABBAGE WITH BURNT LEMON–ANCHOVY VINAIGRETTE

Cabbage makes a solid background player, but it also has the potential to be a star. When you char the humble vegetable, you enhance its sweetness and it takes on a soft crunch. The vinaigrette that trickles between the leaves eats like a bright Caesar dressing with the added complexity that comes from charring lemons before juicing. I provide skillet instructions, but it's awesome on the grill.

LEVEL IT UP

Top with Fried Bread Crumbs (page 256) or Lap Cheong Crumble (page 256).

SWITCH IT UP

Skip the dressing and cheese and brush the charred cabbage generously with Fish Sauce Caramel (page 250) or toss with melted Black Garlic–Anchovy Butter (page 252).

SERVES 4 TO 6

VINAIGRETTE

2 large, juicy lemons, halved

1 medium garlic clove, peeled

Diamond Crystal kosher salt

5 oil-packed anchovy fillets

1 tablespoon Dijon mustard

1 tablespoon minced shallot

Finely ground black pepper

¼ cup extra-virgin olive oil

CABBAGE

1 small head green or Savoy cabbage (about 1 pound)

¼ cup canola oil, plus more as needed

½ teaspoon Diamond Crystal kosher salt

Coarsely ground black pepper

Flaky sea salt

Wedge of Parmigiano-Reggiano, for serving

Make the vinaigrette: Set a large cast-iron skillet or heavy pan over high heat until it smokes lightly. Add the lemons cut-sides down and let them brown and char, undisturbed, about 2 minutes. Set aside.

Combine the garlic and a generous pinch of salt in a mortar and pound to a paste. Add the anchovies and pound to a smooth paste. (Alternatively, mince and mash on a cutting board and scrape into a mixing bowl.) Stir in the mustard, shallot, ½ teaspoon salt, a few turns of pepper, and ¼ cup charred-lemon juice. Slowly drizzle in the olive oil, whisking constantly, until thickened and emulsified.

Make the cabbage: Trim the base of the cabbage and remove any bruised leaves. Cut the cabbage into 1¼-inch wedges through the core, so the wedges stay intact.

Set the skillet over high heat for 2 minutes. Add the canola oil, swirl the pan, and let it smoke lightly. Working in batches to avoid crowding, cook the cabbage wedges cut-sides down and undisturbed until well charred, 2 to 3 minutes. Season the top side of each wedge with a generous pinch of kosher salt and pepper to taste, then flip and char the second side, 2 to 3 minutes more. Add another few tablespoons of oil for subsequent batches.

Arrange the cabbage wedges on a serving plate and drizzle with about half of the vinaigrette (or more to taste), making sure some gets in between the leaves. Sprinkle with flaky salt and black pepper and use a Microplane to grate on a generous amount of Parmigiano. Serve warm.

CORN SOUP WITH CHILI CRISP AND PUFFED WILD RICE

I think of soup as a testament to a chef's skill. With care and technique to build and layer flavors, seemingly simple soup can be a showstopper—and a competition winner. This velvety soup won me a *Top Chef: All Stars* challenge. It captures the beauty of corn at its peak sweetness. I extract as much flavor as possible from summer corn, scraping the cobs for any lingering juices and simmering the cobs (or "corn bones") to make a flavorful stock. Subtle notes of ginger make an unexpected but welcome showing, and playful garnishes like puffed wild rice and chili oil guarantee your guests will ask for seconds.

SWITCH IT UP

For an equally tasty plant-based version, skip the butter and swap in coconut milk for the heavy cream.

SERVES 4 TO 6

CORN STOCK

4 large ears yellow or white corn, shucked

1 medium yellow onion, peeled and quartered

2 by 1-inch knob ginger, peeled and lightly smashed

2 garlic cloves, lightly smashed and peeled

10 cups water

SOUP

1 tablespoon canola oil

1 medium yellow onion, thinly sliced

4 garlic cloves, minced

1 teaspoon finely grated ginger

Diamond Crystal kosher salt

¼ cup water

1 cup heavy cream

½ teaspoon white sugar

4 tablespoons (2 ounces) unsalted butter

1 tablespoon lemon or lime juice

3 tablespoons chili oil from King's Chili Crisp (page 257) or store-bought Chinese chili oil

About ½ cup Puffed Wild Rice (page 257)

Handful of micro cilantro or cilantro leaves

Coarsely ground black pepper

Make the corn stock: Working over a bowl, cut the kernels from the ears of corn, then use the blade of the knife to scrape the cobs over the bowl to access any juices and remaining bits of kernels. Set aside. Break the cobs in half and reserve for the stock.

In a large pot, combine the corn cobs, onion, ginger, garlic, and water. Bring to a boil over high heat. Reduce the heat to cook at a moderate simmer, uncovered, for 1 hour to extract the sweetness and flavor from the cobs. Strain into a container, discarding the solids.

Make the soup: Heat a medium pot over medium-high heat for 1 minute. Add the oil, and let it shimmer. Add the onion, garlic, ginger, and a pinch of salt and cook, stirring frequently, for 1 minute. Add the water, turn the heat down to medium-low, and cook, covered, stirring occasionally, until the onions are soft, 8 to 10 minutes.

Add the kernel mixture, then increase the heat to medium and cook, uncovered and stirring occasionally, until the kernels pick up a little color, about 5 minutes. Add 4 cups of the corn stock and bring to a simmer. Cover the pot and simmer gently, stirring occasionally, for about 30 minutes to extract and meld the flavors. Stir in the heavy cream, sugar, and 1½ teaspoons salt and simmer, uncovered, for 3 minutes more.

Transfer half the corn mixture to a blender and add 2 tablespoons of the butter. Starting on low speed and gradually increasing to high speed, blend until smooth and velvety, about 2 minutes. Pour through a fine-mesh sieve into a clean medium pot, pressing down on the solids to extract as much liquid as possible. Repeat with the remaining corn mixture and butter. Stir in the lemon juice. If necessary, gradually add some of the remaining corn stock or water to thin the soup to the consistency of heavy cream. Season to taste with salt and whisk well before serving.

Serve hot or chilled topped with the chili oil, puffed wild rice, cilantro, and a few turns of black pepper.

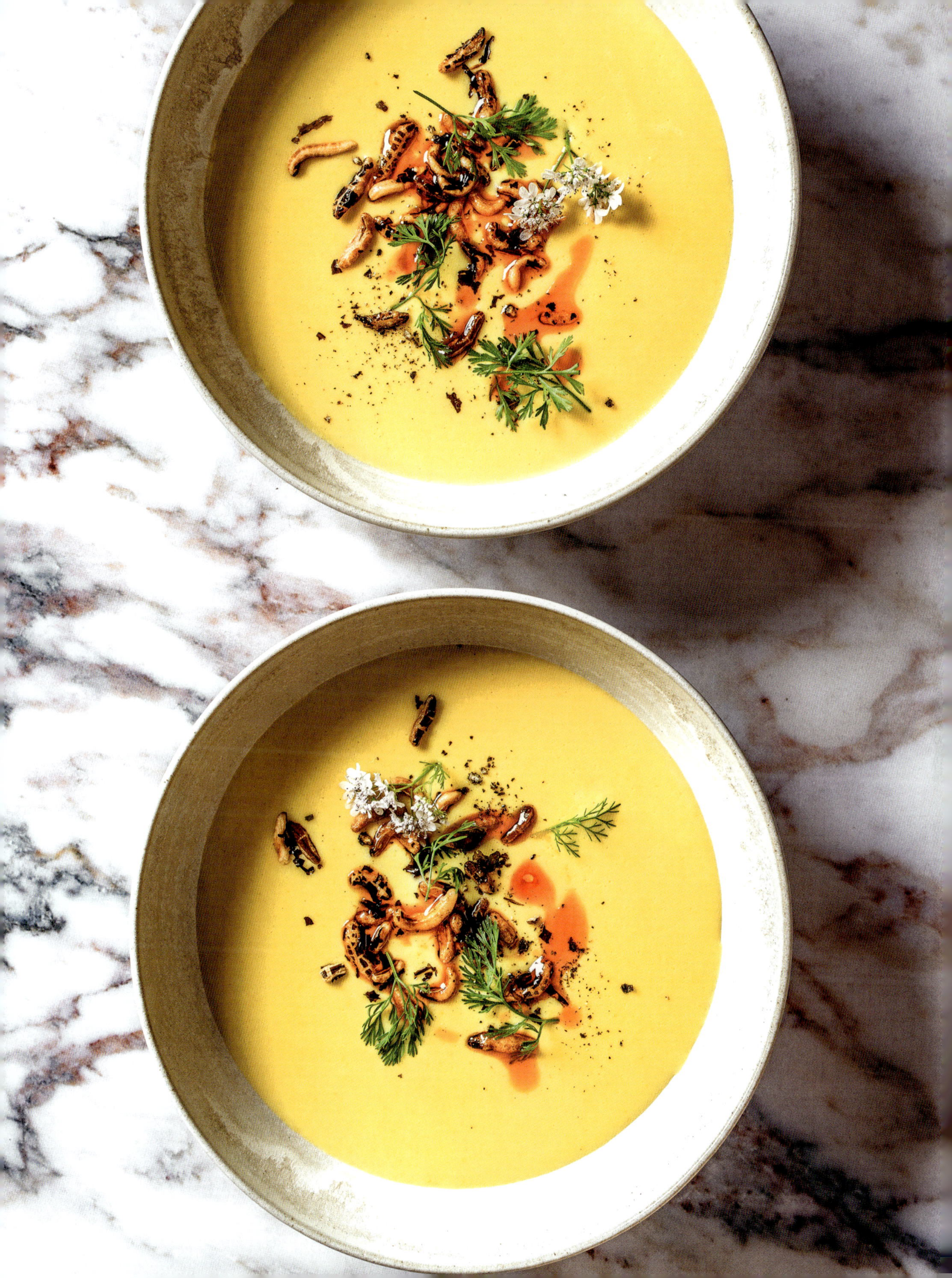

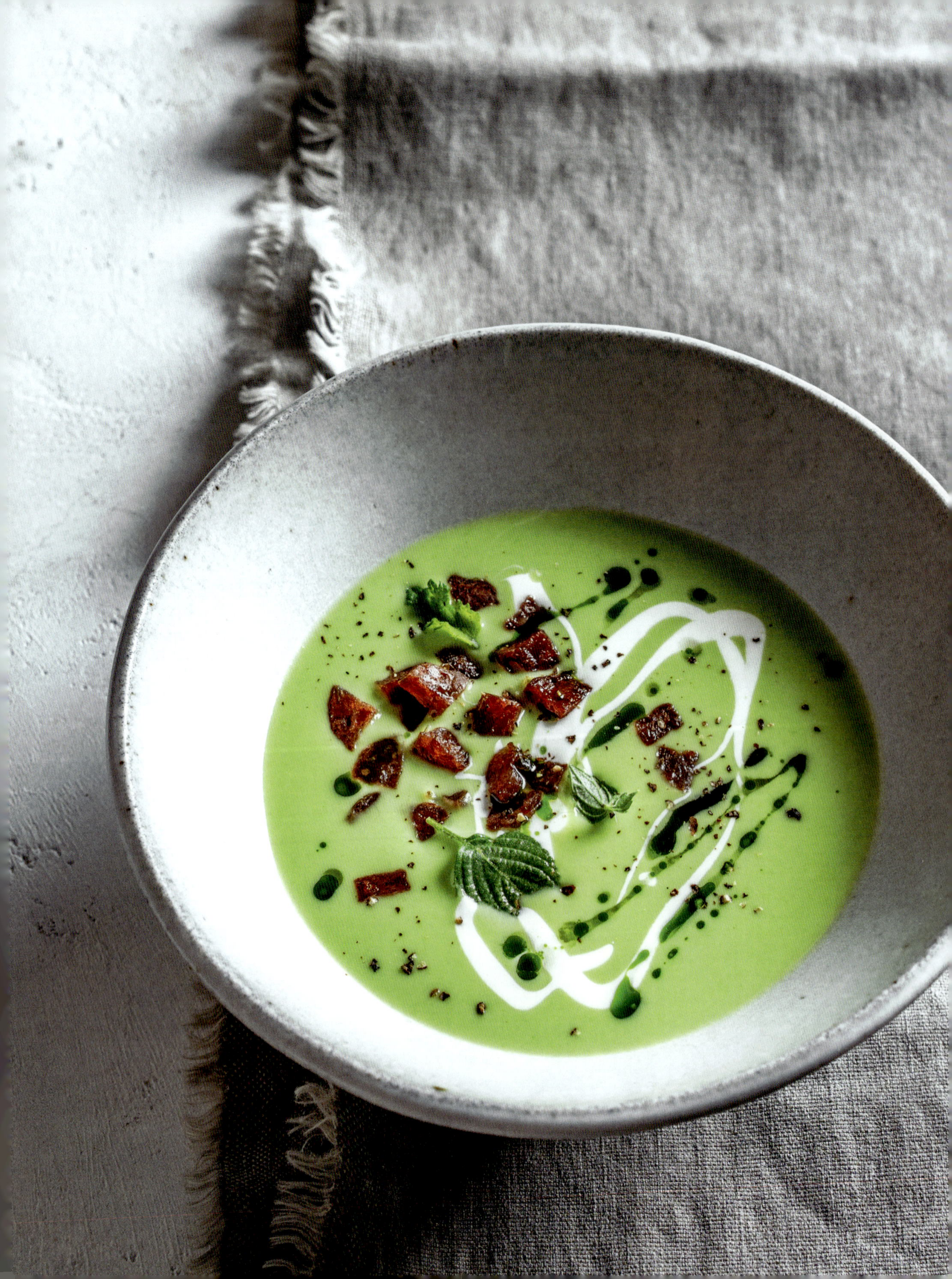

PEA SOUP WITH COCONUT MILK, LAP CHEONG, AND GREEN OIL

I've spent countless hours making pea puree in Michelin-starred kitchens. Not only are fresh peas extremely tedious to shell, but unless they're harvested during a small window in early spring, they're also often overly starchy. But frozen peas, a modern food miracle, spare you endless effort and allow you to make this elegant soup in minutes. Vibrant green and full of spring sweetness (even in the dead of winter), it gets a velvety richness from coconut milk and Agrumato lemon oil, a secret weapon in my pantry that you'll use again and again. Bacon lardons would be lovely on top, but sweet and savory lap cheong is even better.

This soup also tastes great chilled. Before serving, thin with a touch of water, if necessary, and reseason with salt.

LEVEL IT UP

Add texture with Fried Shallots (page 254), Puffed Wild Rice (page 257), or Fried Bread Crumbs (page 256).

SERVES 4

Diamond Crystal kosher salt

One 16-ounce bag frozen peas (3⅓ cups)

One 13.5-ounce can full-fat coconut milk, well shaken

¼ cup Agrumato lemon oil

2 links lap cheong (Chinese pork sausage), diced

Charred Green Oil (page 248), for garnish

A small handful of mint or shiso, torn right before serving

Coarsely ground black pepper

In a medium pot, bring 8 cups water and 3 tablespoons salt to a boil. Meanwhile, fill a large bowl with half ice and half water. Grab a sieve that can hold all the peas comfortably and can fit in the bowl.

When the water is boiling, add the peas and cook, stirring occasionally, until tender all the way through but still vibrant green, 2 to 3 minutes. Drain the peas in the sieve, then transfer the sieve to the bowl of ice water. Briefly stir the peas in the sieve, then let them sit in the ice water for 10 minutes to lock in their vibrant green color. Lift the sieve to drain them well.

Working in batches if necessary, transfer the peas, most of the coconut milk (reserve ¼ cup for garnish), the lemon oil, 1 tablespoon salt, and ½ cup fresh water to a high-powered blender. Start blending on low speed, gradually increasing the speed to high, and blend until velvety smooth, about 2 minutes. Strain through a fine-mesh sieve into a clean medium pot, stirring and gently pressing, then discarding any solids. If necessary, gradually add water until the soup has the texture of heavy cream. Adjust the seasoning with salt to taste and cover to keep warm off the heat.

Cook the lap cheong in a medium skillet over medium heat, stirring occasionally, until golden brown and slightly crispy, 2 to 3 minutes.

Ladle the soup into bowls. Garnish with the sausage and a drizzle of the fat from the pan along with charred green oil and the reserved coconut milk. Tear the mint and shiso leaves and add them to each bowl along with a few turns of pepper. Serve immediately.

GREEN BEANS WITH PANCETTA AND CARAMELIZED SOY SAUCE

When I'm at a Chinese restaurant, I almost always order green beans, which are deep-fried to delicious oblivion. At home, however, I cook them in a hot skillet until crisp-tender and swap out the ground pork found in many Chinese renditions for Italian pancetta, because why not? Bacon or lap cheong (Chinese sausage) would be equally delicious. Dark and light soy sauces and a good dose of sugar make a sweet and savory sauce that coats the beans.

SWITCH IT UP

Try the dish with snow peas, snap peas, asparagus, or bok choy.

SERVES 2 TO 4

1 tablespoon extra-virgin olive oil

¼ cup diced (¼- to ½-inch) pancetta, bacon, or lap cheong (Chinese pork sausage)

½ cup diced (¼-inch) yellow onion

½ pound green beans (or other pole beans), trimmed

2 medium garlic cloves, thinly sliced

2 teaspoons finely grated ginger

1 tablespoon white sugar

1 tablespoon Chinese dark soy sauce

2 teaspoons Chinese light soy sauce

2 teaspoons Shaoxing wine

Finely ground black pepper

Toasted sesame oil, for drizzling

Heat a large skillet over medium heat for 1 minute. Add the oil and swirl to coat the skillet. When the oil shimmers, add the pancetta and cook, stirring occasionally, until it begins to render its fat, about 1 minute. Add the onion and cook, stirring, until the pancetta is golden brown and the onions are translucent with a little color, about 2 minutes.

Increase the heat to high, then add the beans and cook, stirring occasionally, for 3 minutes. Stir in the garlic and ginger and cook, stirring frequently, until the garlic is light golden brown and fragrant, about 15 seconds.

Add the sugar, dark soy sauce, light soy sauce, Shaoxing wine, a few turns of black pepper, and a splash of water and cook for 15 to 30 seconds, stirring until the liquid reduces to a glaze and the beans are tender but still slightly crisp and bright green.

Add a drizzle of sesame oil, stir, and serve immediately.

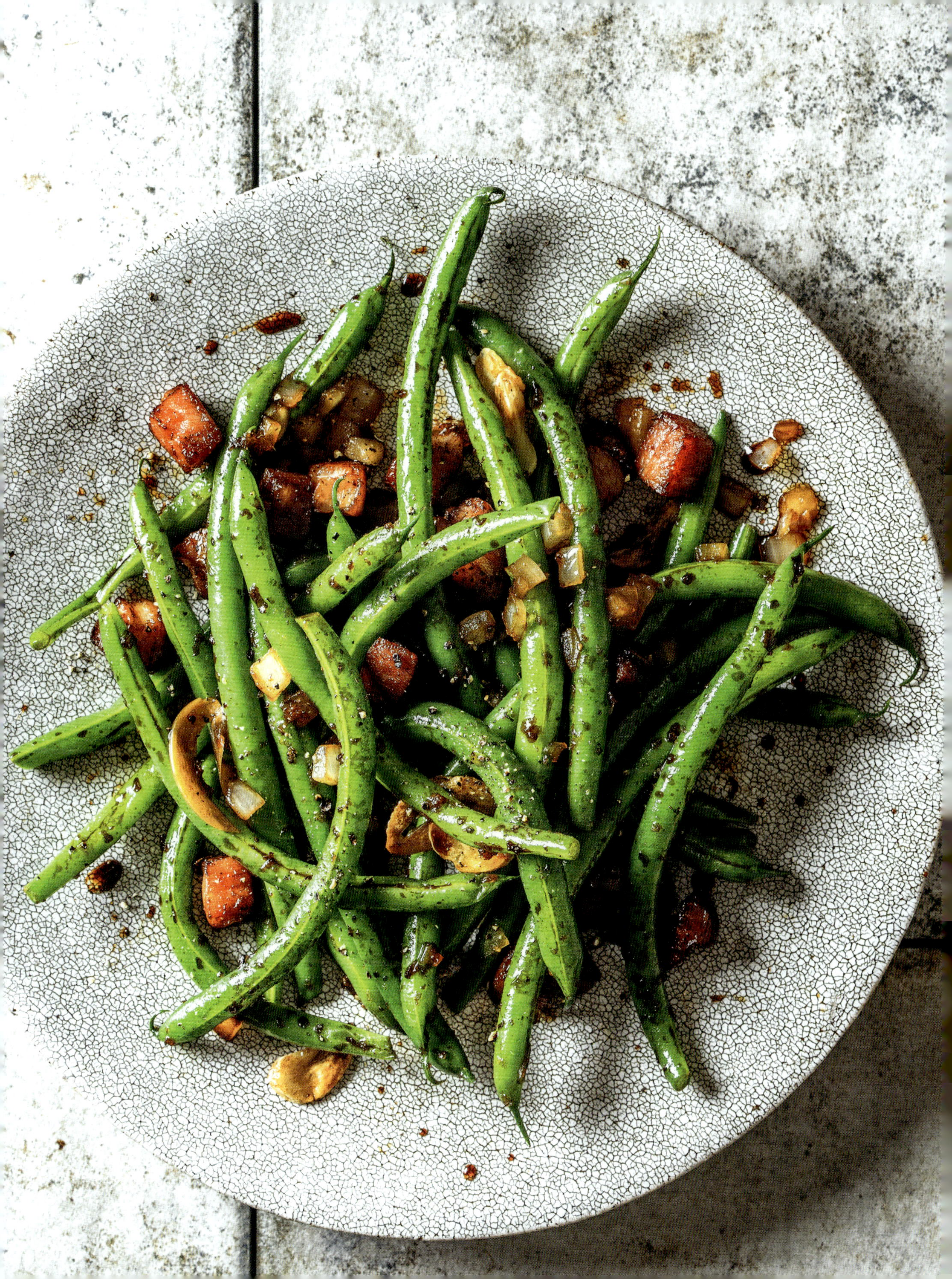

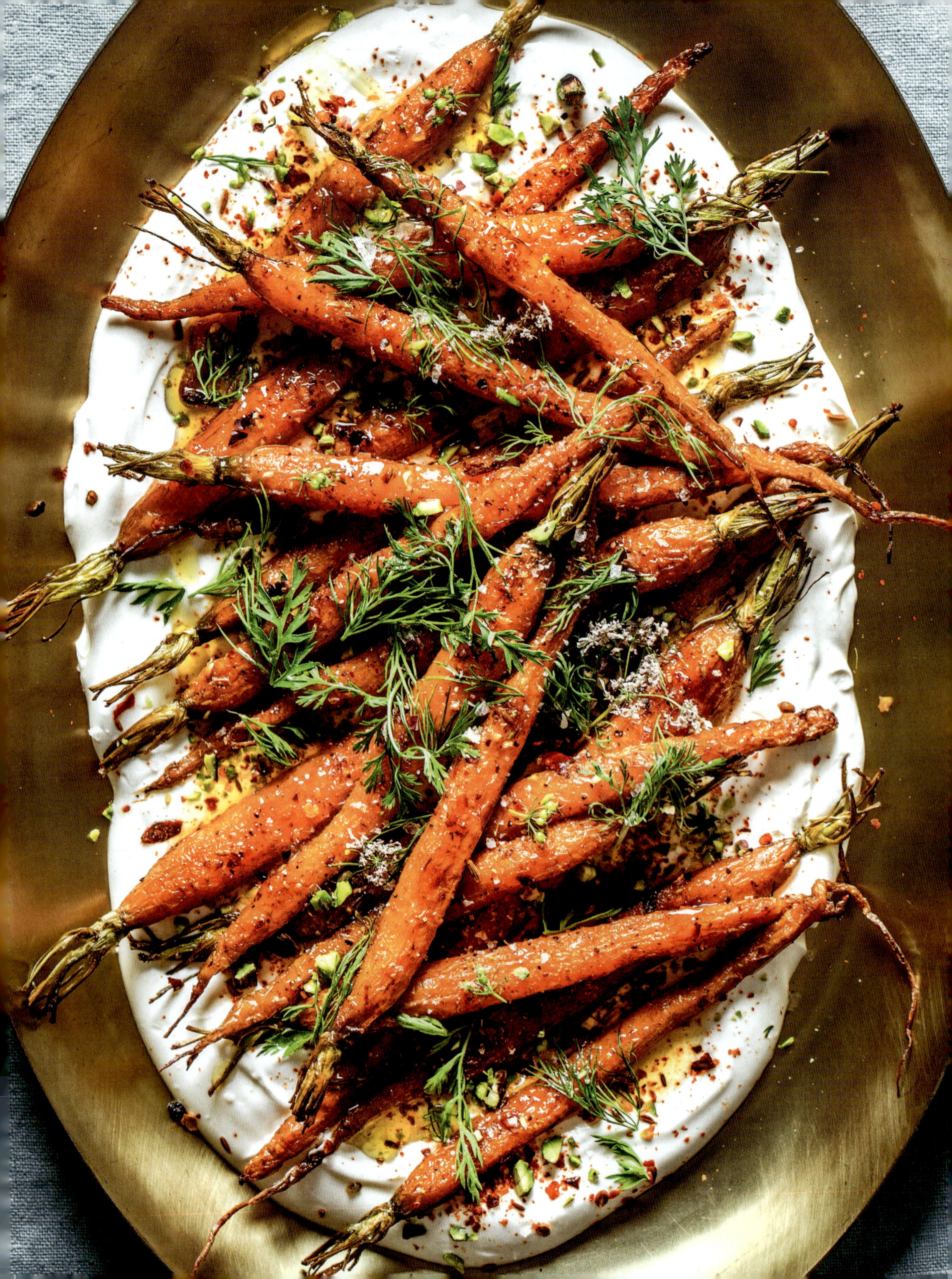

SPICED CARROTS WITH PISTACHIO AND LABNEH

Here's an easy and tasty way to raise your roasted carrot game. After a trip in a hot oven to concentrate their natural sweetness and flavor, these tender carrots are tossed with pistachios, sesame seeds, and a sprinkling of my mala spice mix. A bed of cold, creamy labneh balances the sweetness and heat. Petit carrots, each about the size of your index finger, make a particularly pretty presentation, but larger carrots are great, too, if you cut them to a similar size.

LEVEL IT UP

Drizzle on King's Chili Crisp (page 257) for added punch!

SERVES 4 TO 6

1½ pounds trimmed small carrots (20 to 25), scrubbed but not peeled

2 large garlic cloves, lightly smashed and peeled

3 tablespoons extra-virgin olive oil

½ teaspoon Diamond Crystal kosher salt

Finely ground black pepper

1 teaspoon King's Mala Spice (page 263), plus more for sprinkling

2 tablespoons coarsely chopped unsalted roasted pistachios

1 teaspoon toasted sesame seeds

Squeeze of lemon juice

Agrumato lemon oil or additional olive oil, for drizzling

1 cup labneh, store-bought or homemade (page 32)

Flaky sea salt

Mixed cilantro, mint, dill, and carrot tops, for garnish

Position a rack in the center of the oven and preheat the oven to 400°F.

Put the carrots and garlic on a large (18 by 13-inch) sheet pan. Drizzle with the olive oil, season with the salt and a few turns of pepper, and toss well. Roast until the carrots are fully tender and browned at the edges, 35 to 45 minutes, turning the carrots occasionally and rotating the pan halfway through.

Transfer the warm carrots to a large mixing bowl. Sprinkle on the mala spice, then the pistachios and sesame seeds. Add just enough lemon juice to brighten the flavors and a nice drizzle of lemon oil. Toss well.

Spread the labneh on a serving plate, arrange the carrots nicely on top, and spoon on everything left in the mixing bowl. Drizzle with additional lemon oil, sprinkle with additional mala spice to taste, then sprinkle with flaky salt and the herbs. Serve immediately.

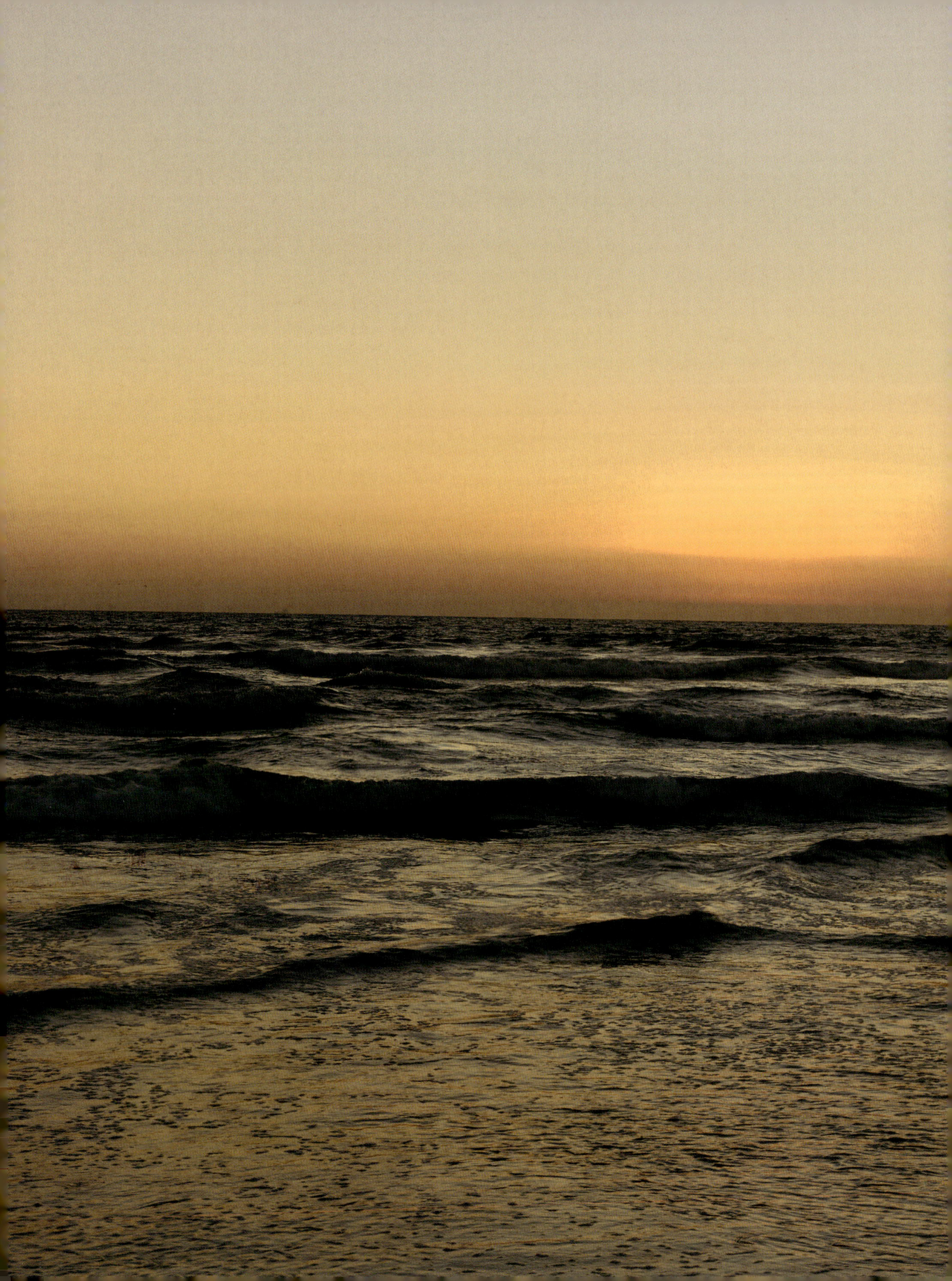

SEAFOOD 6

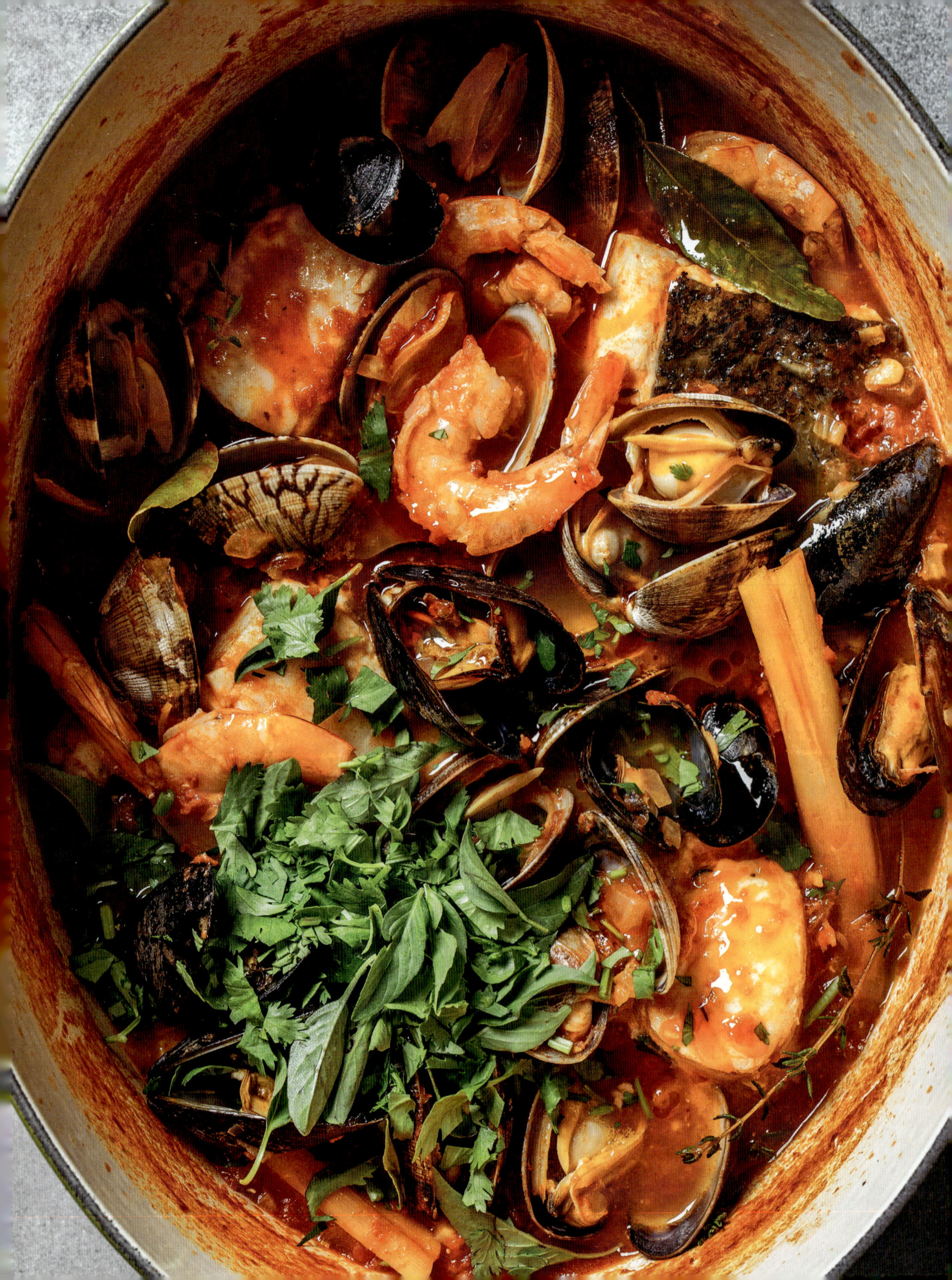

LEMONGRASS CIOPPINO

I had to pay homage to my city's iconic seafood stew, cioppino. Italian immigrant fishermen working on San Francisco's Fisherman's Wharf in the late nineteenth century created this quick, one-pot dish from a base of simmered tomatoes, garlic, and white wine with contributions from the local catch—halibut, Dungeness crab, shrimp, and mussels. I bring in Asian aromatics like lemongrass, ginger, and lime leaves for an even more complex flavor.

You can make the base the night before. The next day, bring it to a simmer before adding the freshest seafood available from your fishmonger.

LEVEL IT UP

Cooked Dungeness or king crab legs combined with the shrimp and fish make a delicious addition.

SERVES 4 TO 6

- 2 tablespoons extra-virgin olive oil, plus more for finishing
- 1 cup finely diced yellow onion
- ½ cup finely diced fennel
- 5 medium garlic cloves, minced
- 3 lemongrass stalks, trimmed (see page 16) and smashed
- 1 by ½-inch knob ginger, peeled and thinly sliced
- Diamond Crystal kosher salt
- 1 teaspoon fennel seeds, finely ground
- ¼ teaspoon red chile flakes
- 1½ cups full-bodied, dry white wine, such as Chardonnay
- A few sprigs thyme
- Finely ground black pepper
- One 28-ounce can crushed tomatoes
- 3 cups (24 ounces) clam juice
- 5 makrut lime leaves
- 1 dozen littleneck or Manila clams (see Note, page 167)
- 1 dozen mussels, cleaned and rinsed
- 1 pound boneless halibut or cod, cut into 1½-inch pieces
- ½ pound large shrimp, peeled and deveined
- Two handfuls mixed cilantro and Thai basil leaves
- Chili oil from King's Chili Crisp (page 257) or store-bought Chinese chili oil
- Garlic Toast (see page 59), for serving

Heat a large wide pot over medium-high heat for 1 minute. Add the oil and swirl to coat the pot. Add the onion, fresh fennel, garlic, lemongrass, ginger, and a generous pinch of salt and cook, stirring occasionally, until softened and translucent, 3 to 4 minutes. Stir in the ground fennel and chile flakes and cook until fragrant, about 10 seconds.

Stir in the wine, thyme, and a few turns of pepper and let it come to a simmer. Turn the heat down to cook at a moderate simmer until the liquid has reduced by half, about 3 minutes. Add the tomatoes and simmer, stirring occasionally, to reduce by half, about 6 minutes more. Add the clam juice and gently simmer, stirring occasionally, for 10 minutes, so the flavors can meld and concentrate.

Add the lime leaves, nestle the clams and mussels in the liquid in a single layer, then cover the pot and cook over medium-high until the clams and mussels open, checking after 1 minute or so. The moment they open, quickly use tongs to transfer the clams and mussels to a large bowl. Discard any that haven't opened after 6 minutes.

Reduce the heat to medium-low. Season the fish and shrimp with ½ teaspoon salt and a few turns of pepper. Add them to the broth, gently nestling them into the liquid if need be, and simmer until just cooked through, about 2 minutes. Gently stir in the clams and mussels, then turn off the heat. Season to taste with salt and pepper.

Remove the lemongrass stalks, if you'd like. Sprinkle on the cilantro and Thai basil and add a drizzle of chili oil and olive oil. Serve immediately with the garlic toast.

SCALLOPS WITH CREAMED CORN AND PROSCIUTTO XO

Learning how to sear scallops to golden perfection will up your dinner game immediately. And it's easier than you might think. Pat them dry, get a pan of oil screaming hot, and in they go to develop a richly golden crust on one side. Then flip them to give the other side just a kiss of heat.

In the summertime, I often choose corn as their partner, whether that's the sauté on page 180 or this "creamed corn." Just a few ingredients transform into an unforgettable creamy side packed with pure sweet corn flavor. (It's also great alongside prime rib, folded into risotto, or as a filling for ravioli.) A few spoonfuls of XO sauce takes it to the next level. Buy the jarred condiment or make my Prosciutto XO, which I promise is worth the effort.

SERVES 4

CREAMED CORN

4 large ears corn, shucked

2 medium garlic cloves, finely grated

¼ teaspoon finely chopped thyme leaves

1 teaspoon Diamond Crystal kosher salt

Finely ground black pepper

ASSEMBLY

¼ cup Prosciutto XO (page 260) or store-bought XO sauce

8 large dry-packed diver scallops, abductor muscle removed

¼ cup canola oil

½ teaspoon Diamond Crystal kosher salt

Finely ground black pepper

2 tablespoons (1 ounce) unsalted butter, cut into two pieces

1 sprig thyme

Make the creamed corn: Set a box grater in a large mixing bowl and use the largest holes to grate the ears of corn to access all of the kernels, including the parts that typically cling to the cob.

Transfer the grated corn to a medium saucepan and add the garlic, thyme, salt, and a few turns of black pepper. Bring to a simmer over medium-high heat, whisking constantly, about 2 minutes. The heat activates the natural starches in the corn, causing the mixture to thicken to the consistency of porridge. Remove from the heat, whisk in the butter, and season to taste with more salt and pepper. Cover to keep warm.

To assemble: In a small saucepan, gently warm the XO sauce. Remove from the heat and set aside.

Pat the scallops dry. Line a large plate with paper towels. Heat a large skillet over high heat for 2 minutes. Add the oil to the skillet and swirl to coat. Season the scallops on both sides with the salt and a few turns of pepper and immediately add the scallops to the skillet in a single layer with some space around each one. Reduce the heat to medium-high and cook, undisturbed (seriously, no peeking!), until the bottoms develop a deep brown crust, about 2 minutes.

Add the butter and thyme, then tilt the pan slightly toward you so the butter pools at the edge of the pan. Use a spoon to constantly baste the scallops for 15 seconds. Flip the scallops and baste again for 10 seconds more. Transfer the scallops to the paper towels for the moment, discarding the butter and thyme.

Spoon the creamed corn onto serving plates, then top with the scallops and the warmed XO sauce. Serve immediately.

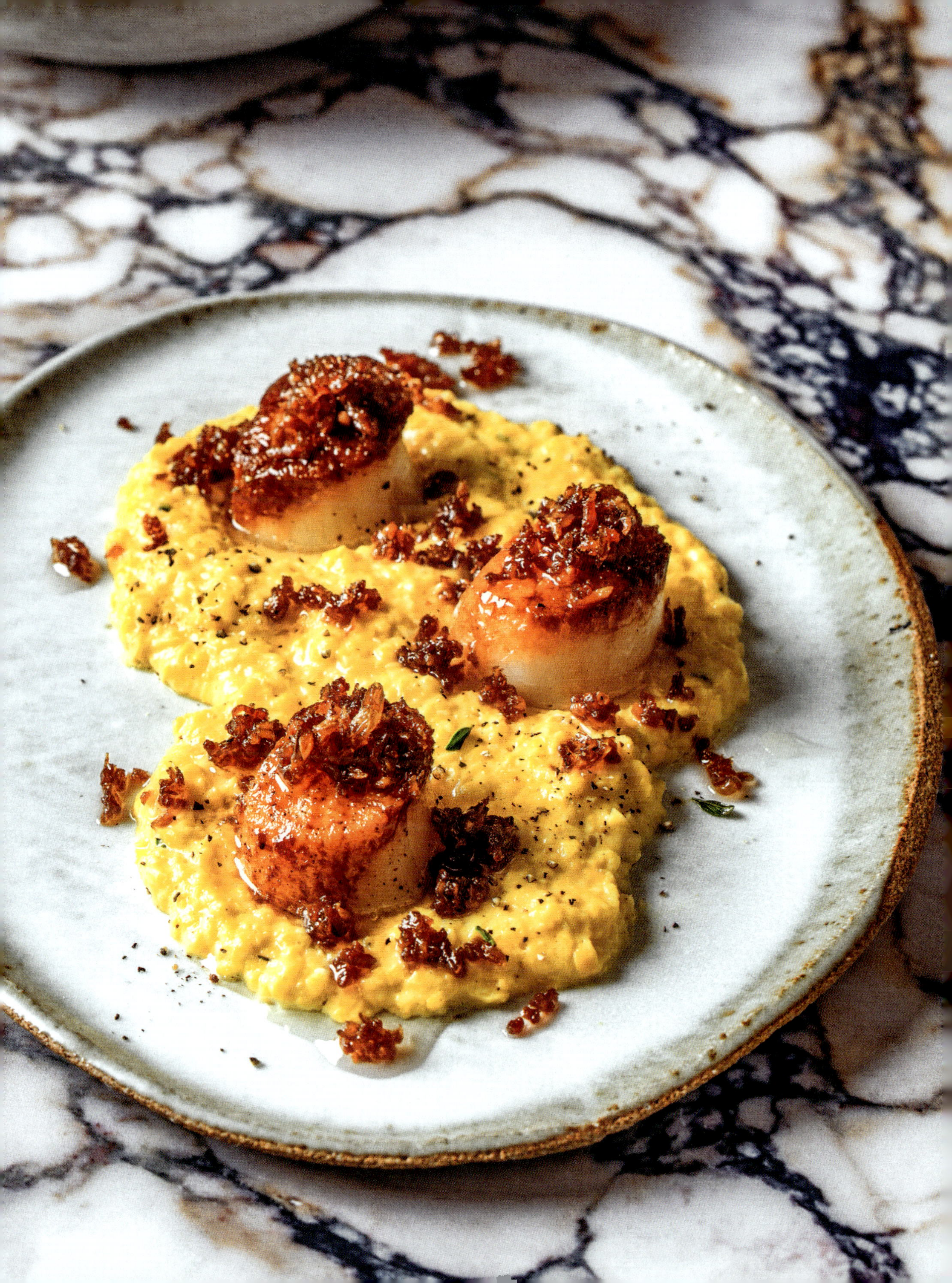

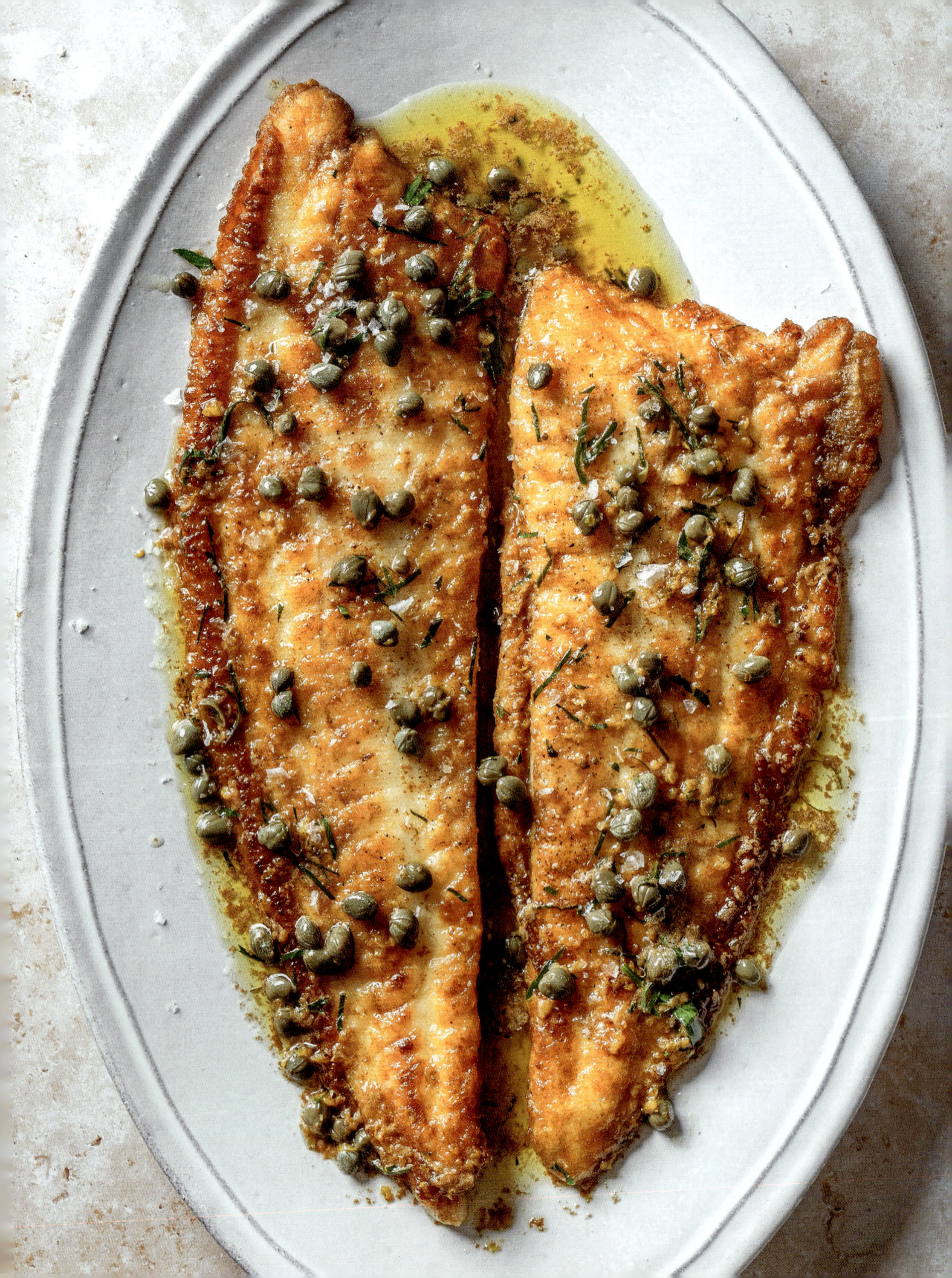

FLOUNDER WITH YUZU BROWN BUTTER AND CAPERS

Sole meunière, the French classic, calls for ingredients that most of us already have in our kitchen. A few tweaks and you have one of my top date-night dishes as well as a couple solid techniques for your other cooking adventures. Flaky, delicate flatfish, such as flounder, turbot, or sole, cooks quickly (and most of the way on one side, for exceptional browning). So does the nutty brown butter that anchors the meunière, so be sure to have everything prepped and ready to go before the butter hits the pan. Instead of the lemon juice that joins parsley and capers in the traditional sauce, I opt for Japanese yuzu, a break from tradition that's similarly bright but even more complex.

LEVEL IT UP

Top with Fried Bread Crumbs (page 256). Instead of yuzu juice, try King's Ponzu (page 258)!

SERVES 2

- One 1-pound or two 6- to 8-ounce skinless flounder or sole fillets
- Diamond Crystal kosher salt and finely ground black pepper
- ⅓ cup all-purpose flour
- 3 tablespoons canola oil
- 1 stick (4 ounces) unsalted butter, cold, cut into 4 pieces
- 2 tablespoons yuzu juice (fresh or bottled) or lemon juice
- 2 tablespoons drained capers
- Finely grated zest of 2 yuzu or lemons
- Small handful of flat-leaf parsley leaves, finely chopped
- Flaky sea salt

Pat the fish dry, put it on a plate, and season on both sides with ¾ teaspoon kosher salt and a few turns of black pepper. Put the flour on a large plate, add the fish, and turn to coat in a thin layer, shaking off any excess.

Heat a skillet (stainless steel or cast iron and large enough to fit the fish comfortably) over high heat until it smokes lightly, about 2 minutes. Add the oil, swirl to coat the pan, and let the oil shimmer. Add the fish rounded-side down and cook, undisturbed, for 30 seconds. Reduce the heat to medium—the goal is a steady sizzle—and cook, again undisturbed, until the bottom is richly browned and releases easily from the pan and most of the flesh is opaque (just a patch on the top will still be translucent), about 4 minutes. Resist the temptation to peek underneath.

Carefully flip the fillet and cook for another 1 minute to cook through. Transfer the fish to a large serving plate.

Pour off and discard any excess oil from the skillet. Return the pan to medium heat and add the butter. Let it melt and bubble, swirling occasionally, until the bubbling subsides and the surface looks frothy. Continue swirling, paying close attention to the color of the butter beneath the froth, and wait for the milk solids to turn a golden brown and for the butter to smell nutty, about 1 to 2 minutes.

Immediately add the yuzu juice to stop the browning, then add the capers, yuzu zest, parsley, and a generous pinch of kosher salt. Remove from the heat, swirl for 10 seconds, and spoon the sauce over the flounder. Sprinkle with flaky salt and serve.

GRILLED FISH COLLARS WITH PICKLED DAIKON AND PONZU

The best part of being a restaurant's fish butcher is that you have access to the delightful cuts that don't often make it to the menu. Behind each fish head destined for the stockpot and in front of the fillets destined for the sauté pan are two oddly shaped collars—my favorite part. Back when I spent my days breaking down salmon and yellowtail, I'd keep a little collection and turn it into staff meal.

Collars char beautifully and the flesh is forgiving, so in many ways, they're the easiest part of the fish to cook. A miso marinade—also great on pork chops, salmon, black cod, and Chilean sea bass fillets—contributes sweetness and depth of flavor, while pickles and ponzu (an umami-packed citrus dipping sauce from Japan) provide contrast with crunch and acidity.

SERVES 2 TO 4

½ cup shiro (white) miso
¼ cup mirin
¼ cup sake
2 tablespoons white sugar
Diamond Crystal kosher salt
4 yellowtail or salmon fish collars (about 6 ounces each)
Pickled Daikon and Ginger (page 245)
King's Ponzu (page 258)

In a small mixing bowl, combine the miso, mirin, sake, sugar, and a generous pinch of salt and whisk until smooth. Put the fish collars in a large resealable bag, add the miso marinade, and seal the bag, forcing the air out. Massage the collars to coat them in the marinade and refrigerate for at least 4 hours or up to 24 hours.

Prepare a grill, preferably charcoal, to cook with medium heat and let the grates get nice and hot. (Alternatively, preheat the broiler and position an oven rack 2 to 4 inches from the heat source. Line a large [18 by 13-inch] sheet pan with aluminum foil.)

Remove the collars from the bag, shaking off any excess marinade. Lightly season both sides of the collars with salt.

Add the collars skin-side down to the grill grates and cook, flipping once, until the skin is slightly crispy and the fish is nicely charred on both sides, 6 to 8 minutes per side. (Alternatively, put the collars skin-side up on the prepared sheet pan with a little space around each one and broil, flipping once, until slightly crispy and charred on both sides, 6 to 8 minutes per side.)

Serve immediately on plates with the pickles and small bowls of the ponzu for dipping.

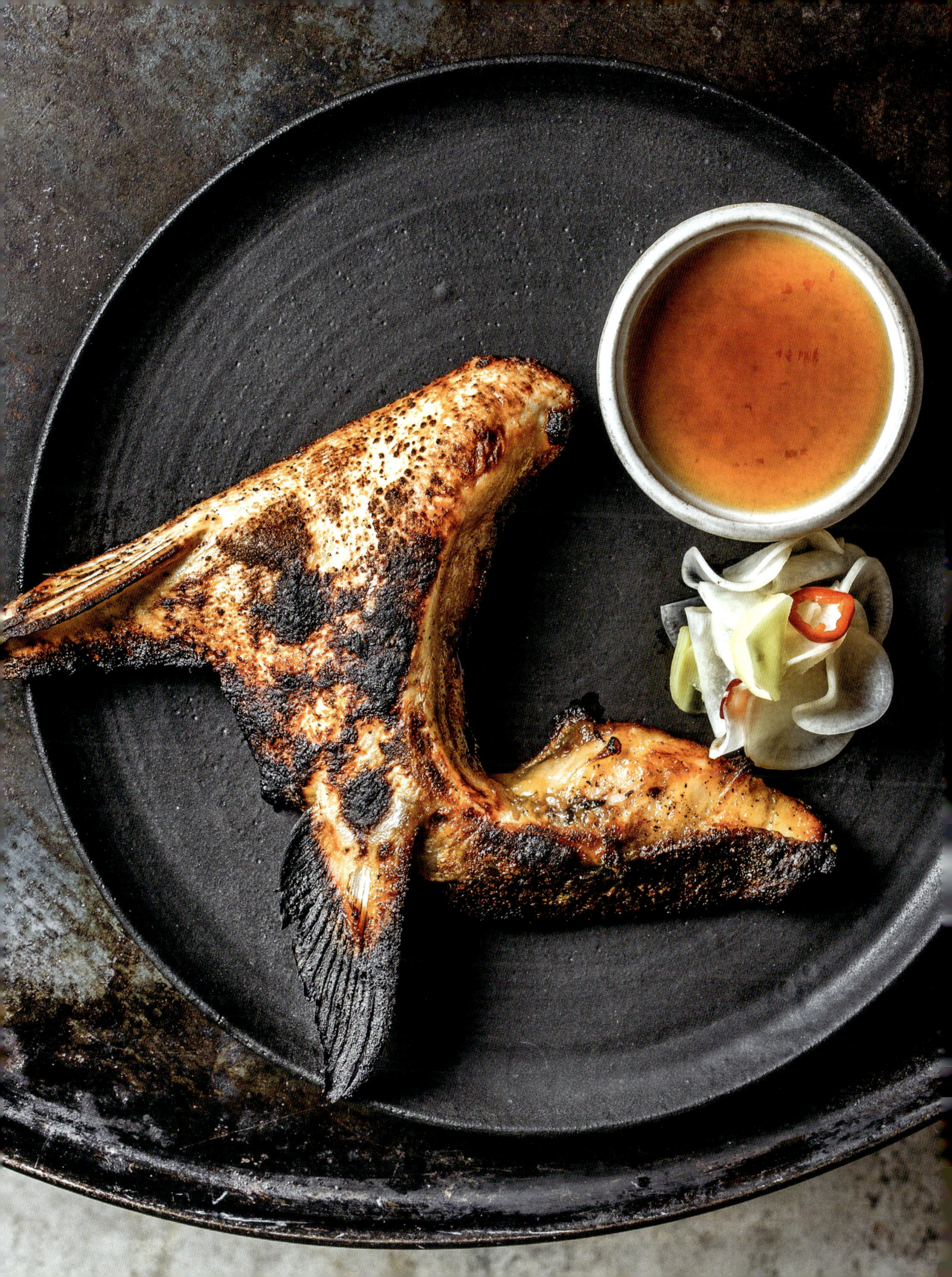

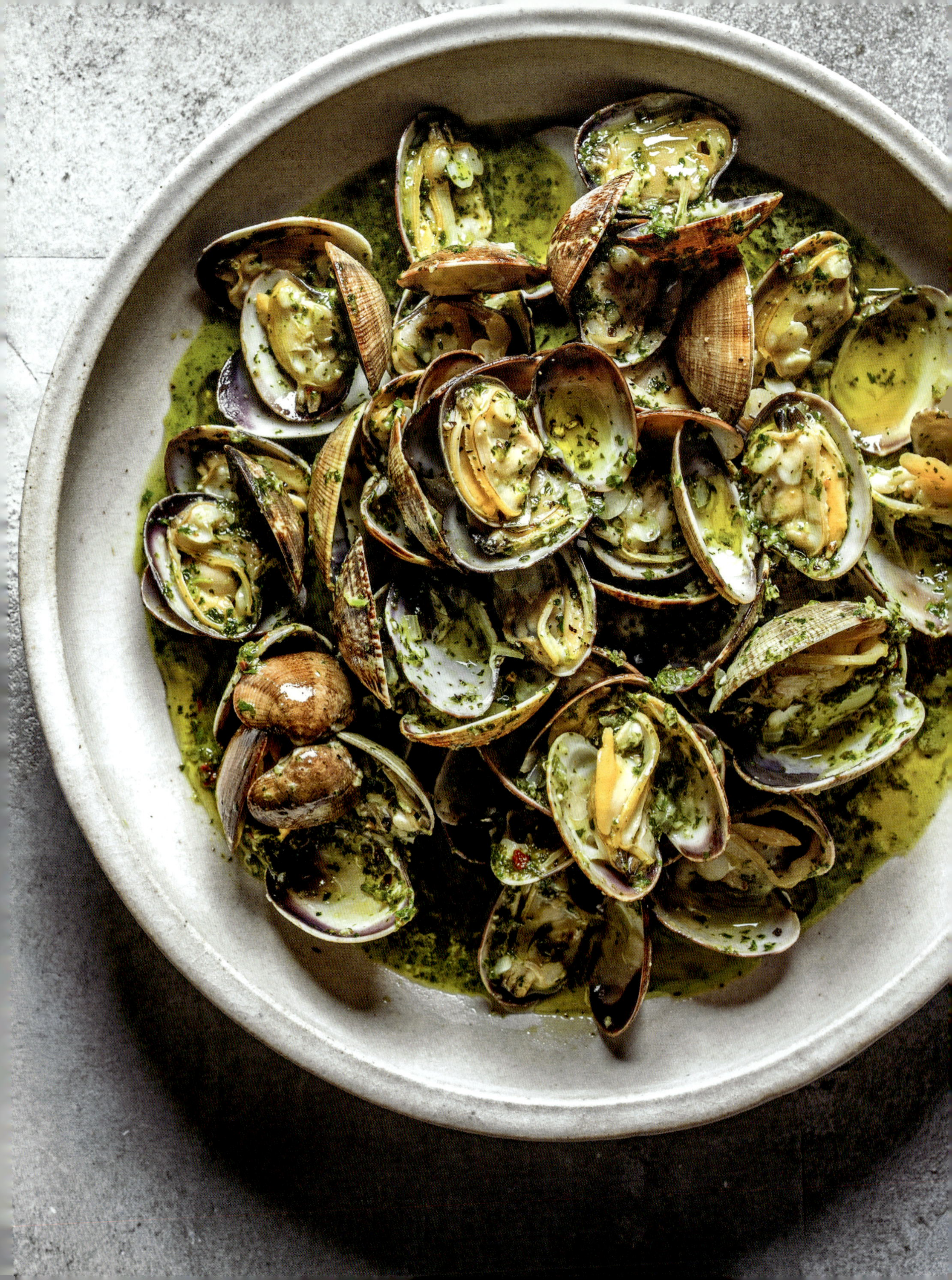

STEAMED CLAMS WITH BURNT LIME–CILANTRO BUTTER

When it comes to clams—and seafood in general—simple is best. That's the spirit behind this recipe, inspired by the incredible steamed clams I had in Lisbon that were cooked with just local white wine, tasty olive oil, garlic, and cilantro. A knob of my burnt lime–cilantro butter—charring citrus before squeezing mellows the juice's acidity and brings out depth and complexity—gives the saucy broth a spark. Serve with crusty bread slathered with that same butter.

SWITCH IT UP

Try it with Sichuan Chile–Bourbon Butter (page 252).

SERVES 2 TO 4

- 3 tablespoons extra-virgin olive oil, plus more for drizzling
- 5 garlic cloves, thinly sliced
- 1 small shallot, minced
- 2 dozen littleneck or Manila clams, scrubbed and rinsed (see Note)
- Generous pinch of Sichuan chile flakes or red chile flakes
- 1 cup vinho verde or other dry white wine
- 6 tablespoons Burnt Lime–Cilantro Butter (page 252)
- Coarsely ground black pepper

Set a wide pan over medium heat for 1 minute. Add the oil, swirl to coat the skillet, and let it shimmer. Add the garlic and shallot and cook, stirring frequently, until fragrant, about 20 seconds.

Increase the heat to high. Add the clams in an even layer, then add the chile flakes and wine. Bring to a boil and cook, uncovered, stirring and jiggling the pan occasionally, until most of the clams have popped open, 4 to 6 minutes. Add the butter and cook, stirring frequently, until the butter melts and more of the clams have opened, 1 to 2 minutes longer. (Discard any clams that haven't opened by this point.)

Transfer to a serving bowl, generously drizzle with olive oil, and season with black pepper. Serve immediately.

NOTE

When you buy clams, scrub and rinse them well, then drain and store in the refrigerator covered with a damp paper towel. Don't store them in an airtight bag or container or submerge them for too long in water, or else they'll die before you cook them. To make sure your clams are alive, only use those with tightly closed shells or those that close when tapped against the counter.

BLACK PEPPER–GARLIC LOBSTER

Hands down this is my favorite way to eat lobster. At its core, it's a Cantonese dish–shell-on and stir-fried with lots of ginger, scallion, soy sauce, and Maggi–though I add a little Vietnamese flair with fish sauce, cracked black pepper, basil, and fresh chile. It makes for intensely satisfying and messy eating. Serve it with steamed rice or Garlic Soy Sauce Noodles (page 109).

SERVES 2 TO 4

One 2-pound live lobster, prepped (see Note), or 1½ pounds shell-on raw tails, cut crosswise into 2-inch pieces

4 tablespoons Shaoxing wine, divided

2 tablespoons Maggi seasoning, divided

2 teaspoons coarsely ground black pepper, plus more for the lobster

¼ cup low-sodium chicken stock

2 tablespoons white sugar

1 tablespoon Chinese oyster sauce

2 teaspoons Chinese light soy sauce

2 teaspoons Chinese dark soy sauce

1 teaspoon fish sauce

½ cup cornstarch

1 cup canola oil

5 garlic cloves, minced

4 scallions, sliced ¼ inch thick

1 small jalapeño, sliced ⅛ inch thick

1 by 1-inch knob ginger, peeled and minced

Large handful of Thai basil leaves

> **NOTE**
>
> To humanely kill the lobster, insert the tip of a large, sharp knife into the center of the back of the head, then quickly and firmly bring the knife down between the eyes to cut the head completely in half. Twist off the tail from the body and cut the tail crosswise into 2-inch pieces. Twist off the claws and then the knuckles, then use the back of the knife to crack the shells in several places.

In a large mixing bowl, combine the lobster pieces, 2 tablespoons of the Shaoxing wine, 1 tablespoon of the Maggi, and a few turns of black pepper and toss to coat well. Let marinate for 10 minutes.

In a small bowl, combine the chicken stock, sugar, remaining 2 tablespoons Shaoxing wine, remaining 1 tablespoon Maggi, the oyster sauce, 2 teaspoons black pepper, light soy sauce, dark soy sauce, and fish sauce and stir well. Set aside.

Pour off and discard the marinade. Add the cornstarch to the bowl with the lobster and toss to coat the pieces, shaking off the excess.

Line a large plate with paper towels. In a large wok or heavy skillet, heat the oil over high heat for 2 to 3 minutes. When the oil is ready, the end of a wooden chopstick or wooden spoon submerged in the oil will immediately release little bubbles.

Working in two batches to avoid crowding, add the lobster pieces to the wok one at a time and cook, flipping occasionally with a wok spatula, until the shells turn red and the coating turns lightly golden and crispy, about 2 minutes per batch. Transfer the lobster pieces to the paper towels to drain.

Discard all but about 3 tablespoons of the hot oil. With the wok over high heat, add the garlic, scallions, jalapeño, and ginger to the oil and cook for 30 seconds, stirring frequently and scraping any browned bits from the pan.

Add the soy sauce mixture and cook, stirring, until thickened slightly, about 1 minute. Return the lobster pieces to the wok and stir-fry for 30 seconds, so the lobster absorbs some of the sauce.

Turn off the heat, add the Thai basil, and toss well. Serve immediately.

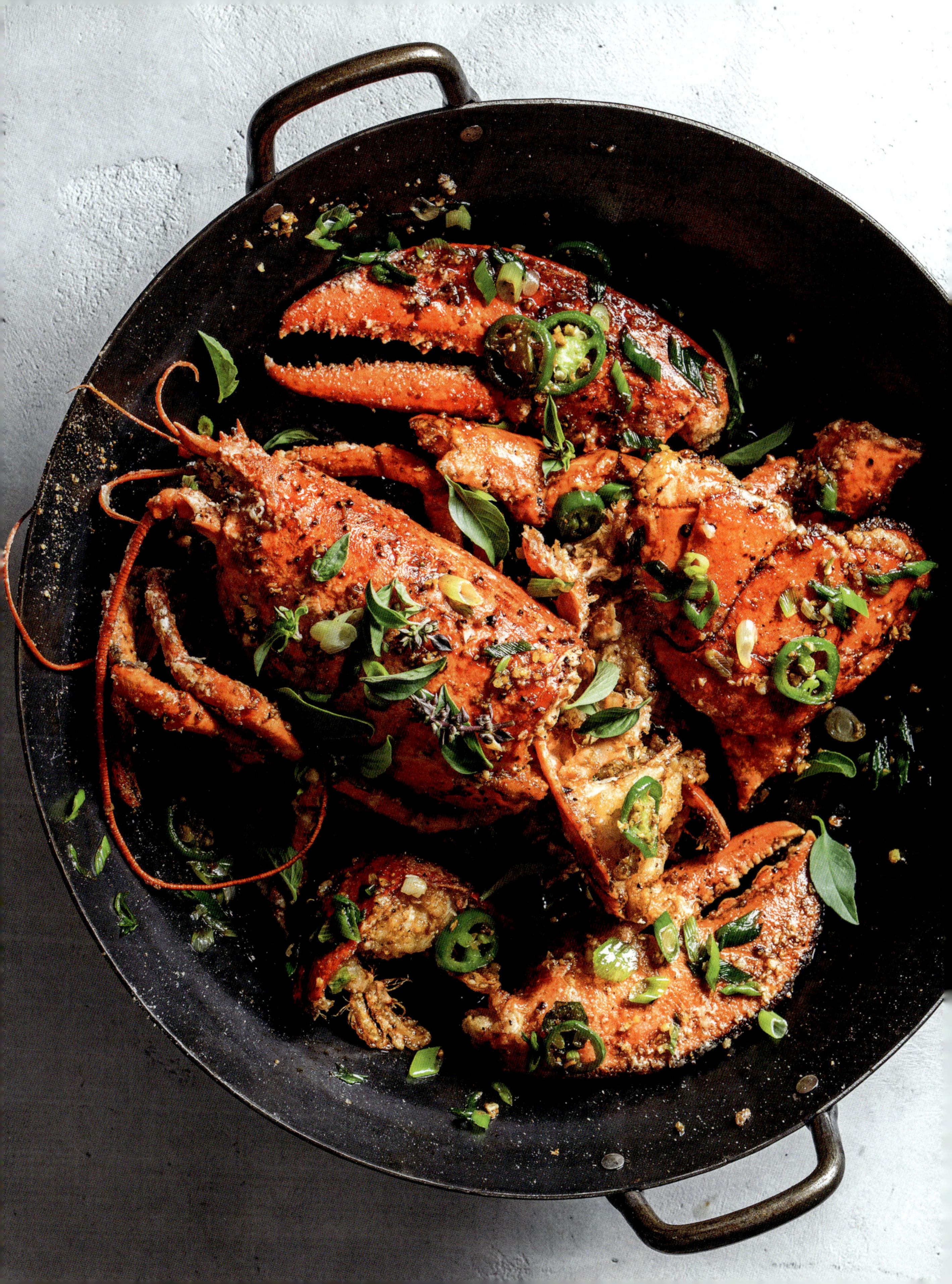

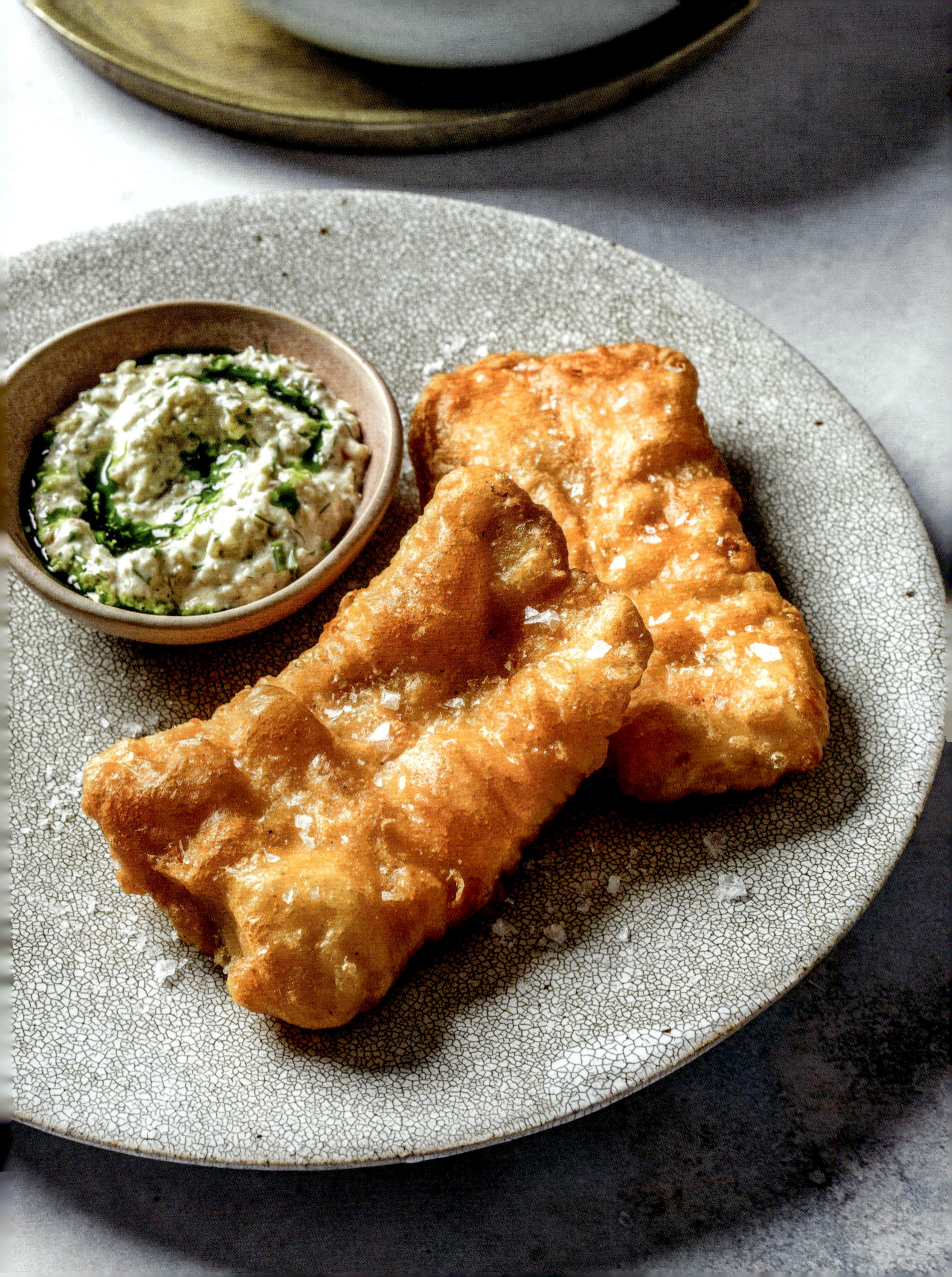

BEER-BATTERED FISH WITH APPLE TARTAR SAUCE

Back when I was a fish butcher, I'd whip up this dish for staff meal using trim from cod and halibut, and beers gifted to us by grateful diners. A good beer batter will serve you well, whether you're frying shrimp, onion rings, pickles, or anything in between. (Choose a brew that's nice and malty, like an amber ale.) For dipping, I add green apple to classic tartar sauce for an unexpected sweet-tart twist.

Like many dishes in this book, the crispy battered fish is a starting point. Try it with leftover pea puree (from Shiso Pea Pappardelle, page 115) for a take on the British mushy peas you often see alongside fish and chips. Tuck it into tortillas topped with King's Guacamole (page 28) and/or Pineapple-Habanero Hot Sauce (page 259), or into Milk Buns (page 86) for the best Filet-O-Fish you've ever had.

LEVEL IT UP

Drizzle Charred Green Oil (page 248) over the tartar sauce.

SERVES 2 TO 4

Equipment: Deep-fry thermometer

1 cup all-purpose flour, plus more for coating the fish

1 teaspoon baking powder

Diamond Crystal kosher salt

Finely ground black pepper

1 cup amber beer, ice cold

1½ pounds cod or halibut fillets, cut into about 5 by 2-inch pieces

Canola oil (about 2 quarts), for deep-frying

Apple Tartar Sauce (page 261), for serving

In a medium mixing bowl, combine the flour, baking powder, 1 teaspoon salt, and a few turns of pepper. Gradually whisk in the beer to make a smooth, foamy batter. Cover and refrigerate for at least 20 minutes or up to 1 hour.

Line a large (18 by 13-inch) sheet pan with a wire rack or paper towels. Spread ¼ cup plus 2 tablespoons salt on a plate, add the fish, and top with another ¼ cup plus 2 tablespoons salt, patting to coat each piece. Let sit at room temperature for 3 minutes, then rinse under cold water and pat dry. This lightly cures the fish and, more important, draws out excess moisture so the batter stays crispy.

Pour 2 inches of oil into a deep 5- to 6-quart pot and heat over medium-high heat until the oil registers 350°F on a deep-fry thermometer.

Lightly season the fish on both sides with pepper. Sprinkle the fish with flour and rub to coat lightly all over, shaking off any excess.

Batter and fry in two batches. One piece at a time, submerge the fish in the beer batter, let the excess drip off, and carefully add it to the oil. Fry, turning occasionally, until golden brown and crispy, 3 to 4 minutes. Transfer to the prepared sheet pan to drain and immediately season lightly with salt. Between batches, use a spider strainer to remove any stray bits from the oil and let the oil come back to temp.

Serve hot with the tartar sauce.

SALT-BAKED WHOLE FISH

Haul this showstopper out of the oven like a superstar chef and crack through the salt crust while your friends ooh, aah, and snap photos. That's the magic of this recipe. Egg whites, water, and a ton of salt form a hard shell around a whole fish as it bakes, locking in the flavors and moisture for the most succulent flesh imaginable. A threeish-pound fish, like red snapper, is appropriate for a grand presentation. Feel free to go smaller (a 1½-pound trout, black bass, or branzino requires less salt mixture and a 30-minute cook time) or larger (a 6- to 7-pound salmon takes twice the salt mixture and 1 hour in the oven).

SWITCH IT UP

Play around with the citrus and herbs—try lime or Meyer lemon, lime leaves and lemongrass.

SERVES 4

1 whole fish (2½ to 3 pounds), scaled and gutted

13 cups kosher salt (4½ pounds), plus more to season the fish

Finely ground black pepper

1 lemon, thinly sliced

2 handfuls of mixed thyme, flat-leaf parsley, and tarragon

6 egg whites

2½ cups cold water

Chimichurri (page 261), King's Ponzu (page 258), Ginger-Scallion Sauce (page 263), or Prosciutto XO (page 260), for serving

Lemon wedges or charred lemon halves, for serving

Flaky sea salt, for serving

Position a rack in the center of the oven and preheat the oven to 450°F.

Lightly season the cavity of the fish with salt and pepper and then stuff it with the lemon slices and herbs.

Put the 13 cups of salt into a large mixing bowl. In a medium mixing bowl, whisk together the egg whites and water. Add the egg white mixture to the bowl of salt, and mix well with your hands. It will resemble the texture of sandcastle sand.

Using your hands, put about one-third of the salt mixture along the diagonal of a large (18 by 13-inch) sheet pan, spreading it into an even layer about 1 inch wider than the width of the fish. Lay the fish on the salt mixture, then top with the rest of the mixture, spreading it to completely cover the fish (make sure there are no holes for steam to escape) and lightly patting to pack it on. Bake until your fish sandcastle has become a hard shell and turned golden brown at the edges, about 40 minutes. Remove the sheet pan from the oven and rest for 5 minutes.

Insert the tip of a sturdy sharp knife through a spot in the salt shell near the belly and make a 3-inch-long lengthwise cut. Give the knife a twist to dislodge a piece of the shell. Repeat the process to remove the top layer of shell and gently brush away any loose salt.

Dig in, avoiding the bones, lemon, herbs, and salt. Serve with chimichurri, lemon wedges, and flaky salt to taste.

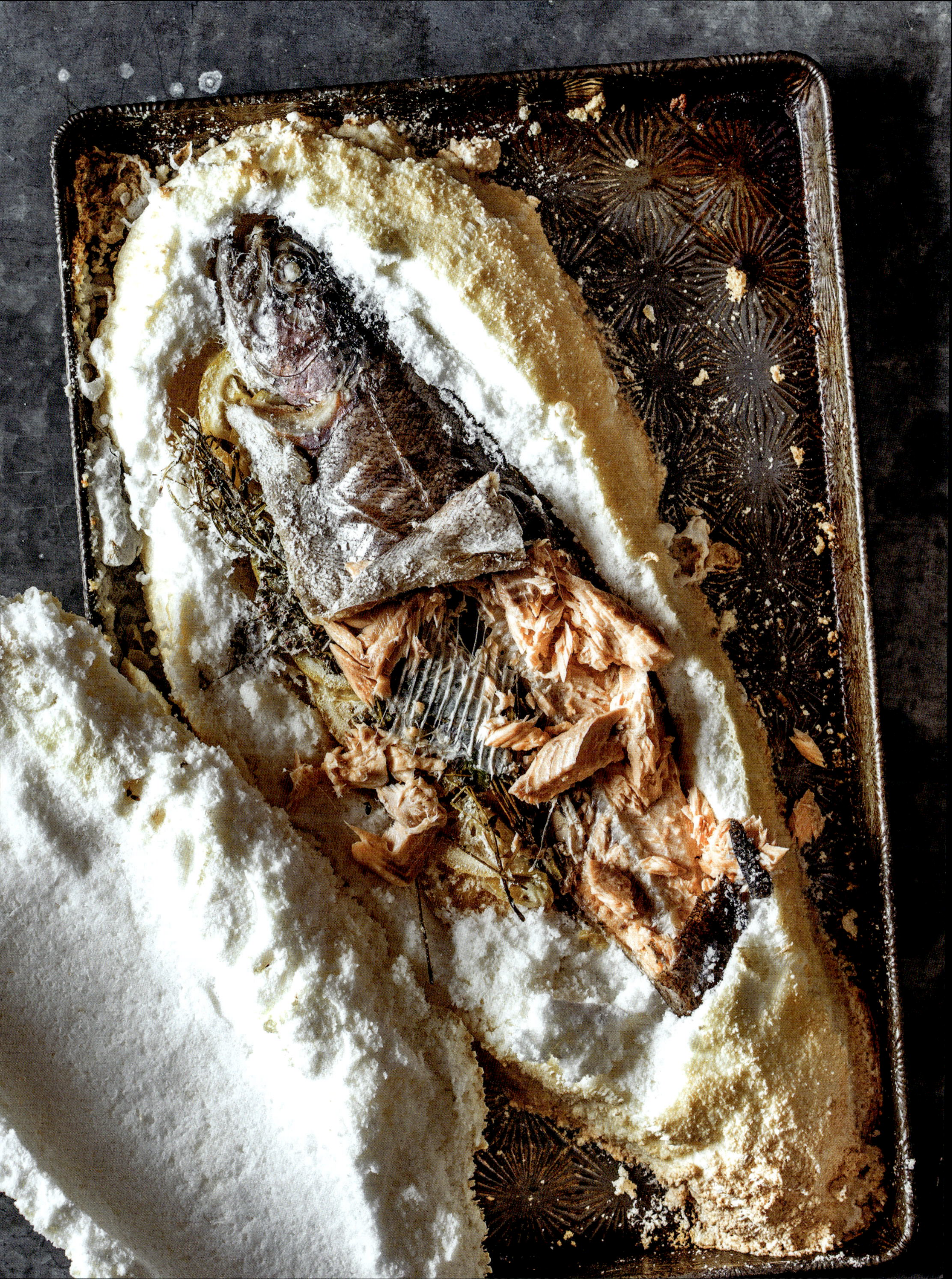

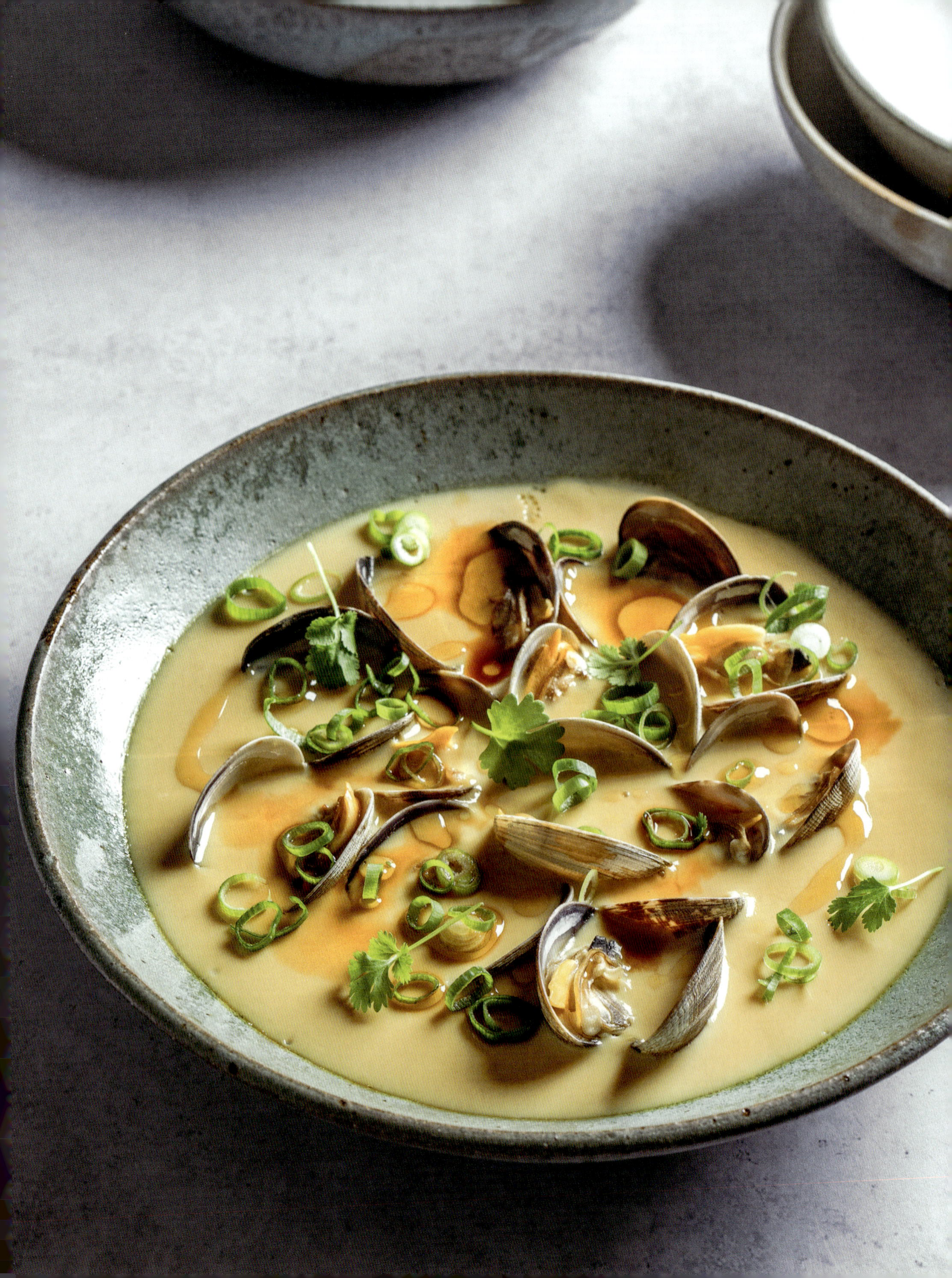

MOM'S STEAMED EGG CUSTARD WITH CLAMS

When I was five, I became my mom's little sous-chef, and I'd "help" her make jing sui dan, a savory Cantonese steamed egg custard with clams. It's a very homey dish: The eggs are whisked with stock and seasoned with a touch of soy sauce, then steamed until jiggly. My mom blew my young mind by making hers in the microwave. I opt for a steamer, which gently cooks the eggs for a silkier texture. The perfectionist in me wants to say it may take a few attempts to completely nail the texture—for instance, if your eggs puff, try a slightly lower heat the next time around. That said, my mom's wasn't always perfect, but it was always delicious.

LEVEL IT UP

Serve with Prosciutto XO (page 260) or King's Chili Crisp (page 257).

SERVES 2 TO 4

Equipment: Wide bamboo steamer or a steamer rack

A dozen littleneck or Manila clams (see Note, page 167), scrubbed and rinsed

1½ cups low-sodium chicken stock, at room temperature

4 large eggs

2 tablespoons mirin

2 teaspoons Chinese light soy sauce, plus more for serving

½ teaspoon Diamond Crystal kosher salt

Dash of ground white pepper

Toasted sesame oil, for serving

Thinly sliced scallions, for garnish

Micro cilantro or cilantro leaves, for garnish

Pour ¾ inch of water in a large wok and bring to a boil over high heat.

Put the clams in a heatproof shallow serving bowl with a 3- to 4-cup capacity that will fit comfortably in the steamer. When the water boils, reduce the heat to maintain a moderate simmer.

Add the bamboo steamer or rack, then add the bowl of clams. Pour 1 cup of the stock into the bowl, cover with the bamboo steamer cover or a tight-fitting lid. Cook, peeking occasionally after 4 minutes and using tongs to transfer the clams to a bowl as soon as they open. Discard any that don't open after 6 minutes.

Strain the clam cooking liquid through a fine-mesh sieve into a large measuring cup and add enough of the remaining chicken stock to make 1½ cups liquid total. Rinse and dry the serving bowl.

In a medium mixing bowl, combine the eggs, mirin, soy sauce, salt, and white pepper and beat until smooth, but no more than 20 seconds. While whisking, pour in the warm clam liquid mixture in a steady stream. Whisk for another 10 seconds or so to combine well.

Arrange the clams in the serving bowl, open-side up and with a little space around each one. Pour the egg mixture through a fine-mesh sieve into an empty spot in the bowl, letting the mixture pool inside the shells. Cover the bowl tightly with plastic wrap.

Top up the water in the steamer setup and bring to a gentle simmer over medium heat. Add the dish to the steamer, cover, and reduce the heat to maintain a low, steamy simmer. Cook until the mixture has set to a jiggly custard, about 15 minutes. If the custard begins to puff or look scrambled, reduce the heat slightly.

When set, carefully remove the dish from the steamer. Uncover the bowl and drizzle with additional soy sauce and sesame oil to taste. Top with scallions and cilantro. Serve immediately.

SICHUAN CHILE BUTTER SHRIMP

With my quick chile-bourbon butter on hand, these flavorful shrimp are just minutes away. The key is to avoid overcooking the shrimp by searing them briefly in a super-hot skillet. Peeled shrimp work, but I highly recommend shell-on, head-on shrimp to maximize flavor. They'll leave you licking every last bit of garlicky chile butter from your fingers.

LEVEL IT UP

Finish with a sprinkling of anise-y, bright fennel pollen.

SWITCH IT UP

Swap out the shrimp for seared scallops (see page 160).

SERVES 2 TO 4

- 9 large shrimp (preferably shell-on and head-on)
- 1 teaspoon Diamond Crystal kosher salt
- ¼ teaspoon finely ground black pepper
- 2 tablespoons extra-virgin olive oil
- 6 tablespoons Sichuan Chile-Bourbon Butter (page 252), or more if desired
- 2 medium garlic cloves, finely chopped
- Finely grated zest of 1 lemon
- Squeeze of lemon juice
- Flaky sea salt

Season the shrimp on both sides with the salt and pepper.

Heat a large skillet over medium-high heat for 1 minute. Add the oil and swirl to coat the skillet. When the oil just begins to smoke, add the shrimp in a single layer with some space around them and cook, undisturbed, until the bottoms turn pink-orange with spots of golden brown, about 1 minute.

Flip the shrimp and cook for 30 seconds. Add the butter and garlic, giving the pan a shake as the butter melts and foams, and cook for 30 seconds more.

Turn off the heat. Add the lemon zest and just enough lemon juice to brighten the flavors, then toss well. Season with flaky salt to taste and serve immediately.

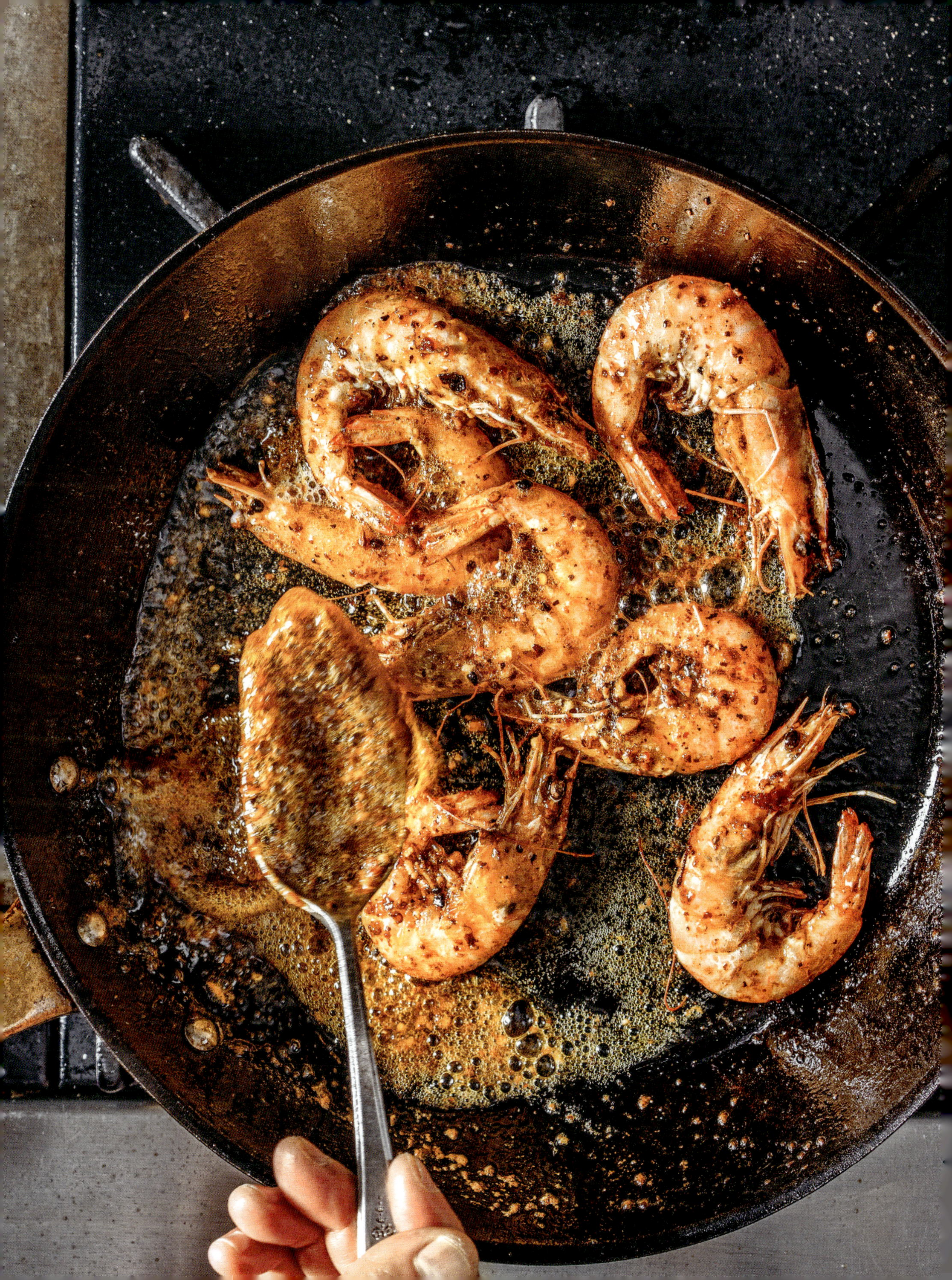

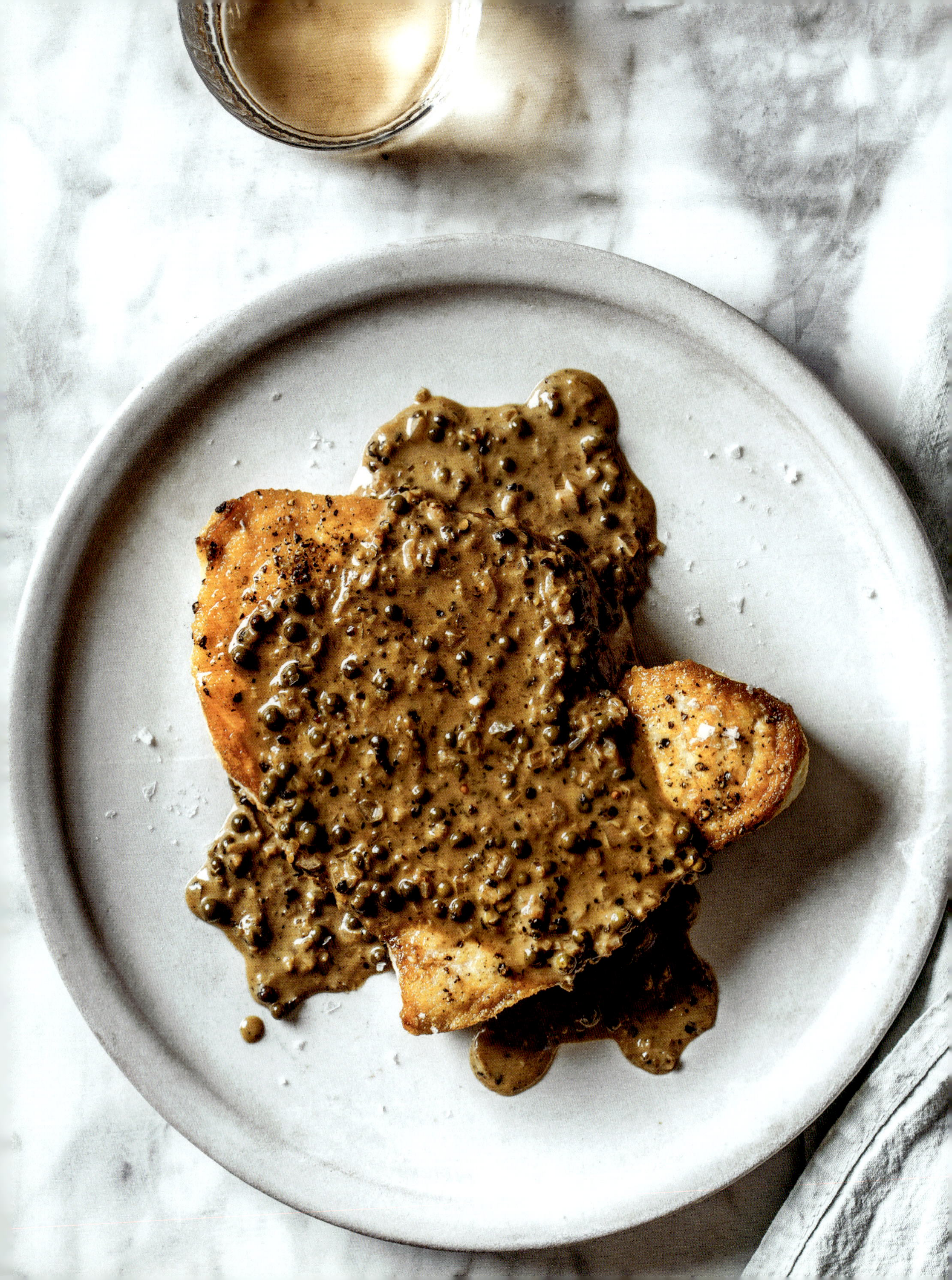

SWORDFISH AU POIVRE

Swordfish is the steak of the sea. Its flesh is so satisfyingly meaty that I often treat it like filet mignon, searing it to create a crisp crust and spooning on a rich sauce of brandy, heavy cream, lots of coarse black pepper, and pickled green peppercorns. The classic French sauce comes together quickly as the fish rests, so make sure you're prepped and ready to go.

SWITCH IT UP

Serve the swordfish with Chimichurri (page 261) or Ginger-Scallion Sauce (page 263). Serve the sauce au poivre with rib eye steak (page 196).

SERVE 2

SWORDFISH

Two 6-ounce swordfish steaks, about 1 inch thick, skinned

1 teaspoon Diamond Crystal kosher salt

½ teaspoon coarsely ground black pepper

2 tablespoons canola oil

SAUCE AU POIVRE

2 tablespoons (1 ounce) unsalted butter, cut into cubes, cold

¼ cup finely chopped shallots

3 tablespoons drained pickled green peppercorns

2 teaspoons coarsely ground black pepper

¼ cup brandy or Cognac

1 cup low-sodium beef stock

3 tablespoons heavy cream

Squeeze of lemon juice

Kosher salt

Flaky sea salt, for serving

Cook the swordfish: Heat a large skillet over high heat for 2 minutes. Meanwhile, season the swordfish on both sides with the salt but only one side with the pepper. Line a plate with paper towels.

Add the oil to the skillet, swirl the pan, and let it smoke lightly. Add the swordfish pepper-side down and cook, undisturbed, for 1 minute. Reduce the heat to medium to medium-low—the goal is a steady sizzle. Continue cooking, undisturbed, until the bottom has developed a crisp, golden brown crust, 3 to 4 minutes more. Use a spatula to carefully flip the fish and cook for 20 seconds more, to give the second side a kiss of heat.

Transfer the fish, seared-side up, to the prepared plate and set aside to rest while you make the sauce.

Make the sauce au poivre: Pour off any oil left in the skillet but keep the browned bits. Set the skillet over medium heat, then add the butter and let it melt and froth. Add the shallots, green peppercorns, and black pepper and cook, stirring, for 30 seconds.

Take the skillet off the heat, add the brandy, then return to the heat. Increase the heat to high and cook, scraping the browned bits from the pan, for 20 seconds. Add the stock, let it come to a boil, and cook until the stock has reduced to about ¼ cup, about 5 minutes.

Add the heavy cream and continue to cook until the sauce turns a deeper brown color and thickens to the consistency of a rich gravy (dragging a spoon through should produce a stripe that reveals the pan and then slowly fills in), about 1 minute more. Add a small squeeze of lemon juice to brighten the sauce, and season to taste with kosher salt. Turn off the heat.

Transfer the fish seared-side up to fresh serving plates. Spoon on the sauce, finish with flaky salt, and serve.

CRISPY SALMON WITH SUMMER CORN AND CHANTERELLES

If you've ever wondered how restaurants make fish with shatteringly crisp skin and a succulent interior, keep reading. Three important factors come into play: patting the skin dry, using plenty of hot oil, and leaving the fish alone as it cooks. Only after the skin browns and releases from the pan and the flesh is almost completely cooked through do you flip once and kiss the opposite side with heat. I often serve this with a simple corn sauté that highlights the best of summer produce. Chanterelles provide an elegant touch, but feel free to use any mushrooms you'd like.

SERVES 4

CORN SAUTÉ

2 tablespoons extra-virgin olive oil

3 cups corn kernels (from 4 ears)

Diamond Crystal kosher salt

½ pound chanterelle or other small mushrooms, trimmed, cleaned, and halved

2 tablespoons (1 ounce) unsalted butter

⅓ cup thinly sliced garlic scapes, green garlic, or scallions

2 garlic cloves, minced

1 small shallot, minced

1 by 1-inch knob ginger, peeled and finely grated on a Microplane

1 cup halved cherry tomatoes, such as Sungolds

Handful of basil leaves, chopped at the last minute

Finely grated zest of 1 lemon

Squeeze of lemon juice

Finely ground black pepper

SALMON

One 1-pound skin-on salmon fillet, pin bones removed

½ teaspoon Diamond Crystal kosher salt

Finely ground black pepper

¼ cup canola oil

Flaky sea salt

Make the corn sauté: Heat a large skillet over medium-high heat for 1 minute. Add the oil, let it shimmer, then add the corn and ½ teaspoon salt. Cook, stirring occasionally, until the kernels soften slightly and pick up some color, 2 to 3 minutes.

Add the mushrooms and ¼ teaspoon kosher salt and cook, stirring and scraping the pan, until any moisture the mushrooms release has evaporated, about 5 minutes.

Add the butter, scapes, garlic, shallot, and ginger and cook, stirring, for 1 minute. Add the tomatoes, basil, lemon zest, just enough lemon juice to brighten the flavors, and a few turns of pepper and stir gently. Season to taste with kosher salt, turn off the heat, and set aside.

Cook the salmon: Pat the salmon skin dry with paper towels. Heat a large skillet (stainless steel or nonstick) over high heat for 2 minutes. Add the oil, swirl the pan, and let it smoke lightly.

Season the fish on both sides with the kosher salt and a few turns of pepper. Add the fish skin-side down and cook, undisturbed, for 30 seconds. Reduce the heat to medium—the goal is a steady sizzle. Continue cooking, undisturbed, for 6 minutes. (Resist the urge to peek underneath.) Meanwhile, gently reheat the corn.

Carefully slide a thin spatula under the fish to take a peek. The skin should release easily from the skillet and be an even golden brown. Continue cooking until the skin is deep brown and crispy and most of the flesh is opaque (just a patch on the top will still be translucent), 1 to 2 minutes more. Carefully flip the fish and cook for 45 seconds, to give the second side a kiss of heat.

Transfer the corn to a plate, add the fish skin-side up, sprinkle the fish with flaky salt, and serve.

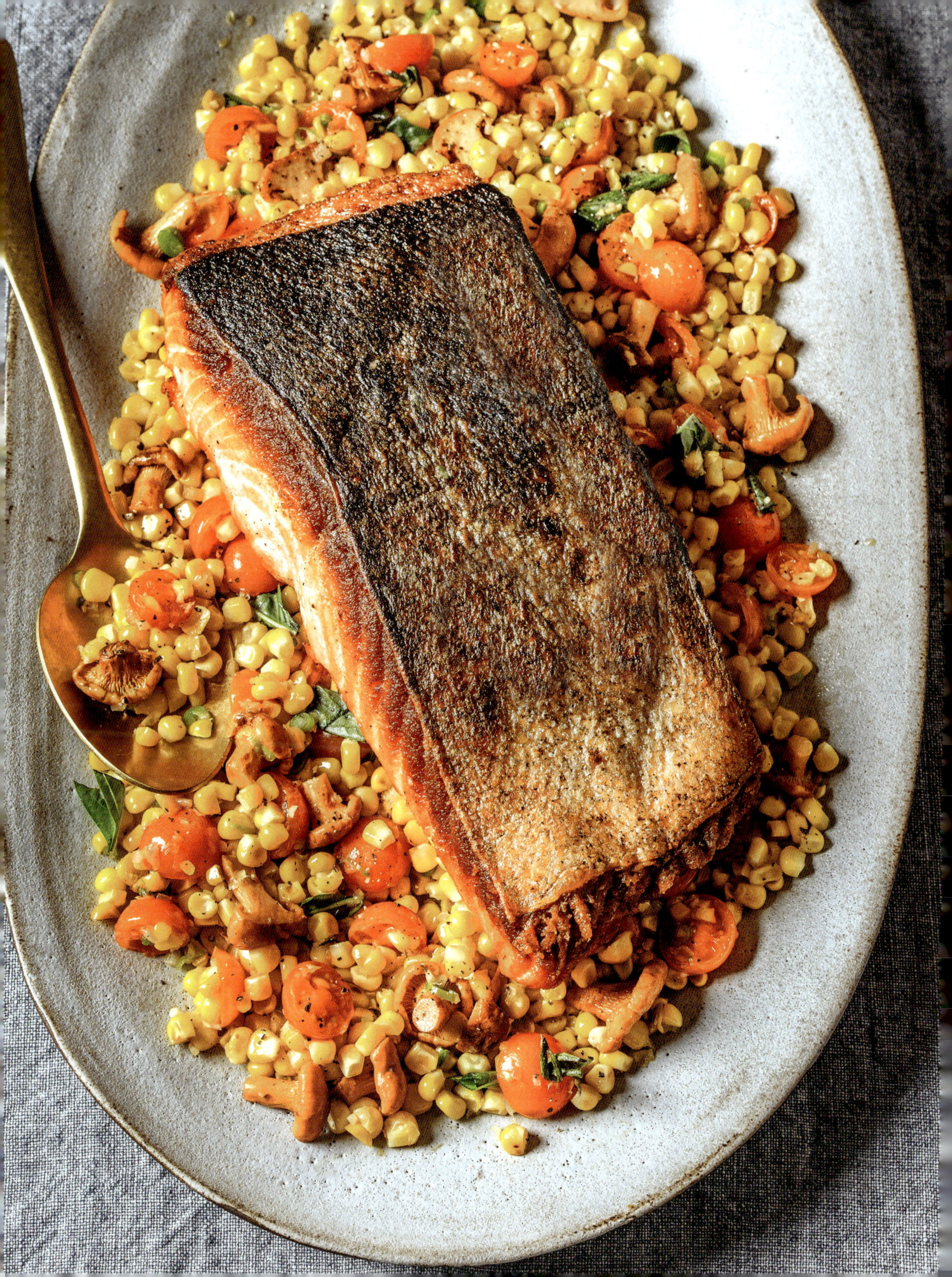

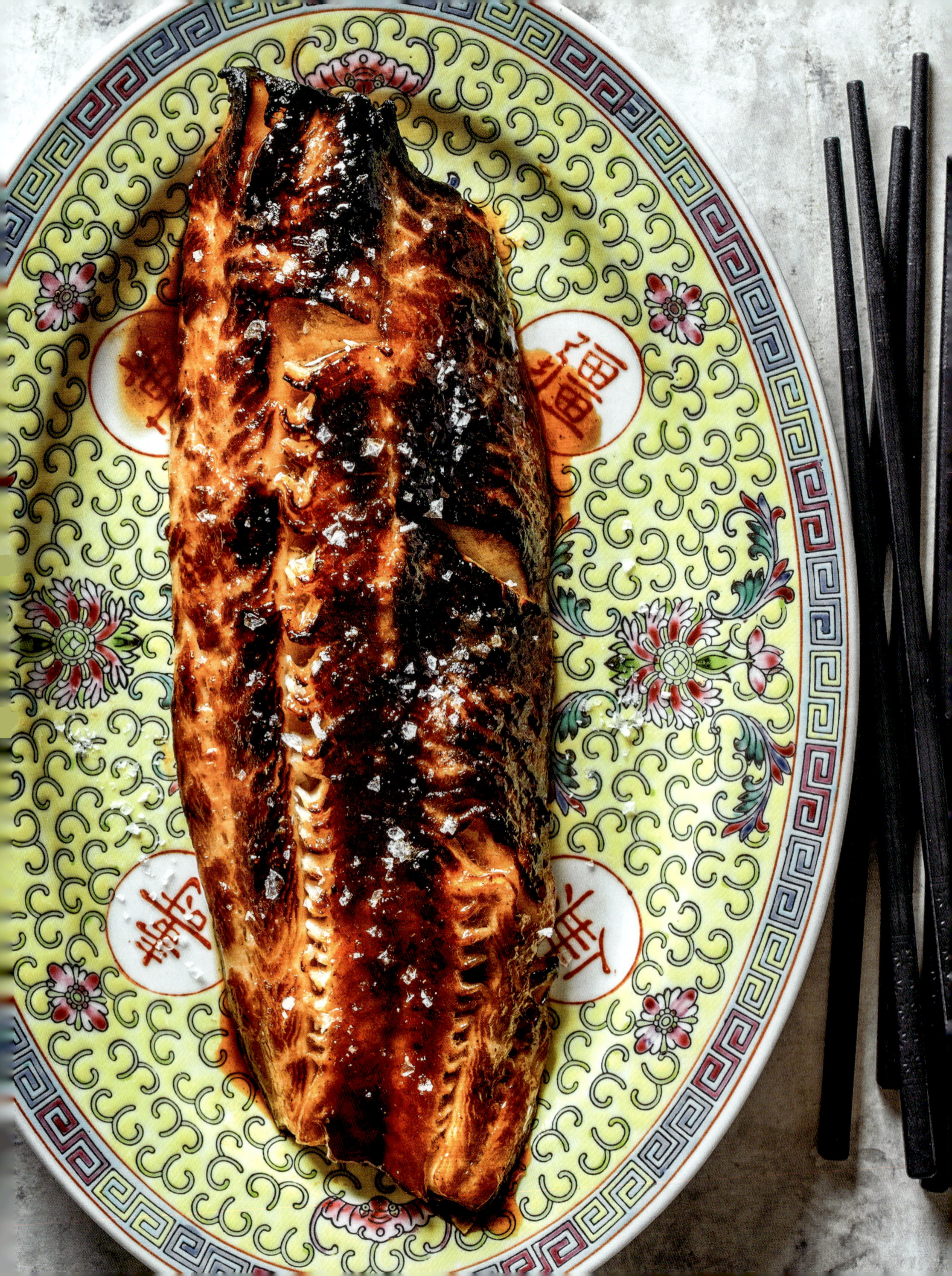

CHAR SIU BLACK COD

When I was a kid, my family would go once a week to Sam Woo BBQ, where I'd gaze at the Cantonese barbecued meats hanging in the window. There were glistening whole roasted ducks and soy sauce chickens and glossy red slabs of char siu, pork shoulder glazed with a mixture of honey, hoisin, and five spice, then charred over an open fire. In my kitchen, I look beyond pork and apply these flavors to so many things, whether I'm lacquering octopus with the sweet, sticky glaze before charring (which helped win me the title of Top Chef) or brushing it onto rich, buttery fish in this riff on the iconic miso black cod.

SWITCH IT UP

Try this glaze on other barbecued meats like baby back pork ribs or beef ribs.

SERVES 4

CHAR SIU MARINADE

¼ cup honey

2 tablespoons light brown sugar

2 tablespoons hoisin sauce

2 tablespoons Shaoxing wine

2 tablespoons Chinese oyster sauce

1 tablespoon Chinese dark soy sauce

1 tablespoon Chinese light soy sauce

1 teaspoon mashed Chinese red fermented bean curd (optional), plus 1 teaspoon of the liquid

½ teaspoon Chinese five spice powder

Dash of ground white pepper

1 large garlic clove, finely grated on a Microplane

1 teaspoon finely grated ginger

BLACK COD

One 1-pound skin-on black cod fillet

Diamond Crystal kosher salt and finely ground black pepper

Flaky sea salt, for serving

Make the char siu marinade: In a medium bowl, stir together all the ingredients.

Marinate the black cod: Transfer the fish to a large resealable bag and add ½ cup of the marinade, reserving the rest in the refrigerator for cooking. Seal the bag, pushing out the air. Massage to coat the fish with the marinade and refrigerate for at least 24 hours or up to 48 hours.

Cook the black cod: Position an oven rack 2 to 4 inches from the heat source, then preheat the broiler. Line a large (18 by 13-inch) sheet pan with aluminum foil.

Remove the fish from the marinade (discarding it) and season lightly on the flesh side with salt and pepper. Set on the sheet pan skin-side down and broil until the flesh develops spots of char, about 4 minutes.

Brush with some of the reserved marinade and continue broiling for 3 to 4 minutes more, rotating the sheet pan and brushing on more marinade a few times, until the flesh is deeply charred and the thicker end flakes open. Any marinade that drips onto the foil will blacken and that's okay!

Slide a spatula between the flesh and skin of the fish and transfer the fish to plates, leaving the skin behind. Remove any pin bones, which are easier to spot after cooking. Sprinkle with flaky salt and serve immediately.

7 POULTRY &

MEAT

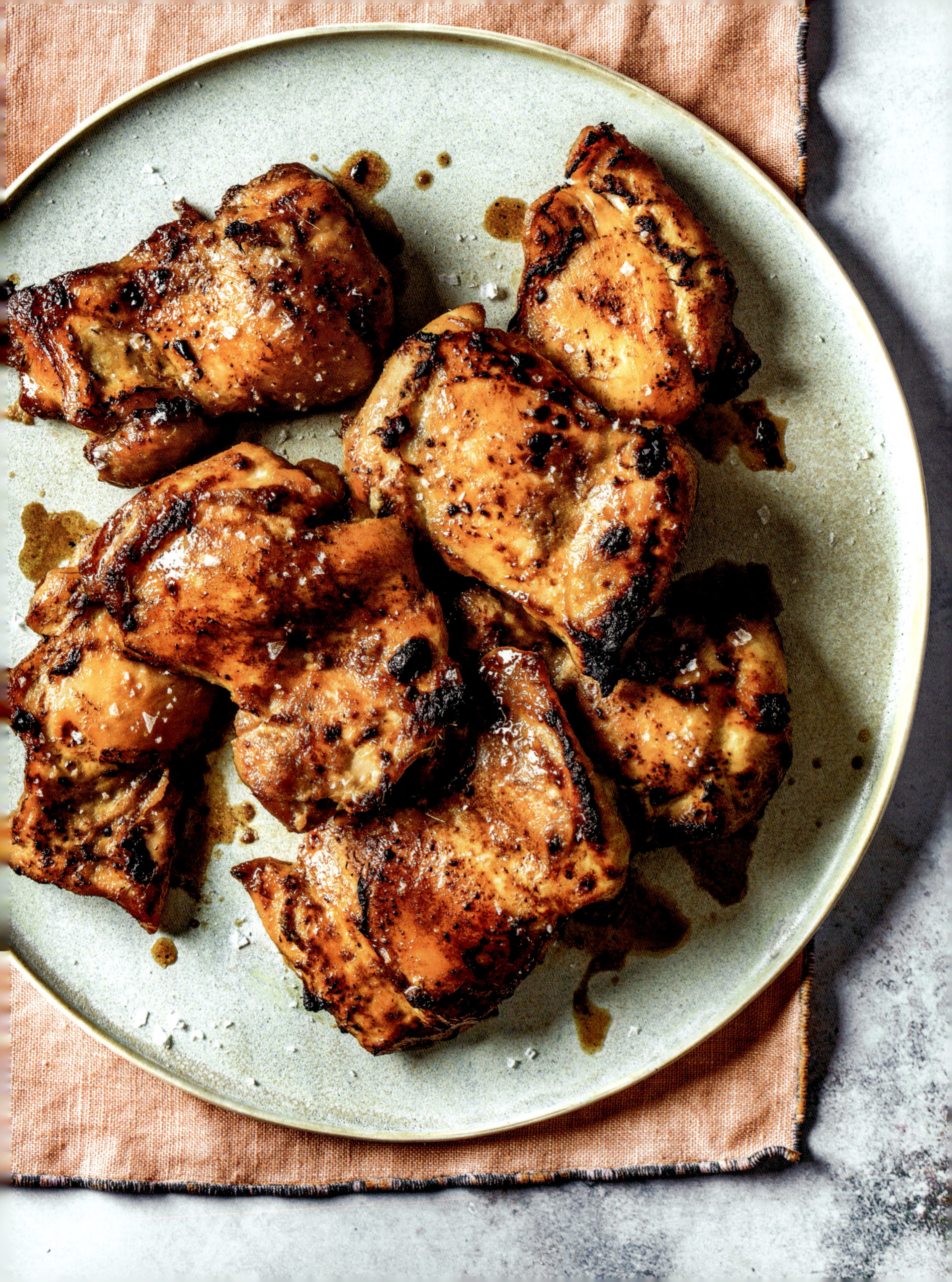

GRILLED LEMONGRASS–SOY SAUCE CHICKEN THIGHS

I've been making variations of this blend-and-go marinade since I was a teen. My first attempt was modeled after my mom's grilled soy sauce chicken wings, and over the years, the marinade has evolved every time I've encountered a new sweet-salty delight, from Japanese teriyaki to Hawaiian huli huli chicken to Vietnamese lemongrass pork chops. One friend told me these glazy chicken thighs remind her of the "Mongolian chicken" she got at the mall as a kid, which I take as the highest compliment.

LEVEL IT UP
Serve with Ginger-Scallion Sauce (page 263) or Calamansi Dipping Sauce (page 218).

SWITCH IT UP
Try the marinade with pork chops (about ½ inch thick will work best) instead of the thighs.

SERVES 4

- ½ cup packed light brown sugar
- ¼ cup Japanese soy sauce
- 2 tablespoons fish sauce (preferably Three Crabs brand)
- 4 medium garlic cloves, peeled
- 2 large lemongrass stalks, trimmed (see page 16) and cut into 1-inch pieces
- 2 by 1-inch knob ginger, peeled and roughly chopped
- Small handful of cilantro stems
- 1 fresh Thai chile or a squeeze of Sriracha sauce (optional)
- 2 pounds boneless chicken thighs (6 to 8 medium), preferably skin on
- Flaky sea salt

In a blender, combine the brown sugar, soy sauce, fish sauce, garlic, lemongrass, ginger, cilantro, and chile (if using). Blend on high, stirring and scraping down the sides, until smooth (some fibrous solids are fine), 1 to 2 minutes.

Put the chicken in the large resealable bag, add the marinade, and seal, pushing out the air. Massage the chicken to coat well and refrigerate for at least 4 hours or up to 18 hours.

Prepare a grill, preferably charcoal, to cook with medium heat—too high and the sugar will burn, not char. (Alternatively, position an oven rack 2 to 4 inches from the heat source and preheat the broiler. Set a large wire rack on a large [18 by 13-inch] sheet pan.)

Remove the chicken from the marinade, shaking off any excess and discarding the marinade. Grill the chicken skin-side down, uncovered and flipping once, until nicely charred and cooked through, 4 to 5 minutes per side. (Alternatively, arrange the chicken thighs skin-side up on the rack in the sheet pan and broil, flipping once, until nicely charred on both sides, 4 to 5 minutes per side.)

Transfer to a cutting board and let rest for 3 minutes. Serve sprinkled with flaky salt.

HAINAN CHICKEN WITH CHICKEN-FAT RICE AND GINGER-SCALLION SAUCE

This dish comes from China's Hainan province and has spread all over the world. While each country—Singapore, Thailand, Malaysia—makes the dish a bit differently, the essence is the same: It's poached chicken served on rice, unassuming but transcendent when it's made with care.

Hainan chicken was popular on our dinner table when I was a kid, whether picked up at our local Hong Kong–style café or cooked by my step-grandma. The method is what makes it special. Rubbing the skin with salt. Bringing the poaching liquid to a boil, then turning it off (twice!) to control the temperature, a grandma's version of sous vide. Dunking the cooked chicken in an ice bath. It's all part of the magic that keeps the chicken tender and moist. Nothing goes to waste either. The fat and poaching liquid are used to cook the rice, so it's full of flavor.

SERVES 4 TO 6

1 whole chicken (3½ to 4 pounds)

¼ cup plus 1 teaspoon Diamond Crystal kosher salt, divided

4 by 1-inch knob ginger, lightly smashed

3 large garlic cloves, lightly smashed and peeled

12 cups low-sodium chicken stock

2 cups water

5 or 6 scallions, white parts only

¼ teaspoon ground white pepper, plus more as needed

1 tablespoon toasted sesame oil

CHICKEN-FAT RICE

3 tablespoons canola oil

4 medium garlic cloves, minced

2 by 1-inch knob ginger, peeled and finely grated on a Microplane

1 large shallot, finely minced

½ teaspoon Diamond Crystal kosher salt

2 cups jasmine rice, rinsed until the water runs clear and drained

TO FINISH

1 teaspoon kosher salt

Ground white pepper

Ginger-Scallion Sauce (page 263), for serving

Sweet Soy Sauce (page 262), for serving

Remove any giblets from the cavity of the chicken and reserve them. Rinse the chicken well, inside and out, with cold water. Next, sprinkle the outside of the bird with ¼ cup of the salt and use your hands to rub the salt against the skin for a minute or two. Let the bird rest for 5 minutes, then rinse the chicken again under cold water to remove the salt.

In a 7- to 9-quart pot, combine the chicken (plus the giblets, if you'd like), ginger, garlic, stock, water, scallion whites, white pepper, and remaining 1 teaspoon salt. If the chicken isn't submerged, add more water. Cover the pot and bring to a boil over high heat, then immediately turn off the heat. Let it stand covered for 30 minutes (set a timer). Bring it back to a boil over high heat, turn off the heat, and let it stand once more, still covered, for another 30 minutes (set the timer again).

A few minutes before the second timer goes off, fill a big bowl with half ice and half water. When the chicken is ready, gently grab it with tongs, and transfer it to the ice water, reserving the cooking liquid. Let the chicken sit in the ice bath for 10 minutes. Transfer it to a cutting board, pat it dry, and rub the chicken with the sesame oil.

Measure 3 cups of broth, making sure to include as much fat as possible, and reserve for making the rice. Strain the remaining broth, transferring any giblets to the cutting board with the chicken and discarding the remaining solids. Return the strained broth to the pot, bring it to a gentle simmer, and cook, uncovered, to reduce slightly while you prepare the rice.

Make the chicken-fat rice: Heat a medium pot over medium heat for 1 minute. Add the oil and swirl to coat the pot. When the oil shimmers, add the garlic, ginger, shallot, and salt and cook, stirring occasionally, until fragrant, about 2 minutes. Stir in the rice and toast, stirring frequently, for 1 minute.

CONTINUED

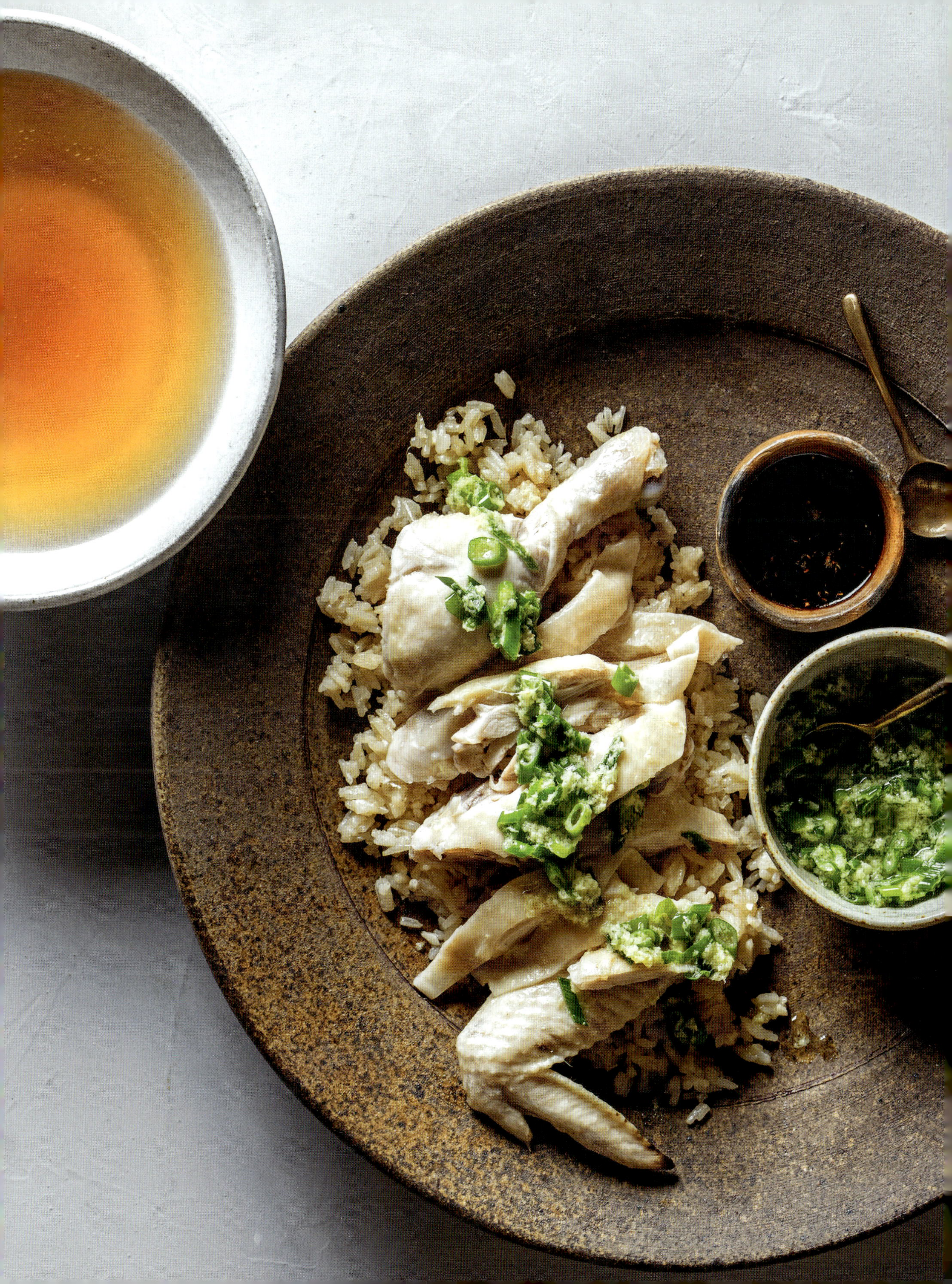

HAINAN CHICKEN WITH CHICKEN-FAT RICE AND GINGER-SCALLION SAUCE
CONTINUED

Add the 3 cups of reserved chicken broth, gently scraping the pot to dislodge any rice grains and flavorful bits. At this point, you can transfer the mixture to a rice cooker (press "cook") or continue in the pot on the stovetop. Increase the heat to high, bring the liquid to a full boil, then immediately cover with the lid and turn off the heat. Let it sit, without peeking, for 20 minutes. Fluff the rice with a fork or rice paddle (gently to avoid smashing the grains), then cover again and let sit for 5 minutes. Fluff again before serving.

To finish: Carve off the legs and wings from the chicken. Carve off the breast meat, and slice it against the grain. Reserve the bones for anyone who likes to gnaw on them. Season the broth in the pot with the kosher salt and a dash of white pepper, and turn off the heat.

Divide the rice among plates, add the chicken on top (along with any giblets). Serve with little bowls of ginger-scallion sauce and sweet soy sauce, and bowls of the broth.

FIVE SPICED DUCK À L'ORANGE

To home cooks, the idea of making tender, rosy slices of duck with crispy skin can feel intimidating, something best left to the professionals. But of all the proteins out there, I find duck breast to be, by far, the simplest to cook. All it takes is the patience to allow the fat to render slowly until the skin is crisp. I cook the breast almost completely on one side, similar to my technique for scallops (page 160) and fish (page 180), flipping just before they leave the pan for a quick butter baste. I treat the duck to a brief five spice cure and pair it with a sauce that plays on both French à l'orange and chop suey–house orange chicken. It makes for an elegant and impressive date night dish and goes great with Chicory Salad with Anchovy, Kumquats, and Smoked Cheese (page 72).

SERVES 2

FOR THE DUCK

2 duck breasts (about 8 ounces each), patted dry

½ cup Diamond Crystal kosher salt, plus more for seasoning

¼ cup white sugar

2 teaspoons Chinese five spice powder

Finely ground black pepper

2 tablespoons (1 ounce) unsalted butter

2 garlic cloves, lightly smashed and peeled

Small handful of mixed rosemary, thyme, and sage sprigs

SAUCE

1 cup freshly squeezed orange juice

1 by 1-inch knob ginger, peeled and finely grated on a Microplane

4 tablespoons (2 ounces) unsalted butter, cut into ½-inch cubes and well chilled

2 tablespoons sliced kumquats (optional)

Dash of Chinese five spice powder

Diamond Crystal kosher salt

Flaky sea salt

For the duck: With a very sharp knife, score the skin of the duck breasts in a diagonal crosshatch pattern. Each cut should be shallow and about ⅛ inch apart.

In a small mixing bowl, stir together the kosher salt, sugar, and five spice. Spread half of the mixture on a plate and add the duck breasts flesh-side down. Top with the remaining five spice mixture, patting to coat all over. Let the duck cure at room temperature for at least 10 minutes or up to 30 minutes.

Rinse the duck breasts, then pat them dry. Season lightly with kosher salt and pepper on both sides. Put the breasts skin-side down in a large heavy skillet and set over medium-low heat. Wait for a gentle sizzle, then cook, occasionally pouring off the rendered fat (reserve it for another day), until the skin is deep brown and very crispy and only a patch of the flesh is raw, about 10 minutes. Slow is best. Don't be tempted to increase the heat.

Pour off the fat once more. Increase the heat to medium-high and flip the breasts. Add the butter, garlic, and herb sprigs and let the butter melt and foam. Tilt the pan slightly toward you so the butter pools at the edge of the pan, then use a spoon to baste the breasts constantly with the butter for 30 seconds.

Transfer the duck skin-side up to a cutting board and let it rest for at least 10 minutes (duck benefits from a little more resting time than other meats).

Make the sauce and serve: While the breasts are resting, in a small saucepan, combine the orange juice and ginger and bring to a boil over high heat. Reduce the heat to cook at a strong simmer, stirring occasionally, until the mixture is thick enough that a flexible spatula dragged through the sauce produces a stripe that reveals the pan and then slowly fills in, 7 to 8 minutes.

CONTINUED

FIVE SPICED DUCK À L'ORANGE
CONTINUED

While whisking, add the butter several cubes at a time. Add the kumquats (if using), five spice, and a pinch of kosher salt and cook, whisking occasionally, for 30 seconds. Remove from the heat and keep warm.

Once the duck breasts have rested, flip the breasts skin-side down (this keeps the skin intact while slicing) and slice about ¼ inch thick against the grain.

Spoon the sauce onto plates, top with the duck, and sprinkle with flaky salt. Serve immediately.

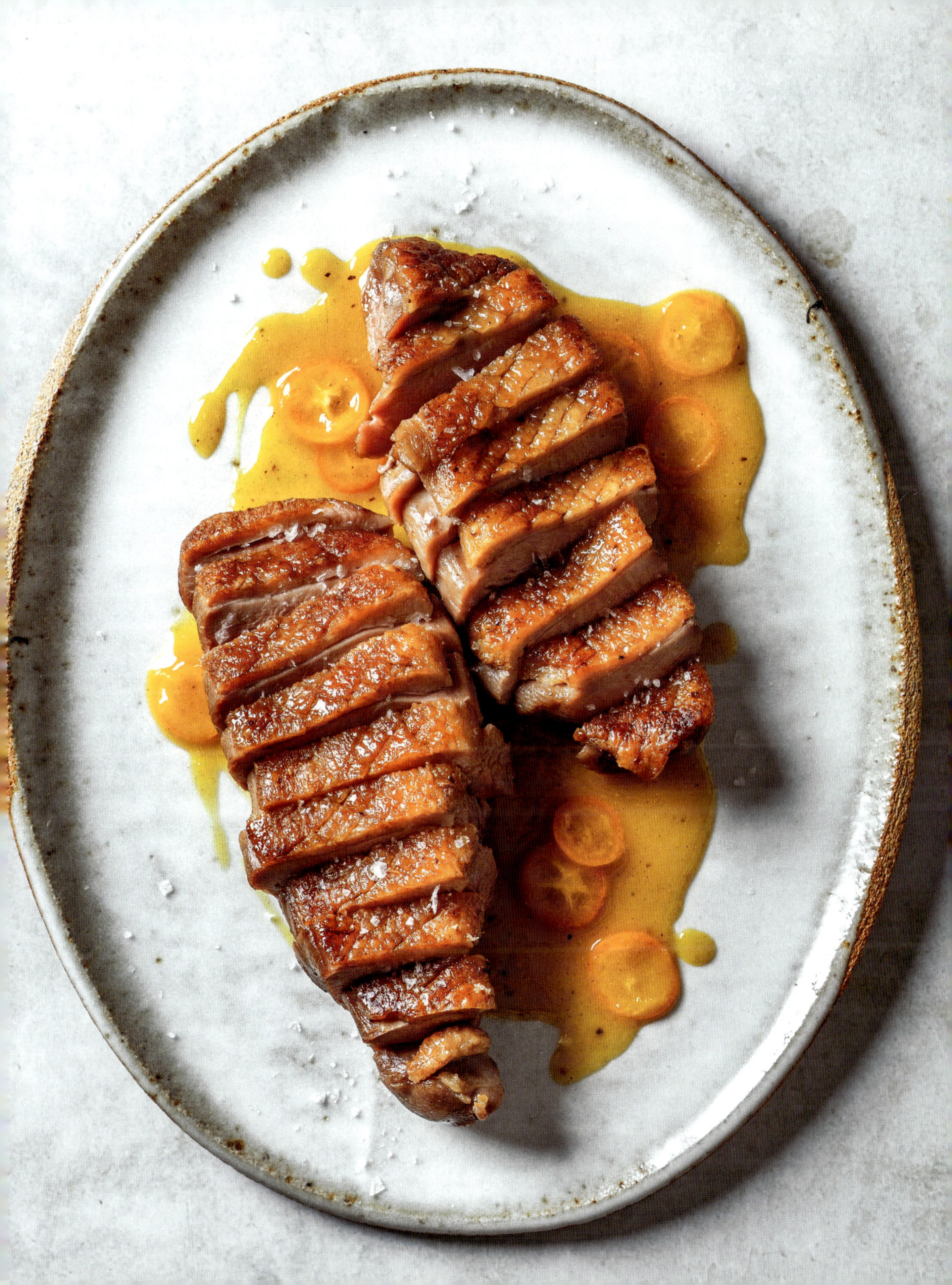

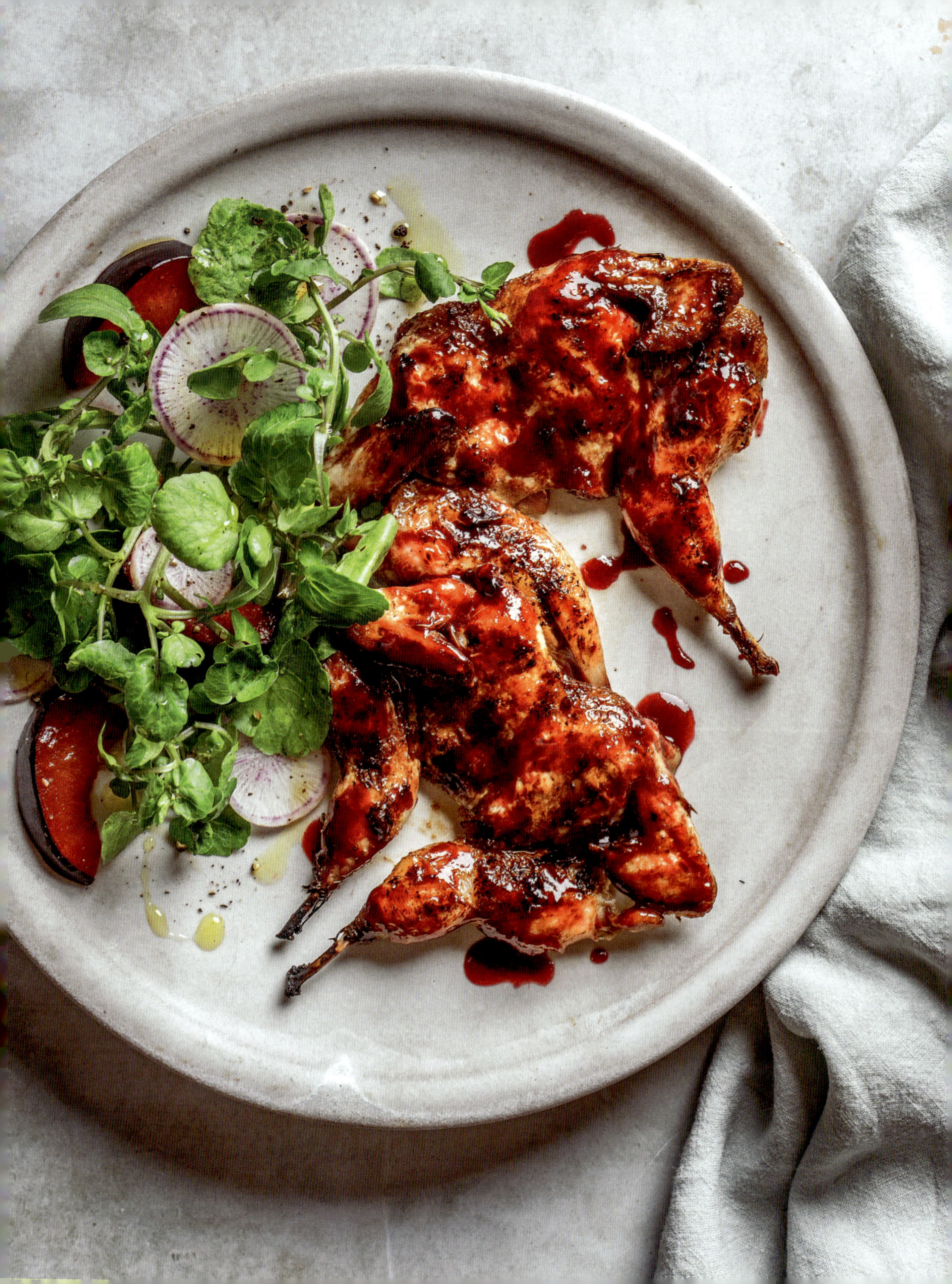

GRILLED QUAIL WITH SWEET AND SOUR PLUM GLAZE

MARINATED QUAIL

4 garlic cloves, finely grated on a Microplane

1 by 1-inch knob ginger, peeled and finely grated on a Microplane

¼ cup Shaoxing wine

¼ cup white sugar

2 tablespoons hoisin sauce

2 tablespoons Chinese light soy sauce

2 tablespoons toasted sesame oil

2 teaspoons fish sauce

½ teaspoon ground white pepper

8 (4-ounce) semi-boneless quail

Diamond Crystal kosher salt

Finely ground black pepper

GLAZE

1 ripe black or red plum or pluot, pitted and roughly chopped

1 garlic clove, finely grated on a Microplane

½ cup blueberries or blackberries

½ medium shallot, thinly sliced

½ small jalapeño, stemmed

½ cup lightly packed light brown sugar

½ cup freshly squeezed orange juice

¼ cup unseasoned rice vinegar

1 by ½-inch knob ginger, peeled and finely grated on a Microplane

1½ teaspoons fish sauce

1½ teaspoons hoisin sauce

1½ teaspoons Shaoxing wine

¼ teaspoon Sriracha sauce

⅛ teaspoon ground white pepper

⅛ teaspoon ground coriander

1 whole star anise

This dish won me a spot in the finals on *Top Chef: All-Stars*, after the sight of gorgeous plums at the farmers' market made me think of the Chinese plum sauce my family ate with roasted squab. To highlight the summer fruit, I made a sweet, spicy, tart glaze and used it to lacquer my favorite bird—the extremely underrated quail.

The glaze is easy—just stir, simmer, and strain—and can be made with whatever stone fruit looks best, including peaches, pluots, and cherries. It tastes incredible on chicken, duck, pork, and grilled radicchio, yet quail is full of flavor and picks up smoky notes from the grill, even though it cooks quickly to a tender, juicy medium-rare.

Pair it with a salad of arugula or watercress and grilled stone fruit with a bright dressing, like Sesame-Lime Vinaigrette (page 250).

SERVES 4 TO 6

Marinate the quail: In a medium mixing bowl, whisk together the garlic, ginger, Shaoxing wine, white sugar, hoisin sauce, soy sauce, sesame oil, fish sauce, and white pepper. Add the quail and turn to coat them well. Let them marinate for at least 20 minutes or in the refrigerator for up to 18 hours (the longer the better).

Make the glaze: In a medium saucepan, combine all the ingredients and bring to a boil over high heat. Turn the heat down to cook at a moderate simmer, stirring occasionally, until the liquid thickens to the consistency of maple syrup, about 25 minutes.

Set a fine-mesh sieve over a heatproof bowl and pour in the glaze, pressing the solids to help extract as much liquid as possible. (Use it right away or let it cool and store in an airtight container in the refrigerator for up to 5 days.)

Cook the quail: Prepare a grill, preferably charcoal, to cook with high heat. Make sure the grill grates are very hot before adding the quail to prevent them from sticking.

Remove the quail from the marinade, letting the excess drip off (discard the marinade). Lightly season the quail on both sides with salt and black pepper. Grill them skin-side down, uncovered, until the skin is crispy and golden brown with spots of char, 3 to 4 minutes.

Reserve a few tablespoons of the glaze in a small bowl for finishing. Generously brush the quail with some of the remaining glaze, then flip and cook for 20 seconds. Brush the skin side with the glaze, then flip and cook for 1 minute more for medium-rare.

Transfer to plates to rest for 3 to 5 minutes. Drizzle with the reserved glaze, then serve right away.

RIB EYE ON THE BONE WITH BLACK GARLIC–ANCHOVY BUTTER

When I trained as a saucier, I was in charge of executing an epic "rib eye for two" experience. I ruined so many before getting it right. Now I want to share my secrets to making perfect steak at home. Sprinkling on a generous amount of salt from 6 inches high helps the salt evenly disperse. A very hot cast-iron skillet with plenty of oil—warning, this will trip your smoke alarm!—and the discipline to not fidget with the steak ensures a gorgeous brown crust. A thick steak gives you the time to develop that crust before the meat hits medium-rare. Finally, resting the steak before slicing allows the juices redistribute so they don't end up on your cutting board. With these tips (and a flavor-packed compound butter), your first attempt will turn out great, but know it'll be even better the more you practice.

SWITCH IT UP

Swap the flavored butter for Sichuan Chile–Bourbon Butter (page 252) or Burnt Lime–Cilantro Butter (page 252).

SERVES 2

1 well-marbled bone-in rib eye steak (1½ to 2 pounds), 1½ to 2 inches thick

1½ to 2 teaspoons Diamond Crystal kosher salt

Coarsely ground black pepper

¼ cup canola oil

2 garlic cloves, lightly smashed and peeled

Small handful of mixed rosemary, thyme, and sage sprigs

3 tablespoons Black Garlic–Anchovy Butter (page 252)

Flaky sea salt

Heat a large cast-iron skillet over high heat until it begins to smoke, about 3 minutes. Meanwhile, pat the steak dry and generously season all over (edges, too) with 1½ teaspoons salt (add an additional ½ teaspoon for a 2-inch-thick steak) and a generous amount of pepper.

Add the oil to the skillet, then carefully add the steak. Cook, flipping once but otherwise undisturbed, until both sides develop an even deep brown crust, about 5 minutes per side for a 1½-inch steak and 7 minutes for a 2-inch steak. Briefly sear the edges of the steak, too.

When juices collect on the surface of the steak (a good indicator the interior is nearing medium-rare), add the garlic, herbs, and butter to the skillet. Tilt the pan slightly toward you so the butter pools at the edge of the pan, then use a spoon to constantly baste the steak (including the bone) with the butter for 1 minute.

Transfer the steak to a cutting board. Let it rest for at least 10 minutes.

To carve, cut the steak off the bone, then slice the steak against the grain into approximately ½-inch-thick slices. Serve the bone and steak on a platter. Stir the delicious fat in the skillet and spoon some over the steak, including the herbs and garlic. Sprinkle with flaky salt and serve.

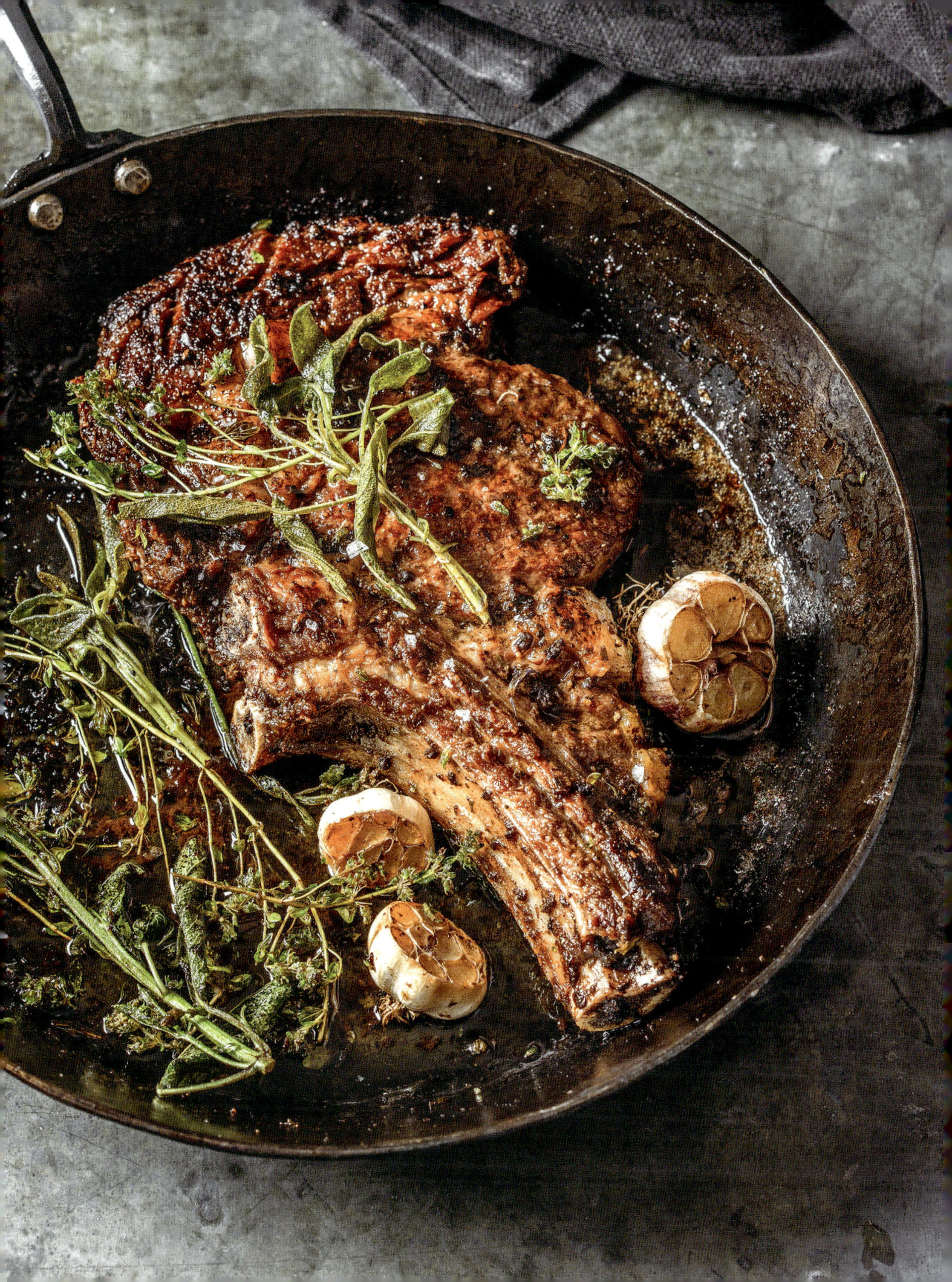

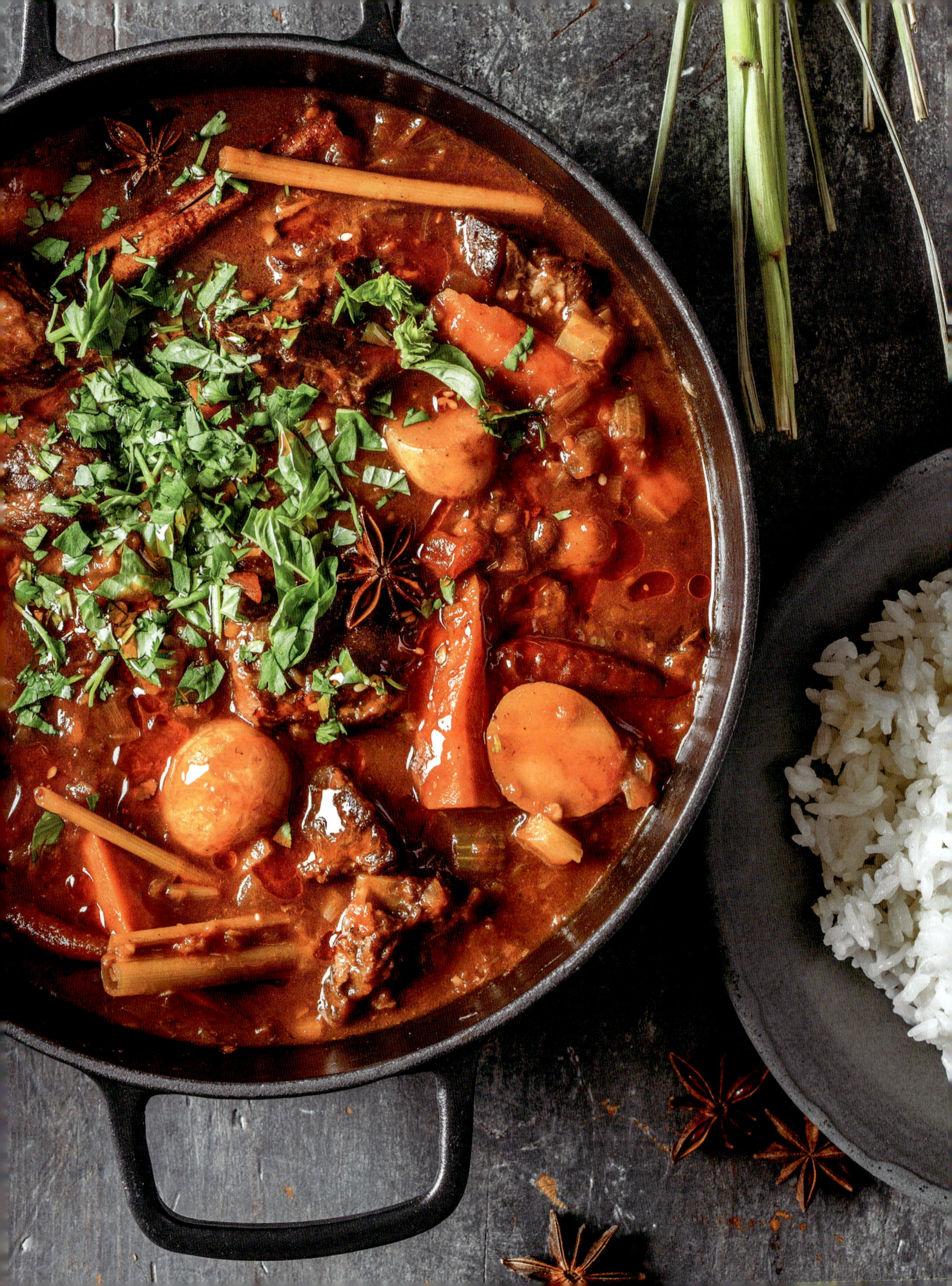

LEMONGRASS BEEF STEW

Equipment: 6- to 8-quart pressure cooker (optional)

2 pounds boneless beef chuck roast, cut into 2-inch chunks

Diamond Crystal kosher salt and finely ground black pepper

2 tablespoons canola oil

2 lemongrass stalks, trimmed (see page 16) and smashed

1 celery stalk, finely diced

1 leek, white and light-green parts only, halved lengthwise, thinly sliced, and rinsed

1 medium yellow onion, finely diced

3 garlic cloves, minced

2 by 1-inch knob ginger, peeled and minced

10 whole cloves

5 whole star anise

3 whole dried Sichuan chiles

2 bay leaves

2 cinnamon sticks

1 scant tablespoon tomato paste

1 cup full-bodied, dry red wine, such as Cabernet Sauvignon or Zinfandel

1⅔ cups canned crushed tomatoes

2 cups low-sodium beef stock

3 tablespoons fish sauce, plus more as needed

1 teaspoon white sugar

1 pound baby, fingerling, or small creamer potatoes (halved or quartered, if large)

3 large carrots, peeled and sliced on the diagonal into 2-inch lengths

Steamed rice, egg noodles, or crusty bread, for serving

Chopped herbs, such as cilantro, scallions, basil, and/or Thai basil, for serving

Chili oil from King's Chili Crisp (page 257) or store-bought Chinese chili oil, for serving

This cozy, flavor-packed stew is a melding of French beef bourguignon and Vietnamese bo kho. The red wine component comes from the Burgundian stew and the lemongrass, fish sauce, and star anise come from the Vietnamese dish, which was shaped by French colonialism but is Vietnamese through and through. The potatoes make it a one-pot meal, though I still like mine over steamed rice or noodles, or with a crusty baguette.

SERVES 4 TO 6

Heat a 5- to 7-quart Dutch oven (or if stewing in a pressure cooker, a large heavy skillet) over medium-high heat for 2 minutes. Meanwhile, season the beef all over with 2 teaspoons of salt and pepper to taste. Add the oil and swirl to coat the pot. Sear the beef in two batches to avoid crowding, turning the pieces occasionally, until deep golden all over, 6 to 8 minutes per batch. Transfer the beef to a plate, leaving the fat behind.

To the pot, add the lemongrass, celery, leek, onion, garlic, ginger, and a pinch of salt and cook, stirring often, for 3 minutes. Add the whole cloves, star anise, chiles, bay leaves, and cinnamon sticks and stir for 1 minute. Add the tomato paste and cook, stirring often, until the oil takes on an orange hue, 1 to 2 minutes. Add the wine, bring to a steady simmer, and cook, stirring and scraping the bottom occasionally, until the wine has reduced by half, about 5 minutes.

In a pressure cooker: Transfer to the cooker. Add the cooked beef (and any juices on the plate), potatoes, carrots, tomatoes, broth, fish sauce, and sugar. Stir well. Lock the lid and cook on high pressure for 35 minutes, until the meat is fork-tender. Quick-release the pressure according to the manufacturer's instructions.

In the oven: Preheat to 300°F. Return the cooked beef to the pot, add the tomatoes, broth, fish sauce, and sugar and bring to a boil over high heat. Cover and cook in the oven until the meat is fork-tender, 2½ to 3 hours, adding the potatoes and carrots for the last 1 hour.

Remove the lemongrass stalks, if you'd like, and season to taste with salt and fish sauce. Serve with rice, noodles, or bread and garnish with the fresh herbs and chili oil. Advise your guests to eat around the remaining whole spices.

MALA LAMB SKEWERS

These are quick-cooking flavor-bombs. Powered by cumin and mala (the gentle mouth-numbing sensation created by combining Sichuan peppercorns and chiles), the skewers of salty, juicy, charred meat have changed the minds of many a lamb-averse friend. Lemon juice is an absolute must, cutting the richness and boosting the complexity of the mala spice. They're best made with a nicely marbled cut of lamb, like shoulder or leg, because that fat will get crispy and absorb the smoky flavors from the hot coals.

LEVEL IT UP

Cheesy Scallion Pancakes (page 93) and Chili Crisp Labneh (page 32) make great partners.

SWITCH IT UP

Chicken thighs, beef sirloin, and pork shoulder are all tasty substitutes for lamb.

MAKES 12 SKEWERS

Equipment: 12 metal or soaked bamboo skewers (about 10 inches long)

2 pounds boneless lamb shoulder or leg

5 large garlic cloves, finely grated on a Microplane

3 tablespoons Shaoxing wine

3 tablespoons Chinese light soy sauce

½ teaspoon cornstarch

½ teaspoon white sugar

½ teaspoon Diamond Crystal kosher salt

½ teaspoon ground cumin

¼ teaspoon ground white pepper

¼ cup King's Mala Spice (page 263), divided

1 lemon, halved

Extra-virgin olive oil, for drizzling

Flaky sea salt, for finishing

Cut the lamb into ¾-inch chunks (no need to trim any fat). Transfer to a medium mixing bowl. Add the garlic, Shaoxing wine, soy sauce, cornstarch, sugar, salt, cumin, and white pepper and mix well. Cover and let marinate in the refrigerator for at least 2 hours or up to 12 hours.

Prepare a grill, preferably charcoal, to cook with medium-high heat. Make sure the grill grates are very hot before adding the lamb.

Thread the lamb onto the skewers, alternating meatier and fattier pieces, so the pieces touch and a few inches at either end of each skewer are empty. Grill, uncovered, flipping the skewers once, until browned with plenty of char, about 4 minutes total. Sprinkle 3 tablespoons of the mala spice mixture on both sides and cook, flipping once, for another 2 minutes total.

While the lamb cooks, squeeze the juice of the lemon onto a serving platter, sprinkle on the remaining 1 tablespoon of the mala spice, and add a generous drizzle of olive oil.

Transfer the cooked lamb to the platter and roll the skewers around to coat the lamb in the mixture. Sprinkle with flaky salt and serve immediately.

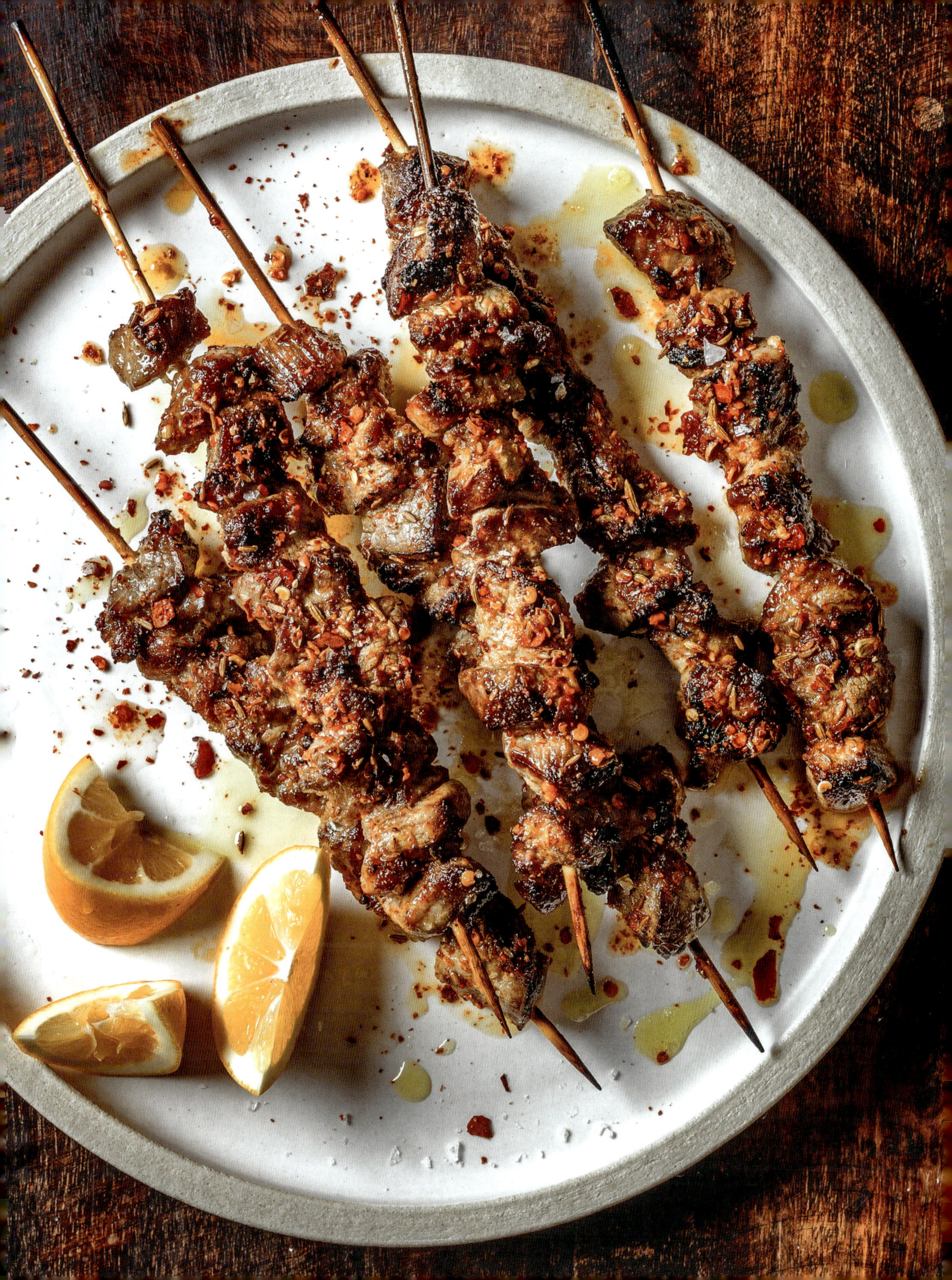

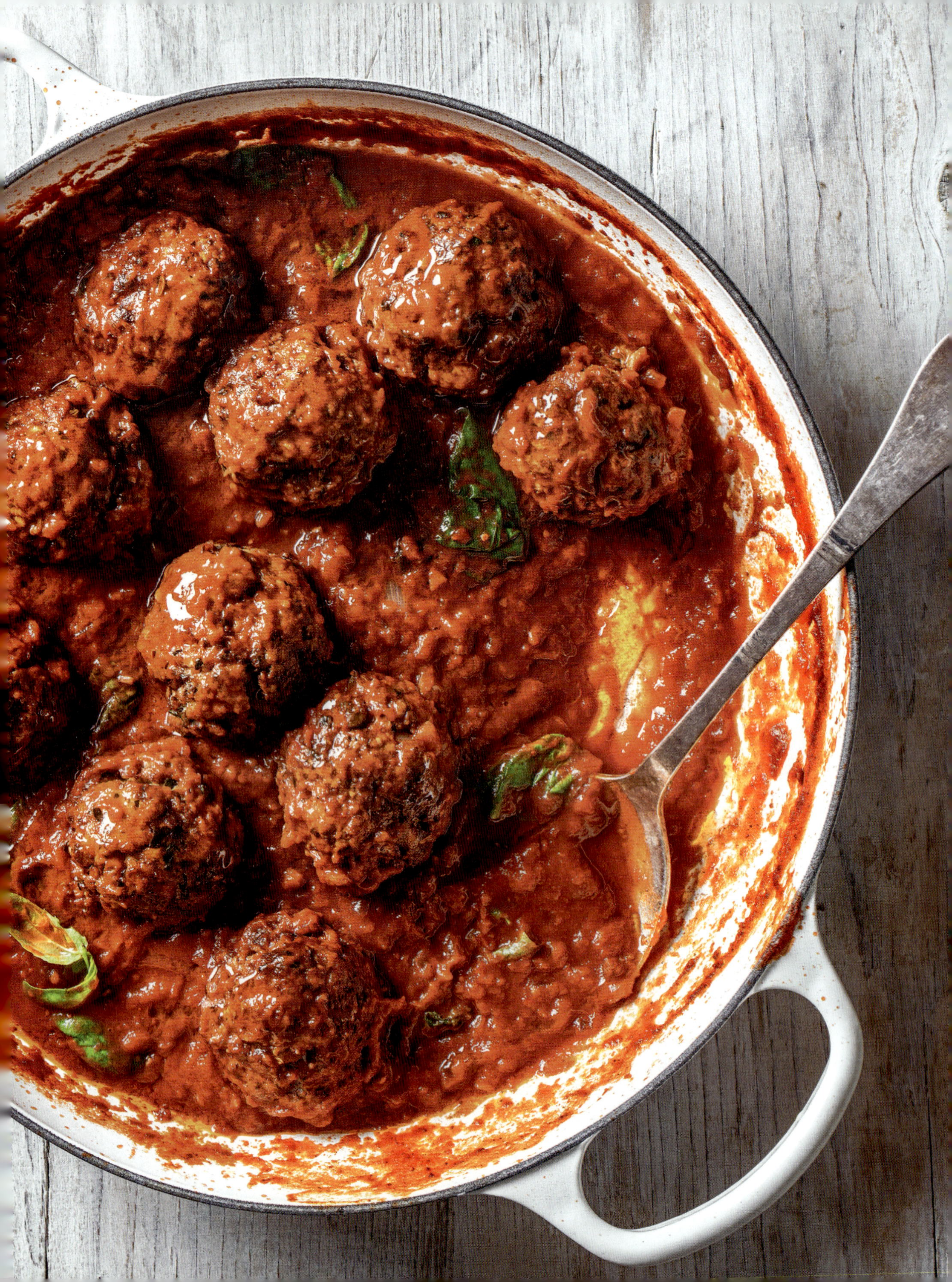

MAMA MEL'S MEATBALLS

My friends call me Mama Mel. That's what happens when cooking is your love language and making feasts is the way you care for your favorite people. These meatballs are one of my go-to dishes for gatherings. No one's mad at a meatball, especially when they're this tender and flavorful thanks to ricotta and, my little secret, chopped capers. They also give you the chance to spend time with your guests, since you can simmer them in cozy pomodoro sauce ahead of time and keep them warm until you're ready to serve. They're great alongside crusty bread (preferably fried in olive oil and rubbed with garlic, see page 59), in a sandwich, or as spaghetti and meatballs. In either case, shaved Parmigiano-Reggiano on top doesn't hurt.

SERVES 4 TO 6

POMODORO SAUCE

½ cup extra-virgin olive oil, divided

1 medium yellow onion, finely diced

4 large garlic cloves, minced

Diamond Crystal kosher salt

½ bottle full-bodied, dry red wine, such as Cabernet Sauvignon or Zinfandel

Two 28-ounce cans crushed tomatoes

1 teaspoon white sugar

½ teaspoon red chile flakes, plus more as needed

Finely ground black pepper

A piece of Parmigiano-Reggiano rind (optional)

Two handfuls of basil leaves

MEATBALLS

3 tablespoons extra-virgin olive oil

1 medium yellow onion, finely diced

4 large garlic cloves, minced

Diamond Crystal kosher salt

1 tablespoon fennel seeds, coarsely ground in a mortar or spice grinder

1 tablespoon chopped oregano leaves

1 tablespoon chopped thyme leaves

1 pound ground beef (20% fat)

1 pound ground pork (20% fat)

1½ cups whole-milk ricotta

¾ cup panko bread crumbs

One 3½-ounce jar capers (scant ½ cup), finely chopped

1 cup finely grated Parmigiano-Reggiano

½ cup finely chopped flat-leaf parsley leaves

Make the pomodoro sauce: Heat a 7- to 8-quart Dutch oven over medium-high heat for 1 minute. Add ¼ cup of the olive oil and heat until it shimmers. Add the onion, garlic, and a pinch of salt and cook, stirring occasionally, until the onion is translucent, about 4 minutes.

Add the wine, bring to a simmer, then cook, stirring occasionally, until it has reduced by about half, 5 to 7 minutes. Stir in the tomatoes, sugar, chile flakes, several turns of black pepper, Parmigiano-Reggiano rind (if using), and 1 tablespoon salt and let it come to a gentle simmer. Reduce the heat to cook at a gentle simmer, partially covered, stirring occasionally, until it has thickened slightly and concentrated in flavor, about 1 hour.

Tear and stir in the basil leaves and the remaining ¼ cup olive oil, and simmer for an additional 5 minutes. Remove from the heat. Remove the Parmigiano-Reggiano rind (discard or snack on it). Season with additional chile flakes, black pepper, and salt to taste. Keep warm while you make the meatballs. (The sauce keeps in the refrigerator for up to 5 days or in the freezer for up to 2 months.)

Form the meatballs: Heat a medium skillet over medium heat for 1 minute. Add the olive oil and heat until it shimmers. Add the onion, garlic, and a pinch of salt and cook, stirring occasionally, until the onion is translucent and softened, about 4 minutes. Stir in the fennel, oregano, and thyme and cook for an additional minute. Transfer to a shallow bowl and refrigerate until fully cooled.

In a large mixing bowl, combine the cooled onion mixture, beef, pork, ricotta, panko, capers, Parmigiano-Reggiano, parsley, chile flakes, black pepper, egg, and 1 tablespoon salt. Use your hands to mix until the ingredients are evenly dispersed, no longer than 2 minutes.

Use wet hands to roll the meat mixture into roughly 2½-inch balls, transferring them to a tray in a single layer. Cover and refrigerate for at least 20 minutes, to help hold their shape when seared, or up to 24 hours.

CONTINUED

MAMA MEL'S MEATBALLS
CONTINUED

1 teaspoon red chile flakes, or more as needed

¼ teaspoon finely ground black pepper

1 large egg

Canola oil (about 1 quart), for shallow-frying

Finish the dish: Bring the sauce to a gentle simmer. Lightly season the meatballs all over with additional salt.

Pour 1 inch of canola oil into a large skillet and heat over high heat for 5 minutes. When the oil is ready, the end of a wooden chopstick or wooden spoon submerged in the oil will immediately release little bubbles.

Working in batches to avoid crowding, gently add the meatballs to the hot oil one by one, leaving a little space around each one. Cook, flipping once halfway through, until deep brown all over, about 8 minutes per batch. Between batches, use a spider strainer to remove any stray bits from the oil. As they're done, transfer the meatballs to the simmering sauce, nestling them so they're mostly submerged.

Cover the pot and simmer, gently rotating the meatballs occasionally, for at least 15 minutes or up to 1 hour. Serve hot.

PORK KATSU WITH SNOW PEAS, HERBS, AND YUZU VINAIGRETTE

People around the world love a crispy cutlet, from the schnitzel of Germany to the cotoletta of Italy to the milanesa of Mexico. My version is most similar to Japanese tonkatsu. The pork is pounded thin, coated in panko, and pan-fried until golden, then served with a sweet and tangy sauce made with Worcestershire and sesame. All that crunch yearns for something fresh and bright, like the heaps of thinly sliced cabbage that come with classic katsu or the slivered snow peas and celery tossed with delicate herbs and yuzu juice I like to pile on at home.

SWITCH IT UP

Pounded chicken breasts make a great stand-in for pork and portobello caps make a lovely replacement for meat.

SERVES 4

TONKATSU SAUCE

½ cup ketchup

¼ cup plus 2 tablespoons Worcestershire sauce

1½ tablespoons Japanese soy sauce

1 tablespoon Dijon mustard

2 teaspoons white sugar

2 tablespoons lemon juice

2 tablespoons toasted sesame seeds

PORK CUTLETS

1 cup all-purpose flour

Diamond Crystal kosher salt and finely ground black pepper

2 large eggs

2 cups panko bread crumbs

4 boneless pork loin chops (about 6 ounces each)

YUZU VINAIGRETTE

1 tablespoon minced shallot

3 tablespoons bottled yuzu juice

1 tablespoon lemon juice

1 tablespoon honey

1 tablespoon Dijon mustard

Finely grated zest of 1 lemon

½ teaspoon Diamond Crystal kosher salt

Finely ground black pepper

¼ cup extra-virgin olive oil

Make the tonkatsu sauce: In a small saucepan, combine the ketchup, Worcestershire sauce, soy sauce, mustard, and sugar and cook over medium heat, whisking occasionally, until the sugar has dissolved, 1 to 2 minutes. Cool to room temperature and stir in the lemon juice. Finely grind the sesame seeds in a mortar and stir into the sauce. (The sauce keeps in an airtight container in the refrigerator for up to 5 days.)

Prepare the pork cutlets: Set up a dredging station in three shallow dishes. In one dish, stir together the flour, 1 teaspoon salt, and a few turns of pepper. In a second dish, beat the eggs with a pinch of salt and 2 tablespoons water. In the third dish, put the panko.

One at a time, put the pork chops between two pieces of plastic wrap and lightly pound with the flat side of a meat mallet or the back of a small heavy skillet to make even cutlets that are between ¼ and ½ inch thick.

One at a time, lightly season the cutlets on both sides with salt and pepper. Dredge them in the flour mixture, shaking off any excess. Add them to the egg mixture, turning to coat completely, then immediately transfer to the panko, patting to coat well. As they're breaded, transfer to a sheet pan and repeat with the other cutlets. (The breaded cutlets can be refrigerated, covered, for up to 12 hours.)

Make the yuzu vinaigrette: In a small mixing bowl, stir together the shallot, yuzu juice, and lemon juice and let sit for 2 minutes to tame the shallot's sharp flavor. Whisk in the honey, mustard, lemon zest, salt, and pepper to taste. Slowly drizzle in the olive oil, whisking constantly, until thickened and emulsified.

When ready to assemble: Preheat the oven to its lowest setting. Line a sheet pan with a wire rack or paper towels.

CONTINUED

PORK KATSU WITH SNOW PEAS, HERBS, AND YUZU VINAIGRETTE

CONTINUED

ASSEMBLY

Canola oil (about 2 cups), for shallow-frying

Diamond Crystal kosher salt

6 ounces snow peas, trimmed, julienned, and chilled

1 cup sliced (¼-inch) celery, chilled, plus a handful of tender leaves

Small handful of tarragon leaves

Small handful of picked dill

Small handful of mint leaves

Finely ground black pepper

Lemon wedges or charred lemon (see Note)

> **NOTE**
>
> To char citrus, set a large cast-iron skillet over high heat until it smokes lightly. Add citrus halves cut-sides down and let them brown and char, undisturbed, about 2 minutes.

Pour ½ inch canola oil into a large heavy skillet and heat over medium heat for 5 minutes. When the oil is ready, the end of a wooden chopstick or wooden spoon submerged in the oil will immediately release little bubbles.

Working in two batches to avoid crowding, fry the cutlets until deep golden brown on both sides, adjusting the heat if necessary and flipping once halfway through, 5 to 6 minutes per batch. Between batches, use a spider strainer to remove any stray bits from the oil. Transfer the cutlets to the rack or towels, immediately sprinkle lightly with salt, and keep warm in the oven.

In a medium bowl, combine the snow peas, celery, celery leaves, tarragon, and dill. Roughly chop the mint leaves and add them to the bowl. Whisk the yuzu vinaigrette well and drizzle over the salad. Add a pinch of salt and a few turns of pepper. Mix gently with your hands.

Serve the katsu on plates topped with the salad and with the lemon wedges and tonkatsu sauce on the side.

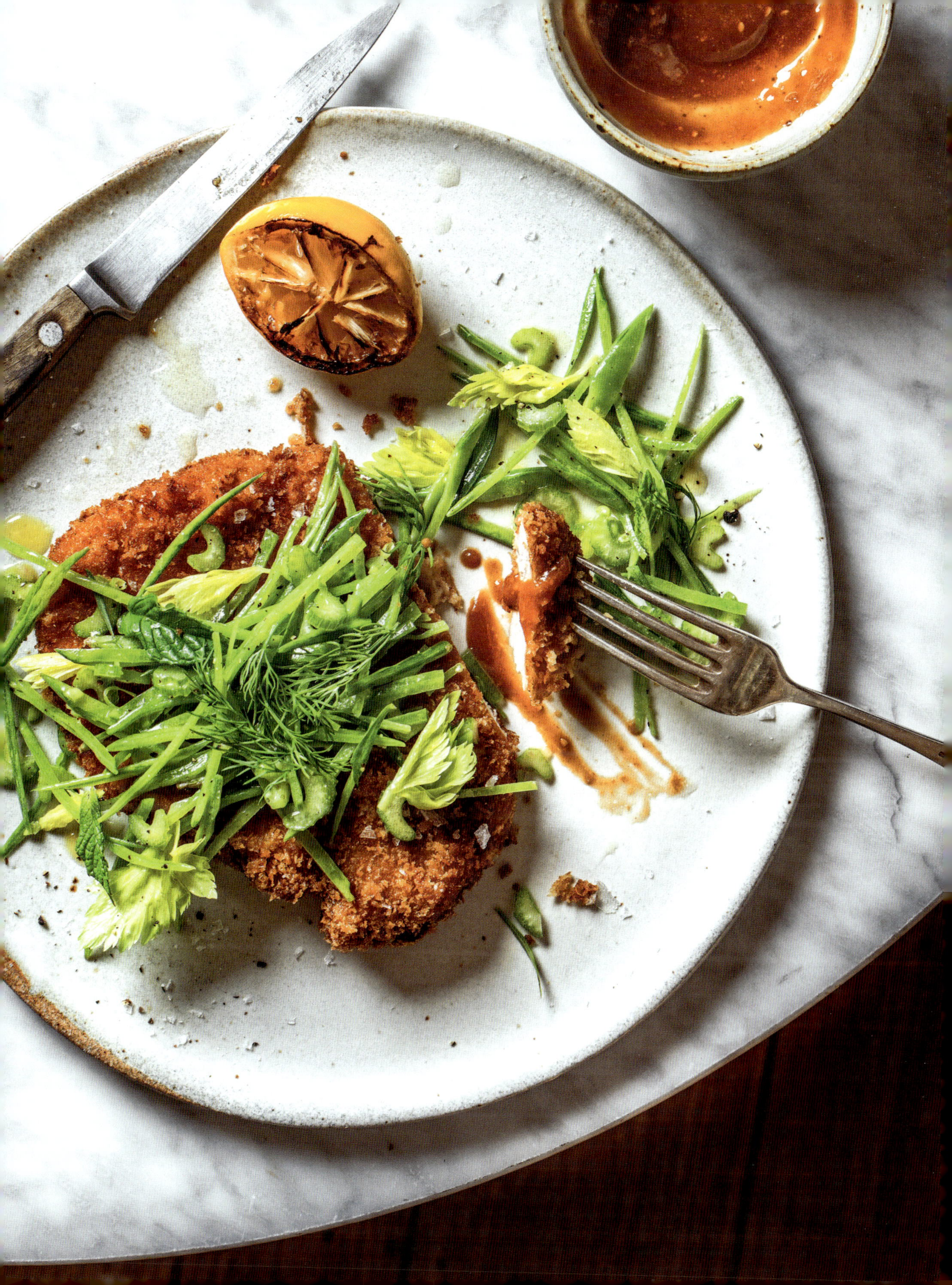

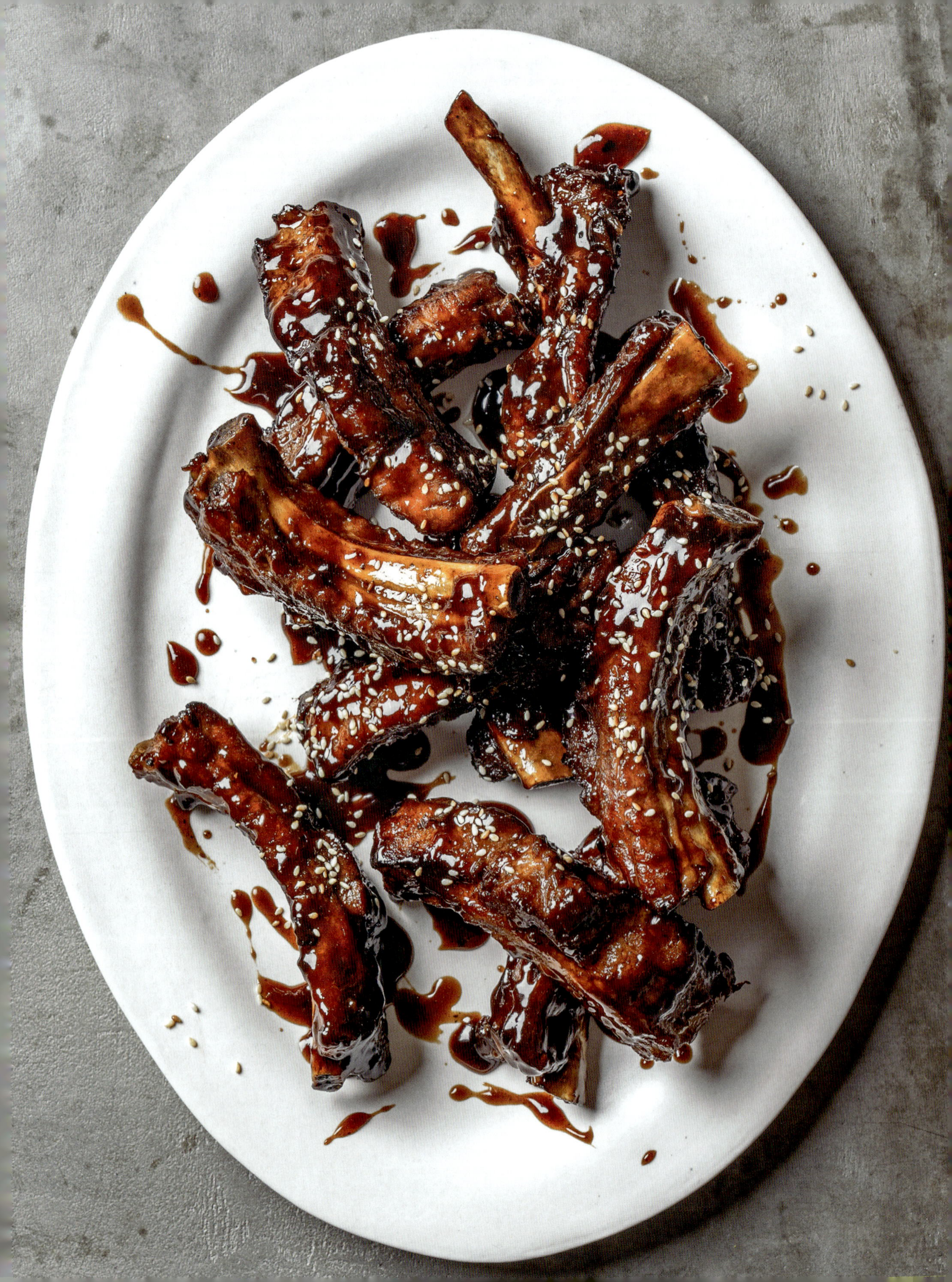

BLACK VINEGAR RIBS

These are baby back ribs, Shanghainese style. As a kid, I'd stand on a wooden stool next to the stove and watch my mom simmer pork ribs in a wok until they were just tender. She'd remove the cover and crank up the heat to reduce the sauce into a sweet, sticky, umami glaze. Zhenjiang black vinegar gives these ribs a unique malty tang.

SERVES 4

MARINATED RIBS

¼ cup Shaoxing wine

2 tablespoons Chinese light soy sauce

1 tablespoon Chinese dark soy sauce

1 tablespoon packed dark brown sugar

1 tablespoon cornstarch

Dash of ground white pepper

One 2-pound rack baby back pork ribs (about 12), membrane removed, cut into individual ribs

TO FINISH

½ cup water

½ cup Zhenjiang black vinegar

½ cup Shaoxing wine

2 tablespoons Chinese dark soy sauce

1 tablespoon Chinese light soy sauce

1 tablespoon Maggi seasoning

Dash of ground white pepper

Diamond Crystal kosher salt

3 tablespoons canola oil

2 by 1-inch knob ginger, peeled and finely grated on a Microplane

2 large garlic cloves, finely grated on a Microplane

½ cup packed dark brown sugar or Chinese rock sugar

Coarsely ground black pepper

1 teaspoon toasted sesame seeds, for garnish

Marinate the ribs: In a small mixing bowl, combine the Shaoxing wine, light soy sauce, dark soy sauce, brown sugar, cornstarch, and white pepper and stir to dissolve the sugar. Transfer to a large resealable bag, add the ribs, and seal, pushing out the air. Massage to coat in the marinade and refrigerate for at least 2 hours or up to 24 hours.

To finish: In a medium mixing bowl, stir together the water, black vinegar, Shaoxing wine, dark soy sauce, light soy sauce, Maggi, and white pepper. Set the vinegar mixture aside.

Remove the ribs from the marinade, discarding it, and lightly season all over with salt.

Heat a large skillet or wok that has a tight-fitting lid over high heat for 1 minute. Add the canola oil, swirl the pan, and let it smoke lightly. Working in batches, add the ribs (one at a time to prevent splatter), then reduce the heat to medium-high and cook, turning occasionally, until golden brown all over, 4 to 5 minutes per batch.

Return all the ribs to the skillet, then add the ginger and garlic to an empty space in the pan and stir them for 10 seconds or so. Add the brown sugar and let it melt and bubble, stirring occasionally, 1 to 2 minutes. Toss well to coat the ribs in the melted sugar.

Add the vinegar mixture and stir. Bring to a boil, then turn the heat down to cook at a steady simmer, covered, stirring and flipping the ribs occasionally, until the meat is tender and pulls easily from the bone, about 50 minutes.

Remove the ribs and increase the heat to cook at a vigorous simmer, uncovered, until the liquid thickens to a sticky glaze that's as thick as honey, 8 to 12 minutes more.

Return the ribs to the pan along with a few turns of the black pepper and toss to coat well. Serve the ribs on a plate, drizzle with the glaze, and top with the toasted sesame seeds.

CHICKEN AND GINSENG BONE BROTH WITH GOJI BERRIES

This is the most Cantonese recipe I can think of: a clear, healing bone broth that reminds me of my childhood. It was the first thing I made on my own when I was about eight years old. By that time, I had already earned the nickname tong wong, or "soup king," from my family, because of how much I love drinking broth. It's made from black Silkie chicken, prized for its high collagen content (drinking it is a major part of my skincare routine—I'm not even joking!). The ginseng, ginger, goji berries, and jujubes are there for flavor and for their curative properties, according to traditional Chinese medicine. As kids, my sister and I had to hold our noses to get through the earthy, slightly sweet ginseng notes and weren't allowed to leave the table until we'd finished every last drop. But as an adult, I crave the soothing flavors and make this broth regularly for myself and often for friends who aren't feeling their best.

Black chicken is commonly available in the frozen section at Chinese markets. You can totally chicken out and use a standard bird, but you won't get the same collagen boost.

SERVES 4 TO 6

1 whole Silkie (black) chicken (2 to 3 pounds)

2 by 1-inch knob ginger, peeled and sliced

2 ounces dried ginseng root (about 6), rinsed

6 dried jujubes

Handful of dried goji berries

1½ tablespoons Diamond Crystal kosher salt

1 teaspoon Shaoxing wine

In a large pot, combine the chicken and 16 cups water. Cover and bring to a boil over high heat. Uncover and boil for 10 minutes, turning the chicken over halfway through. Drain, then rinse the chicken well under cold water. The blanching process removes coagulated blood and other impurities from the bones and gives the broth a cleaner flavor.

Rinse out the pot, then add the chicken to the pot along with the ginger and 18 cups fresh water. Cover and bring to a boil. Immediately reduce the heat to cook at a gentle simmer, partially covered, for 3 hours, skimming and adjusting the heat as necessary. Long and slow is the key to a clear, flavorful broth.

Add the ginseng and continue to cook for another 2 hours, skimming occasionally. Add the jujubes and cook for 1 hour more, for a total cooking time of 6 hours.

Use a ladle to skim off any fat from the surface of the broth. Add the goji berries and simmer, uncovered, until they plump, about 5 minutes. Stir in the salt and Shaoxing wine, then season with more salt to taste.

Ladle the broth, jujubes, and goji berries into bowls, leaving the rest behind and discarding it. Serve hot.

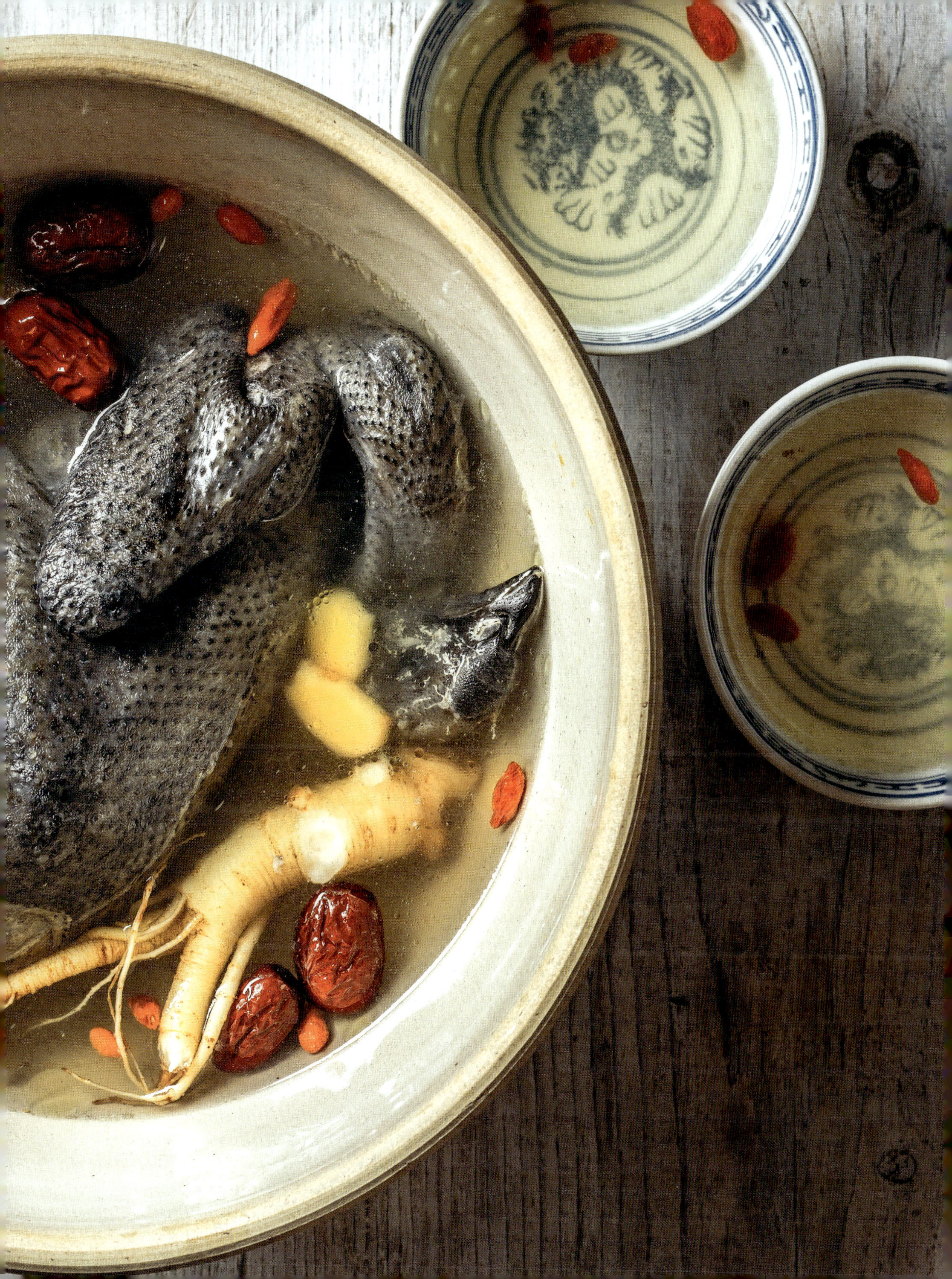

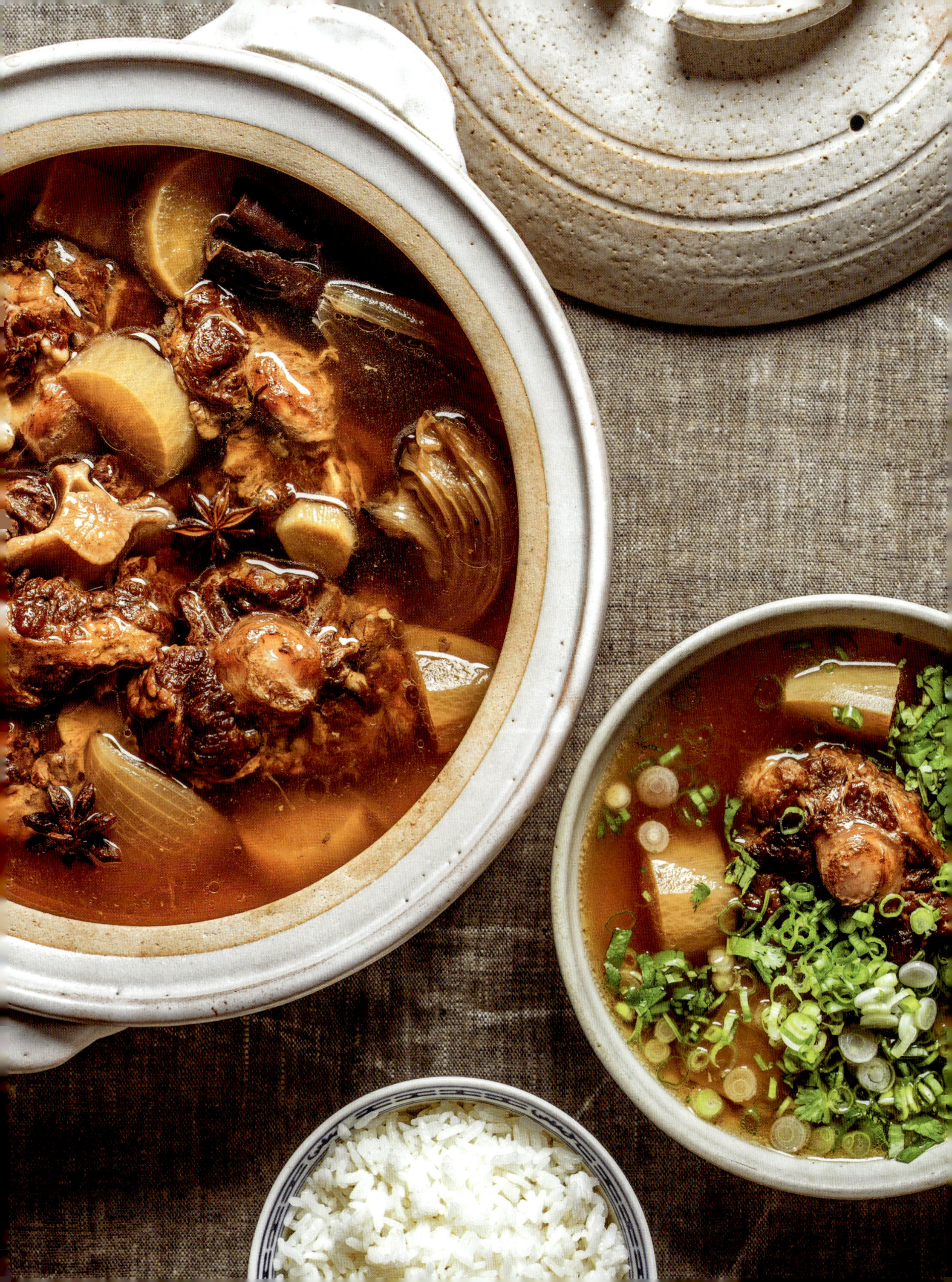

OXTAIL AND DAIKON SOUP

This warm hug in a bowl combines so many things I love in one pot. It takes cues from Cantonese ching tong lam, beef brisket braised with sweet, tender daikon radish and star anise, and Hawaiian oxtail soup. When I make it, I infuse the flavorful broth with warm spices and aromatics like ginger and shallots charred in the style of Vietnamese phở. And I stew oxtails, a collagen-rich cut once considered scraps and transformed into fall-off-the-bone gold by resourceful cooks around the world. Use a heavy hand with cilantro and scallions to finish each bowl for a welcome freshness.

SERVES 4

Equipment: 6- to 8-quart pressure cooker (optional)

½ pound ginger, cut into ¼-inch slices
2 medium shallots, halved lengthwise
1 large yellow onion, quartered
3 pounds meaty oxtail, cut by a butcher into 2-inch segments
2½ teaspoons Diamond Crystal kosher salt, divided, plus more as needed
Finely ground black pepper
3 tablespoons canola oil
2 bay leaves
1 whole star anise
1 cinnamon stick
¼ teaspoon coriander seeds
6 whole cloves
4 cups beef stock, homemade or low-sodium store-bought
4 cups water
2 tablespoons fish sauce, plus more as needed
1 tablespoon white sugar, plus more as needed
1 pound daikon radish, peeled, halved lengthwise, and cut crosswise into 1½-inch pieces
4 medium garlic cloves, peeled
1 medium bunch of cilantro, stems separated, leaves chopped
4 or 5 scallions, thinly sliced
Steamed jasmine rice, for serving

Preheat the broiler and position an oven rack 2 to 4 inches from the heat source. Spread the ginger, shallots, and onion on a large (18 by 13-inch) sheet pan and broil, flipping once, until well charred but not completely blackened on both sides, about 4 minutes. Set aside.

Heat a large, wide pot over high heat for 1 minute. Meanwhile, season the oxtail all over with 1½ teaspoons of the salt and pepper to taste. Add the oil and swirl to coat the bottom. Sear the oxtail until golden brown all over, including the edges, 5 to 7 minutes total. The process will produce smoke, so consider opening a window.

Reduce the heat to medium, add the bay leaves, star anise, cinnamon, coriander, and cloves and cook, stirring frequently, until fragrant, about 1 minute. Add the stock, water, fish sauce, sugar, and remaining 1 teaspoon salt.

On the stovetop: Cover and bring to a boil. Reduce the heat to cook at a gentle simmer, covered, for 3 hours, occasionally skimming off any fat or foam.

Add the daikon, garlic, and cilantro stems along with the charred ginger, shallots, and onion and continue to simmer gently, partially covered, until the meat pulls very easily from the bone, about 1 hour.

In a pressure cooker: Transfer to the cooker, then add the daikon, garlic, and cilantro stems along with the charred ginger, shallots, and onion. Lock the lid and cook on high pressure for 1 hour. Quick-release the pressure, according to the manufacturer's instructions. Skim off any fat or foam.

To serve the dish: Season to taste with salt, sugar, and fish sauce. Ladle the broth, oxtails, and daikon into bowls (avoiding the aromatics and spices). Garnish with the chopped cilantro and scallions and serve with rice.

SHANGHAINESE "LION'S HEAD" MEATBALLS

When I was a kid, my dad cooked just one thing: si zi tau ("lion's head meatballs"), a homey Shanghainese dish of pork meatballs simmered with napa cabbage and glass noodles in a flavorful, gingery chicken broth and served with rice. As a kid, I'd watch him vigorously mix ground pork with egg whites, cornstarch, and water with his hands, part of the alchemy behind their signature tender, silky texture. I'd help him shape the large orbs (big, like a lion's head) while he talked up the importance of refrigerating them before cooking and never, ever skipping the egg whites. He'd tell me that lion's head meatballs reminded him of Shanghai and his mom's cooking. At the time, they reminded me of "stinky lunch box" embarrassment—a typical tale of the first-generation American experience. Now they remind me of him.

SERVES 4

MEATBALLS

1 pound ground pork (preferably 20% fat)

2 tablespoons Shaoxing wine

2 teaspoons cornstarch

2 teaspoons chicken bouillon powder

1 teaspoon Diamond Crystal kosher salt

1 teaspoon Chinese light soy sauce

½ teaspoon white sugar

¼ teaspoon ground white pepper

2 large egg whites

2 scallions, minced

1 by 1-inch knob ginger, peeled and finely grated on a Microplane

2 tablespoons water

TO FINISH

Canola oil (about 4 cups), for shallow-frying

5 cups 2-inch pieces napa cabbage

6 cups low-sodium chicken stock

1 teaspoon Chinese light soy sauce

1 teaspoon Chinese oyster sauce

½ teaspoon white sugar

¼ teaspoon Diamond Crystal kosher salt, plus more as needed

¼ teaspoon ground white pepper, plus more as needed

2 slices peeled ginger

3 ounces dried bean threads (thin mung bean noodles)

2 tablespoons cornstarch

2 tablespoons water

Make the meatballs: In a large bowl, combine all the ingredients except the water and mix and squeeze the mixture by hand to distribute the ingredients well, about 1 minute. Add the water and continue to mix and squeeze until the mixture is smooth and homogenous, about 2 minutes more. Do not be gentle. This process emulsifies the mixture and helps give the cooked meatballs their distinctive texture. Don't be alarmed by the looseness of the mixture. Cover and refrigerate for at least 30 minutes, to let the mixture firm up, or up to 4 hours.

To finish: Pour 1 inch of canola oil into a large wok or skillet and heat over high heat for 5 minutes. When the oil is ready, the end of a wooden chopstick or wooden spoon submerged in the oil will immediately release little bubbles.

Using wet hands, scoop out about one-fifth of the mixture, shape into a meatball as best you can, and carefully add it to the oil. Repeat with the rest of the mixture, leaving a little space around each meatball. Cook, flipping once halfway through, until deeply browned all over, 5 to 6 minutes. As they're done, use a slotted spoon or spider strainer to transfer to a 10-inch clay pot or 3½- to 5-quart Dutch oven.

Add the cabbage, chicken stock, light soy sauce, oyster sauce, sugar, salt, white pepper, and ginger. Cover and bring to a boil over high heat. Reduce the heat to cook at a gentle simmer, covered, for 15 minutes. Add the noodles, stirring so they submerge in the liquid, and cook, uncovered and stirring, until the noodles are translucent and tender, 2 to 3 minutes more.

In a small bowl, stir together the cornstarch and water until smooth. Bring the broth to a boil, then drizzle the cornstarch slurry directly into the broth, and simmer until the broth thickens slightly, about 1 minute. Season to taste with salt and pepper. Serve hot.

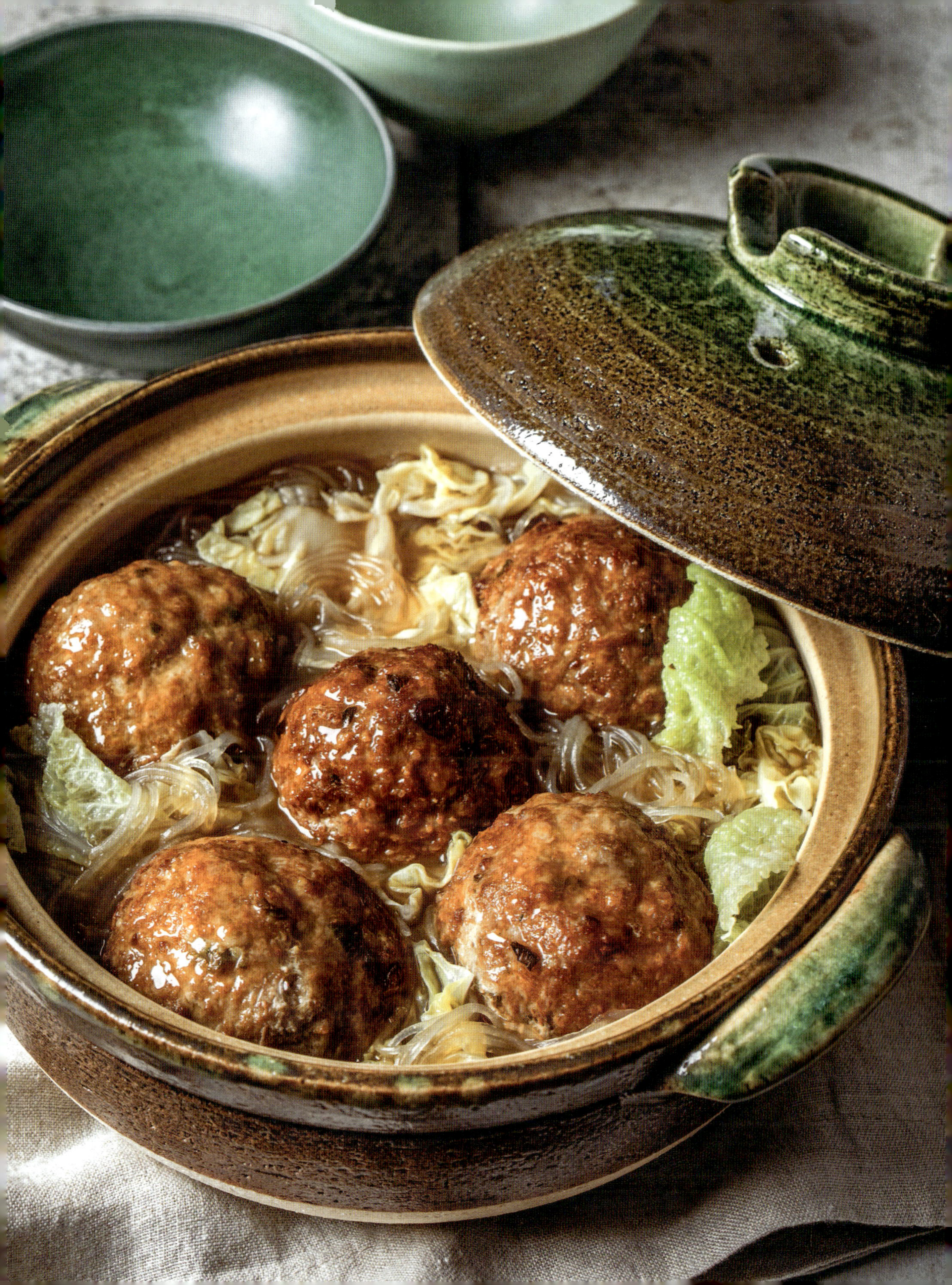

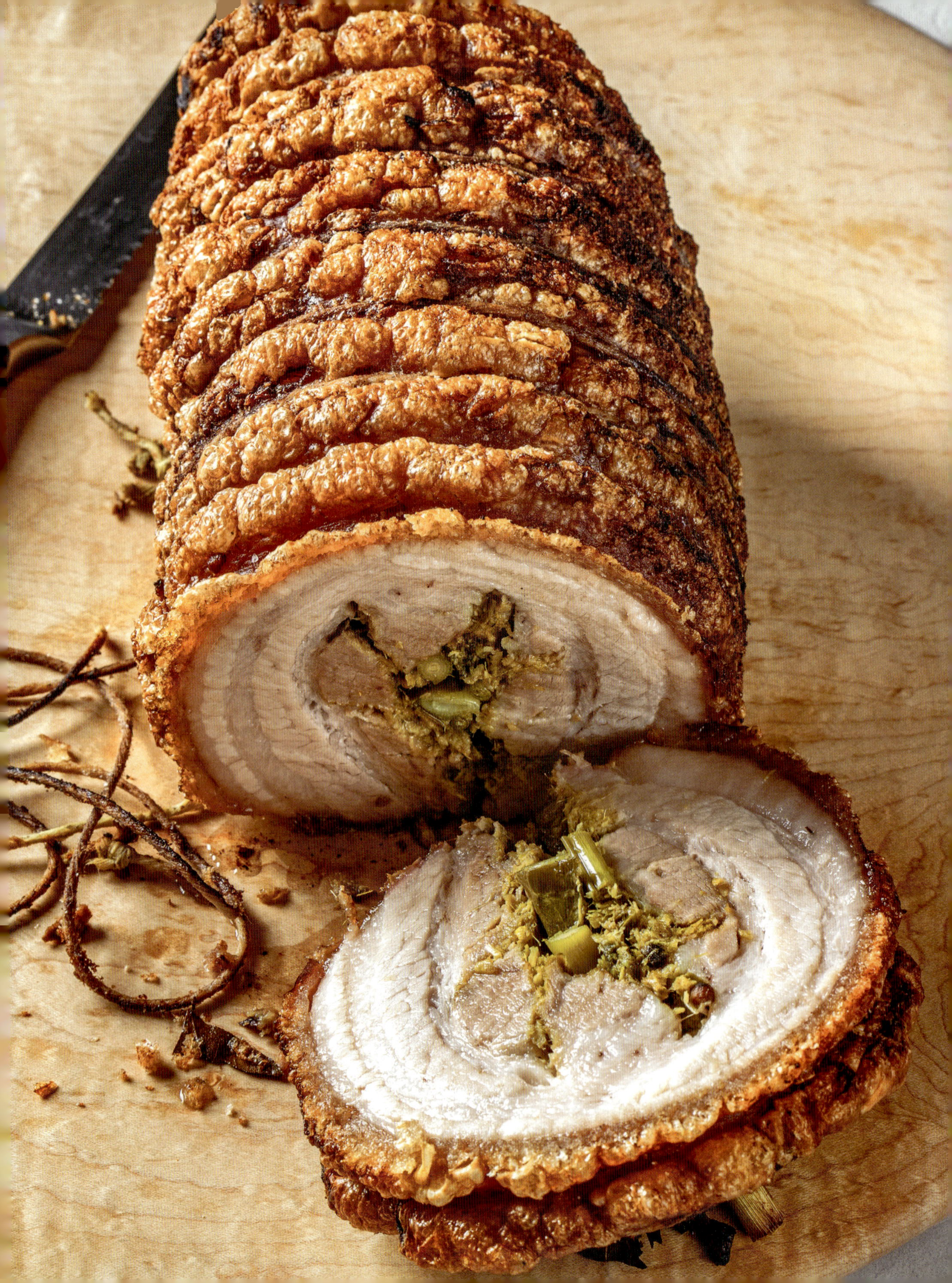

TURMERIC-LEMONGRASS PORK BELLY ROAST

While cruising on a little scooter around Bali a few years back, I stopped on the roadside and ate one of the most delicious things: babi guling, a whole suckling pig stuffed with lemongrass, lime leaves, and turmeric, then basted with coconut water as it roasted over an open fire until the skin was crackly crisp. Back home, I couldn't get those flavors off my mind. Because rolled pork belly is a bit more manageable for home cooks, I created a mash-up with babi guling and my favorite belly preparations, like Italian porchetta and Filipino lechon liempo. I also apply the poking technique that gives siu yuk (Chinese crispy roasted pork) its airy, puffed skin. When you slice, loudly, through this roast to reveal the juicy, tender meat, you'll have this moment of surprise and pride: Did I really make this? Yes, you did!

LEVEL IT UP

Make it a feast with Coconut Rice (page 251) or jicama salad (page 79), Pickled Daikon and Ginger (page 245), Cheesy Scallion Pancakes (page 93), and a basket of lettuce leaves and fresh herbs to make wraps.

SERVES 8 TO 10

Equipment: Eight 20-inch lengths of butcher's twine

One 6- to 7-pound piece skin-on boneless pork belly (see Note on page 218)

Diamond Crystal kosher salt

TURMERIC PASTE

¼ cup canola oil

1 tablespoon sliced Thai chiles (or jalapeño for less heat)

1 tablespoon coriander seeds

2 teaspoons black peppercorns

2 teaspoons Diamond Crystal kosher salt

10 garlic cloves, peeled

5 medium shallots, roughly chopped

4 lemongrass stalks, trimmed (see page 16; tops reserved and set aside), smashed, and roughly chopped

4 makrut lime leaves, roughly chopped

3 by ½-inch piece fresh turmeric root, peeled and roughly chopped, or 1 teaspoon ground turmeric

1 by 1-inch knob ginger, peeled and roughly chopped

Pat the pork belly dry. Use a pork skin poker or the tip of a sharp paring knife (I use two or three at a time to speed up the process) to pierce the skin (stopping short of the flesh) all over to make a hundred or so holes. This helps the skin render its fat and turn bubbly and crackling-crisp when roasted.

Set a wire rack over a large (18 by 13-inch) sheet pan, put the belly skin-side up on the wire rack, and evenly sprinkle 1½ tablespoons salt onto the skin. Refrigerate uncovered for 10 to 12 hours.

Make the turmeric paste: In a blender, combine all the ingredients and blend for 1 to 2 minutes, occasionally stopping to stir and scrape down the sides, until it's a fairly smooth paste (small bits and fibers are just fine). If necessary, add a splash of water to help the paste catch in the blades.

Prepare the roast: Use paper towels to wipe away any salt or moisture from the pork and transfer it skin-side down to a cutting board, reserving the wire rack and sheet pan. Score the flesh in a crosshatch pattern, making diagonal cuts that are about ¼ inch deep and 1 inch apart. Sprinkle the flesh side with 1 tablespoon kosher salt and a few turns of pepper. Wearing gloves to avoid staining your fingers yellow, rub the turmeric paste onto the flesh, including into the slits created by the crosshatch cuts.

Lay the reserved lemongrass tops, lime leaves, bay leaves, scallions, and cilantro sprigs widthwise along the center of the pork. Starting with a short side, roll the belly over the stuffing into a tight log, then turn the log seam-side down. Carefully slide one piece of twine under and in the middle of the log, snugly tie it around the pork belly (tightly enough to

CONTINUED

TURMERIC-LEMONGRASS PORK BELLY ROAST
CONTINUED

ROAST

Diamond Crystal kosher salt and finely ground black pepper

10 makrut lime leaves, scrunched to bruise slightly

6 bay leaves

3 scallions, trimmed but whole

Handful of cilantro sprigs

Canola oil, for rubbing the skin

Flaky sea salt, for finishing

Calamansi Dipping Sauce (recipe follows)

> **NOTE**
>
> For this recipe, it's particularly important to use the correct cut of meat. Tell a butcher you're looking for a single piece of skin-on, boneless pork belly that's roughly 14 by 10 inches—essentially, half a side of belly that has been cut the short way. If given the choice, choose the half from the front of the pig, which has a slightly higher ratio of meat to fat.

½ cup finely chopped red or yellow onion

¼ cup coconut vinegar or distilled white vinegar

3 tablespoons calamansi or yuzu juice (fresh or bottled) or lime juice

2 tablespoons Japanese soy sauce

1½ tablespoons light brown sugar

¼ teaspoon Diamond Crystal kosher salt

1 large garlic clove, finely grated on a Microplane

Several turns of coarsely ground black pepper

Finely chopped fresh hot chiles, such as Thai or jalapeño, to taste

make the slightest indentation in the skin), then double-knot the twine. Use the remaining twine to tie the belly in the same manner at 1-inch intervals. Snip off any excess string.

Return the pork to the wire rack set over the sheet pan, pat dry, and refrigerate uncovered for at least 12 hours and up to 24 hours to further dry out the skin. The dryer the skin, the crispier the results.

To finish: When you're ready to roast, position an oven rack in the lowest slot, remove the other racks, and preheat the oven to 300°F.

Rub the skin with canola oil to lightly coat all sides, then sprinkle all over with 1 teaspoon kosher salt (for beautifully blistered skin, do not rub on the salt). Transfer the wire rack and belly to a large roasting pan (a deep pan is necessary to catch the rendered fat). Roast until a meat thermometer registers 160°F, 3 to 3½ hours, basting occasionally with any rendered fat and rotating the pan halfway through. Be sure to insert the thermometer prong directly into the meat, not through the tough skin.

When the pork reaches 160°F, turn on the broiler and continue to cook, occasionally turning the belly on its side and basting, until evenly golden brown, puffed, and blistered all over, 15 to 30 minutes. Turn more frequently if the skin threatens to blacken.

Remove from the oven and let rest for 30 minutes. Remove the strings and then use a serrated knife to carve into thick slices (eat around the filling). Sprinkle with flaky salt to taste and serve with the dipping sauce alongside.

CALAMANSI DIPPING SAUCE

This tart dipping sauce, inspired by Filipino toyomansi, is fueled by fragrant citrus like calamansi or yuzu to cut the richness of anything it is served with.

MAKES ABOUT ¾ CUP

In a small bowl, stir together all the ingredients until the brown sugar has dissolved. Before serving, set aside for at least 1 hour to let the onion pickle and the flavors develop. (The sauce can be stored in an airtight container in the refrigerator for several weeks.)

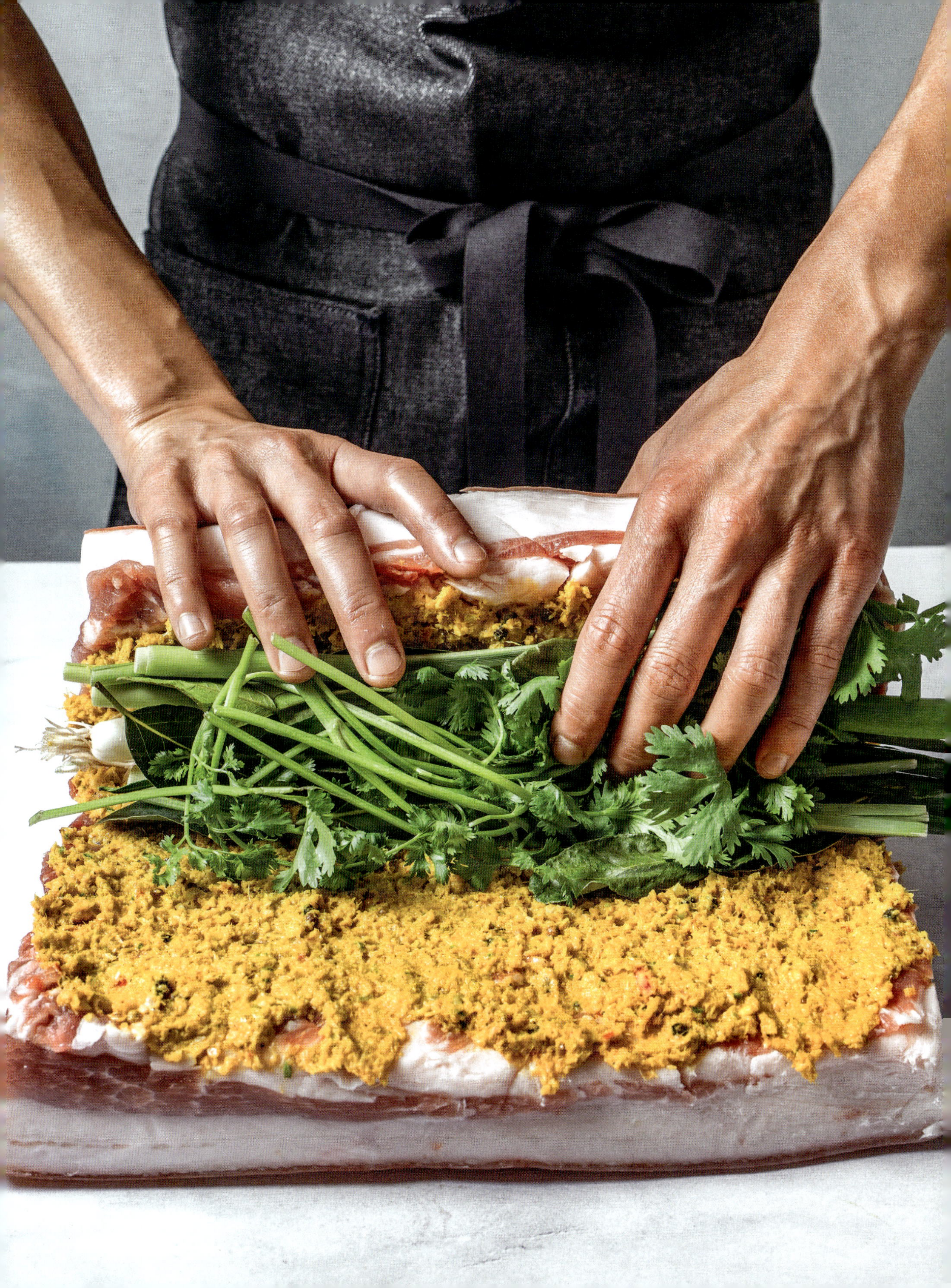

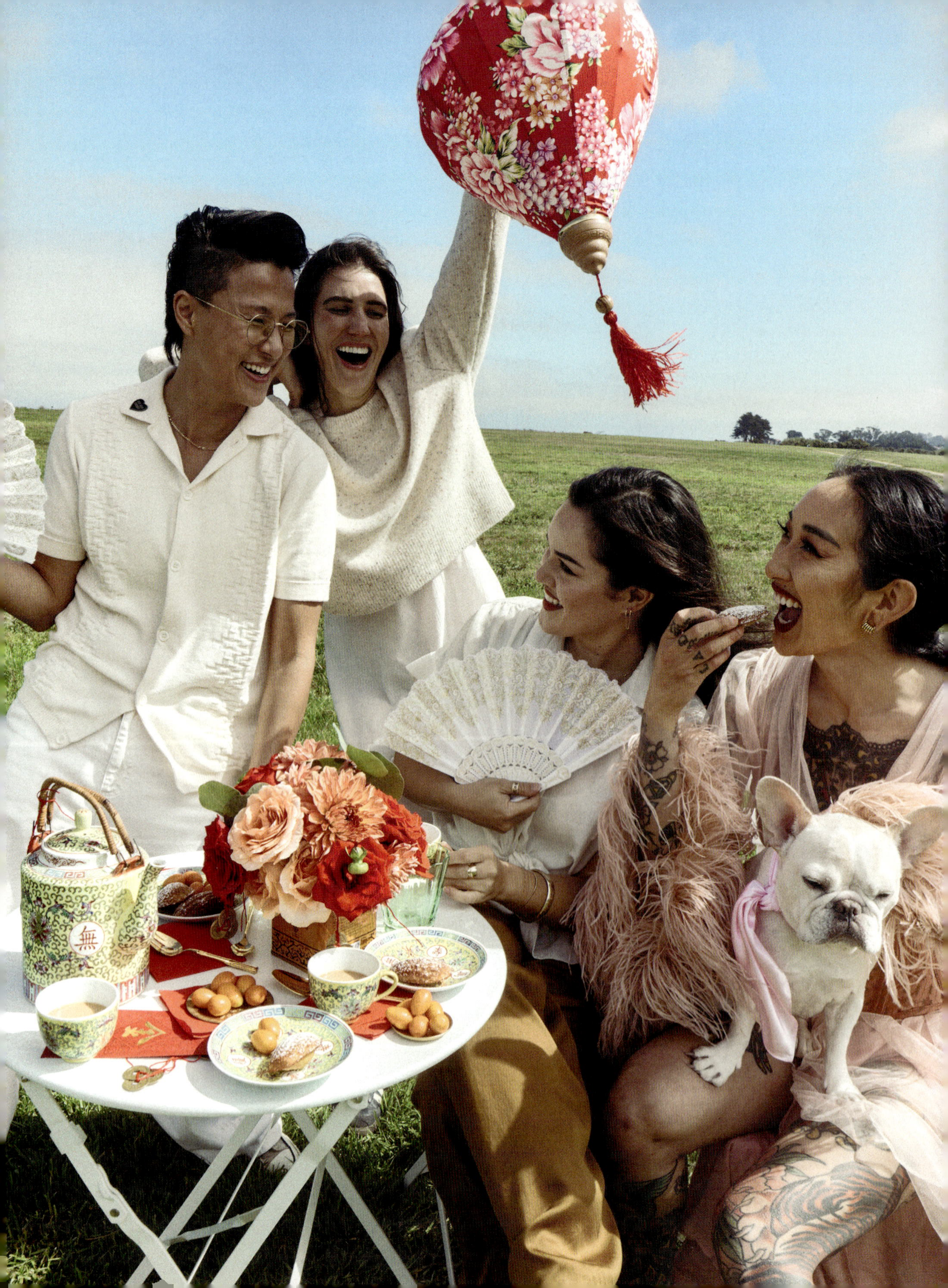
無

8 SWEETS

HONG KONG MILK TEA TIRAMISU

This dessert holds a very special place in my heart. Not only did it leave the famed Italian butcher Dario Cecchini teary-eyed, but it also won me *Top Chef: All-Stars*. It's essentially a classic tiramisu, the chilled layered Italian dessert, but with the espresso element replaced with a vivid memory of my childhood home: the *lai cha* (Hong Kong milk tea) my parents drank every morning. Like so much of the food I create, the secret is a lot of care and a little bit of me.

The tiramisu is great for entertaining, because it's made and chilled in advance. For the brand of tea, I highly recommend Dai Pai Dong 2-in-1.

SWITCH IT UP

Make it your own by swapping in other unsweetened instant teas, like Thai tea, Earl Grey, or matcha.

SERVES 10 TO 12

Equipment: Stand mixer

MASCARPONE CUSTARD

8 large egg yolks
½ cup sweetened condensed milk
½ cup white sugar
3 tablespoons unsweetened instant Hong Kong milk tea powder
⅔ cup whole milk
¾ teaspoon Diamond Crystal kosher salt
24 ounces (3¾ cups) mascarpone, cold

WHIPPED CREAM

2 cups heavy cream, cold
1½ teaspoons white sugar
2 vanilla beans, split lengthwise

TO ASSEMBLE

2 cups boiling water
¾ cup unsweetened instant Hong Kong milk tea powder
½ cup sweet or dry Marsala or Madeira
¾ cup sweetened condensed milk
About 40 savoiardi (Italian ladyfingers)
1 bar milk chocolate, cold, for grating

Make the mascarpone custard: Find a large metal bowl that can sit in a medium saucepan filled with 1 inch of water without touching the water. In the bowl, combine the egg yolks, sweetened condensed milk, sugar, tea powder, whole milk, and salt. Whisk until well combined.

Fill a slightly larger bowl with half ice and half water. Set up a double boiler: In the saucepan, bring 1 inch of water to a gentle simmer over medium to medium-low heat, and set the bowl with the egg yolk mixture in the pan. Constantly and vigorously whisk side to side until the mixture has doubled in volume and thickened slightly, 4 to 6 minutes.

Remove the bowl from the heat and set it in the bowl of ice water. With one hand, hold a rubber spatula in the custard and against the side of the bowl; with the other, spin the bowl until the mixture is well chilled, 4 to 6 minutes. This allows you to cool the mixture quickly without losing much of the air you beat in earlier.

In a stand mixer fitted with the whisk, combine the custard and mascarpone and whisk on medium-high speed, scraping down the bowl once or twice, to medium peaks, about 3 minutes. Refrigerate the mascarpone custard.

Make the whipped cream: In a stand mixer fitted with the whisk, combine the heavy cream and sugar. Use a paring knife to scrape the seeds of the vanilla beans into the bowl, reserving the pods for another day. Beat on medium-high speed until soft peaks form, 2 to 3 minutes. Whisk by hand until medium peaks form, about 15 seconds more. Refrigerate the whipped cream.

CONTINUED

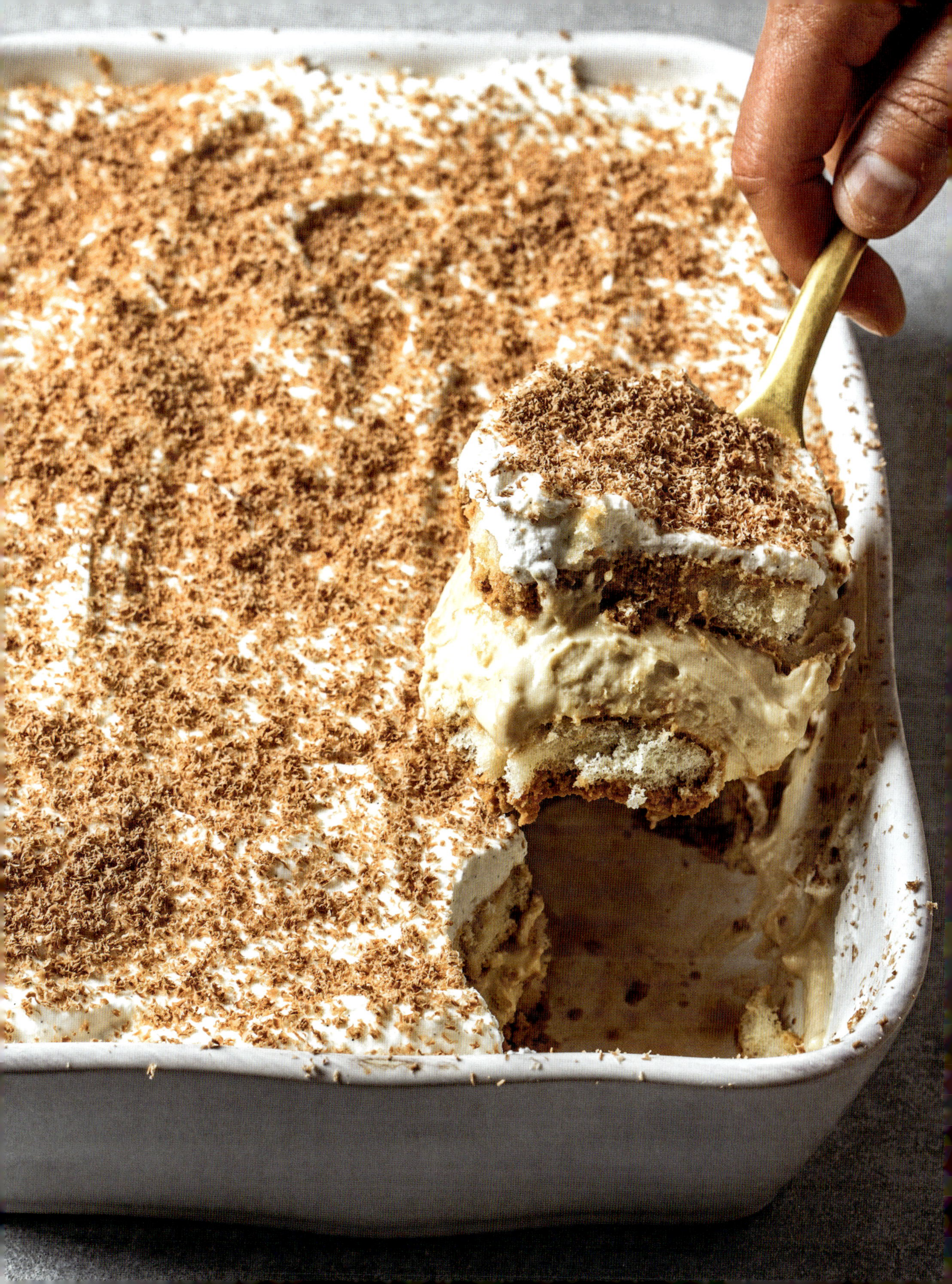

HONG KONG MILK TEA TIRAMISU
CONTINUED

Assemble the tiramisu: In a wide shallow bowl, stir together the boiling water and tea powder until the powder dissolves. Add the Marsala and the sweetened condensed milk and stir well.

Set a heavy 9 by 13-inch baking dish that's at least 3 inches deep near the tea mixture. One by one, briefly submerge 16 to 20 of the ladyfingers in the tea mixture for 3 to 4 seconds to saturate them (any longer and they'll fall apart) and add them to the baking dish to cover it in a single layer. Use a rubber spatula to spread the mascarpone custard evenly on top.

One by one, briefly submerge and add enough ladyfingers to make a second layer. (Discard any leftover tea mixture.) Spread the whipped cream evenly on top. Use a Microplane to finely grate enough of the chocolate bar over the tiramisu to generously cover the surface.

Cover and refrigerate for at least 24 hours or up to 72 hours (for me, the sweet spot is 48 hours). Serve cold.

TORCHED BANANA PUDDING WITH CHINESE ALMOND COOKIES

Sometimes changing just one ingredient can completely transform a dish. When my dear friend Andrew Zimmern and I collaborated on an event, we created a cozy, indulgent banana pudding with a little King twist. We swapped out vanilla wafers for the Chinese almond cookies I'd sneak from my Cantonese grandma Sabrina PoPo's pantry (the ones in the signature pink box), bringing a toasty, nutty flavor to this crowd favorite.

SWITCH IT UP

Torched peaks of Italian meringue provide a striking presentation and toasted-marshmallow vibes, but if you don't have the time or the torch, a simple whipped cream topping is lovely.

SERVES 12

Equipment: 1 large trifle bowl (at least 3 quarts) or twelve 8-ounce glass cups, bowls, or jars; stand mixer; parchment paper; candy thermometer; kitchen blowtorch

PASTRY CREAM

1 vanilla bean, split lengthwise
2 cups / 480g whole milk
6 large egg yolks
⅔ cup / 142g white sugar
½ teaspoon / 2g Diamond Crystal kosher salt
¼ cup / 28g cornstarch
1 tablespoon / 14g unsalted butter

BANANA PUDDING

One 15-ounce box Chinese almond cookies (preferably Twin Dragon brand)
6 large ripe bananas
2 cups / 480g heavy cream, cold
1 cup / 312g sweetened condensed milk
1 teaspoon / 4g almond extract

MERINGUE AND FOR SERVING

¼ cup / 20g sliced almonds
4 large egg whites
½ cup / 113g water
1½ cups / 300g white sugar

Make the pastry cream: Scrape the vanilla seeds into a small pot. Add the vanilla pod and the milk and cook over medium-high heat, stirring once or twice, just until it steams and begins to foam, 3 to 4 minutes.

Meanwhile, in a large mixing bowl, whisk together the yolks, sugar, and salt until smooth. Whisk in the cornstarch.

Once the milk is ready, discard the vanilla pod, then in a thin, steady stream, pour the hot milk mixture into the egg mixture, whisking constantly.

Clean and dry the small pot. Pour the egg mixture back into the pot, set over medium heat, and cook, constantly whisking, until the mixture begins to simmer, about 3 minutes. Continue whisking until it thickens to a pudding consistency, about 1 minute more. Remove from the heat, stir in the butter until melted, then immediately transfer to a medium mixing bowl. Cover with plastic wrap pressed against the surface of the pudding, and refrigerate until cooled completely, at least 2 hours or up to 24 hours.

Assemble and chill the banana pudding: Break the almond cookies roughly into quarters. Cut the bananas into ½-inch chunks.

Set a fine-mesh sieve over a large mixing bowl. Once the pastry cream has fully cooled, pour it into the sieve, stirring and pressing to pass it through, and set aside.

In a stand mixer fitted with the whisk, whip the heavy cream and condensed milk on medium-high speed to medium peaks. Stir the almond extract into the pastry cream, then use a flexible spatula to gently fold the whipped cream mixture into the pastry cream until no streaks remain.

CONTINUED

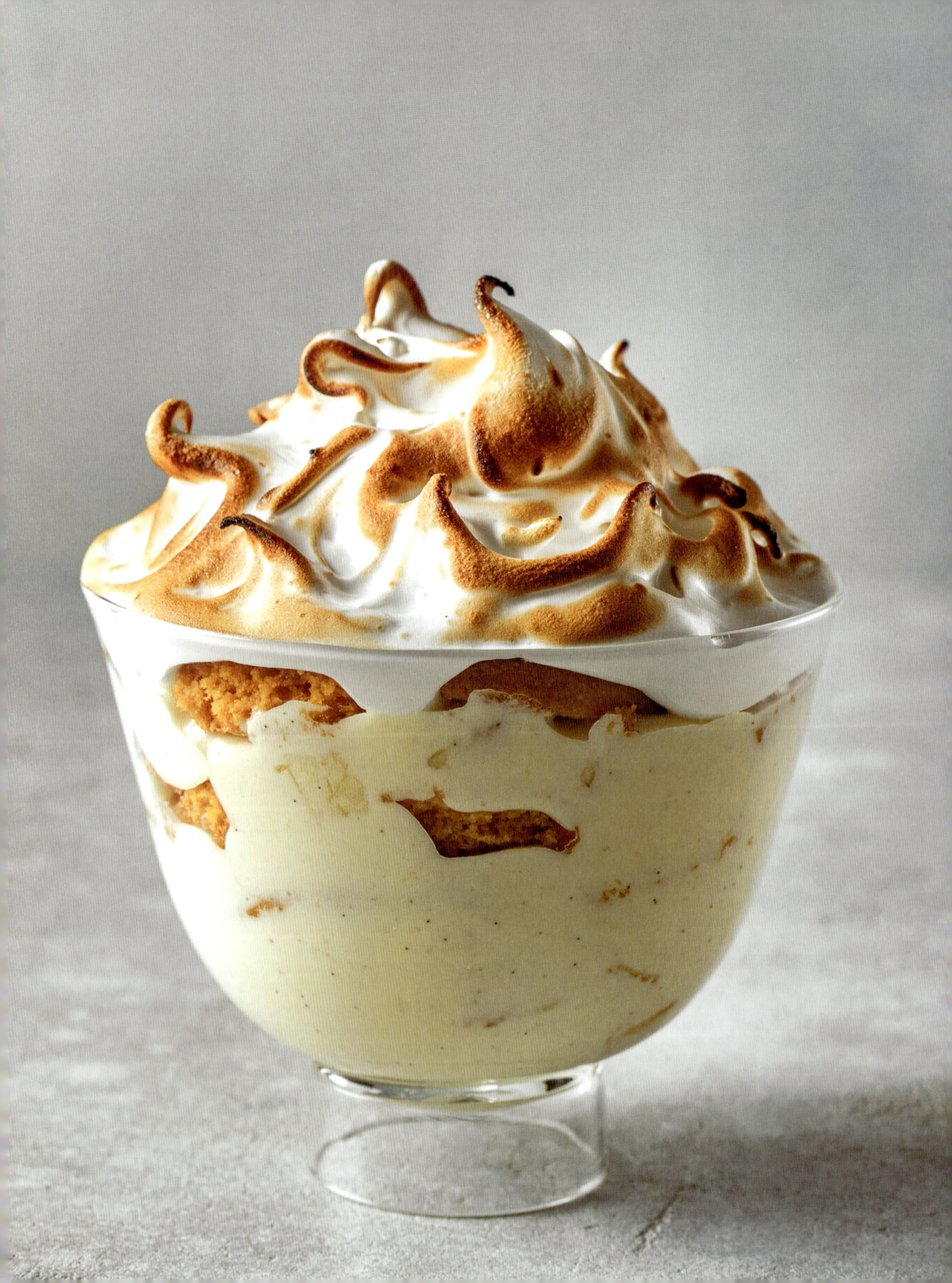

TORCHED BANANA PUDDING WITH CHINESE ALMOND COOKIES
CONTINUED

For making a large pudding, layer one-third of the whipped cream mixture into the dish. Top with one-third of the cookies then one-third of the bananas. Repeat the layers. For making individual puddings, fold bananas into the whipped cream mixture. Divide half the mixture among the serving containers, add a layer of cookies, and top with the remaining whipped cream mixture. Cover and refrigerate for at least 12 hours or up to 36 hours.

Make the meringue and serve: About 30 minutes before serving, preheat the oven to 350°F. Line a small (9 by 13-inch) sheet pan with parchment paper.

Spread the almonds on the prepared sheet pan in a single layer and toast in the oven, stirring occasionally, until an even golden brown, 5 to 7 minutes. Set aside to cool.

In a stand mixer fitted with the whisk, whisk the egg whites on low speed. Meanwhile, pour the water into a small saucepan and carefully spoon in the sugar, making sure it doesn't touch the sides of the pan. Gently stir to make sure all the sugar is wet without dry pockets. Attach a candy thermometer and bring to a boil over high heat, without stirring. Boil until the mixture reaches 240°F, about 5 minutes. Immediately turn off the heat.

Working quickly but carefully, increase the mixer speed to high. In a thin steady stream, pour the hot sugar mixture against the edge of the bowl so it drips into the egg whites (do not pour it on directly). Continue whisking on high until the peaks are stiff and the bowl is no longer hot to the touch (warm is fine), about 6 minutes.

Remove the pudding(s) from the fridge and sprinkle with the toasted almonds. Dollop on the meringue and spread evenly. If any spills, use a hot, wet towel to clean the edges. Use your fingers to haphazardly pinch and pull the meringue to form small peaks. Holding the blowtorch a few inches away, lightly torch the meringue all over. Serve immediately.

ALMOND MADELEINES WITH CITRUS MARMALADE

Madeleines were one of the first desserts I memorized how to make. A cookie-size buttery cake with a soft crumb and pretty fluted shape, they became my back-pocket pastry, one I could whip out for a dinner party at a friend's place or a cooking competition because they're so easy to make.

A dedicated madeleine pan gives you that seashell look, but the time I busted these out in a *Top Chef* quickfire challenge, I only had access to a muffin pan and the results were still delicious. The simple batter is easy to double or triple, and because it can be made ahead and refrigerated up to a day before use, serving warm madeleines is even easier than you may have thought. Serve them as is or with Citrus Marmalade (page 258) or Strawberry-Ginger Jam (page 231), and a hot cup of Hong Kong Milk Tea (page 259).

MAKES 8 MADELEINES

Equipment: Madeleine pan with at least 8 molds

3 tablespoons / 42g unsalted butter, plus ½ tablespoon melted butter for greasing the pan

2 teaspoons / 5g light brown sugar

½ teaspoon / 5g honey

3 tablespoons / 40g white sugar

3 tablespoons / 24g all-purpose flour, sifted

3 tablespoons / 25g almond meal, sifted

½ teaspoon / 1g baking powder

1 large egg

1 teaspoon / 5g almond extract

Finely grated zest of 1 lemon

Powdered sugar, for dusting

Citrus Marmalade (page 258)

In a small saucepan, combine the butter, brown sugar, and honey and cook over medium heat, stirring, until the butter and sugar melt, 1 to 2 minutes. Turn off the heat.

In a medium mixing bowl, combine the white sugar, flour, almond meal, and baking powder and whisk to combine. Whisk in the egg and continue whisking as you slowly pour in the melted butter mixture. Whisk in the almond extract and lemon zest. Cover and refrigerate for at least 1 hour or up to 24 hours.

Position a rack in the center of the oven and preheat the oven to 350°F. Put the madeleine pan in the oven for 5 minutes to let it heat up.

Carefully remove the pan and brush 8 of the molds with melted butter. Spoon the batter into the buttered molds, stopping just shy of the rim.

Bake until the madeleines rise slightly and turn golden (a skewer inserted into the center will come out clean), 7 to 8 minutes, rotating the pan halfway through.

Carefully remove the madeleines from the pan. Serve immediately dusted with powdered sugar and with the marmalade on the side.

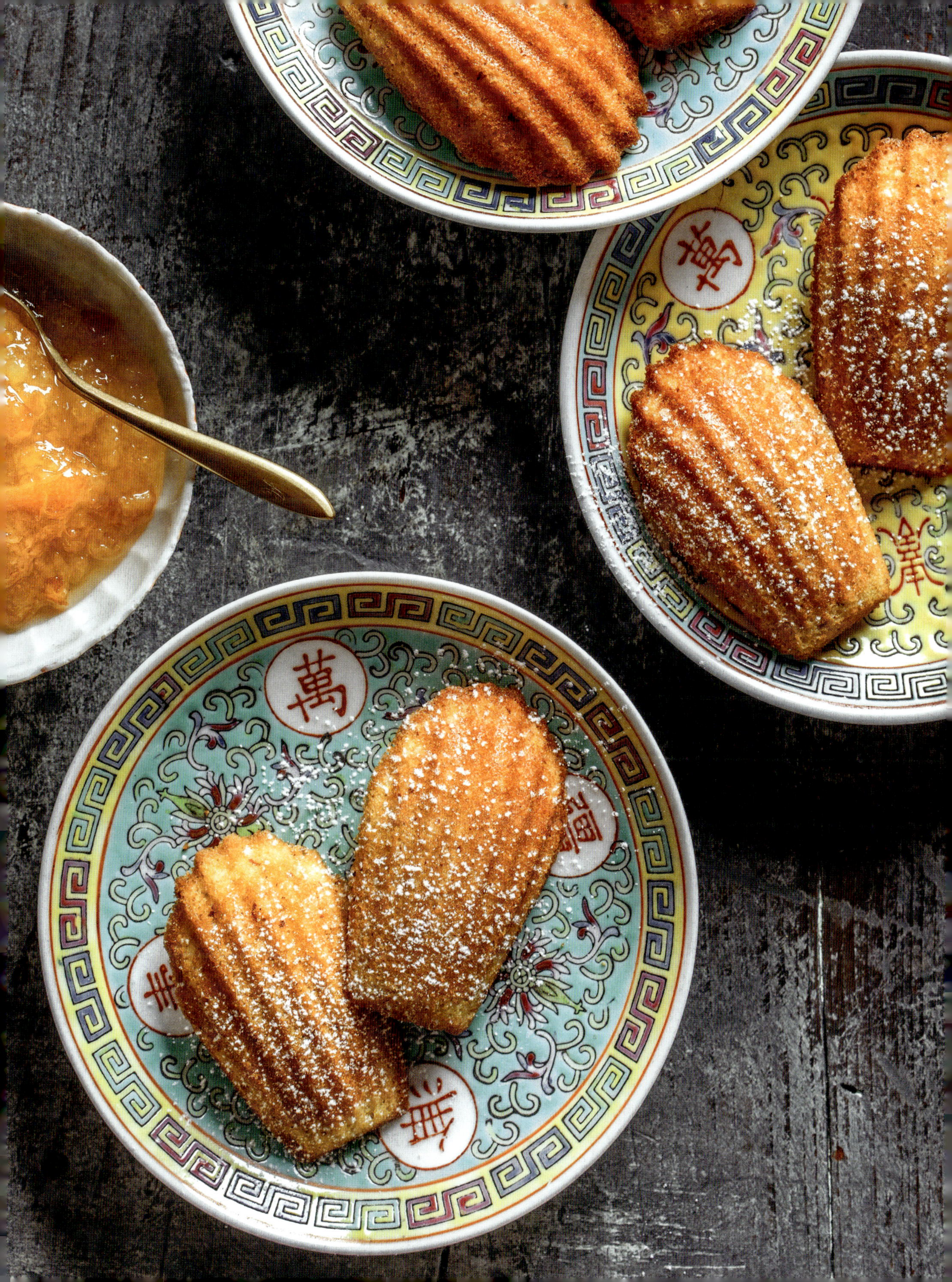
萬
萬

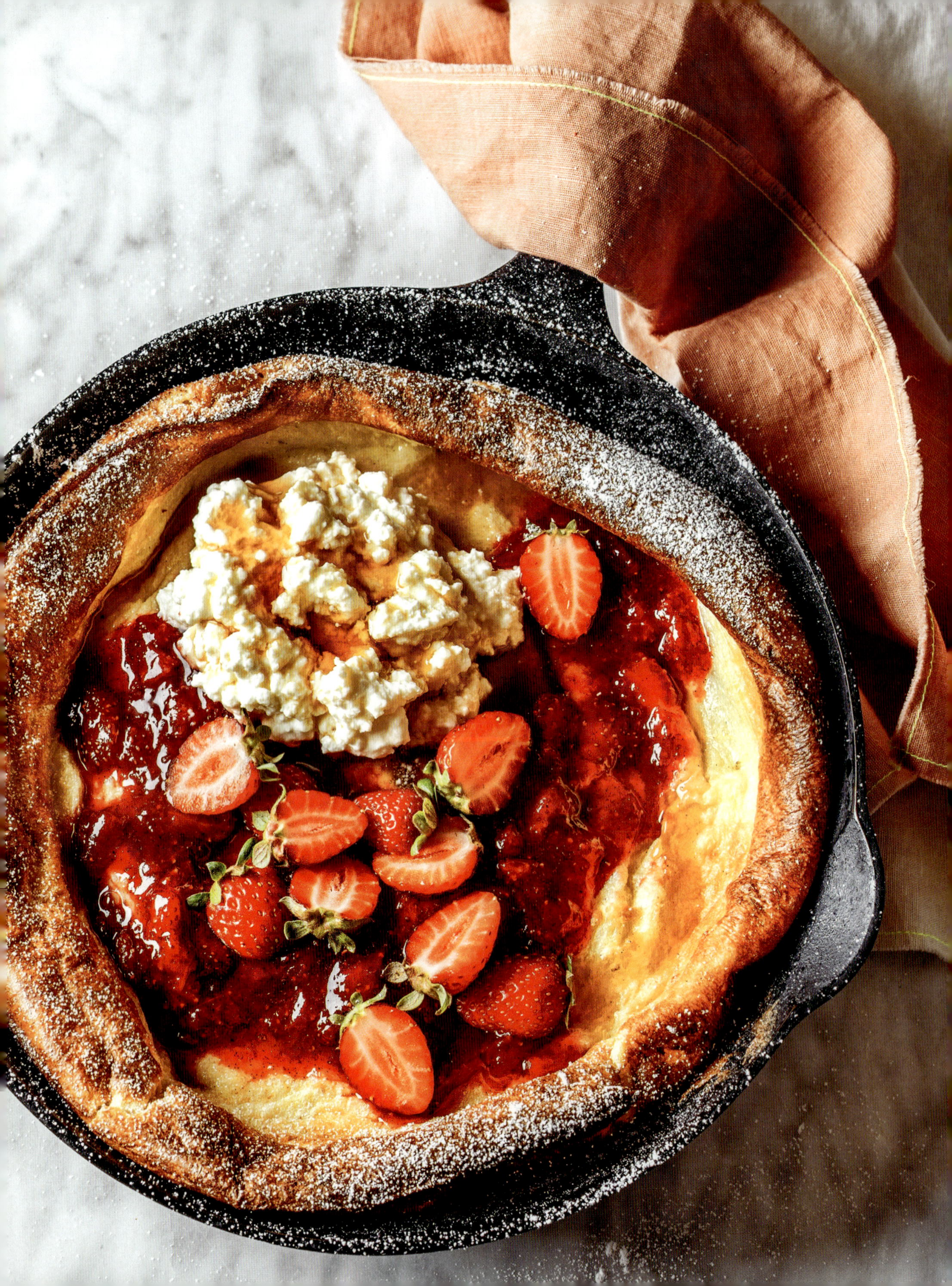

DUTCH PANCAKE WITH RICOTTA AND STRAWBERRY-GINGER JAM

Be a Sunday hero and make your family and friends a Dutch pancake or two. A simple batter poured into a super-hot skillet and baked transforms into a dramatic sight, the edges puffed and crisped and the center custardy. Ginger-spiked strawberry jam and ricotta is just one way to serve it, so choose your own sweet accompaniments, or add crispy bacon strips or Lap Cheong Crumble (page 256) for a salty/sweet brunch. Skip the vanilla and sugar in the batter and you have savory Yorkshire pudding that's incredible with roasts.

SERVES 2 TO 4

- ¾ cup all-purpose flour
- 2 tablespoons white sugar
- ½ teaspoon Diamond Crystal kosher salt
- 1½ cups whole milk
- 3 large eggs
- 1 vanilla bean, split lengthwise, or 1 teaspoon vanilla extract
- 3 tablespoons (1½ ounces) unsalted butter, cut into cubes
- Powdered sugar, for dusting
- Maple syrup, warm, for serving
- Strawberries, halved, for garnish
- Strawberry-Ginger Jam (recipe follows)
- A large dollop fresh whole-milk ricotta

Position a rack in the center of the oven and remove any racks above it. For the prettiest rise, use a 10-inch ovenproof skillet, though one up to 11½ inches still works nicely. Put the skillet on the center rack, and preheat the oven to 450°F with the skillet inside. It's important that the skillet and the oven be sufficiently hot to ensure a proper soufflé effect.

Meanwhile, in a large mixing bowl, whisk together the flour, sugar, and salt. In a medium mixing bowl, combine the milk and eggs, scrape in the vanilla seeds or add the extract, and whisk well. Add the milk mixture to the flour mixture and whisk until smooth, about 1 minute. It will be looser than pancake batter.

Working quickly, carefully transfer the skillet to the stovetop, add the butter, and swirl to coat the bottom of the skillet. As soon as it's melted, pour the batter into the skillet and return the skillet to the oven. Bake, resisting the urge to open the oven, until the edges are puffed and golden brown and the center is lightly browned, 15 to 20 minutes.

Remove the skillet from the oven. Dust with powdered sugar and drizzle with maple syrup. Serve immediately with fresh strawberries, jam, and ricotta.

STRAWBERRY-GINGER JAM

MAKES ABOUT 1½ CUPS

- 2 pints strawberries, hulled and quartered
- ½ cup white sugar
- 1 by 1-inch knob ginger, peeled and finely grated on a Microplane
- Finely grated zest and juice of 2 limes
- 2 tablespoons water
- 2 vanilla beans, split lengthwise, or 2 teaspoons vanilla extract

In a medium saucepan, combine the strawberries, sugar, ginger, lime zest, lime juice, and water. Scrape the vanilla seeds into the pot and add the pods. Stir well, and bring to a boil over medium-high heat. Turn the heat down to cook at a moderate simmer, stirring occasionally, until the berries break down and the mixture has a jam-like consistency, 20 to 25 minutes.

Remove from the heat and discard the vanilla pods. Keep warm if serving right away, or cool and store in an airtight container in the refrigerator for up to 1 week.

SALTED EGG YOLK BASQUE CHEESECAKE

I think of this as my best-of-both-worlds cheesecake. It has the decadent creaminess of Basque cheesecake, with its trademark "burnt" caramelized top, as well as the graham cracker crust of a classic New York cheesecake. The salted duck egg yolks, a common ingredient in Chinese desserts, give the crust a savory edge.

SERVES 8 TO 10

Equipment: Parchment paper, stand mixer or hand mixer

CRUST

20 squares (10 full sheets) / 150g graham crackers

⅓ cup / 70g white sugar

1 teaspoon / 3g Diamond Crystal kosher salt

4 Cured Duck Egg Yolks (page 247) / 57g or store-bought salted duck egg yolks (thawed if frozen)

8 tablespoons / 114g unsalted butter, melted

FILLING

Three 8-ounce / 226g packages cream cheese, at room temperature

1 cup / 200g white sugar

½ teaspoon / 2g Diamond Crystal kosher salt

1 teaspoon vanilla paste or vanilla extract

3 large eggs

1½ cups / 340g heavy cream

⅓ cup / 43g all-purpose flour

Position a rack in the center of the oven and preheat the oven to 350°F. Coat an 8-inch round cake pan with cooking spray or butter. Crumple two 13 by 13-inch pieces of parchment paper. Line the cake pan with one of the pieces, pressing it against the bottom and sides so it adheres, then add the other, rotated 45 degrees.

Make the crust: In a food processor, pulse the graham crackers to the texture of fine bread crumbs (or crush the crackers in a resealable bag). Transfer to a medium mixing bowl and add the sugar and salt. Using a Microplane, finely grate in the salted egg yolks. Mix well. Drizzle in the melted butter and mix to evenly coat.

Transfer the mixture to the cake pan and press down firmly with the bottom of a glass to make an even, compact layer. Bake until the color deepens and the crumbs fuse together to make a firm crust, about 12 minutes. Remove from the oven, press again with the glass, and set aside to cool.

Transfer the cake pan to a large (18 by 13-inch) sheet pan. Increase the oven temperature to 400°F.

Make the filling: In a stand mixer fitted with the paddle (or in a bowl using a hand mixer with the beater attachment), beat the cream cheese, sugar, salt, and vanilla together on medium speed, stopping to scrape down the sides, until pale and fluffy, about 1 minute. Stop the machine, add one of the eggs, and mix until fully incorporated. Repeat with the remaining eggs.

Reduce the speed to low, pour in the cream in a steady stream, and mix until smooth, scraping down the sides. Stop the machine, add the flour, and mix on low, scraping down the sides, just until smooth, about 30 seconds.

Pour the cream cheese mixture over the prepared crust. Carefully tap the cake pan against the sheet pan a few times and then smooth the surface with a rubber spatula. Transfer, sheet pan and all, to the oven and bake until the entire surface is deep brown, 40 to 45 minutes, rotating the pan halfway through. The cake will still be very jiggly.

Remove from the oven and let cool for 1 hour. Use the parchment paper to carefully lift the cake from the pan. Let cool further to room temperature, about 30 minutes. To cut neat slices, use a hot knife (run under hot water, then dried), wiping it clean between cuts.

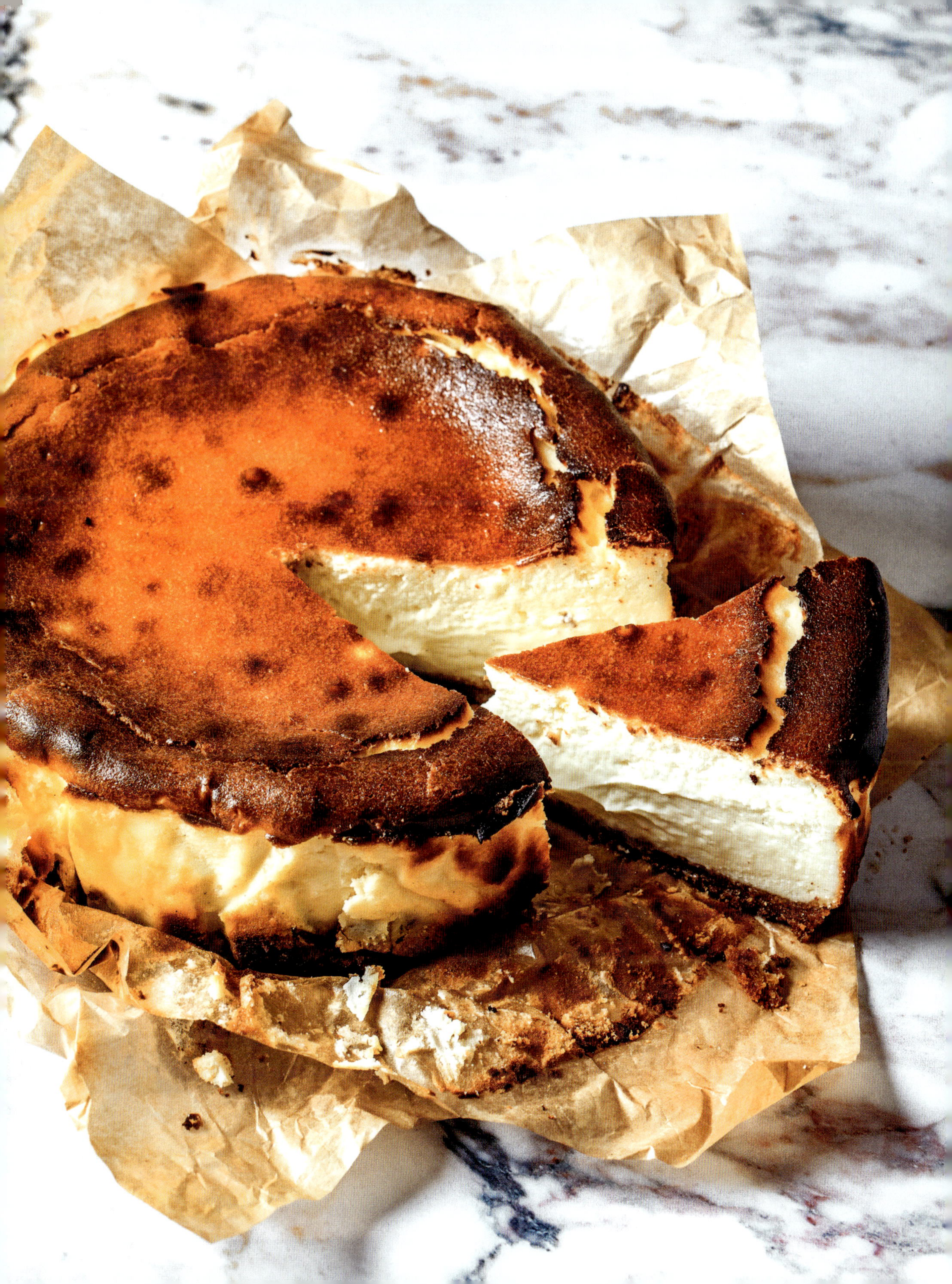

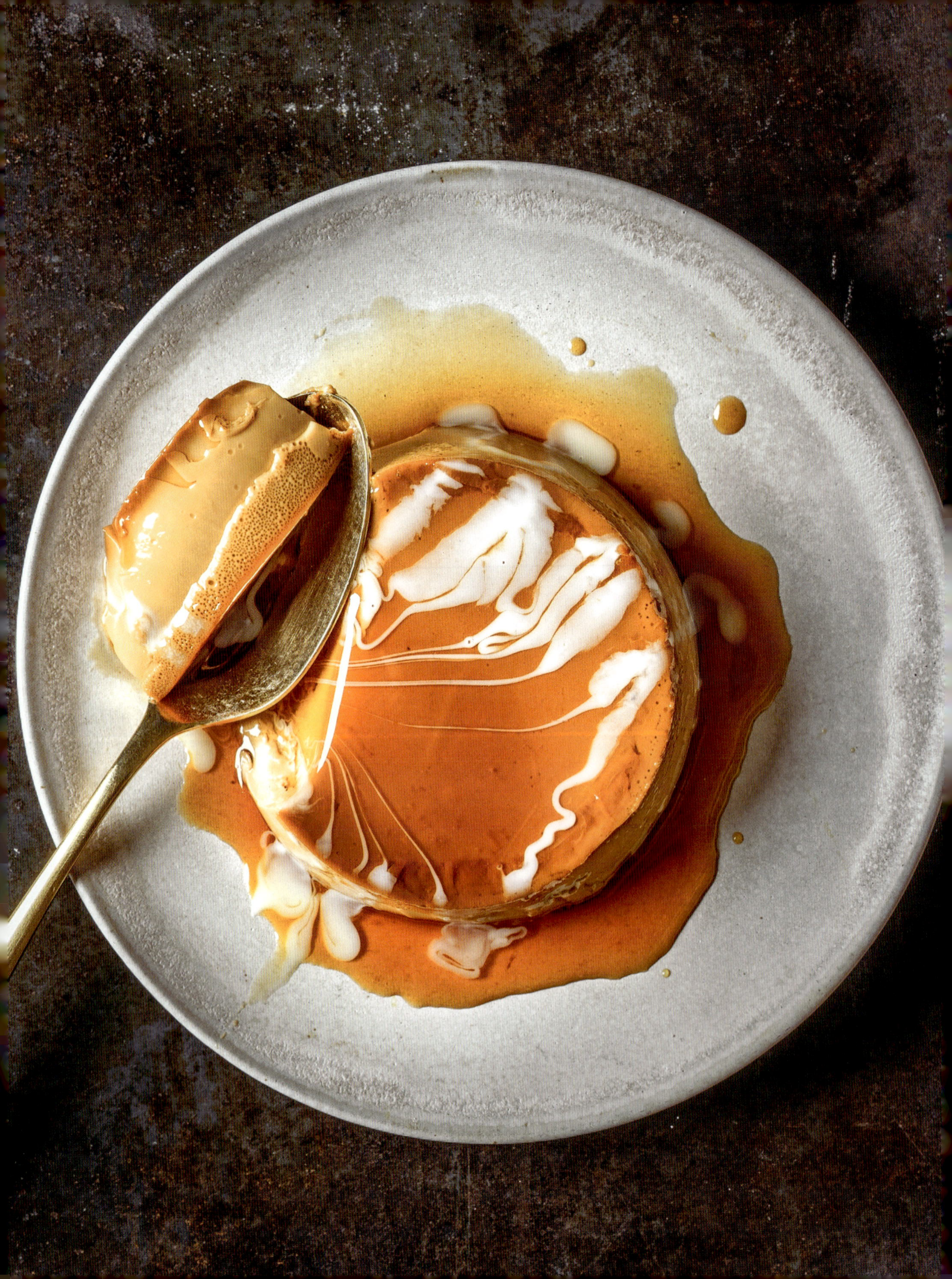

VIETNAMESE COFFEE FLAN

I'm a big fan of jiggly custard desserts like flan. Because flan often calls for sweetened condensed milk, it got me thinking about the flavors of boldly brewed Vietnamese coffee, which relies on the sugary, creamy product to temper its delightful bitterness. To infuse the flan with a robust chicory-coffee kick to balance the sweet, drippy caramel, I just had to use Café Du Monde coffee, whose iconic yellow can is a common sight in Vietnamese American homes—and my grandma Sabrina's.

SERVES 8

Equipment: Eight 5- to 6-ounce ramekins

½ cup / 113g water

1½ cups / 300g white sugar

2⅔ cups / 624g whole milk

⅓ cup / 28g ground chicory coffee (preferably Café Du Monde)

½ cup / 156g sweetened condensed milk, plus more for serving

2 large eggs

3 large egg yolks

½ teaspoon / 2g Diamond Crystal kosher salt

Set the ramekins in a large baking dish or roasting pan with some space around each one.

Pour the water into a small saucepan, then carefully spoon in the sugar so it doesn't touch the sides of the pan. Gently stir to make sure all the sugar is wet. Bring to a boil over high heat, without stirring, and cook until the bubbles are slower and larger, about 5 minutes. Continue cooking for 2 to 3 minutes, gently swirling if necessary to ensure even coloring, until slightly darker than honey.

Turn off the heat. Working carefully but quickly so the caramel doesn't set, pour a ¼-inch layer of caramel into each ramekin and swirl to coat about ½ inch up the sides. Discard any leftover caramel. Set aside to let the caramel harden, 10 to 15 minutes.

Line a fine-mesh sieve with cheesecloth and set it over a heatproof container. In a medium saucepan, heat the milk over medium heat just until it bubbles at the edges and a skin forms on the surface, 5 to 6 minutes. Turn off the heat, stir in the coffee, then cover and let steep for 4 minutes (or up to 6 minutes for a bolder coffee flavor).

In a large mixing bowl, combine the sweetened condensed milk, whole eggs, egg yolks, and salt and whisk until smooth. Once the coffee has steeped, strain through the lined sieve, discarding the grounds. By the ladleful and in a thin, steady stream, add the hot coffee milk to the egg mixture while whisking constantly. Strain through a fine-mesh sieve into a container.

Position a rack in the center of the oven and preheat the oven to 300°F. Bring about 4 cups water to a boil.

Stir the coffee mixture and then divide it evenly among the ramekins. Carefully pour enough boiling water into the baking dish to reach halfway up the side of the ramekins. Cover tightly with foil, carefully transfer to the oven, and bake until the middle is set but still jiggly, 30 to 40 minutes.

Carefully remove the hot ramekins and let them cool completely. Cover and refrigerate at least 8 hours or up to 12 hours.

To serve, run the tip of a paring knife around the sides of the custard, then invert each onto serving plates. Drizzle with some sweetened condensed milk and serve.

HONG KONG STUFFED FRENCH TOAST

My Cantonese grandma, Sabrina PoPo, used to take me for breakfast at the Chinese cafés in the San Gabriel Valley. They were like Chinese IHOPs, with giant diner-style menus and big, affordable breakfast combinations like wok-fried eggs with Spam, jook (page 122), see yow mein (see Garlic Soy Sauce Noodles, page 109), and a Hong Kong Milk Tea (page 259). She had a sweet tooth, so her combo almost always included her favorite: Hong Kong–style French toast. Unlike American French toast, Hong Kong–style is two slices of thick-cut milk bread stuffed with peanut butter, battered, and deep-fried until crispy and gooey. Then it's drizzled with maple syrup and condensed milk. Did your brain explode yet? I hope so.

LEVEL IT UP

Play around with toppings like whipped butter, ice cream, crushed peanuts, or Lap Cheong Crumble (page 256).

SWITCH IT UP

Get creative by adding bananas or jam to the filling, swapping Nutella for peanut butter, or going triple decker instead of double.

SERVES 2

- 4 slices (about ¾ inch thick) milk bread or brioche, slightly stale
- 2 tablespoons creamy peanut butter
- 4 large eggs
- 1 cup half-and-half
- 1 tablespoon white sugar
- 1 teaspoon vanilla extract
- Dash of ground cinnamon
- Pinch of Diamond Crystal kosher salt
- 1 cup sweetened condensed milk
- 2 tablespoons buttermilk
- Finely grated zest of 1 lemon
- 2 tablespoons lemon juice
- Canola oil (2 to 3 cups), for shallow-frying
- Room-temperature unsalted butter, for serving
- Flaky sea salt

Make 2 peanut butter sandwiches, then trim off the crusts with a sharp knife. Put the sandwiches side by side in a baking dish.

In a medium mixing bowl, whisk together the eggs, half-and-half, sugar, vanilla, cinnamon, and kosher salt until smooth. Pour the mixture over the tops of the sandwiches. Cover, transfer to the fridge, and let soak, carefully flipping them halfway through, for at least 30 minutes and up to 1 hour.

When ready to cook, in a small saucepan, combine the condensed milk, buttermilk, lemon zest, and lemon juice. Gently warm over low heat. Remove from the heat and cover to keep warm.

Line a sheet pan with paper towels. Pour ¾ inch of oil into a 12- to 14-inch skillet and heat over medium-high heat for 3 minutes. When the oil is ready, the end of a wooden chopstick or wooden spoon submerged in the oil will immediately release little bubbles.

Gently transfer the sandwiches to the oil in a single layer. Fry, flipping once, until golden brown and crispy on both sides, 1 to 2 minutes per side. Transfer to the paper towels.

Serve on plates topped with a pat of butter, a generous drizzle of the warm condensed milk mixture, and a sprinkle of flaky salt.

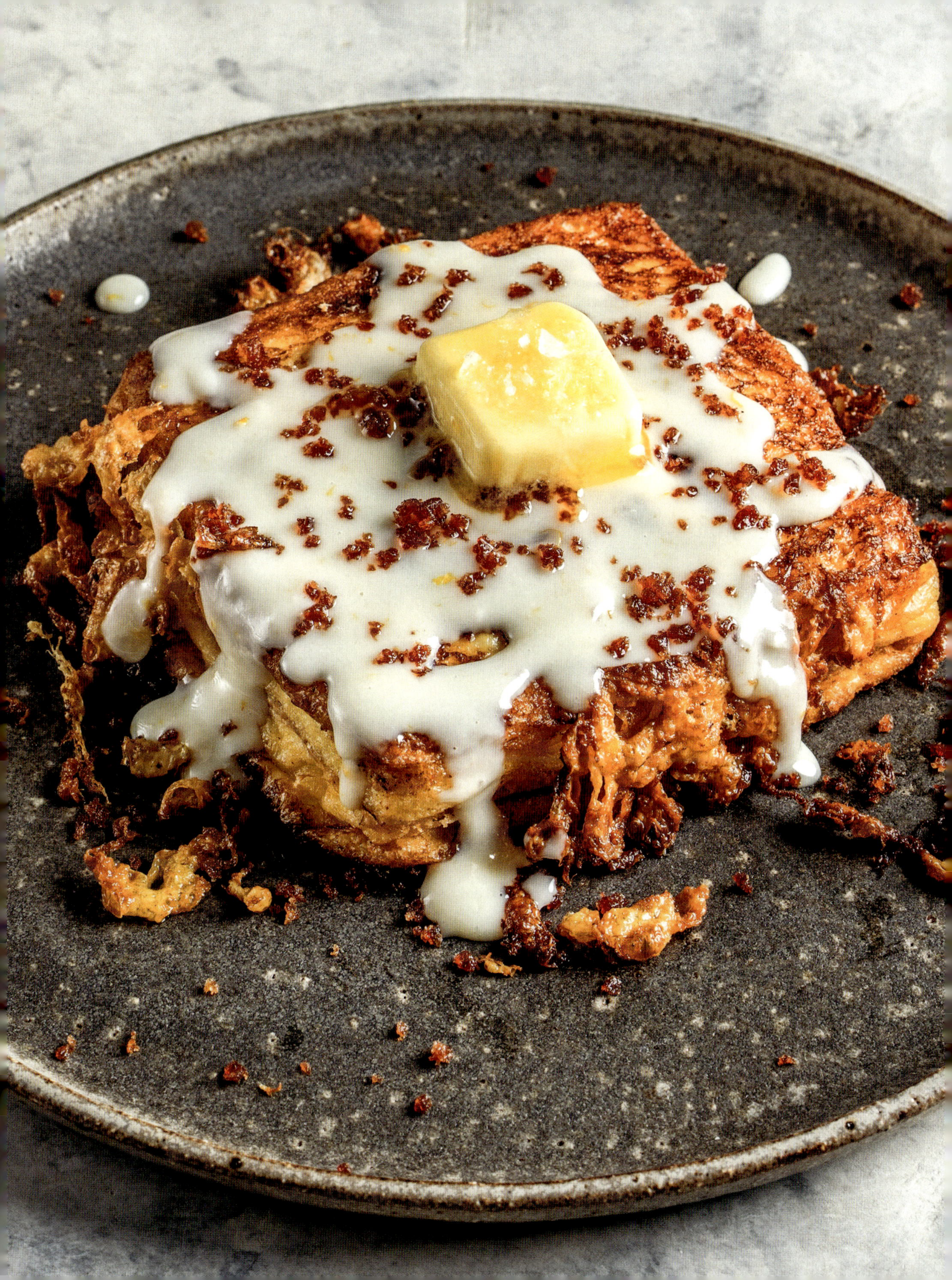

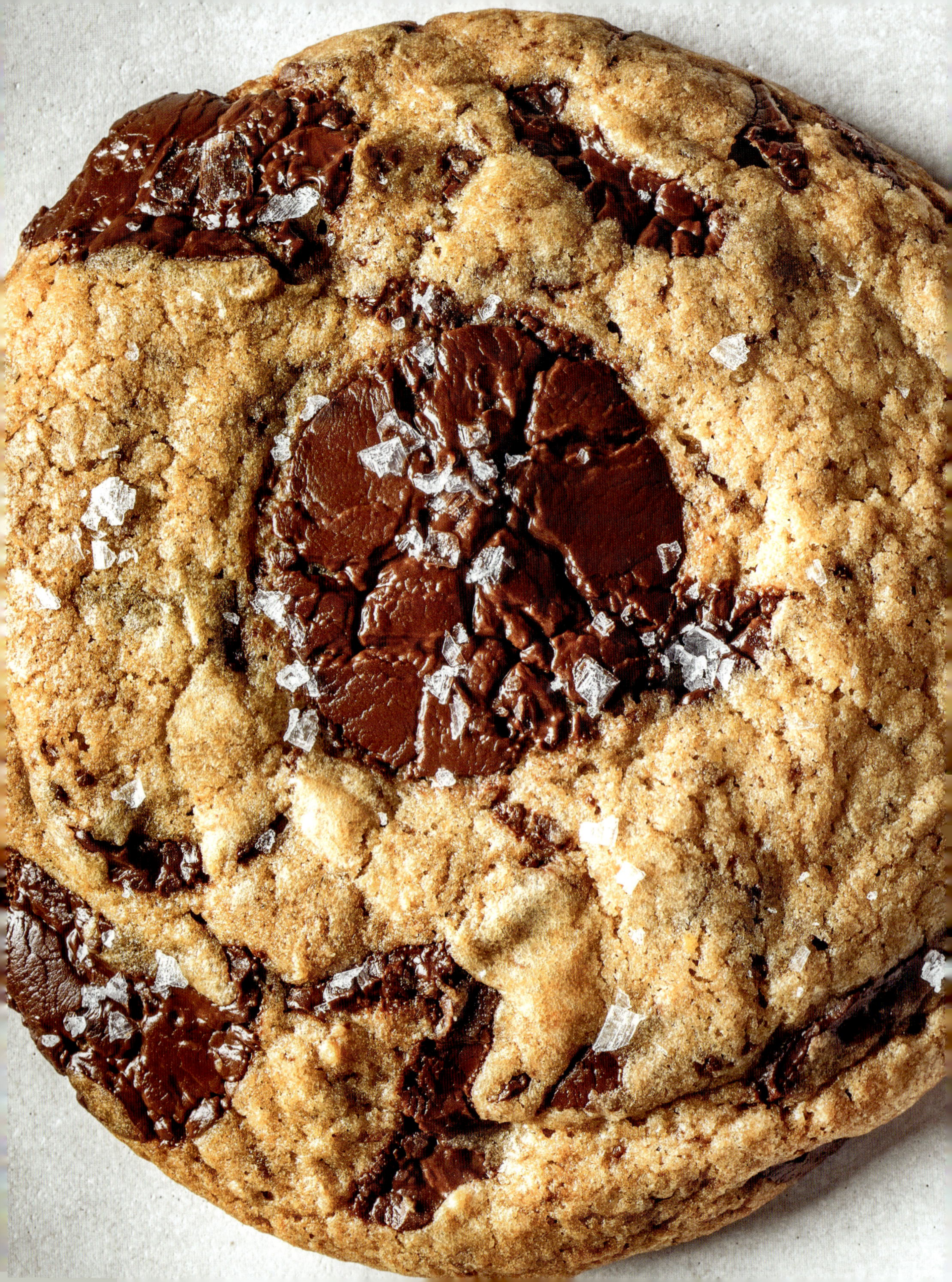

CHOCOLATE CHUNK COOKIES

One of my peak career moments was appearing on *Sesame Street* and cooking with Cookie Monster, my blue, fuzzy sous-chef. I too am a bit of a cookie monster. Of all the desserts out there, a good chocolate chip cookie is the way to my heart. And while much of my food features surprising combinations of flavors, I'm a purist when it comes to cookies. So, you won't find any chile or miso here, just a nice thick cookie, slightly crispy on the outside and soft and chewy inside, with gooey pockets of chocolate goodness and a sprinkle of flaky salt. If you can't find chocolate wafers (also labeled feves), chop a bar of good-quality dark chocolate. Chips won't give you the big gooey chunks I'm after here.

MAKES 18 COOKIES

1½ cups / 283g packed light brown sugar

⅔ cup / 142g white sugar

2 large eggs

2 large yolks

1 tablespoon / 14g vanilla extract

1½ teaspoons / 7g coffee extract

2 teaspoons / 7g Diamond Crystal kosher salt

13½ tablespoons / 190g unsalted butter, melted

1¼ teaspoons / 7g baking soda

3 cups / 425g all-purpose flour

3 cups / 400g dark chocolate wafers (55% to 70% cacao), roughly chopped, plus 18 whole wafers

Flaky sea salt, for sprinkling

In a medium mixing bowl, whisk together the brown sugar, white sugar, whole eggs, egg yolks, vanilla, coffee extract, and kosher salt. Add the melted butter and whisk until fully incorporated. Add the baking soda and about half the flour and whisk until smooth. Add the remaining flour, then switch to a wooden spoon and stir until smooth with no lumps. Stir in the chopped chocolate.

Line a small (9 by 13-inch) sheet pan with parchment paper. Portion the dough into roughly 18 equal portions (about ¼ cup each), roll into balls, and arrange in a single layer on the prepared sheet pan. To each ball, add a chocolate wafer and press down gently, just so it adheres to the top.

For best results, cover tightly and either refrigerate for at least 24 hours or up to 72 hours or freeze until fully frozen, about 2 hours. (Once frozen, transfer to an airtight container for up to 3 months. Thaw completely in the refrigerator before baking.)

When ready to bake, preheat the oven to 335°F. Line as many large (18 by 13-inch) sheet pans as needed with parchment paper. Evenly space out 6 cookies per sheet.

Bake until the edges are golden brown and the surface looks dry, 16 to 20 minutes, rotating the pan halfway through.

Remove from the oven, sprinkle flaky salt over the melty chocolate on top, and let the cookies cool to warm or room temperature on the pan before serving.

YUZU–COCONUT OLIVE OIL CAKE WITH BERRIES

This play on Italian olive oil cake is as impressive to serve as it is easy to make. Fragrant yuzu stands in for the classic lemon, and coconut milk joins olive oil for richness. A dead-simple glaze and the seasonal fruit of your choice, like summer berries briefly macerated to enhance their flavor, enliven this moist, delicate plant-based dessert. If you're open to dairy, a dollop of whipped cream or scoop of ice cream is a fantastic addition.

SWITCH IT UP

Lemon, Meyer lemon, mandarin, and blood orange are all welcome in place of the yuzu. Instead of macerated berries, try diced mango or charred pineapple.

MAKES ONE 8-INCH CAKE

Equipment: Parchment paper

MACERATED BERRIES

2 pints / 660g hulled strawberries or blackberries, halved or quartered

3 tablespoons / 37g white sugar

1 vanilla bean, split lengthwise, or 1 teaspoon / 6g vanilla bean paste

CAKE

½ cup plus 2 tablespoons / 135g extra-virgin olive oil, plus more for the pan

1 cup plus 2 tablespoons / 270g well-shaken full-fat coconut milk

⅓ cup / 76g bottled yuzu juice

2¼ cups / 316g all-purpose flour

1¼ cups / 255g white sugar

2½ teaspoons / 9g baking powder

Finely grated zest of 1 lemon

GLAZE

1¼ cups / 140g powdered sugar

2 tablespoons plus 2 teaspoons / 40g bottled yuzu juice

Macerate the berries: In a medium mixing bowl, combine the berries, sugar, and vanilla seeds or vanilla bean paste. Toss gently but well, and let macerate while preparing the cake.

Make the cake: Position a rack in the center of the oven and preheat the oven to 350°F. Lightly grease the bottom and sides of an 8-inch round cake pan with olive oil. Line the bottom with a round of parchment paper, then put the cake pan on a sheet pan.

In a medium mixing bowl, whisk together the coconut milk, olive oil, and yuzu juice and set aside. In a large mixing bowl, whisk together the flour, white sugar, baking powder, and lemon zest. Add the coconut milk mixture to the flour mixture and whisk until smooth. Transfer the batter to the prepared pan and gently tap on the counter to level the batter.

Bake until a skewer inserted into the center comes out clean, about 40 minutes, rotating the pan halfway through. Remove from the oven and let cool for 15 minutes.

Run a knife around the edge of the cake to loosen it from the pan. Invert a large plate onto the cake pan, hold the plate and pan together with both hands, and flip. Remove the pan and the parchment paper. (Before it's glazed, the cake keeps in an airtight container at room temperature for up to 24 hours.)

Glaze and serve: In a medium mixing bowl, whisk together the powdered sugar and yuzu juice until smooth.

Carefully flip the cake onto a large serving plate, so it's right-side up. Pour the glaze onto the center of the cake and let it run down the sides. Let the glaze set, about 15 minutes.

Slice the cake and serve with the macerated berries.

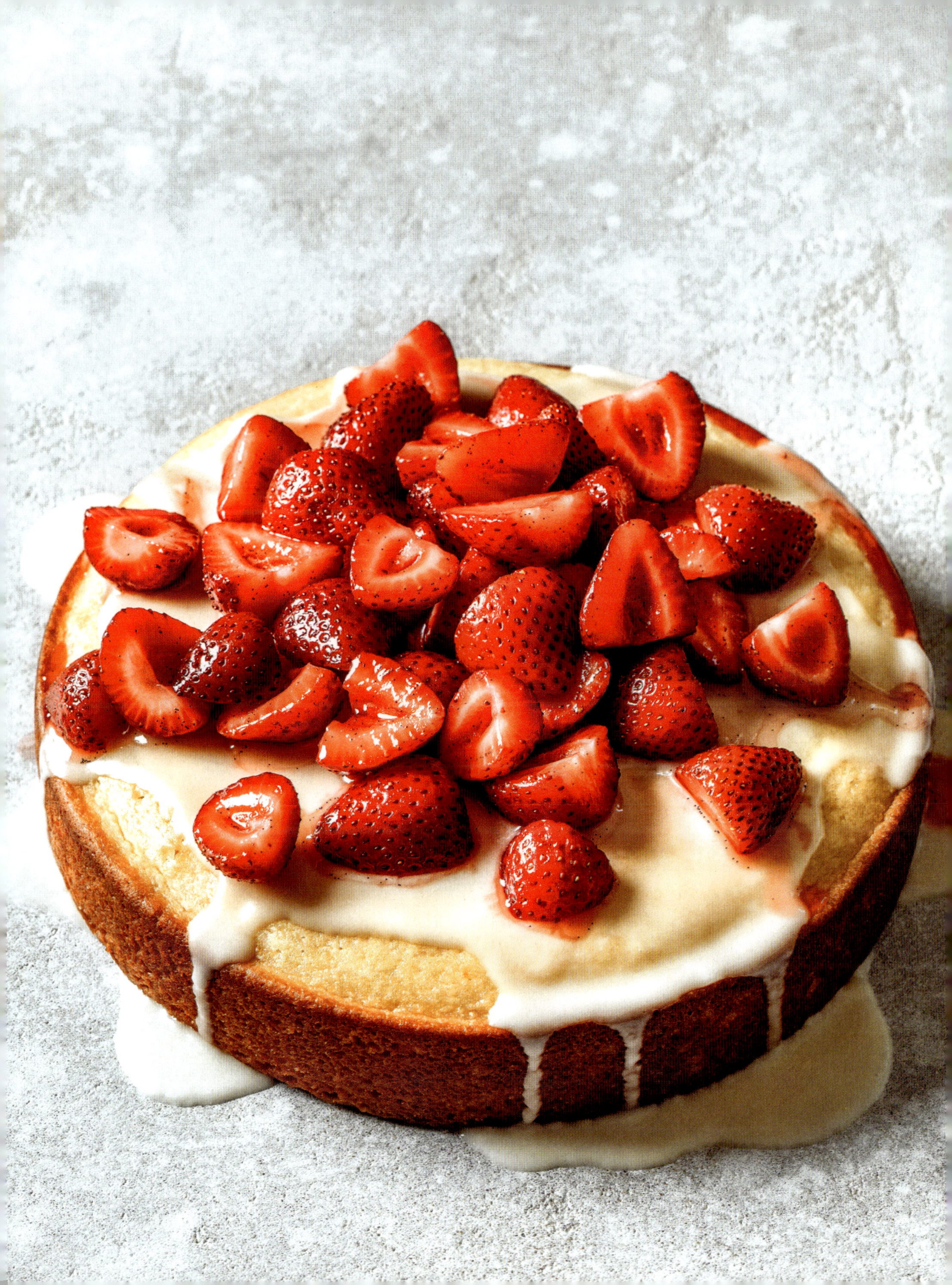

9

SAUCES,

CONDIMENTS
& OTHER FUN

WEEKEND BROTH

At the end of every week, I rummage through my fridge and freezer for gold and turn it into a big pot of delicious broth. The foundation is typically the same: onions with their peels, carrot and celery ends, and ginger nubs. (I've gotten into the habit of saving trim from the week in a resealable bag.) The rest depends on what you have on hand. I use a combination of flavorful ingredients—often including corn cobs (aka corn bones) and umami-giving ones, everything from mushroom stems and kombu to chicken bones and fish heads. The broth tastes different every week and that's part of the fun.

No matter what combination you choose from the ingredients here, be sure to use large pieces (small ones dissolve during the long cooking time) and simmer gently to ensure a clear, clean broth.

LEVEL IT UP

Before serving, add a squeeze of lime, finely diced onions, ground black pepper, chopped cilantro, and shredded rotisserie chicken.

MAKES 3 TO 4 QUARTS

BASE INGREDIENTS

2 to 4 garlic cloves, peeled

1 small onion, halved, or the equivalent in trim

1 celery stalk, halved, or the equivalent in trim

1 carrot, halved, or the equivalent in trim

3 by 1-inch knob ginger, roughly sliced

4 quarts water

UMAMI
(MIX AND MATCH)

Fresh mushrooms (whole, stems, or other trim)

Dried mushrooms

Kombu (dried kelp)

Katsuobushi (bonito flakes)

Chicken, pork, or beef bones or rotisserie chicken carcass

Fish heads, bones, or other trim

Lobster or shrimp heads and shells

Dried scallops

FLAVOR BOOSTERS
(MIX AND MATCH)

Corn bones (aka stripped corn cobs), broken in half

Cabbage cores

Tomato trim

Roughly chopped leeks or scallions or trim

Lemongrass trim, smashed

Roughly chopped winter squash or trim

Herbs (thyme sprigs, parsley sprigs, and/or bay leaves)

Goji berries and dried jujubes

Apple or pear cores

SEASONING

Kosher salt

Fish sauce

White sugar

In a 5- to 7-quart pot (you can also use a slow cooker), combine the base ingredients and any umami-giving ingredients and flavor boosters, and bring to a boil over high heat.

Reduce to a bare simmer, cover, and cook for 4 hours (and up to 8 hours in the slow cooker), occasionally adjusting the heat to maintain the simmer and skimming off any scum from the surface. Season to taste with salt, fish sauce, and sugar.

Ladle the broth directly into bowls or heatproof containers, doing your best to avoid any solids. (The fully cooled broth keeps in an airtight container in the fridge for up to 4 days and in the freezer for up to 3 months.)

QUICK PICKLES

Fermented pickles take weeks to make. These sweet, tangy quick pickles are ready to eat in about 30 minutes. I use this brine no matter what I'm pickling, so choose your own adventure with 2 to 2½ cups of the four vegetables and fruits I suggest below or go with sliced cucumbers, cauliflower, green beans, carrots, beets—the options are endless!

SWITCH IT UP

Add dried Sichuan or fresh Thai chiles for heat, or change up the flavor profile with spices and aromatics like coriander seeds, bay leaves, or lemongrass.

MAKES ABOUT 2 CUPS

BRINE

2 cups unseasoned rice vinegar

1½ cups white sugar

2 teaspoons Diamond Crystal kosher salt

2 by 1-inch knob ginger, peeled and thinly sliced

2 garlic cloves, lightly smashed and peeled

1 whole star anise

PICKLED DAIKON AND GINGER

½ pound daikon radish (about 2½ inches wide), peeled, halved, and very thinly sliced on a mandoline

½ cup very thinly sliced (on a mandoline) peeled ginger

1 or 2 fresh Thai chiles, thinly sliced

PICKLED RED ONION

2½ cups thinly sliced red onion (about 1 medium)

PICKLED KUMQUATS

2½ cups kumquats (about 14 ounces), cut into ⅛-inch rounds, large seeds removed

PICKLED CHILES

2½ cups thinly sliced Fresno chiles (about 10), seeded if you prefer less heat

Make the brine: In a medium saucepan, bring the ingredients to a boil over high heat, stirring occasionally to ensure the sugar dissolves.

Make the pickles: Combine whatever you're pickling in a heatproof 1-quart jar with a wide mouth. Once the brine boils, immediately pour it into the jar. Stir well, then gently press so the brine submerges the pickles.

Let cool to room temperature, uncovered, about 30 minutes. I like to chill them in the refrigerator before eating. (The pickles keep in an airtight container in the refrigerator for up to 2 months.)

SLOW-ROASTED CHERRY TOMATOES WITH GARLIC, FENNEL, AND CORIANDER

Slow-roasting cherry tomatoes with lots of good olive oil concentrates their flavor, turning even your wintertime haul into something tasty. It's a great cold-weather hack, but it's truly incredible made with beautiful summer tomatoes, whether you spoon them on eggs, toast, labneh (page 32), charred steak (page 196), or roasted fish. Don't neglect the oil either, which is infused with the flavor of those tomatoes, garlic, and spices and is lovely in salad dressings, as a dip for crusty bread, or used to make the next batch of roasted tomatoes.

MAKES ABOUT 3 CUPS

2 pints cherry tomatoes, halved through the stem end

8 garlic cloves, lightly smashed and peeled

A few sprigs of hardy herbs, such as thyme, rosemary, and/or oregano

1 tablespoon coriander seeds, lightly crushed in a mortar

1 tablespoon fennel seeds, lightly crushed in a mortar

1 teaspoon Diamond Crystal kosher salt

¼ teaspoon finely ground black pepper

About 1¾ cups extra-virgin olive oil, plus more if necessary

CONTINUED

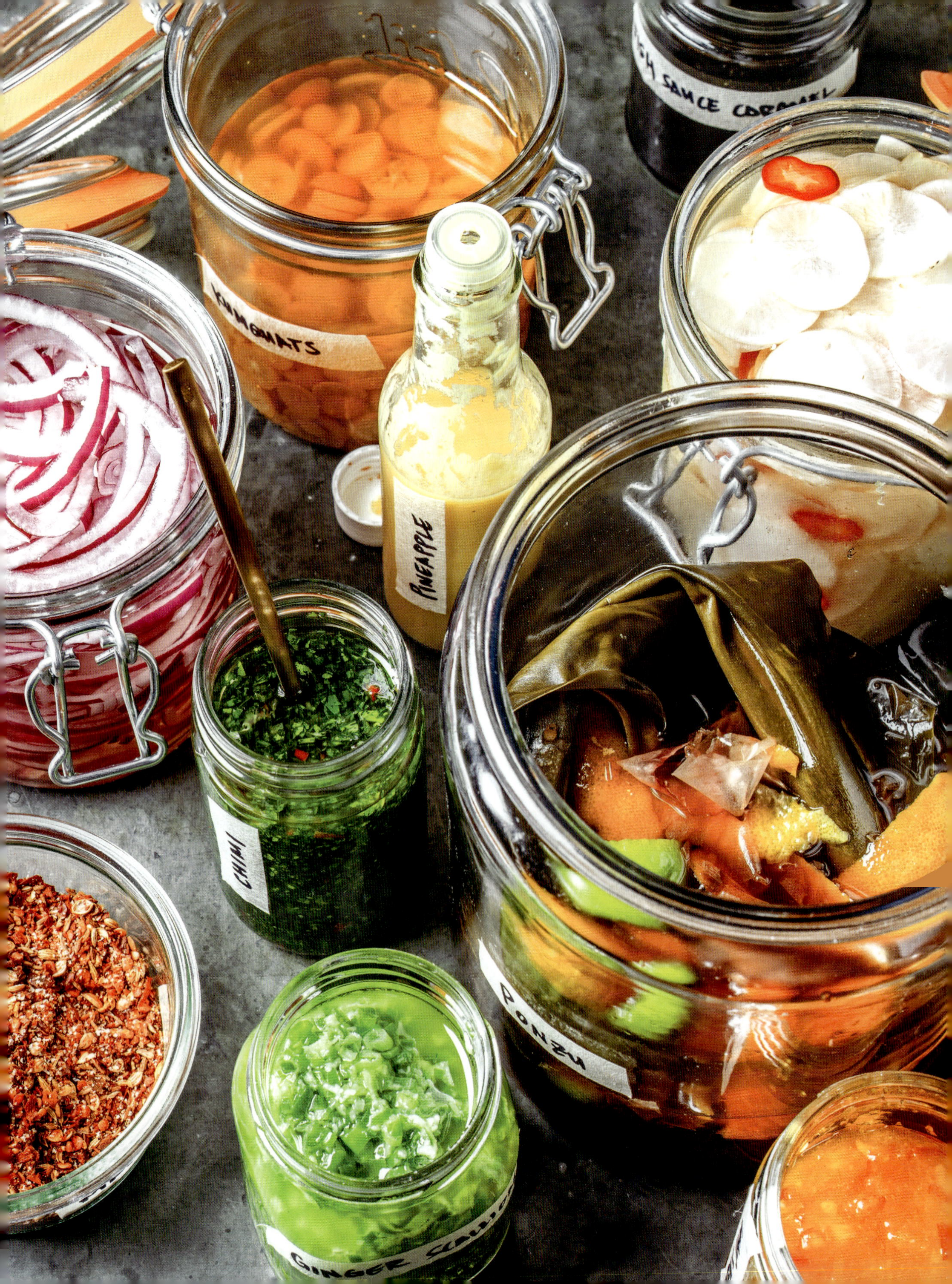
KUMQUATS
SAUCE
PINEAPPLE
CHIMI
PONZU
GINGER

Position a rack in the center of the oven and preheat the oven to 350°F.

Find a shallow baking dish small enough that the tomatoes fit in one snug layer. Combine the tomatoes, garlic, and herbs in the baking dish. Sprinkle on the coriander, fennel, salt, and pepper. Pour in enough oil to just about cover the tomatoes. Gently toss with your hands to mix well and turn the tomatoes cut-sides up.

Roast until the tomatoes have shrunk and caramelized at the edges, 1½ to 2 hours.

Serve warm or at room temperature. Store the tomatoes in the oil in an airtight container in the refrigerator for up to 5 days.

CURED DUCK EGG YOLKS

I have so many childhood memories of ham dan, or "salted egg" in Cantonese. These golden beauties were often in my mom's steamed pork patties with salted fish, nestled in clay pot rice with Chinese sausage, or inside mooncakes my parents would bring home from Hong Kong. Traditionally, whole duck eggs—chosen for their richness and for higher yolk-to-white ratio—are submerged in a wet brine of water, salt, Shaoxing wine, and star anise. The result is raw whites with firm, slightly jammy yolks. Here, I cure the yolks only—the only other ingredients are salt and time—until they're firm enough to grate over pastas and salads as you would Parmigiano-Reggiano. They give a similar salty, umami boost to practically any dish, including Sichuan Steak Tartare (page 31), Blistered Snap and Snow Peas with Cumin-Shiso Tzatziki (page 126), and Miso Caesar (page 67).

Keep in mind that duck eggs have strong shells and take a little extra force to break. Because the recipe requires intact yolks, buy a few extra in case any get punctured. Use the leftover egg whites to make the meringue for Torched Banana Pudding (page 225) or in your next omelet.

MAKES 12 CURED YOLKS

Equipment: Cheesecloth, butcher's twine

6 cups / 2 pounds Diamond Crystal kosher salt

12 duck eggs

Make an even ½-inch layer of salt in a 9 by 13-inch baking dish. Use the wider end of one of the eggs to make 12 evenly spaced divots ¼ inch deep in the salt.

Carefully crack an egg into a small bowl. Use your hands to gently separate the yolk from the white and carefully transfer the yolk into one of the divots. Repeat with the remaining eggs, reserving the whites for another day. Gently pour on the remaining salt to completely cover the yolks, taking care not to break them. Cover the dish and refrigerate for 4 days.

After 4 days, remove the now-firm yolks from the salt and brush off the excess. Cut out a 32 by 9-inch length of cheesecloth and lay it on a work surface. Line up the yolks on the cheesecloth an inch or so from the edge, leaving about 1 inch of space between the yolks. Gently fold the edge over the yolks and roll the cloth to make a tube. Use a piece of twine to tie each end closed, then use a piece to tie a knot around the cheesecloth in between the yolks. Use bowknots, so you can easily untie the twine to check the yolks.

In a dark, cool spot below 50°F, such as a refrigerator or closet, hang the two cheesecloth packages to let the yolks dry until they're as firm as Parmigiano-Reggiano, 7 to 9 days.

Remove the cured yolks from the cheesecloth and transfer to an airtight container. They keep in the refrigerator for up to 1 month.

BLACK VINEGAR–CARAMELIZED ONIONS

These are classic caramelized onions, cooked until their sugars concentrate and develop a deeper, more complex sweetness. The only difference is that I deglaze the pan with Chinese black vinegar for a bright, malty lift. Try them wherever you'd use the classic—on burgers, focaccia (page 82), or sandwiches like Shanghainese Pork Belly Cubanos (page 100).

MAKES ABOUT 2 CUPS

¼ cup canola oil

12 cups thinly sliced yellow onion (about 4 large)

2 teaspoons Diamond Crystal kosher salt

8 to 10 tablespoons water

6 tablespoons Zhenjiang black vinegar

Heat a large Dutch oven over medium heat for 1 minute. Add the oil and swirl to coat the pan. When the oil shimmers, add the onions and salt and cook, stirring occasionally, until the onions have softened and started to take on some color, 13 to 15 minutes.

Add 2 tablespoons water, stir and scrape up any browned bits from the pan with a wooden spoon. Continue to cook, stirring frequently and adding 2 tablespoons of water every 5 minutes or so, until the onions are very soft and deeply caramelized, 15 to 20 minutes. When they're done, the onions will be a deep, even golden-brown color all the way through. Reduce the heat slightly if necessary.

Stir in the black vinegar and cook, stirring for 20 seconds. To store, let the onions cool and keep in an airtight container in the refrigerator for up to 4 days.

CHARRED GREEN OIL

Drizzling this vibrant green oil over noodles, crudos, and soups will make you feel like a Michelin-starred chef. The fact that it's made from trim that would otherwise be tossed in a compost bin is a zero-waste moment to be proud of.

First, you blend oil with dark green leek tops—green garlic or scallion tops work, too—then briefly cook the puree in a screaming hot pan, charring it so it turns a striking bright green. I promise it's ridiculously easy to do, though I can't promise it won't trip your smoke detector (sorry!). Once it's strained, you're left with an emerald oil that will give any dish a savory-sweet allium boost. Use it to sauté noodles or vegetables, dress your salads, add to soups, or drizzle over Cheesy Scallion Pancakes (page 93), Cumin-Shiso Tzatziki (page 128) or labneh (page 32).

MAKES ABOUT ½ CUP

Equipment: High-powered blender (like a Vitamix), cheesecloth

6 cups roughly chopped leek tops (dark greens only), from 2 large leeks

1 cup canola oil, plus more if necessary

¼ teaspoon Diamond Crystal kosher salt

Put the leek tops in a big bowl of water, swish them around to dislodge any dirt, then drain well.

In a high-powered blender, combine the oil, leek tops, and salt. Start blending on low speed, gradually increasing the speed to high, and blend until completely smooth, 1 to 2 minutes. If necessary, gradually add more oil to help the blades catch.

Line a fine-mesh sieve with a double layer of cheesecloth and set it over a heatproof container. Consider opening a window, turning on a fan, and turning off your smoke alarms, because this step gets smoky. Heat a large sauté pan over high heat until it starts to smoke, 2 to 3 minutes. Carefully and quickly add the puree to the pan—it will sputter and splatter—then use a flexible spatula to stir frequently until the oil turns a vibrant emerald green, separates from the solids, and pools at the surface, about 2 minutes.

Pour the mixture into the prepared sieve and set aside, gently stirring after 15 minutes but not pressing, to extract the oil, about 30 minutes. Use the oil right away or store in an airtight container in the freezer (to maintain its color) for up to 3 months. Scoop out the green oil as needed, leaving any clear liquid behind. The oil will thaw in no time.

CIPOLLINI ONIONS AGRODOLCE

A sleeper-hit side dish for roasts, steak (page 196), and crisp-skinned salmon (page 180), these onions are done in the style of agrodolce, which means sweet and sour in Italian. Roasting cipollinis (pre-peeled is just fine) brings out their natural sugars, and vinegar, stock, and butter create a tart glaze for the caramelized onions. They're also great as a topping for focaccia (page 82) or mixed into Eggplant Caponata (page 141).

SERVES 4 TO 6

1 pound cippolini or pearl onions
¼ cup extra-virgin olive oil
¼ cup champagne vinegar
¼ cup low-sodium chicken stock or water
1 tablespoon white sugar
½ teaspoon Diamond Crystal kosher salt
5 large garlic cloves, smashed and peeled
Handful of thyme sprigs
Coarsely ground black pepper
2 tablespoons (1 ounce) unsalted butter, cut into 6 or so pieces

Position a rack in the center of the oven and preheat the oven to 450°F.

Peel the onions by trimming the tops and root ends from each one, then using a paring knife to peel off the papery skin. Halve each onion through the core.

On a small (9 by 13-inch) sheet pan, combine the onions, olive oil, vinegar, stock, sugar, salt, garlic, thyme, and a few turns of pepper and toss gently but well. Arrange the onions cut-sides up. Distribute the butter evenly throughout the pan and cover tightly with foil.

Roast for 10 minutes. Remove the foil, then use a spoon to baste the onions with the liquid in the pan. Rotate the pan and roast uncovered, basting occasionally, until the onions are tender and caramelized at the edges, about 20 minutes more.

Serve warm or at room temperature.

SESAME-LIME VINAIGRETTE

This might be the dressing I make most often: a versatile, everyday vinaigrette that's bright from lime zest and juice, slightly sweet from honey, and nutty from toasted sesame oil.

MAKES ABOUT 1 CUP

1 tablespoon minced shallot
¼ cup champagne vinegar
2 tablespoons honey
Finely grated zest of 2 limes
2 tablespoons lime juice
1 teaspoon Diamond Crystal kosher salt
½ cup extra-virgin olive oil
1 tablespoon toasted sesame oil
1 tablespoon toasted sesame seeds
Freshly ground black pepper

In a small mixing bowl, combine the shallot and vinegar, stir well, and let sit for 2 minutes to tame its sharp flavor.

Whisk in the honey, lime zest, lime juice, and salt. Slowly drizzle in the olive oil and sesame oil, whisking constantly, until thickened and emulsified. Stir in the sesame seeds and several turns of pepper. (It will keep in an airtight container in the refrigerator for up to 4 days. Bring to room temperature and whisk well before using.)

FISH SAUCE CARAMEL

Inspired by the caramel sauce popular in Vietnamese cooking, this sticky drizzle uses fish sauce to explore the savory side of scalded sugar. Spoon it onto roasted Brussels sprouts, steamed fish, and grilled chicken wings (page 47).

MAKES A GENEROUS 1 CUP

1½ cups packed light brown sugar
½ cup fish sauce (Three Crabs is a must here)
½ cup water
3 large garlic cloves, finely grated on a Microplane
2 tablespoons finely grated ginger
¼ teaspoon ground white pepper
¼ teaspoon ground coriander
¼ teaspoon ground ginger
A few cilantro stems

In a medium saucepan, combine all the ingredients and whisk well. Bring to a boil over high heat. Reduce the heat to cook at a gentle simmer, whisking occasionally, until thickened to a consistency a little looser than honey, 18 to 22 minutes. Keep a close eye as it reduces, lowering the heat if it threatens to bubble up and overflow. To test if it's done, chill a plate, add a few drops of the caramel, and wait 15 seconds or so. If the drops hold their shape like honey, it's ready.

Set a fine-mesh sieve over a heatproof container and pour in the glaze, pressing to extract as much flavor as possible. Discard the solids. (Cooled completely, the glaze keeps in an airtight container in the refrigerator for up to 1 week.)

KING'S HOT HONEY

Once you learn how to make hot honey yourself, you might never buy another bottle. My no-mess method infuses honey with the distinctive flavor of Sichuan chile flakes. Try it on anything that could use a sweet, spicy kick like Roasted Kabocha (page 142), fried chicken, Pork Katsu (page 205), your favorite slice of pizza, or my Sheet Pan Pizza (page 89).

MAKES ABOUT 1½ CUPS

- One 16-ounce jar honey (1¼ cups)
- ¼ cup plus 1 tablespoon Sichuan chile flakes

In a clean jar, combine the honey and chile flakes. Cover with a tight-fitting lid. There's no need to stir.

Set the jar in a medium saucepan, add enough water to come about halfway up the honey, and bring to a simmer over medium-low heat. As the honey warms, give the jar a few good swirls to distribute the chile flakes. Once the honey simmers, turn off the heat and let the honey cool completely in the pan, swirling the jar a few times as it cools. (The honey keeps in an airtight container at room temperature for up to 6 months. Stir well before using.)

COCONUT RICE

Three ingredients transform plain rice into fragrant coconut rice. I use just enough coconut milk to give the grains a touch of nutty sweetness. I make mine in a rice cooker, but since not everyone has one, I've provided instructions for stovetop cooking as well. Serve it as is or stir in a handful of chopped cilantro and a squeeze of lime for some freshness and brightness.

For the fluffiest result, avoid coconut milk made with guar gum.

SERVES 4

- 2 cups white jasmine rice
- 1½ cups well-shaken full-fat coconut milk
- 1 teaspoon Diamond Crystal kosher salt
- 1 teaspoon white sugar

Put the rice in the bowl of a rice cooker or in a large pot. Cover with cold water, use your hands to briefly agitate the rice, then pour out the starchy water. Repeat until the water is just barely cloudy, at least three times. Drain the rice well in a mesh sieve.

Wipe out the bowl or pot and add the drained rice, coconut milk, salt, sugar, and 1½ cups fresh water. Stir briefly.

If using the rice cooker, cook according to the manufacturer's instructions.

If using the pot, cover and bring to a boil over high heat. Immediately turn the heat down to cook at a gentle simmer, covered, for 10 minutes, trying your best not to open the lid. You may have to switch burners to ensure the heat is low enough.

Turn off the heat and keep covered for an additional 10 minutes.

Fluff again with a fork and serve.

FLAVORED BUTTERS

With compound butter in your fridge, you can add flavor and dimension to dishes any time. Slather them on crusty bread or freshly baked Milk Buns (page 86). Dollop them into a hot pan of shrimp (page 176) or steamed clams (page 167). Use them to top grilled oysters (page 43) or tender vegetables just after they leave the oven.

Each butter keeps in an airtight container in the refrigerator for up to 2 weeks.

MAKES ABOUT 1½ CUPS

KING'S HOT HONEY BUTTER

- 2 sticks (8 ounces) unsalted butter, at room temperature
- ¼ cup well-stirred King's Hot Honey (page 251)
- ¼ teaspoon Diamond Crystal kosher salt

In a small food processor, combine all the ingredients and process, stopping to scrape down the sides, until fairly smooth, about 30 seconds. Alternatively, mix the ingredients together in a bowl.

BLACK GARLIC–ANCHOVY BUTTER

- 2 sticks (8 ounces) unsalted butter, unsalted, at room temperature
- 2 heads black garlic (about 20 cloves), peeled
- 10 oil-packed anchovy fillets
- 1 medium shallot, chopped
- Finely grated zest of 2 lemons
- 2 tablespoons lemon juice
- Handful of flat-leaf parsley leaves
- Several turns of ground black pepper
- 2 teaspoons Dijon mustard
- 2 teaspoons Maggi seasoning
- 2 teaspoons Worcestershire sauce
- ½ teaspoon Diamond Crystal kosher salt

In a small food processor, combine all the ingredients and process, stopping occasionally to scrape down the sides, until fairly smooth, about 30 seconds.

BURNT LIME–CILANTRO BUTTER

- 2 sticks (8 ounces) unsalted butter, at room temperature
- 2 cups packed cilantro leaves
- 1 cup packed flat-leaf parsley leaves
- ¾ teaspoon Diamond Crystal kosher salt
- ½ teaspoon coarsely ground black pepper
- ¼ teaspoon Sichuan chile flakes or red chile flakes
- 3 garlic cloves, peeled
- 1 small shallot, chopped
- 2 juicy limes

In a small food processor, combine all the ingredients except for the limes. Finely grate in the lime zest. Halve then char the limes (see Note, page 206).

Squeeze the juice into the food processor and process, stopping occasionally to scrape down the sides, until bright green, 1 to 2 minutes.

YUZU–BLACK PEPPER HONEY BUTTER

- 2 sticks (8 ounces) unsalted butter, at room temperature
- 2 tablespoons finely grated yuzu zest (or Meyer lemon or regular lemon zest)
- 2 tablespoons yuzu juice, bottled or fresh
- 2 tablespoons honey
- 2 teaspoons coarsely ground black pepper
- ¼ teaspoon Diamond Crystal kosher salt

In a small food processor, combine all the ingredients and process, stopping occasionally to scrape down the sides, until fairly smooth and well combined, about 30 seconds.

SICHUAN CHILE–BOURBON BUTTER

- 2 sticks (8 ounces) unsalted butter, at room temperature
- 4 garlic cloves, peeled
- ¼ cup King's Chili Crisp (page 257) or store-bought Chinese chili crisp
- 2 tablespoons bourbon
- 2 tablespoons amber maple syrup or packed light brown sugar
- 2 teaspoons finely grated lemon zest
- ½ teaspoon Diamond Crystal kosher salt
- Several turns of finely ground black pepper

In a small food processor, combine all the ingredients and process, stopping occasionally to scrape down the sides, until the garlic is minced and everything is well combined, about 30 seconds.

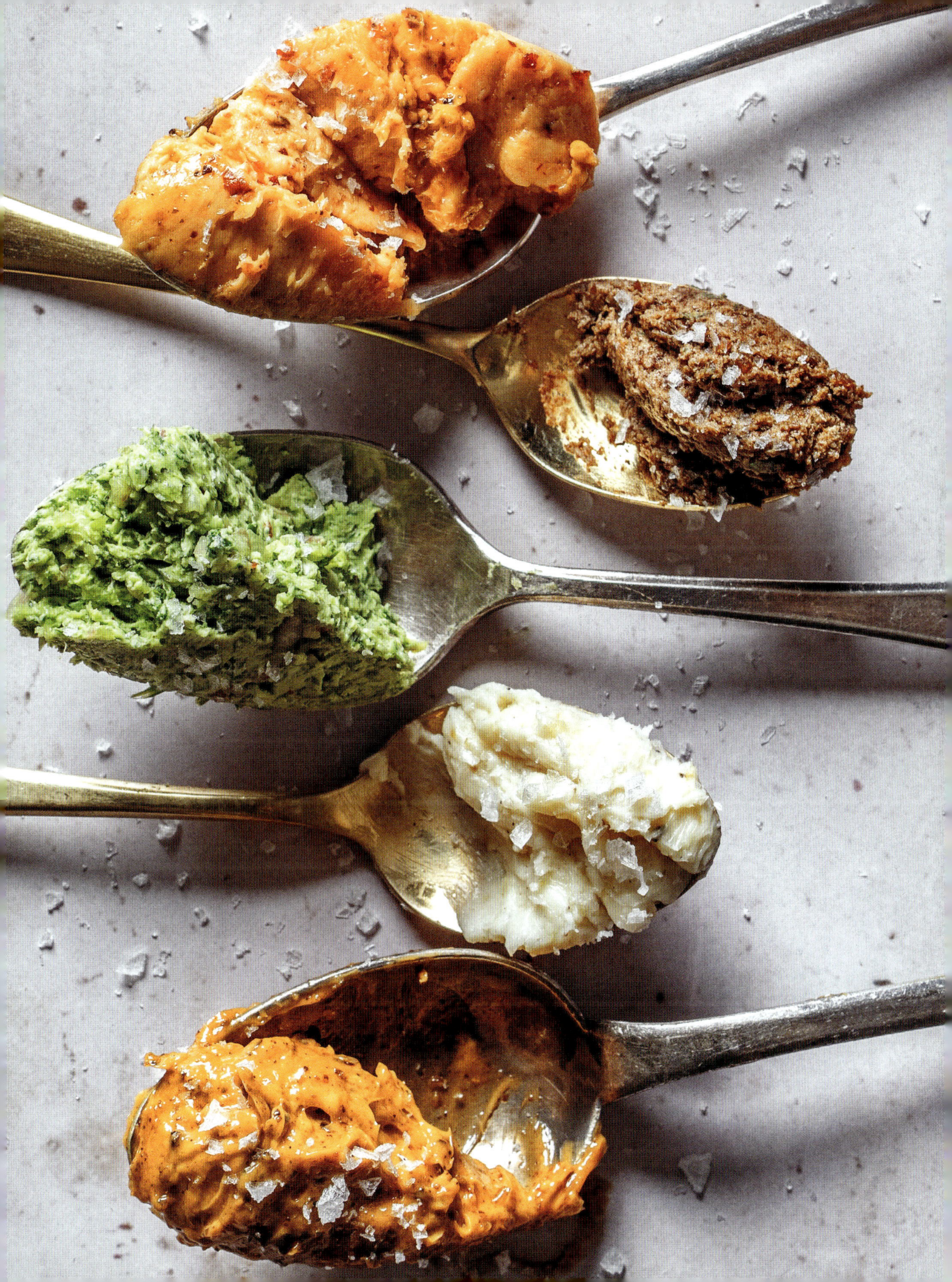

FRIED SHALLOTS

This recipe is a two-for-one deal. Not only does it give you an irresistible crunchy garnish, it also yields lots of fragrant, tasty oil that's great for drizzling over noodles, in vinaigrettes, and for bringing even more flavor to King's Chili Crisp (page 257) and Prosciutto XO sauce (page 260).

MAKES ABOUT 1¼ CUPS FRIED SHALLOTS AND 3½ CUPS SHALLOT OIL

12 ounces large shallots, peeled
4 cups canola oil
½ teaspoon Diamond Crystal kosher salt

Use a sharp knife or mandoline to slice the shallots into 1/16-inch rounds. Gently separate the rings. You'll have about 4 cups.

Line a sheet pan with several layers of paper towels. In a 3- to 4-quart pot, combine the shallots and oil. Bring to a vigorous bubble over medium heat, about 5 minutes, stirring as the shallots begin to sizzle. Cook, stirring occasionally, until the shallots turn an even, light golden brown (they won't be crisp just yet), 15 to 18 minutes, lowering the heat slightly if necessary to avoid bubbling over. Use a spider strainer to transfer the shallots to the paper towels and spread in a single layer. Sprinkle with the salt.

Let cool before using. As the shallots cool, they'll get slightly darker and turn crisp. Reserve the flavorful cooking oil and let it cool completely.

The fried shallots keep in an airtight container (lined with a paper towel to soak up excess oil) in a cool and dry place for up to 1 week. The oil keeps in an airtight container in the refrigerator for up to 1 month.

STEAMED BAO

If the thought of making these pillowy Chinese steamed buns feels intimidating, just know I believe in you! And I'm here to help. The simple dough steams to fluffy perfection, just like the bao you've probably seen on a lazy Susan alongside Peking duck. They're a great vehicle for many of the fun items in this book, including Shanghainese pork belly (page 100), al pastor (page 97), Five Spiced Duck à l'Orange (page 191), and Shoyu Butter Mushrooms (page 138).

Their bright white color comes from bleached flour, but feel free to substitute unbleached flour. Once they're steamed, the buns can be frozen, then thawed fully and rewarmed in a steamer just before serving.

MAKES 16 BUNS

Equipment: Stand mixer, rolling pin, sixteen 4-inch squares of parchment paper, a bamboo steamer (your best option) or a flat steamer basket

2⅔ cups / 320g bread flour (bleached or unbleached)

¾ cup / 175g water, at room temperature (70° to 90°F)

3 tablespoons / 40g white sugar

2½ tablespoons / 35g unsalted butter, at room temperature

2 teaspoons / 6g instant yeast

1¼ teaspoons / 5g Diamond Crystal kosher salt

½ teaspoon / 2g baking powder

Canola oil, for brushing

In a stand mixer fitted with the dough hook, combine all the ingredients except for the oil and mix on medium-low speed for 10 minutes, to combine well and properly develop the gluten. Cover the bowl loosely with a kitchen towel and let the dough rise in a place in your kitchen where it's slightly warmer than room temperature until roughly doubled in size, 1 to 1½ hours.

Transfer the dough to a clean work surface, cut it in half, then keep halving the halves until you have 16 equal portions (about 35g each). Roll each portion into a ball by hand. Arrange them an inch or so apart, then cover loosely with a kitchen towel and let them rest for 20 minutes.

Set out sixteen 4-inch squares of parchment paper. One at a time, use a lightly oiled rolling pin to roll each ball into an oval that's about ¼ inch thick. Lightly brush the top with oil, fold in half, and transfer to one of the parchment paper pieces. Cover loosely with a towel and let them rise until the dough springs right back when you press it with your finger, 30 to 45 minutes.

To steam the buns, bring 1 inch of water to a boil in a pot over high heat. Steam in batches: Transfer the buns (including the parchment paper) to a steamer basket, leaving a little space around each bun. Set the steamer basket in the pot, cover, and cook until the buns look fluffy and spring back when poked, about 12 minutes. Between batches, top up the pot with water and let it return to a boil.

As they're steamed, carefully transfer them (parchment paper included) from the steamer basket to a large plate or tray. Let cool to room temperature, then cover loosely with a kitchen towel. They'll stay fresh for up to 1 hour.

To freeze, steam the bao, cool, then freeze (parchment paper included) in a single layer in an airtight container for up to 2 weeks.

To reheat the buns, remove from the container, cover loosely, and let thaw completely at room temperature, about 30 minutes. Steam the buns until hot and fluffy, about 5 minutes.

OLIVE OIL–FRIED SOURDOUGH CROUTONS

These croutons barely make it to the table. All you do is tear great bread (the San Franciscan in me picks sourdough) into rustic pieces, then soak it in really good olive oil before pan-frying. The result is crispy at the edges, tender on the inside, and bursting with the flavor of delicious olive oil. They're so good, they inspire sneaky friends to hang out next to the stove, waiting for a chance to snatch a few. Just make sure there's some left to top the Miso Caesar (page 67).

MAKES ABOUT 3 CUPS

4 cups torn (about 1-inch pieces) sourdough (crust removed)

⅓ cup plus 3 tablespoons extra-virgin olive oil, divided

2 large garlic cloves, smashed and peeled

Leaves from 2 sprigs thyme

½ teaspoon Diamond Crystal kosher salt

Line a plate with paper towels and set aside. Put the bread in a large mixing bowl, drizzle with ⅓ cup of the oil, and toss together with your hands, gently squeezing the pieces to help them evenly absorb the oil.

Heat a large skillet over medium-high heat for 1 minute. Add the remaining 3 tablespoons oil and the garlic and swirl to coat the surface of the skillet. Add the bread and fry for about 4 minutes, stirring and turning the bread often so the sides brown evenly, until the pieces are crispy and light golden brown all over but still soft inside.

Add the thyme and stir for a minute more to infuse its flavor into the croutons. Turn off the heat, sprinkle on the salt, and toss well.

Transfer the fried sourdough to the paper towels in a single layer and let them drain for a few minutes (discard the garlic). They're best enjoyed warm.

FRIED BREAD CRUMBS

These crispy olive oil bread crumbs are simple to make and will give a boost to your pastas, salads, roasted vegetables, and really anything that benefits from a little crunch.

MAKES ABOUT 1½ CUPS

3 cups cubed sourdough (crust removed), preferably stale

½ cup extra-virgin olive oil

2 large garlic cloves, smashed and peeled

2 sprigs thyme

½ teaspoon Diamond Crystal kosher salt

If the bread is fresh, let the cubes sit out for 1 to 3 hours to stale. (Alternatively, bake at 200°F, stirring once, for 20 minutes. Let cool fully before proceeding.)

In a food processor, working in batches if necessary so the processor is no more than one-third full, pulse the bread to coarse bread crumbs, about 15 seconds per batch.

Line a plate with paper towels. Heat a large skillet over medium-high heat for 1 minute. Add the olive oil and garlic and cook, stirring, until lightly golden, about 3 minutes. Add the bread crumbs and thyme sprigs, stir to coat the crumbs in the olive oil, and cook, stirring and tossing constantly, until golden brown and crispy, about 2 minutes.

Turn off the heat, sprinkle with the salt, and toss well. Transfer to the paper towels to drain and let cool before using. If not using within 1 hour, cover and store in an airtight container at room temperature for up to 24 hours.

LAP CHEONG CRUMBLE

Think bacon bits, Chinese-style. These crispy, chewy bites are full of sweet-savory lap cheong flavor. It levels up everything from roasted vegetables like Charred Cabbage (page 147) to salads like my Miso Caesar (page 67) and Classic Wedge (page 68) to vibrant-green spring pea soup (page 151) and even Hong Kong Stuffed French Toast (page 236).

The flavorful oil leftover can be used to fry eggs, make Fried Bread Crumbs (at left), or drizzle into vinaigrettes.

MAKES ABOUT 1 CUP

4 links lap cheong (Chinese pork sausage), chilled

3 tablespoons canola oil

Peel off the sausage casings (it takes a little patience, but it's easy once you get the hang of it). Slice the sausages into ½-inch rounds. Transfer to a food processor, pulse a few times, then process continuously to the size of coarse bread crumbs, about 15 seconds.

Line a small (9 by 13-inch) sheet pan with paper towels. In a large skillet, combine the ground sausage and oil and stir well. Set over medium-low heat and cook gently, stirring frequently to prevent the sugars in the sausage from burning and adjusting the heat if necessary to maintain a gentle sizzle, until the bits of sausage turn a shade or two darker in color and are slightly crispy, 6 to 8 minutes.

Use a slotted spoon to transfer the sausage to the paper towels in a single layer to drain, leaving the flavorful fat in the skillet (reserving it for another use). Let cool completely.

The lap cheong crumble is best made a few hours before serving. It's also great the next day—cooled and stored in an airtight container in the fridge—just not quite as crispy.

PUFFED WILD RICE

Puffed grains, a staple in many Michelin-starred kitchens, can be a hassle to make. Wheat berries, quinoa, and rice, for instance, need to be thoroughly cooked and dehydrated overnight before they'll puff in the fryer. But not wild rice, which can go directly from raw to hot oil, quickly puffing to an airy, delicate crunch. It's a back-pocket garnish that adds nuttiness and texture to elevate your dishes.

There are countless ways to use it—sprinkled on corn soup (page 148), wedge salad (page 68), and Yellowtail Crudo in Ginger-Citrus Broth (page 39). Leftovers even make awesome Rice Krispies treats.

MAKES ABOUT 1¾ CUPS

Equipment: Deep-fry thermometer

Canola oil (about 6 cups), for deep-frying

½ cup wild rice

Diamond Crystal kosher salt

Line a large (18 by 13-inch) sheet pan with paper towels and set near the stove. Pour 1½ inches of oil into a deep medium pot and heat over medium-high heat until it registers 380°F.

With a spider strainer in one hand, use your other hand to carefully sprinkle half of the rice into the oil. Immediately start stirring with the spider and continue until the rice floats to the surface and puffs (it will double in volume and split to reveal a light golden brown interior), about 10 seconds.

Immediately use the spider to transfer the puffed rice to the paper towels, spreading out the grains to encourage cooling and draining. Lightly season with salt. Let the oil heat back up and repeat with the remaining rice. (Cool completely before storing. The puffed rice keeps in an airtight container at room temperature for up to 4 hours or, with silica packets, up to 2 days.)

KING'S CHILI CRISP

I'm obsessed with this chili crisp—a simpler version of the one I sell in my small-batch line of products—and I use it on everything! Infused with aromatic spices, Sichuan peppercorns, and chile flakes, it lends a pleasantly numbing, full-flavored kick of heat.

MAKES ABOUT 2½ CUPS

2 cups canola oil

2 teaspoons red Sichuan peppercorns

1 teaspoon whole cloves

1 teaspoon coriander seeds

6 dried bay leaves

6 garlic cloves, lightly smashed and peeled

3 whole star anise

2 by 1-inch knob ginger, peeled and thinly sliced

1 cinnamon stick

1 cup Sichuan chile flakes

2 tablespoons store-bought fried garlic or shallots (optional)

2 tablespoons toasted sesame seeds

½ teaspoon Diamond Crystal kosher salt

In a medium saucepan, combine the oil, Sichuan peppercorns, cloves, coriander, bay leaves, garlic, star anise, ginger, and cinnamon stick. Set it over medium-high heat until the spices and garlic begin to bubble, 3 to 4 minutes. Continue cooking, stirring occasionally, until the garlic turns deep golden brown, 4 to 6 minutes.

Turn off the heat, then use a spider strainer to scoop out and discard the solids. Set over medium-high heat and add the chile flakes, fried garlic (if using), sesame seeds, and salt. Cook, stirring frequently, until the oil turns a vibrant red color, about 2 minutes.

Turn off the heat and let cool to room temperature. (The chili crisp keeps in an airtight container in the refrigerator for up to 3 months. Stir well before serving.)

CITRUS MARMALADE

Every year, I harvest the SoCal citrus bounty in my family's yard—kumquats and Meyer lemons, mandarinquats, and sour Seville oranges—and turn them into this sweet fruit preserve, warmed with just a touch of ginger. And it's so easy—a quick trip in the blender and a simmer on the stove. Recommended for madeleines (page 228), the marmalade is also a fantastic addition to any charcuterie board, great slathered on goat cheese or ricotta toasts, and healing when stirred into hot water for a quick citrus tisane to bring on the coziness.

MAKES ABOUT 3 CUPS

12 ounces assorted citrus (kumquats, mandarins, oranges, lemons)

1 Meyer lemon or lemon (about 4 ounces)

¼ cup water

2½ cups white sugar

¼ teaspoon Diamond Crystal kosher salt

3 by 1-inch knob ginger, peeled and finely grated on a Microplane

Remove any stems from the assorted citrus and the lemon, and cut the fruit into quarters (or eighths, if especially large). Discard any seeds.

In a blender, combine the citrus and water and blend, starting on low speed and gradually increasing the speed to medium, to a coarse paste with pea-size pieces of citrus, about 30 seconds. Do not blend until smooth.

Pour the mixture into a medium saucepan, add the sugar, salt, and ginger and stir well. Bring to a boil over high heat, stirring occasionally. Turn the heat down to cook at a gentle simmer, stirring frequently to prevent burning, until the mixture registers 220°F on a candy thermometer, about 30 minutes. (Alternatively, chill a plate, add a teaspoon of the marmalade, and wait 30 seconds. If the liquid has set like jelly, it's ready.) Let cool completely before serving. (The marmalade keeps in an airtight container in the refrigerator for up to 2 months.)

KING'S PONZU

You can purchase ponzu, the much-loved Japanese condiment made of soy sauce and citrus, but I want to show you just how easy and rewarding it is to make it yourself. Along with fragrant yuzu juice, I like to play with other citrus: orange, lemon, and lime—including the zest—to build brightness. Since you most likely won't use it all in one go, you'll also get the chance to taste the magic of aging ponzu, experiencing the way steeping katsuobushi (bonito flakes) and kombu (dried kelp) deepens the flavors over time. Ponzu benefits from an artisanal soy sauce, which brings nuance and complexity.

Try it as a dipping sauce for fried maitake (page 133), raw fish, or grilled seafood, such as the Grilled Fish Collars (page 164).

MAKES ABOUT 3 CUPS

2 or 3 large juicy oranges

2 or 3 juicy lemons

2 or 3 juicy limes

1 cup mirin

1 cup Japanese soy sauce

½ cup bottled yuzu juice

¼ cup unseasoned rice vinegar

2 lightly packed cups / 20g katsuobushi (bonito flakes)

5 by 7 inches kombu, broken into a few pieces

Use a peeler to remove long wide strips of zest from 2 of the oranges, 2 of the lemons, and 2 of the limes. Trim off any white pith from the strips and add them to a wide-mouthed 32-ounce mason jar.

Halve and squeeze enough of the citrus to yield ½ cup orange juice, ¼ cup lemon juice, and ¼ cup lime juice. Add the juices and the remaining ingredients to the jar, stir, and cover. Refrigerate for at least 2 hours. Before using, stir well, then pour the amount you need through a sieve, returning any solids to the jar. (The ponzu keeps in the refrigerator for up to 2 months and gets even better as it "ages.")

PINEAPPLE-HABANERO HOT SAUCE

There's something special about making your own hot sauce. So whip up this vibrant condiment (no fermentation necessary) that highlights the tropical sweetness of pineapple and the fruity heat of habanero. Then use it on pretty much anything—from Al Pastor Bao (page 97) to Tuna Tostadas (page 36) and from Grilled Lemongrass–Soy Sauce Chicken Thighs (page 187) to Yellowtail Crudo (page 39), not to mention pizza, barbecued ribs, and even soups and stews. You'll have plenty, so bottle it up with some cute labels for gifting.

SWITCH IT UP

Make it your own by using mango, papaya, or peaches instead of pineapple, adding fresh turmeric along with the ginger, and using whatever fresh chiles you've got—jalapeños and Fresnos for less heat and ghost peppers if you dare.

MAKES ABOUT 4 CUPS

- 1 tablespoon canola oil
- 2 fresh habanero or datil chiles, halved, seeded, and deveined (wear gloves!)
- 1 yellow bell pepper, roughly chopped
- ½ cup sliced yellow onion
- 2 by 1-inch knob ginger, peeled and sliced
- Diamond Crystal kosher salt
- 2 cups peeled fresh pineapple chunks
- 1 cup distilled white or apple cider vinegar
- 3 tablespoons lime juice (from 2 limes), plus more as needed
- 1 tablespoon honey, plus more as needed
- 2 medium garlic cloves, peeled

Heat a large skillet over medium heat for 1 minute. Add the oil and swirl to coat. When the oil shimmers, add the chiles, bell pepper, onion, ginger, and a pinch of salt and cook, stirring occasionally, until the onions are translucent, about 3 minutes. Add the pineapple and cook, stirring occasionally, until lightly caramelized, about 3 minutes.

Transfer to a blender, add the vinegar, lime juice, honey, garlic, and 1 teaspoon salt and blend until completely smooth, about 1 minute. Season to taste with additional salt, lime juice, and honey. Let it cool completely. (The hot sauce keeps in an airtight container in the refrigerator for up to 3 months. Stir well before serving.)

HONG KONG MILK TEA

Growing up in the former British colony of Hong Kong, my parents became accustomed to having their tea with milk. For them lai cha (or "milk tea") was their caffeine source, not coffee. They still have the habit of making theirs with sachets of Lipton black tea, one of the few options available when they first arrived in America in the 1960s. My mom drinks her lai cha at the kitchen table with a slice of toasted milk bread slathered with butter and condensed milk. At Hong Kong–style cafés, it's often served alongside jook (page 122), rice noodle rolls, and bolo bao (pineapple buns).

There's an art to making a good cup. The best places in Hong Kong "pull" the bold brewed tea, pouring it multiple times through a strainer that resembles a silk stocking to aerate it for a smooth mouthfeel. At home, I brew high-quality Ceylon or English breakfast tea long and strong to a rich red color and then pour it over evaporated and sweetened condensed milk. For a truly authentic experience, Black and White brand evaporated and sweetened condensed milk is a must. Serve it alongside Almond Madeleines (page 228), Hong Kong Stuffed French Toast (page 236), Hong Kong Milk Tea Tiramisu (page 222), or Basque Cheesecake (page 232).

CONTINUED

SERVES 4

Equipment: Cheesecloth

4 cups water

½ cup loose Ceylon or English breakfast tea

One 12-ounce can evaporated milk

¼ cup sweetened condensed milk, plus more as needed

In a medium pot, bring the water to a boil, covered. Stir in the tea leaves and reduce the heat to cook at a moderate simmer, uncovered, for 15 minutes.

Turn off the heat. Line a sieve with cheesecloth, set over a heatproof container, and pour in the tea, discarding the solids. You'll have about 2½ cups brewed tea.

Divide the evaporated milk among four large teacups or coffee mugs and add 1 tablespoon sweetened condensed milk (or more to taste) to each cup. Divide the hot brewed tea among the cups and stir well. Serve hot or let cool completely and serve over ice.

PROSCIUTTO XO

During my *Top Chef: All-Stars* season, we were in Parma for the last competition before the finale. Our challenge was to make a dish with prosciutto di Parma, the city's famous ham. I was running frantically through a marketplace in a timed shopping spree, unsure of what to make. Until I spotted pristine diver scallops in their shells, and it hit me.

Suddenly, I was back at my family's table with my mom, dipping into a tiny, pricey jar of XO sauce. We'd ration it, spooning dabs on our rice or dumplings, savoring its umami goodness. The Hong Kong–born condiment is made of shallots, chiles, and garlic along with premium ingredients like dried scallops and shrimp, XO ("extra old") Cognac, and a touch of Chinese ham. I was in Italy with no access to most of these ingredients, but inspiration took over. I flipped the XO script, highlighting the cured meat and serving it over seared scallops. To replace the briny flavor bomb from the missing dried seafood, I picked up bottarga, Italy's cured fish roe.

At Judge's Table, the dish was a huge hit, though I got a kick out of the tender teasing of one Italian judge. The sauce is so good, he said, now please never heat up prosciutto again. It was sacrilegious but delicious, a good way to describe so much of the food I love. Spoon it on dumplings, noodles, steamed rice, or Scallops with Creamed Corn (page 160).

MAKES ABOUT 2½ CUPS

Equipment: Meat grinder fitted with a medium (4mm) die plate

One 6-ounce piece prosciutto (or trimmed prosciutto ends), cut into 1-inch pieces, cold

2 cups canola oil

1 cup roughly chopped shallots (about 4 medium)

¾ cup peeled garlic cloves (about 20 large)

1 ounce dried bottarga (optional), finely grated on a Microplane

2 fresh red Thai chiles, minced

1 tablespoon white sugar, plus more as needed

1 teaspoon fish sauce (preferably Three Crabs), plus more as needed

¼ teaspoon Diamond Crystal kosher salt, plus more as needed

3 tablespoons XO Cognac or other Cognac, brandy, or Shaoxing wine

Run the prosciutto pieces through a meat grinder fitted with a 4mm die plate.

In a medium saucepan, combine the oil and prosciutto and stir well. Set over medium heat and let the oil reach a rapid bubble. Fry, stirring frequently, until the prosciutto turns deep brown as it caramelizes and gets slightly crispy, about 5 minutes.

Turn off the heat, then use a fine-mesh sieve to scoop out the prosciutto and transfer it to a bowl. Let the oil cool for 10 minutes to prevent overflow later.

Meanwhile, in a food processor, pulse the shallots and garlic, scraping down the sides as necessary, until finely minced.

When the oil has cooled for 10 minutes, stir in the shallot/garlic mixture. Set the pan over medium heat and cook, stirring frequently, until golden brown, 10 to 12 minutes.

Stir in the reserved prosciutto along with the bottarga (if using), chiles, sugar, fish sauce, and salt and cook for 2 minutes. Turn off the heat, stir in the Cognac (it will bubble rapidly), and cool to room temperature. Season to taste with additional salt, sugar, and fish sauce. (It keeps in an airtight container in the refrigerator for up to 4 months. Stir well before using.)

CHIMICHURRI

I treat the gorgeous, drizzly Argentinian herb sauce as a jumping-off point. Classic parsley and fresh oregano are fantastic, but I'll often finely chop whatever herbs I have on hand—cilantro, mint, shiso—then add the other components (chile, salt, vinegar, olive oil) until I'm happy. Try it on Salt-Baked Whole Fish (page 172), crispy salmon (page 180), rib eye steak (page 196), or roasted veggies.

SWITCH IT UP

Make chimichurri your own by adding chopped olives or capers, mashed anchovies, suprêmed segments of lemon, halved cherry tomatoes, or thinly sliced garlic scapes.

MAKES ABOUT ¾ CUP

- 2 tablespoons red wine vinegar, plus more as needed
- 2 teaspoons minced shallot
- 2 medium garlic cloves, finely grated on a Microplane
- Diamond Crystal kosher salt
- 2 handfuls of mixed delicate leafy herbs, such as shiso, cilantro, and flat-leaf parsley leaves
- 2 big pinches of oregano leaves, or ½ teaspoon dried
- 2 tablespoons minced seeded red Fresno chile, or ¼ teaspoon red chile flakes
- Finely ground black pepper
- ½ cup extra-virgin olive oil, plus more as needed

In a medium bowl, combine the vinegar, shallot, garlic, and a pinch of salt. Stir well and let sit for 2 minutes to tame their sharp flavors. Stir again to distribute any clumps of garlic.

Use a very sharp chef's knife and a rocking motion to finely chop the herbs, including the oregano, without bruising them. You'll have about ½ cup.

Add the herbs, chiles, 1 teaspoon salt, and several turns of black pepper to the bowl and stir well. Slowly drizzle in the olive oil while stirring. The chimichurri should be loose enough to drip easily off a spoon, so gradually add more olive oil if needed.

Season to taste with more salt, pepper, and vinegar and stir well. Serve within 30 minutes.

APPLE TARTAR SAUCE

Green apple is surprisingly welcome in this otherwise classic tartar sauce meant for Beer-Battered Fish (page 171). It adds a sweet-tart dimension and another element of texture.

MAKES ABOUT 2 CUPS

- ½ cup mayonnaise
- 1 tablespoon drained capers
- Finely grated zest of 1 lemon
- 2 teaspoons lemon juice
- ½ teaspoon Diamond Crystal kosher salt
- 8 cornichons, plus 1 teaspoon cornichon brine
- 1 small shallot, roughly chopped
- ½ medium Granny Smith apple, peeled, cored, and cut into 2-inch chunks
- Small handful of dill fronds
- Small handful of chopped chives
- A few turns of finely ground black pepper

In a food processor, combine all the ingredients and pulse, scraping down the sides, until the cornichons, apples, and shallots are minced, about 30 seconds. Refrigerate until chilled, at least 30 minutes or up to 4 hours.

SWEET SOY SAUCE

Classically served with Hainan Chicken (page 188), this sauce is welcome with virtually anything—drizzle it over steamed fish, add it to noodles in a hot wok, or serve it as a dip for poached shrimp.

MAKES ABOUT ½ CUP

¼ cup white sugar

3 tablespoons Chinese dark soy sauce

3 tablespoons Chinese light soy sauce

2 tablespoons Shaoxing wine

1 medium garlic clove, finely grated on a Microplane

½ teaspoon finely grated ginger

Dash of ground white pepper

In a small saucepan, combine all the ingredients, stir well, and bring to a simmer over medium-high heat. Turn the heat down to cook at a steady simmer, stirring occasionally, until thickened to the consistency of warm maple syrup, 2 to 3 minutes. Turn off the heat and let cool before serving. (The sauce keeps covered in the refrigerator for up to 1 week. Let it come to room temperature before serving.)

OLIVE TAPENADE

Tapenade may feel a little old-school, but I love it and think everyone should have one in their back pocket to elevate simple dishes. Mine is full of earthy Kalamata olives and briny capers brightened with red wine vinegar and fresh herbs. It's a winner on crispy salmon (page 180), rib eye steak (page 196), lamb chops, and sweet potatoes (page 134). It's also a great addition to a grazing board: think Chili Crisp Labneh (page 32), Miso Baba Ghanoush (page 24), and Black Vinegar–Marinated Sweet Peppers (page 35) with focaccia (page 82) for dipping.

MAKES ABOUT 1½ CUPS

2 tablespoons red wine vinegar, plus more as needed

2 teaspoons minced shallot

2 medium garlic cloves, finely grated on a Microplane

Diamond Crystal kosher salt

Small handful of flat-leaf parsley leaves, finely chopped

Finely grated zest of 1 lemon

1 cup drained Kalamata olives, pitted and finely chopped

1 teaspoon drained capers, finely chopped

¼ cup plus 2 tablespoons extra-virgin olive oil

Finely ground black pepper

In a medium bowl, combine the vinegar, shallot, garlic, and a pinch of salt. Stir well and let sit for 3 minutes to tame the sharp flavors of the garlic and shallots.

Stir in the parsley and lemon zest, then add the olives, capers, and olive oil and stir well. Season to taste with pepper and more vinegar and/or salt.

(The tapenade keeps in an airtight container in the refrigerator for up to 2 weeks.)

GINGER-SCALLION SAUCE

Rarely does this Cantonese sauce last in my fridge for more than a day. When hot oil hits ginger and scallion, it tempers their sharpness but ignites their flavors, making the three-ingredient condiment so delicious you'll find yourself searching for any excuse to eat it.

MAKES ABOUT 1 CUP

- 1 cup thinly sliced scallions (about 1 bunch)
- ¼ cup finely grated ginger (from two 4 by 1-inch knobs)
- 1 teaspoon Diamond Crystal kosher salt
- ½ cup canola oil

In a heatproof medium mixing bowl, combine the scallions, ginger, and salt. Stir briefly and put the bowl near the stove.

In a small saucepan, heat the oil over high heat and wait for it to start smoking, 2 to 3 minutes. Pour it evenly and quickly over the scallion mixture, then immediately stir well. Let it cool completely. (It keeps in an airtight container in the fridge for up to 4 days.)

BLACK VINEGAR–CHILI DIPPING SAUCE

MAKES ABOUT ⅓ CUP

- ¼ cup Zhenjiang black vinegar
- 2 tablespoons Chinese light soy sauce
- 1 teaspoon finely grated ginger
- ½ teaspoon toasted sesame seeds
- ½ teaspoon King's Chili Crisp (page 257) or store-bought Chinese chili crisp
- ½ teaspoon white sugar
- Large pinch of finely chopped cilantro (leaves and stems)
- Large pinch of thinly sliced scallions

In a small bowl, combine all of the ingredients and stir well. (It keeps in an airtight container in the refrigerator for up to 2 days. Stir before serving.)

KING'S MALA SPICE

This special spice blend embraces mala, the spicy-numbing flavor profile beloved in Sichuan cooking, and spices like coriander, cumin, and fennel seeds. It's the key to my Lamb Skewers (page 200), but I also sprinkle it on everything from roasted carrots (page 155), buttered popcorn, whole chickens before roasting, fried eggs, and my morning avocado toast.

MAKES ABOUT 1¼ CUPS

- ¼ cup cumin seeds
- 1 tablespoon coriander seeds
- 1 tablespoon fennel seeds
- 1 tablespoon red Sichuan peppercorns
- 1 tablespoon toasted sesame seeds
- ¾ cup Sichuan chile flakes
- ¼ cup Diamond Crystal kosher salt
- 2 tablespoons white sugar
- 1 teaspoon ground ginger
- ½ teaspoon ground white pepper

In a small skillet, toast the cumin, coriander, and fennel seeds over medium-low heat, stirring frequently, until fragrant, 2 to 3 minutes. Transfer to a mortar or spice grinder and pound or grind to a coarse powder. Transfer to a container.

Pound or grind the Sichuan peppercorns to a fine powder and transfer to the container. Pound or grind the sesame seeds in a mortar to a fine powder, and transfer to the container. Add the remaining spice mix ingredients to the container and stir well. (The spice mix keeps in an airtight container in a cool, dark place for up to 6 months.)

ACKNOWLEDGMENTS

They say it's a passion project, and it's so true: You don't understand how long a cookbook takes to make until you actually make it. This book began in 2016 as an idea after my first run on *Top Chef*. After my All-Star season in 2020, I wrote the first words. More than four years later, I'm proudly, finally, writing these acknowledgments. I have so many people to thank for making this dream come to life.

First and foremost, thank you to my parents, my sister, Stephanie, and the rest of my family for your love and support. You were the first people to taste my cooking and my first fans, eating my early creations without complaint even when the food was oversalted or burnt. You taught me to welcome mistakes in the kitchen and in life, and that the most important thing is to continue improving and try your best.

Thank you to all of you, especially my mom and dad, for teaching me the value of hard work and persistence, which has carried me through my career. Extra thanks to my mom for the late nights putting together humble dinners to nourish our family and for letting me be your little sous-chef. So many of these recipes I experienced or learned to make with you before I turned 12. You continue to be my biggest cheerleader.

Thank you to my grandmas on both sides for teaching me about our culture through the dishes that your mothers taught you. Special thanks to Sabrina PoPo. Your spirit and our memories together flow through this book. Thank you to all the "uncles" and "aunties" who have supported me and my cooking since I was a kid. I'm proud to continue passing on the flavor memories of my family, my home, and my culture through this book.

To my eight-year-old twin nieces, Sophia and Elizabeth, for being my favorite "helper chefs." Many of these dishes we have made together—dumplings, sheet pan pizza, meatballs, Dutch pancakes, even the Sicilian crudo! They now get to live on in this book for you two. Both of you inspire me to continue building new food memories.

To my coauthor and friend, JJ Goode. You made this entire process feel wildly insane, but in the best possible way. I could not have written this without you. Your attention to detail and neurotic obsessiveness was a match for mine, and your positivity, sassy-ass humor, and levity is what truly anchored us. You challenged me in all the right places, and you were the voice of reason for the home cook every time I'd default to "Eh, they'll figure it out!" I laughed and ate way too much while writing this with you, and I could not have asked for a better work wife/bagel queen.

To my culinary team, who helped get these recipes out of my head and onto paper. To my assistant, Callyn Humm, who wears all the hats. I'm very lucky to have shared this cookbook experience with you. You've diligently tested these recipes to ensure success for our readers. To Connie Collica for obsessing over bubbles, techniques, and recipe words together like we were in an episode of *Schitt's Creek*. And to Brian Collica for the baos. Thank you to my pastry chef, Laura Monge, for running with my random dessert ideas and bringing them to life with your expertise. And to Tao Romalis, who at just fifteen years old approached retests with poise, curiosity, and diligence.

To my culinary mentors and chef friends at every restaurant I've worked at throughout my career. You have all shared invaluable knowledge and fundamentals with me that have trickled into each and every recipe in this book. I would not be the chef I am today without your guidance—Roberto Desales, Shawn Smith, Megan Garrelts, Dan Corey, Gavin Schmidt, Connie Collica, and the Ritz-Carlton fam. A special thank you to chef Ron Siegel, my culinary father, who patiently taught me how to butcher whole animals, make pasta, turn trim into deliciousness, cook with the California seasons, and be a leader.

To my amazing, feisty book agent, Sabrina Taitz. I could not have done any of this without you. Thank you for always being in my corner and believing in me. I'm never letting you convince me to bring a book baby into the world again—at least, not until I take a vacation. To my supportive managers at M88, Phil Sun and Carrie Wiener, and agents at WME, Jeff Googel and Ginger Chan.

To my editors, Kelly Snowden and Claire Yee. Kelly, you believed in me and this project from our very first coffee meeting at The Mill way back in 2016. Claire, what a joy to have a Canto sister on this project! To Emma Campion for obsessing over design with me and putting your heart into every detail. Thank you to the entire Ten Speed team—Liana Faughnan, Philip Leung, Jina Stanfill, Monica Stanton, Mari Gill, and Faith Hague—for fully supporting my vision and allowing me the freedom to create a book that I feel so proud of and represents all of me (head-on black chicken and all).

To my incredible photo team, whose obsessive attention to detail and easy-going, collaborative energy let us create such beauty together. To photographer Ed Anderson, for your beautiful eye for lighting and shadows, your ability to capture the heart of each dish in the most stunning way. To food stylist Lillian Kang and her assistant Paige Arnett, the culinary backbones of the shoot, for producing more than 121 recipes in 11 days and adding touches to the images that we can all be proud of. Lillian, I learned so much from you and I'm so honored we got to create this together. To Ashley Batz, my ride-or-die portrait photographer and dear friend, for bringing the California vibes and effortless style to our lifestyle images. I'm in awe of your artistry, passion, and deep humility. Thank you for putting so much of your heart into my projects. To Glenn Jenkins, for all the beautiful props and ceramics that captured my personality.

To the fashion designer Thom Browne and team, especially Kelly Connor and Cameron Cipolla, for keeping me looking sharp. And a nod to my other favorite brands—Dior, Saint Laurent, Valentino, Golf Wang, Rowing Blazers, The Elder Statesman, Bode—which brought so much life to the images in this book.

To *Top Chef*, a twice-in-a-lifetime experience that changed me. So many of these dishes were birthed during the competition, in moments when stress turned into revelation. To Padma Lakshmi, Tom Colicchio, and Gail Simmons—your guidance, advice, and support have made me a better chef. You each have challenged me to dig deep, explore my identity, and draw out the stories I have to tell through my food. To my *Top Chef* family and friends I made along the way—in particular, Mei Lin, Shirley Chung, Silvia Barban, Nini Nguyen, Dale Talde, Kwame Onwuachi, and Gregory Gourdet—who changed the way I think about food, who challenged me to become a better chef each day.

To my musician friends—Drama, The Beaches, Brijean and the rest of Crying in the Club—for the songs that played on repeat in my kitchen and carried me through the highs and lows of writing this book.

To all my loving friends and chosen family who supported me while I disappeared in a hole to write this book. Thank you for listening to me obsess over recipes every time you saw me and for continuing to cheer me on throughout my career. Thank you for eating my experiments, testing my recipes, repping my merch, yelling at TV screens, and yelling how proud you are of me. To Rachel Helzer, Frankie Fictitious, Sam Hoffman, and Emi Grannis for joining the photoshoot fun. Special thanks to Emi, my unofficial art director, for always taking time to be my creative sounding board, for always picking up my calls to obsess over fonts and scribbling ideas on napkins during lunch hangouts. I trust your artistic eye most! To Caroline Blaike, who when I asked what I should call my cookbook, nonchalantly blurted out the title while spinning pirouettes in a green leopard leotard and cat-eye sunglasses. To Phoenix, my fire mother, for the flames.

Thank you to old and new friends reading this book right now. Thank you for your support. I hope these recipes become part of your life and that you share them with the people you care about most. And to every ex-girlfriend who has experienced the magic of Mama Mel's Meatballs. I hope they made you feel loved.

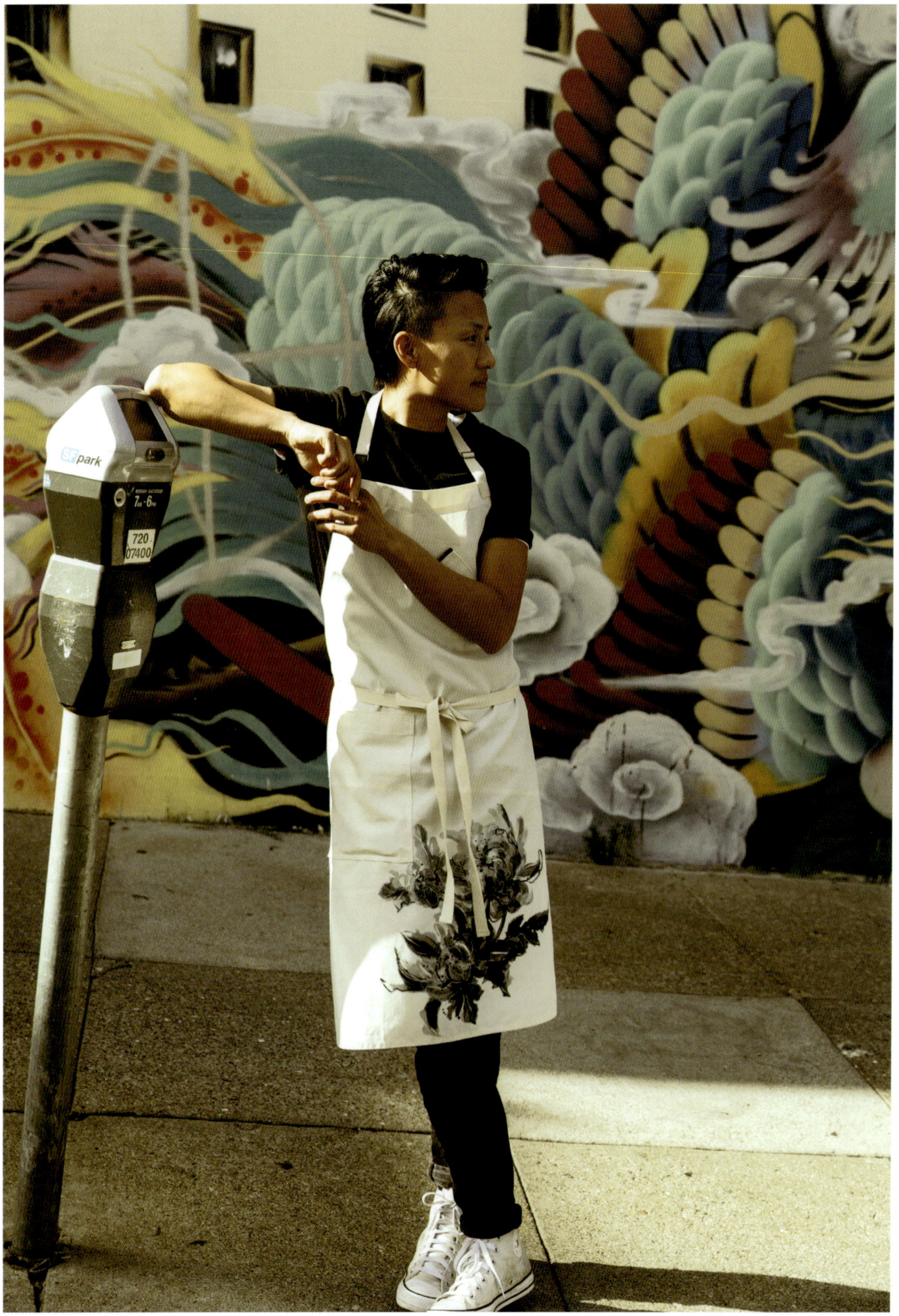
SFpark
720
07400

ABOUT THE AUTHORS

Chef Melissa King is a Chinese American, Bay Area Michelin-star trained chef. She's most known as the winner of *Top Chef: All-Stars,* winning the most challenges of any season, and the host of *Tasting Wild with National Geographic.* She's an award-winning chef entrepreneur, TV personality, model, and LGBTQ and AAPI philanthropist. She's curated menus for events such as the Met Gala and was also featured on an AAPI special for *Sesame Street.* Her unique style of cooking combines modern California cuisine with Asian flavors.

JJ Goode helps people write books, and mostly cookbooks, which are the best books. He has coauthored several *New York Times* bestsellers and has won two James Beard awards. He writes essays and articles sometimes, too. The editors of *The Norton Reader* selected his *Gourmet* magazine essay on cooking with one arm for their anthology of nonfiction, which includes writing from Nora Ephron, Barack Obama, and Jesus.

INDEX

A
almond:
    Cookies, Chinese, Torched Banana Pudding with, 225
    Madeleines with Citrus Marmalade, 228
Al Pastor Bao, 97
anchovy(ies):
    Black Garlic–Anchovy Butter, 252
    Burnt Lemon–Anchovy Vinaigrette, 147
    Caesar salad dressing, 67
    dressing, lemony, 72
apple(s):
    Asian Pear Sauce, 137
    Tartar Sauce, 261
        Beer-Battered Fish with, 171
avocado(s):
    Jicama with Avocado, Macadamia Nuts, and Sesame-Lime Vinaigrette, 79
    King's Guacamole, 28
    Tuna Tostadas with Avocado, Ginger, and Scallion, 36

B
Baba Ghanoush, Miso, 24
bacon, in Classic Wedge with Shiso Ranch, 68
Banana Pudding, Torched, with Chinese Almond Cookies, 225
Bao, Steamed, 254. *See also* Al Pastor Bao
Basque Cheesecake, Salted Egg Yolk, 232
beef:
    Chilled Beef Shank Salad with Celery and Radish, 71
    Kimchi-Beef Filling, 110
    Mama Mel's Meatballs, 203
    Oxtail and Daikon Soup, 213
    Rib Eye on the Bone with Black Garlic–Anchovy Butter, 196
    Sichuan Steak Tartare, 31
    Stew, Lemongrass, 199
    Taiwanese Beef Noodle Soup, 106
Beer-Battered Fish with Apple Tartar Sauce, 171
Berries, Yuzu–Coconut Olive Oil Cake with, 240. *See also* Strawberry-Ginger Jam
Black Garlic–Anchovy Butter, 252
    Rib Eye on the Bone with, 196
Black Pepper–Garlic Lobster, 168
black vinegar, 18
    –Caramelized Onions, 248
    –Chili Dipping Sauce, 263
    –Marinated Sweet Peppers, 35
    Mayo, 130
    Ribs, 209
Bone Broth, Chicken and Ginseng, with Goji Berries, 210
bourbon:
    Sichuan Chile–Bourbon Butter, 252
Bread Crumbs, Fried, 256
Brine, 245
broth. *See also* Bone Broth
    Weekend, 244
    Yuzu, 116
buns:
    Milk Buns, 86
    Steamed Bao, 254
Burnt Lemon–Anchovy Vinaigrette, 147
Burnt Lime–Cilantro Butter, 252
    Steamed Clams with, 167
burrata, in Shiso Pea Pappardelle, 115
Butters, Flavored, 252

C
cabbage:
    Charred, with Burnt Lemon–Anchovy Vinaigrette, 147
    Pork and Salted Cabbage Filling, 110
    Shanghainese "Lion's Head" Meatballs, 214
Caesar salad:
    Miso Caesar with Gai Lan and Chrysanthemum Greens, 67
Cake, Yuzu–Coconut Olive Oil, with Berries, 240. *See also* Madeleines, Almond
Calabrian Chile Mayo, 130
Calamansi Dipping Sauce, 218
    Turmeric-Lemongrass Pork Belly Roast with, 217
capers:
    Flounder with Yuzu Brown Butter and, 163
    Mama Mel's Meatballs, 203
Caponata, Eggplant, 141
Carrots, Spiced, with Pistachio and Labneh, 155
Century Duck Eggs with Chilled Tofu, 51
Charred Green Oil, 248
Char Siu Black Cod, 183
Char Siu Marinade, 183
cheese. *See also specific cheeses*
    Cheesy Scallion Pancakes, 93
    Smoked Cheese, Chicory Salad with Anchovy, Kumquats, and, 72
Cheesecake, Salted Egg Yolk Basque, 232
chicken:
    and Ginger Jook, 122
    and Ginseng Bone Broth with Goji Berries, 210
    Grilled Fish Sauce–Caramel Chicken Wings, 47
    Grilled Lemongrass–Soy Sauce Chicken Thighs, 187
    Hainan, with Chicken-Fat Rice and Ginger-Scallion Sauce, 188
    King's Wings, 44
    Taiwanese Popcorn Chicken, 48
Chicory Salad with Anchovy, Kumquats, and Smoked Cheese, 72
Chile Mayo, Calabrian, 130
chile peppers, 14
    Al Pastor Bao, 97
    Calabrian Chile Mayo, 130
    Hot Honey–Cured Egg Yolks on Garlic Toast, 59
    King's Chili Crisp, 257
    King's Guacamole, 28
    Pickled Chiles, 245
    Pineapple-Habanero Hot Sauce, 259
    Prosciutto XO, 260
    Salt and Pepper Maitake, 133
    Sweet and Sour Plum Glaze, 195
    sweet and spicy glaze, 44
    Taiwanese Beef Noodle Soup, 106
chili crisp, 14
Chili Crisp, King's, 257
    Century Duck Eggs with, 51
    Chili Crisp Labneh with, 32
    Chilled Beef Shank Salad with, 71
    Corn Soup with, and Puffed Wild Rice, 148
    Sichuan Chile–Bourbon Butter with, 252
    Sichuan Steak Tartare with, 31
Chili Crisp Labneh, 32
Chili-Lime Melon and Prosciutto, 63
Chocolate Chunk Cookies, 239
cilantro:
    Burnt Lime–Cilantro Butter, 252
Cioppino, Lemongrass, 159
Cipollini Onions Agrodolce, 249
    Eggplant Caponata with, 141
citrus. *See also* yuzu
    Ginger-Citrus Broth, 39
    King's Ponzu, 258
    Marmalade, 258
        Almond Madeleines with, 228
clams:
    Lemongrass Cioppino, 159
    Mom's Steamed Egg Custard with, 175
    Steamed, with Burnt Lime–Cilantro Butter, 167
coconut:
    Pea Soup with Coconut Milk, Lap Cheong, and Green Oil, 151
    Rice, 251
    Shrimp Toast, 27

cod:
    Beer-Battered Fish with Apple Tartar Sauce, 171
    Char Siu Black, 183
Coffee Flan, Vietnamese, 235
cookies:
    Chinese Almond, Torched Banana Pudding with, 225
    Chocolate Chunk, 239
Coriander, Slow-Roasted Cherry Tomatoes with Garlic, Fennel, and, 245
corn:
    Crispy Salmon with Summer Corn and Chanterelles, 180
    Scallops with Creamed, and Prosciutto XO, 160
    Soup with Chili Crisp and Puffed Wild Rice, 148
    Street Corn Three Ways: Thai, Sichuan, and Italian, 129
Cornichons, Really F***ing Crispy Potatoes with Raclette and, 144
cream cheese, in Salted Egg Yolk Basque Cheesecake, 232
Croutons, Olive Oil–Fried Sourdough, 255
crudo:
    Sicilian-Style, with Shoyu-Cured Salmon Roe, 40
    Yellowtail, in Ginger-Citrus Broth, 39
Cubanos, Shanghainese Pork Belly, 100
Cumin-Shiso Tzatziki, 128
    Blistered Snap and Snow Peas with, 126
Cured Duck Egg Yolks, 247
    Salted Egg Yolk Basque Cheesecake with, 232

D

daikon:
    and Ginger, Pickled, 245
    Oxtail and Daikon Soup, 213
Dan Dan Mein, 105
dipping sauce:
    Black Vinegar–Chili, 263
    Calamansi, 218
dips:
    Chili Crisp Labneh, 32
    Cumin-Shiso Tzatziki, 128
    King's Guacamole, 28
    Miso Baba Ghanoush, 24
dressing. *See also* fish sauce; vinaigrette
    Caesar salad, 67
    lemony anchovy, 72
    Shiso Ranch, 68
duck:
    à l'Orange, Five Spiced, 191
    Eggs with Chilled Tofu, Century, 51
    Egg Yolks, Cured, 247
dumplings:
    Crispy Lace, Two Ways: Kimchi Beef & Pork and Salted Cabbage, 110
    Lobster Wontons in Yuzu Broth, 116
Dutch Pancake with Ricotta and Strawberry-Ginger Jam, 231

E

eggplant:
    Caponata, 141
    Miso Baba Ghanoush, 24
egg(s)
    Custard, Mascarpone, 222
    Custard, Mom's Steamed, with Clams, 175
    Duck Eggs with Chilled Tofu, Century, 51
    Duck Egg Yolks, Cured, 247
    Hot Honey–Cured Egg Yolks on Garlic Toast, 59
    Salted Egg Yolk Basque Cheesecake, 232
    Smoky Tea Eggs, 23
    Vietnamese Coffee Flan, 235
Endive Salad with Asian Pear and Walnuts, Fennel and, 64

F

fennel:
    and Endive Salad with Asian Pear and Walnuts, 64
    Slow-Roasted Cherry Tomatoes with Garlic, Fennel, and Coriander, 245
feta:
    Spiced Charred Peaches with Olives, Feta, and Orange Zest, 75
fish and seafood. *See also specific types*
    Beer-Battered Fish with Apple Tartar Sauce, 171
    Grilled Fish Collars with Pickled Daikon and Ponzu, 164
    My Shanghainese Grandma's Fish, 55
    Salt-Baked Whole Fish, 172
fish sauce, 16
    Caramel, 250
    –Caramel Chicken Wings, Grilled, 47
    Vinaigrette, 76
Five Spiced Duck à l'Orange, 191
five spice powder, 14
Flan, Vietnamese Coffee, 235
Flounder with Yuzu Brown Butter and Capers, 163
Focaccia, King's, 82
French Toast, Hong Kong Stuffed, 236
Fried Bread Crumbs, 256
Fried Shallots, 254
    Heirloom Tomatoes with Fish Sauce, Mint, and, 76

G

garlic:
    Butter, 86
    Soy Sauce Noodles, 109
    Toast, 59
ginger, 16
    -Citrus Broth, 39
    Scallion Lobster Rolls, 98
    -Scallion Sauce, 263
        Hainan Chicken with Chicken-Fat Rice and, 188
    Strawberry-Ginger Jam, 231

glaze:
    Sweet and Sour Plum, 195
    sweet and spicy, 44
    yuzu, 240
Goji Berries, Chicken and Ginseng Bone Broth with, 210
graham cracker crust, in Salted Egg Yolk Basque Cheesecake, 232
Green Beans with Pancetta and Caramelized Soy Sauce, 152
Guacamole, King's, 28

H

Hainan Chicken with Chicken-Fat Rice and Ginger-Scallion Sauce, 188
halibut:
    Beer-Battered Fish with Apple Tartar Sauce, 171
    Lemongrass Cioppino, 159
Hash Browns, Scallion, with Crème Fraîche and Asian Pear, 137
honey:
    King's Hot, 251
    King's Hot Honey Butter, 252
    Yuzu–Black Pepper Honey Butter, 252
Hong Kong Milk Tea, 259
Hong Kong Milk Tea Tiramisu, 222
Hong Kong Stuffed French Toast, 236
Hong Sew Yuk, 100
Hot Honey–Cured Egg Yolks on Garlic Toast, 59
Hot Sauce, Pineapple-Habanero, 259

I

Italian Street Corn, 130

J

jicama:
    with Avocado, Macadamia Nuts, and Sesame-Lime Vinaigrette, 79
    Pork Lettuce Wraps, 56
Jook, Chicken and Ginger, 122

K

Kabocha, Roasted, with Five Spice and Hot Honey, 142
Katsu, Pork, with Snow Peas, Herbs, and Yuzu Vinaigrette, 205
Kimchi-Beef Filling, 110
King's Chili Crisp, 257
King's Focaccia, 82
King's Guacamole, 28
King's Hot Honey, 251
King's Hot Honey Butter, 252
King's Mala Spice, 263
King's Ponzu, 258
King's Wings, 44
kombu, 16
    in Yuzu Broth, 116
kumquats:
    Chicory Salad with Anchovy, Kumquats, and Smoked Cheese, 72
    Pickled, 245

L

Labneh, Chili Crisp, 32
lamb:
    Skewers, Mala, 200
lap cheong, 16
    Crumble, 256
    Pea Soup with Coconut Milk, Lap Cheong, and Green Oil, 151
leeks, in Charred Green Oil, 248
Lemon–Anchovy Vinaigrette, Burnt, 147
lemongrass, 16
    Beef Stew, 199
    Cioppino, 159
    Shrimp Cocktail with Michelada Mayo, 52
    -Soy Sauce Chicken Thighs, Grilled, 187
    Turmeric-Lemongrass Pork Belly Roast, 217
Lettuce Wraps, Pork, 56
lime:
    Burnt Lime–Cilantro Butter, 252
    Chili-Lime Melon and Prosciutto, 63
    Sesame-Lime Vinaigrette, 250
lobster:
    Black Pepper–Garlic, 168
    Rolls, Ginger Scallion, 98
    Wontons in Yuzu Broth, 116

M

macadamia nuts:
    Jicama with Avocado, Macadamia Nuts, and Sesame-Lime Vinaigrette, 79
Madeleines, Almond, with Citrus Marmalade, 228
Maitake, Salt and Pepper, 133
Mala Lamb Skewers, 200
Mala Spice, King's, 263
Mama Mel's Meatballs, 203
Marinade, Char Siu, 183
Marmalade, Citrus, 258
Marsala wine, in Hong Kong Milk Tea Tiramisu, 222
Mascarpone Custard, 222
Mayo, Michelada, 52
meat. *See* beef; lamb; pork
meatballs:
    Mama Mel's, 203
    Shanghainese "Lion's Head," 214
Melon, Chili-Lime, and Prosciutto, 63
Meringue, Italian, 225
Michelada Mayo, Lemongrass Shrimp Cocktail with, 52
Milk Buns, 86
Milk Tea Tiramisu, Hong Kong, 222
miso, 16
    Baba Ghanoush, 24
    Caesar with Gai Lan and Chrysanthemum Greens, 67
    -Tahini, Roasted Japanese Sweet Potato with Olives, Walnuts, and, 134
Mom's Steamed Egg Custard with Clams, 175
mushrooms:
    Chinese Sticky Rice with Dried Seafood and Sausage, 119
    Crispy Salmon with Summer Corn and Chanterelles, 180
    Salt and Pepper Maitake, 133
    Shoyu Butter Mushrooms, 138
mussels, in Lemongrass Cioppino, 159

N

noodles:
    Dan Dan Mein, 105
    Garlic Soy Sauce, 109
    Shiso Pea Pappardelle, 115
    Taiwanese Beef Noodle Soup, 106
nuts. *See specific types*

O

Olive Tapenade, 262
onion(s):
    Black Vinegar–Caramelized, 248
    Cipollini Onions Agrodolce, 249
    Pickled Red, 245
orange(s):
    Chicory Salad with Anchovy, Kumquats, and Smoked Cheese, 72
    Spiced Charred Peaches with Olive, Feta, and Orange Zest, 75
Oxtail and Daikon Soup, 213
Oysters, Grilled, with Sichuan Chile–Bourbon Butter, 43

P

pancake(s):
    Cheesy Scallion, 93
    Dutch Pancake with Ricotta and Strawberry-Ginger Jam, 231
pancetta:
    Green Beans with, and Caramelized Soy Sauce, 152
pantry ingredients, 14–18
Pappardelle, Shiso Pea, 115
Pastry Cream, 225
Peaches, Spiced Charred, with Olives, Feta, and Orange Zest, 75
peanut(s):
    Butter, in Hong Kong Stuffed French Toast, 236
    Sauce, 129
pears:
    Fennel and Endive Salad with Asian Pear and Walnuts, 64
pea(s). *See also* snow peas
    Shiso Pea Pappardelle, 115
    Soup with Coconut Milk, Lap Cheong, and Green Oil, 151
peppercorns, pickled green, in Swordfish au Poivre, 179
pepperoni:
    Sheet Pan Pizza with Stracciatella, Pepperoni, and King's Hot Honey, 89
peppers. *See* chile peppers; sweet peppers
Pickled Chiles, 245
    Sichuan Steak Tartare with, 31
Pickled Daikon and Ginger, 245
    Grilled Fish Collars with, 164
    Shanghainese Pork Belly Cubanos with, 100
Pickled Kumquats, 245
Pickled Red Onion, 245
    Al Pastor Bao with, 97
Pickles, Quick, 245
Pineapple-Habanero Hot Sauce, 259
Pistachio, Spiced Carrots with, and Labneh, 155
Pizza, Sheet Pan, with Stracciatella, Pepperoni, and King's Hot Honey, 89
Plum Glaze, Sweet and Sour, 195
ponzu:
    Grilled Fish Collars with Pickled Daikon and, 164
    King's, 258
Popcorn Chicken, Taiwanese, 48
pork. *See also* bacon; pancetta; pepperoni; prosciutto; sausage
    Al Pastor Bao, 97
    Black Vinegar Ribs, 209
    Dan Dan Mein, 105
    Katsu with Snow Peas, Herbs, and Yuzu Vinaigrette, 205
    Lettuce Wraps, 56
    Mama Mel's Meatballs, 203
    and Salted Cabbage Filling, 110
    Shanghainese "Lion's Head" Meatballs, 214
    Shanghainese Pork Belly Cubanos, 100
    Turmeric-Lemongrass Pork Belly Roast, 217
potatoes:
    Really F***ing Crispy, with Raclette and Cornichons, 144
    Scallion Hash Browns with Crème Fraiche and Asian Pear, 137
poultry. *See* chicken; duck; quail
prosciutto:
    Chili-Lime Melon and, 63
    Prosciutto XO, 260
Pudding, Torched Banana, with Chinese Almond Cookies, 225
Puffed Wild Rice, 257
    Corn Soup with Chili Crisp and, 148

Q

quail:
    Grilled, with Sweet and Sour Plum Glaze, 195

R

Raclette Mornay, 144
Radish, Chilled Beef Shank Salad with Celery and, 71. *See also* daikon
ranch dressing. *See* Shiso Ranch
Rib Eye on the Bone with Black Garlic–Anchovy Butter, 196
rice:
    Chicken and Ginger Jook, 122
    Chicken-Fat Rice, 188
    Chinese Sticky Rice with Dried Seafood and Sausage, 119

Coconut Rice, 251
Puffed Wild, 257

S

salmon:
    Crispy, with Summer Corn and Chanterelles, 180
    Grilled Fish Collars with Pickled Daikon and Ponzu, 164
    Roe, Shoyu-Cured, 40
Salt and Pepper Maitake, 133
Salt-Baked Whole Fish, 172
Salted Egg Yolk Basque Cheesecake, 232
sauce. *See also* dipping sauce; fish sauce, soy sauce
    Apple Tartar, 171, 261
    Asian Pear, 137
    Ginger-Scallion, 263
    Peanut, 129
    Pineapple-Habanero Hot, 258
    Pomodoro, 203
    Tonkatsu Sauce, 205
sausage. *See also* lap cheong
    Chinese Sticky Rice with Dried Seafood and, 119
scallion(s):
    Cheesy Scallion Pancakes, 93
    Ginger Scallion Lobster Rolls, 98
    Ginger-Scallion Sauce, 263
    Hash Browns with Crème Fraîche and Asian Pear, 137
scallops:
    Chinese Sticky Rice with Dried Seafood and Sausage, 119
    with Creamed Corn and Prosciutto XO, 160
seafood. *See specific types*
Sesame-Lime Vinaigrette, Jicama with Avocado, Macadamia Nuts, and, 79
Shallots, Fried, 254
Shanghainese Grandma's Fish, My, 55
Shanghainese "Lion's Head" Meatballs, 214
Shanghainese Pork Belly Cubanos, 100
Sheet Pan Pizza with Stracciatella, Pepperoni, and King's Hot Honey, 89
Shiso Pea Pappardelle, 115
Shiso Ranch, 68
Shoyu Butter Mushrooms, 138
shrimp:
    Chinese Sticky Rice with Dried Seafood and Sausage, 119
    Coconut Shrimp Toast, 27
    Lemongrass Cioppino, 159
    Lemongrass Shrimp Cocktail with Michelada Mayo, 52
    Sichuan Chile Butter Shrimp, 176
Sichuan Chile–Bourbon Butter, 252
    Grilled Oysters with, 43
Sichuan Chile Butter Shrimp, 176
Sichuan Steak Tartare, 31
Sichuan Street Corn, 129, 130
Sicilian-Style Crudo with Shoyu-Cured Salmon Roe, 40
Smoky Tea Eggs, 23
snow peas:
    Pork Katsu with Snow Peas, Herbs, and Yuzu Vinaigrette, 205
    Snap and Snow Peas, Blistered, with Cumin-Shiso Tzatziki, 126
soup:
    Corn, with Chili Crisp and Puffed Wild Rice, 148
    Oxtail and Daikon, 213
    Pea, with Coconut Milk, Lap Cheong, and Green Oil, 151
    Taiwanese Beef Noodle Soup, 106
Sourdough Croutons, Olive Oil–Fried, 255
soy sauce, 18
    Garlic Soy Sauce Noodles, 109
    Green Beans with Pancetta and Caramelized, 152
    Sweet, 262
Spice Mix, 133
squash:
    Roasted Kabocha with Five Spice and Hot Honey, 142
Steak Tartare, Sichuan, 31
Steamed Bao, 254
    Al Pastor Bao with, 97
stracciatella:
    Sheet Pan Pizza with Stracciatella, Pepperoni, and King's Hot Honey, 89
Strawberry-Ginger Jam, 231
Street Corn Three Ways: Thai, Sichuan, and Italian, 129
Sweet and Sour Plum Glaze, 195
sweet peppers:
    Black Vinegar–Marinated, 35
Sweet Potato, Roasted Japanese, with Olives, Walnuts, and Miso-Tahini, 134
Sweet Soy Sauce, 262
Swordfish au Poivre, 179

T

tahini:
    Roasted Japanese Sweet Potato with Olives, Walnut, and Miso-Tahini, 134
Taiwanese Beef Noodle Soup, 106
Taiwanese Popcorn Chicken, 48
Tangzhong, 86
Tapenade, Olive, 262
Tartar Sauce, Apple, 171, 261
Tea, Hong Kong Milk, 259
Thai Street Corn, 129, 130
Tiramisu, Hong Kong Milk Tea, 222
toast:
    Coconut Shrimp, 27
    Hot Honey–Cured Egg Yolks on Garlic Toast, 59
Tofu, Century Duck Eggs with Chilled, 51
tomatoes:
    Heirloom, with Fish Sauce, Mint, and Fried Shallots, 76
    Pomodoro Sauce, 203
    Slow-Roasted Cherry, with Garlic, Fennel, and Coriander, 245
Tonkatsu Sauce, 205
Tostadas, Tuna, 36
Tuna Tostadas with Avocado, Ginger, and Scallion, 36
turmeric:
    -Lemongrass Pork Belly Roast, 217
    Paste, 217
Tzatziki, Cumin-Shiso, 128

V

vegetables. *See specific vegetables*
Vietnamese Coffee Flan, 235
vinaigrette:
    Fish Sauce, 76
    Lemon–Anchovy, 147
    Sesame-Lime, 250
    Yuzu, 205

W

walnuts:
    Fennel and Endive Salad with Asian Pear and, 64
    Roasted Japanese Sweet Potato with Olives, Walnuts, and Miso-Tahini, 134
Wedge with Shiso Ranch, Classic, 68
wine, in Pomodoro Sauce, 203. *See also* Marsala wine
Wontons, Lobster, in Yuzu Broth, 116

Y

Yellowtail Crudo in Ginger-Citrus Broth, 39
yogurt:
    Chile Crisp Labneh, 32
    Cumin-Shiso Tzatziki, 128
yuzu, 18
    –Black Pepper Honey Butter, 252
    Broth, Lobster Wontons in, 116
    Brown Butter and Capers, Flounder with, 163
    –Coconut Olive Oil Cake with Berries, 240
    Vinaigrette, 205

Ten Speed Press
An imprint of the Crown Publishing Group
A division of Penguin Random House LLC
1745 Broadway, New York, NY 10019
tenspeed.com
penguinrandomhouse.com

Text copyright © 2025 by Melissa King
Food photographs copyright © 2025
by Ed Anderson
Lifestyle photographs copyright © 2025
by Ashley Batz

Penguin Random House values and supports copyright. Copyright fuels creativity, encourages diverse voices, promotes free speech, and creates a vibrant culture. Thank you for buying an authorized edition of this book and for complying with copyright laws by not reproducing, scanning, or distributing any part of it in any form without permission. You are supporting writers and allowing Penguin Random House to continue to publish books for every reader. Please note that no part of this book may be used or reproduced in any manner for the purpose of training artificial intelligence technologies or systems.

TEN SPEED PRESS and the Ten Speed Press colophon are registered trademarks of Penguin Random House LLC.

Typefaces: General Type's Cambon and ATF's Alternate Gothic

Library of Congress Cataloging-in-Publication Data
Names: King, Melissa (Writer on cooking), author. | Goode, J. J., author. | Anderson, Ed (Edward Charles), food photographer. | Batz, Ashley, lifestyle photographer.
Title: Cook like a King : recipes from my California Chinese kitchen / by Melissa King with JJ Goode ; food photographs by Ed Anderson ; lifestyle photographs by Ashley Batz.
Description: First edition. | California ; New York : Ten Speed Press, [2025] | Includes index.
Identifiers: LCCN 2024039569 (print) | LCCN 2024039570 (ebook) | ISBN 9781984861924 (hardcover) | ISBN 9781984861931 (ebook)
Subjects: LCSH: Cooking. | LCGFT: Cookbooks.
Classification: LCC TX714 .K56623 2025 (print) | LCC TX714 (ebook) | DDC 641.5—dc23/eng/20240907
LC record available at https://lccn.loc.gov/2024039569
LC ebook record available at https://lccn.loc.gov/2024039570

Hardcover ISBN: 978-1-9848-6192-4
Ebook ISBN: 978-1-9848-6193-1

Acquiring editor: Kelly Snowden | Project editors: Claire Yee and Kelly Snowden | Production editor: Liana Faughnan | Editorial assistant: Gabriela Ureña Matos
Art director & designer: Emma Campion
Production designers: Mari Gill and Faith Hague
Production: Philip Leung
Food stylist: Lillian Kang | Food stylist assistants: Paige Arnett and Callyn Humm
Prop stylist: Glenn Jenkins
Copy editor: Kate Slate | Proofreaders: Eldes Tran, Hope Clarke, Sigi Nacson, Mark McCauslin, Tess Rossi, and Miriam Taveras
Indexer: Barbara Mortenson
Publicist: Jina Stanfill | Marketer: Monica Stanton

Manufactured in Malaysia

10 9 8 7 6 5 4 3 2 1

First Edition

The authorized representative in the EU for product safety and compliance is Penguin Random House Ireland, Morrison Chambers, 32 Nassau Street, Dublin D02 YH68, Ireland, https://eu-contact.penguin.ie.